Evergreen
WITH READINGS

Evergreen
WITH READINGS

A Guide to Writing

FIFTH EDITION

Susan Fawcett   Alvin Sandberg

Houghton Mifflin Company ▪ Boston ▪ Toronto
Geneva, Illinois ▪ Palo Alto ▪ Princeton, New Jersey

Sponsoring editor: Renée Deljon
Associate editor: Melody Davies
Senior project editor: Rosemary Winfield
Senior production/design coordinator: Sarah Ambrose
Senior manufacturing coordinator: Priscilla Bailey
Marketing manager: Charles Cavaliere

Cover design: Judy Arisman, Arisman Design. Cover image: John Marshall, Western Hemlock from the Olympic Mountains of Washington state.

Photo credits: We are grateful to the following individuals for permission to reproduce their photographs in this text: page 40—*Self-Portrait with Monkey*, by Frida Kahlo, 1938, oil on masonite. Albright-Knox Art Gallery, Buffalo, New York. Bequest of A. Conger Goodyear, 1966; page 49—Bettmann Archive; page 84—© James Carroll; page 95—Frank Ward/© 1995 Amherst College; page 96—© 1991 Jonathan A. Meyers; page 101—© Grant Heilman; page 110—© 1993 Anne-Marie Webert/The Stock Market; page 131—© James Carroll; page 136—© 1986 Deborah Kahn Kalas/Stock Boston; page 137—© 1995 Michael Zide; page 217—© 1995 Jonathan A. Meyers; page 234—René Magritte, *Le Therapeute*, 1941. Private collection. Giraudon/Art Resource; page 424—Half-Dome, Winter. Photograph by Ansel Adams © 1995 by the Trustees of the Ansel Adams Publishing Rights Trust. All rights reserved.

Text credits: pages 478–479—"How Sunglasses Spanned the World" from *Panati's Extraordinary Origins of Everyday Things* (pages 267–268) by Charles Panati. Copyright © 1987 by Charles Panati. Reprinted by permission of HarperCollins Publishers and the author.
Text credits continue on page 538.

Printed in the U.S.A.

Student edition ISBN: 0-395-76024-0

Instructor's annotated edition ISBN: 0-395-75035-0

DEFGHIJ-WC-00 99 98 97

Contents

Answer Questions
Read

UNIT 6   Reviewing the Basics

Contents

Preface

Evergreen with Readings combines in one volume the new Fifth Edition of our popular college writing text *Evergreen* and fifteen high-interest reading selections. Based on our classroom experience at Bronx Community College of the City University of New York, *Evergreen* was designed for students who need to improve the writing skills so necessary to success in college and in most careers. Again and again, we hear from instructors and students alike that *"Evergreen* works," and we consider this the greatest possible compliment. The text's clear, paced lessons, numerous high-interest practices, and engaging writing assignments have guided over a million students through the process of writing effectively, from prewriting to final draft.

By choosing *Evergreen with Readings,* those instructors who wish to include reading in their writing classes may choose from richly varied and provocative reading selections by such writers as Alice Walker, Judith Ortiz Cofer, Arthur Ashe, Russell Baker, and Anna Quindlen. Each selection is accompanied by a headnote, glosses, comprehension questions, and writing assignments. We are excited about this Fifth Edition, which has been strengthened by several new features.

Features of *Evergreen with Readings,* Fifth Edition

- **Increased Coverage of Prewriting.** The section on keeping a journal has been expanded to include numerous specific writing suggestions, as well as two sample entries from actual student journals.

- **New Section on Summary Writing.** Instruction and practice in the useful skill of summarizing have been added to Chapter 20, now called "The Essay Question and the Summary."

- **Three New Reading Selections.** Based on instructor and student responses to the last edition of *Evergreen with Readings,* we have replaced three of the reading selections with strong new pieces by Arthur Ashe, Russell Baker, and Suzanne Britt.

- **New Introduction to the Readings.** A reader's introduction has been added, featuring ten tips on how most effectively to read the selections and prepare for class discussion. A short essay, "How Sunglasses Spanned the World," is included here, with sample student annotations.

- **New High-Interest Practice Material.** Nearly fifty practices have been replaced with high-interest paragraphs, short essays, and continuous discourses for proofreading and other tasks. New topics include the fax revolution, photographer Ansel Adams, the story of Levi's jeans, Navaho code talkers in the U.S. Marines, the Internet, Mariah Carey's rise to stardom, Langston Hughes, Joyce Chen, who introduced authentic Chinese cuisine to the United States, and more. These exercises motivate students to read on while improving their writing skills.

- **New Model Paragraphs and Essays.** We have replaced many written models with fresh examples of student and professional work. Subjects range from youth violence to Steven Spielberg's special effects to "random acts of kindness."

- **Quotation Bank.** This new feature consists of 85 wise and witty quotations from a wide range of authors. On such topics as education, work and success, love, friends and family, ourselves in society, and wisdom for living, these quotations can be used to stimulate class discussion and to inspire students' writing.

- **Quick Reference Guide for Students with ESL Backgrounds.** A brief index specifically geared to the ESL student provides quick reference to commonly encountered writing problems and solutions.

- **Extensive Ancillary Package.** Available on adoption of the text, the following ancillaries provide the instructor with excellent support material and expand teaching options. New to this edition are the *Evergreen Grammar Review Exercises*, which provide additional grammar practice, and the *Evergreen Community*, a collection of teaching ideas from instructors across the country who are using *Evergreen* in their classes.

    Instructor's Annotated Edition

    Evergreen Grammar Review Exercises

    Evergreen Editing Exercises

    Test Package

    Computerized Diagnostic/Mastery Tests

    Test Bank Data Disk

    Evergreen Community

    Student Answer Key

Organization of the Text

Evergreen with Readings begins with an overview of the writing process, audience, and purpose and then introduces five prewriting techniques. Unit 2 guides students through the paragraph-writing process: planning, writing topic sentences, generating ideas, organizing, making smooth transitions, and revising. Unit 3 moves on to the rhetorical modes most often required in college writing (illustration, narration, description, process, definition, comparison/contrast, classification, and persuasion). Unit 4 covers the more subtle skills of sentence variety and language awareness. In Unit 5, the techniques of paragraph writing are applied step by step to the process of writing essays, answering essay examination questions, and writing summaries. Unit 6 thoroughly reviews basic grammar, highlighting such major problem areas as verbs, punctuation, and mechanics; Unit 7 covers spelling and homonyms.

Evergreen with Readings, with its full range of materials and flexible organization, adapts easily to almost any course design and to a wide range of student needs. Because each chapter is self-contained, the text also works well for tutorials, laboratory work, and self-teaching.

Acknowledgments

We wish to thank those people whose thoughtful comments and suggestions helped us develop the Fifth Edition.

Debra Anderson, Indian River Community College, FL

Marilyn Athmann, Alexandria Technical College, MN

William O. Boggs, Slippery Rock University, PA

Muriel M. Brennan, College of San Mateo, CA

Gay Brookes, Borough of Manhattan Community College, NY

Cynthia A. Brouse, George Brown College, Ontario

Michael A. Douglas, Savannah State College, GA

Debra Callen, Harold Washington College, IL

Julie Hawthorne, Sacramento City College, CA

Irma Luna, San Antonio College, TX

Bonnie Orr, Wenatchee Valley College, WA

Betty Owen, Broward County Community College, FL

John Thornburg, San Jacinto College—Central, TX

Meredith Wilson, Solano Community College, CA

Linda Wishnant, Guilford Technical Community College, NC

Our terrific editor, Melody Davies, contributed fine ideas and a balancing energy—always with her characteristic patience and ready laughter. We value our years-long relationship with her. Thanks to Dr. Neil Grill of Bronx Community College and his students for sharing with us some of their journal entries and to Troy Bethune for permission to adapt his poem. We have missed working with Barry Kwalick, a skilled writer and fine human being who lent his talents to the last edition of *Evergreen with Readings* but tragically lost his life in 1992.

Susan Fawcett thanks her husband, Richard Donovan, for his ongoing love and support—and for reading drafts and inventing sports examples with only minimal pestering. Alvin Sandberg would like to thank Beth for her encouragement and support and Miriam for her many suggestions for improvement to the manuscript. He would also like to thank Marilyn Weissman for her editorial assistance. And of course we thank our students, who daily teach us the power of words.

Susan Fawcett and Alvin Sandberg

Evergreen

WITH READINGS

Unit 1

Getting Started

1

Exploring the Writing Process

PART A The Writing Process
PART B Subject, Audience, and Purpose

This chapter will give you a brief overview of the writing process, which is explored in greater depth throughout this book. By surveying the steps that many writers take and some of the factors they consider, you will see that writing is not a magic ability some are born with, but a skill that can be learned—the result of planning, hard work, and a positive attitude toward your work.

The Writing Process

Many students mistakenly think that good writers simply sit down and write out a perfect letter, paragraph, or essay from start to finish. In fact, writing is a **process** consisting of a number of steps:

1. Thinking about a topic
2. Freely jotting down ideas about the topic
3. Narrowing the topic and writing it in one sentence   ⎫ prewriting
4. Selecting and dropping ideas
5. Arranging ideas in a plan or an outline
6. Writing a first draft   ⎱ writing
7. Rethinking and rewriting as necessary
8. Writing one or more new drafts   ⎱ revising and proofreading
9. Proofreading for errors

Not all writers perform all the steps in this order. Actually, writing can be a messy process of thinking, writing, reading what has been written, and writing again. Sometimes steps overlap or must be repeated. The important thing is that writing the first draft is just one stage in the process. "I love being a writer," jokes Peter De Vries. "What I can't stand is the paperwork."

Before they write, good writers spend time **prewriting**—thinking about and planning for a paper. Steps 1 through 5 above are prewriting steps. Here writers think, let their imaginations run free, jot down ideas, decide which ideas to use, and come up with a plan for writing. Many beginning writers get into trouble by skipping the prewriting phase. They don't realize that doing this early work saves time and frustration later and usually creates a much better piece of writing than just sitting down and starting to write.

Next comes **writing** the first draft. Writers who have planned ahead are now free to concentrate on writing the best possible draft. The focus is on presenting ideas, feelings, and experiences as convincingly as possible, rather than on correction.

The next phase of the process—and one that many writers rush through or omit altogether—is **revising.** Steps 7 and 8 are revising steps. Experienced writers do not accept the first words that flow from their pens; they are like sculptors, shaping and reworking rough material into something meaningful. Writers do this by letting the first draft sit for five minutes, an hour, or a day. Then they read it again with a fresh, critical eye and rewrite—adding, dropping, or rearranging ideas; changing words to achieve more clarity and punch; and so on. Many writers revise two or three times until they get it right—until their writing says clearly and effectively what they want it to say. Finally, they **proofread** for grammar and spelling errors, so that their writing seems to say, "I am proud to put my name on this work."

PART B

Subject, Audience, and Purpose

Early in the prewriting phase, writers should give some thought to their subject, audience, and purpose.

Whenever possible, choose a **subject** that you know and care about: life in Cleveland, working with learning-disabled children, repairing motorcycles, overcoming shyness, watching a friend struggle with drug addiction, succeeding in college. You may not realize how many subjects you do know or have strong opinions about. What special experience or expertise do you have? What angers you, inspires you, saddens you? What do you love to do? The answers to these questions will suggest good subjects to write about. In college courses, your instructor often will assign you a broad subject. Try to direct this subject toward some aspect that intrigues you. If you have interest, energy, and passion about a topic, then probably your readers will too.

Just how you approach your subject will depend on your readers—your **audience.** Ask yourself just who these readers are: your classmates, your professor, other students at your college, your boss, youngsters in your community, people who probably agree with you, people who don't? Keeping your audience in mind will help you know what information to include and what to leave out. For example, if you were writing about rap music for an audience of middle-aged parents, you would explain your subject differently than you would to an audience of eighteen-year-old rap fans. What do your readers already know about your subject? What might they need or want to learn?

Next you will want to think about your **purpose** in writing. Do you want to explain something to your readers, persuade them that a certain view is correct, entertain them, tell a good story, or some combination of these? Keeping your purpose in mind will help you write more effectively. For example, if your purpose is to persuade your company to recycle its paper and glass, you might want to write about ways in which recycling would benefit the company: Recycling could earn or save money, improve the company's image, or make employees proud to work there.

PRACTICE 1   List five subjects about which you might like to write. For ideas, reread the list of possible subjects and the questions in Part B, page 3.

1. _____

2. _____

3. _____

4. _____

5. _____

PRACTICE 2   Jot down ideas for these three assignments, by yourself or with a group of classmates. Notice how your ideas and details differ, depending on the audience and purpose.

1. You have been asked to write a description of your college for local high school students. Your purpose is to encourage them to enroll in your college after being graduated from high school. What kinds of information should you include? What will your audience want to know?

2. You have been asked to write a description of your college for the governor of your state. Your purpose is to persuade her or him to spend more money to improve your college. What information should you include? What will your audience want to know?

3. You have been asked to write a description of your college for your best friend, who attends a college out of state. Your purpose is to share your personal impressions and experiences. What information should you include? What will your audience want to know?

2

Generating Ideas

PART A Freewriting
PART B Brainstorming
PART C Clustering
PART D Asking Questions
PART E Keeping a Journal

This chapter presents five effective prewriting techniques that will help you get your ideas onto paper and overcome the "blank page jitters" that many people face when they sit down to write. Try all five and see which ones, alone or in combination, work best for *you*.

PART A

Freewriting

Freewriting is an excellent method that many writers use to warm up and get ideas. These are the guidelines: for five, ten, or fifteen minutes, write rapidly, without stopping, about anything that comes into your head. If you feel stuck, just repeat or rhyme the last word you wrote, but *don't stop writing*. And don't worry about grammar, logic, complete sentences, or grades.

The point of freewriting is to write so quickly that ideas can flow without comments from your inner critic. The *inner critic* is the voice inside that says, every time you have an idea, "That's dumb; that's no good; cross that out." Freewriting helps you tell this voice, "Thank you for your opinion. Once I have lots of ideas and words on paper, I'll invite you back for comment."

After you freewrite, read what you have written, underlining any parts you like.

Here is one student's first freewriting, with his own underlinings:

> Boy I wish this class was over and I could go home and get out of this building, boy was my day miserable and this sure is a crazy thing to do if a shrink could see us now. My I just remember I've got to buy that cassette my my my I am running out of stuff to write but dont worry teach because this is really the nuttiest thing but lots of fun you probably like reading this mixed up thing That girl's remark sounded dumb but impressing. You know this writing sure puts muscles in your fingers if I stop writing oh boy this is the most incredible assignment in the world think and write without worrying about sentence structure and other English garbage to stall you down boy that guy next to me is writing like crazy so he looks crazy you know this is outrageous I'm writing and writing I never realized the extent of mental and physical concentration it takes to do this constantly dont mind the legibility of my hand my hand oh my hand is ready to drop off please this is crazy crazy and too much work for a poor guy like myself. Imagine me putting on paper all I have to say and faster than a speeding bullet.

■ This example has the lively energy of many freewritings. Why do you think the student underlined what he did? Would you have underlined other words or phrases? Why?

Freewriting is a powerful tool for helping you turn thoughts and feelings into words, especially when you are unsure about what you want to say. Sometimes freewriting produces only nonsense; often, however, it can help you zoom in on possible topics, interests, and worthwhile writing you can use later.

PRACTICE 1

1. Set a timer for ten minutes or have someone time you. Freewrite without stopping for the full ten minutes. If you get stuck, repeat or rhyme the last word you wrote until words start flowing again but *don't stop writing!*

2. When you finish, write down one or two words that describe how you felt while freewriting.

_____

_____

3. Next, read your freewriting. Underline any words or lines you like—anything that strikes you as interesting, thoughtful, or funny. If nothing strikes you, that's okay.

PRACTICE 2

Try three more freewritings at home—each one ten minutes long. Do them at different times of day or night when you have a quiet moment. If possible, use a timer. Set it for ten minutes; then write quickly and freely until it rings. Later, read over your freewritings and underline any striking lines or ideas.

Focused Freewriting

In **focused freewriting**, you simply try to focus your thoughts on one subject as you freewrite. The subject might be one assigned by your instructor, one you choose, or one you have discovered in unfocused freewriting. The goal of most writing is a polished, organized piece of writing; focused freewriting can help you generate ideas or narrow a topic to one aspect that interests you.

Here is one student's focused freewriting on the topic *someone who strongly influenced you:*

> Gran, you started me in music. High cheekbones, dark skin, she took me in. Lived for her albums, trophies and plaques, photos in robes and flowery dresses, Gran turning the pages she taught me to believe in myself, to reach for my dream—my music—gospel was her thing and her voice rocked the church on Sundays, navy dress, white hat, head thrown back she belted out the glory of the lord, she sang and sang till the power fell down, she prayed and prayed till she began to moan. Then the singing stopped, the turning stopped, I saw her last on a bed of satin in a box.

- This student later used her focused freewriting—its vivid details about Gran and her influence—as the basis for a strong paper. Underline any words or lines *you* find especially striking or appealing. Be prepared to explain why you like what you underline.

PRACTICE 3   Do a three-minute focused freewriting on three of these words:

highway	red
success	parent (or child)
rain	friendship

Underline as usual. Did you surprise yourself by having so much to say about any one word? Perhaps you would like to write more about this word or topic.

PRACTICE 4   1. Read over your earlier freewritings and notice your underlinings. Would you like to write more about any underlined words or ideas? Write two or three such words or ideas here:

_____

_____

_____

2. Now choose one word or idea. Focus your thoughts on it and do a ten-minute focused freewriting. Try to stick to the topic as you write but don't worry too much about keeping on track; just keep writing.

Brainstorming

Another prewriting technique that may work for you is **brainstorming** or freely jotting down ideas about a topic. As in freewriting, the purpose is to get lots of ideas on paper so you have something to work with and choose from. Write everything that comes to you about a topic—words and phrases, ideas, details, examples.

After you have brainstormed, read over your list, underlining interesting or exciting ideas you might develop further. As with freewriting, many writers brainstorm on a general subject, underline, then brainstorm again as they focus on one aspect of that subject to write about.

Here is one student's brainstorm list on the topic *computers:*

> They're everywhere
>
> Advertisements in the paper daily
>
> Words I don't understand—*bytes, RAM, modem*
>
> Ron and Wanda have a computer
>
> Computers scare me
>
> In the bank, at work, hospital, learning center
>
> My little brother knows more than I do
>
> Classes for kids
>
> He's not afraid—loves problems to solve, games
>
> Whole different generation
>
> Kids get used to the keyboard, the screen—to them, it's a game
>
> All kids should learn young

As he brainstormed, this writer moved toward a more focused topic—*All kids should learn young.* Once he had discovered a topic about which he had something to say—that all children should receive computer training when they are young—the writer could brainstorm again for more reasons, details, and examples to support this idea.

PRACTICE 5   Choose one of the following topics that interests you and write it at the top of your paper. Then brainstorm. Write anything that comes into your head about the topic. Just let ideas pour onto paper!

1. a place I never want to go back to   4. a lesson

2. dealing with difficult people   5. my best/worst job

3. an unforgettable person in politics,   6. dating
   sports, or religious life

Once you fill a page with your list, read it over, underlining the most interesting ideas. Draw arrows to connect related ideas. Is there one idea that might be the subject of a paper?

PART C

Clustering

Some writers use still another method—called **clustering** or **mapping**—to get their ideas onto paper. To begin clustering, simply write an idea or a topic, usually one word, in the center of your paper. Then let your mind make associations, and write these associations, branching out from the center.

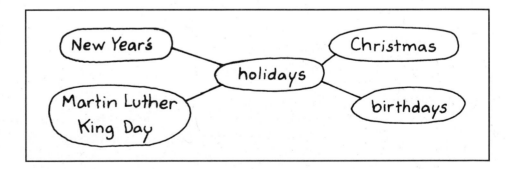

When one idea suggests other ideas, details, and examples, write these around it in a "cluster." After you finish, pick the cluster that most interests you. You may wish to freewrite for more ideas.

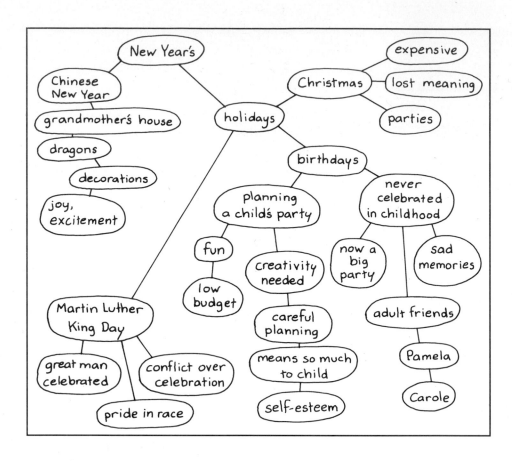

PRACTICE 6   Choose one of these topics or another topic that interests you. Write it in the center of a piece of paper and then try clustering. Keep writing down associations until you have filled most of the page.

1. heroes   4. inspiration

2. holidays   5. a dream

3. exercise   6. movies

PART D

Asking Questions

Many writers get ideas about a subject by asking questions and trying to answer them. This section describes two ways to do so.

The Reporter's Six Questions

Newspaper reporters often answer six basic questions at the beginning of an article: **Who? What? Where? When? Why? How?** Here is the way one student used these questions to explore the general subject of *sports* assigned by his instructor:

Who?	Players, basketball and football players, coaches, fans. Violence—I'm tired of that subject. Loyal crazy screaming fans—Giants fans.
What?	Excitement. Stadium on the day of a game. Tailgate parties. Cookouts. Incredible spreads—Italian families with peppers, stuff to spread on sandwiches. All day partying. Radios, TVs, grills, Giants caps.
Where?	Giants Stadium parking lot. People gather in certain areas—meet me in 10-B. Stadiums all over the country, same thing. People party on tailgates, in cars, on cars, plastic chairs, blankets.
When?	People arrive early morning—cook breakfast, lunch. After the game, many stay on in parking lot, talking, drinking beer. Year after year they come back.
Why?	Big social occasion, emotional outlet.
How?	They come early to get space. Some stadiums now rent parking spaces. Some families pass on season tickets in their wills!

Notice the way this writer used the questions to focus his ideas about tailgate parties at Giants Stadium. He has already come up with many interesting details for a good paper.

Ask Your Own Questions

If the reporter's six questions seem too confining, just ask the questions *you* want answered about a subject. Let each answer suggest the next question. Here is how one student responded to the subject of *teenage pregnancy:*

What do I know about teenage pregnancy? I saw my sister's plans for her future cut short by pregnancy. She won a high-school fashion design award, was spunky, full of fun. Now, with a child to raise, she works in a diner. The father of the child disappeared two years ago.

What would I like to know? Why do teenagers get pregnant? Teenage girls think they can't get pregnant. Teenage boys think it's macho to get a girl pregnant. Lack of knowledge of birth control methods. Teenage girls think that having a baby will keep their boyfriends from leaving them. They think that babies are fun to have around, to play with.

Where can I get more information? Guidance counselors at my old school. Planned Parenthood. Interview my friends who had babies when they were still teenagers. Talk to my sister.

What would I like to focus on? What interests me? I would like to know what pressures, fears, and hopes teenage girls feel that would allow them to take the chance of becoming pregnant.

What is my point of view? I would like teenagers to be aware of how their lives will be forever changed by a pregnancy.

Who is my audience? I would like to write for teenagers—primarily girls—to help them understand the problems of teenage pregnancy.

PRACTICE 7   Answer the reporter's six questions on one of the following topics or on a topic of your own choice.

1. drug addiction   5. music

2. sports   6. family get-togethers

3. career goals   7. replacing negatives with positives

4. coping with stress   8. choosing a major or concentration

PRACTICE 8   Ask and answer at least five questions of your own about one of the topics in Practice 7. Use these questions if you wish: What do I know about this subject? What would I like to know? Where can I find answers to my questions? What would I like to focus on? What is my point of view about this subject? Who is my audience?

PART E

Keeping a Journal

Keeping a journal is an excellent way to practice your writing skills and discover ideas for further writing. Mostly, your journal is for you—a private place where you record your experiences and your inner life; it is the place where, as one writer says, "I discover what I really think by writing it down."

Get yourself an attractive notebook with $8\frac{1}{2}$-by-11-inch paper. Then every morning or night, or several times a week, write for at least fifteen minutes in this journal. Don't just record the day's events ("I went to the store. It rained. I came home.") Instead, write in detail about what most angered, moved, or amused you that day.

Write about what you really care about—motorcycles, loneliness, working in a doughnut shop, family relationships, turkey farming, ending or starting a relationship. You may be surprised by how much you know. Write, think, and write some more. Your journal is private, so don't worry about grammar or correctness. Instead, aim to capture your truth so exactly that someone reading your words might experience it too.

Carry journal paper with you during the day for "fast sketches," jotting down things that catch your attention: a man playing drums in the street; a baby wearing a bib that reads *Spit Happens*; a compliment you receive at work; something your child just learned to do.

Every journal is unique—and usually private—but here are two sample journal entries to suggest possibilities. The first student links a quotation he has just learned to a disturbing "lesson of love":

Apr. 11. Two weeks ago, our professor mentioned a famous quote: "It is better to have loved and lost than never to have loved at all." The words had no particular meaning for me. How wrong I was. Last Sunday I received some very distressing news that will change my life from now on.

My wife has asked me why I never notified any family members except my mother of the birth of our children. My reply has been an argument or an angry stare. Our daughter Angelica is now two months shy of her second birthday, and we were also blessed with the birth of a son, who is five months old. I don't know whether it was maturity or my conscience, but last Sunday I decided it was time to let past grievances be forgotten. Nothing on this green earth would shelter me from what I was to hear that day.

I went to my father's address, knocked on his door, but got no response. Nervous but excited, I knocked again. Silence. On leaving the building, I bumped into his neighbor and asked for the possible whereabouts of my father. I couldn't brace myself for the cold shock of hearing from him that my father had died. I was angry as well as saddened, for my father was a quiet and gentle man whose love of women, liquor, and good times exceeded the love of his son.

Yes, it would have been better to have loved my father as he was than never to have gotten the opportunity to love such a man. A lesson of love truly woke me up to the need to hold dearly the ones you care for and overcome unnecessary grudges. "I love you, Pop, and may you rest in peace. Que Díos te quide."

—Anthony Falu (Student)

In the journal entry that follows, another student writes in order to sort out her feelings. As you read, ask yourself what seems to be bothering her. Is it really a cold? Is it the cat?

Nov. 5. The coffee and the egg can wait—not particularly in the mood for that now. Not in the mood for this journal either, but maybe I'll find out what's going on or why I feel so bad. I'm a little sleepy, have less patience lately, especially stupidity—questions asked without thinking. Why do I feel my time's wasted? Shouldn't. Just a little irritable, worried about this cold I'm developing and why Don seemed upset when I questioned him about visiting his sister. I didn't sleep very well last night. Maybe the cat's at fault. She must have been cold and crawled under the covers, so I pushed her out and Don woke up. Or he shoved her off the bed when her whiskers tickled his nose and that woke me up. So we fought again. Now I'm the one who gets up at 7 a.m., and he's the one in the beautiful picture of a tired sleeping male form under the covers, calico cat curled up, sleeping off the breakfast I just gave her. Wish I didn't have to leave.

The uses of a journal are limited only by your imagination. Here are some ideas:

- Write down your goals and dreams; then brainstorm steps you can take to make them reality. (Notice negative thoughts—"I can't do that. That will never work." Focus on positive thoughts—"Of course I can! If X can do it, so can I.")

- Write about a problem you are having and creative ways in which you might solve it.

- Analyze yourself as a student. What are your strengths and weaknesses? What can you do to build on the strengths and overcome the weaknesses?

- What class at this college have you most enjoyed? Why?

- Who believes in you? Who seems not to believe in you? How do their attitudes make you feel?

- Imagine five other lives you might want to live. Who would you be: a figure skater? an inventor? a surgeon?

- If you could change one thing about yourself, what would it be? What might you do to change it?

- If you could spend time with one famous person, living or dead, who would it be? Why?

- List ten things you would love to do if they didn't seem so crazy.

- Do you have an important secret? Kept from whom? How do you feel about keeping this secret? Why *do* people have secrets?

- Name three people you are supposed to admire; then name three you really do admire. Do the differences teach you anything about yourself?

- If money were no object, what place in the world would you visit and why? What would you do there, whom would you take, and how long would you stay?

- Use your journal as a place to "think on paper" about material that you have read in a textbook, newspaper, or magazine.

- What news story most upset you in the past month? Why?

- Write down facts that impress you—the average young American watches 18,000 TV murders before he or she graduates from high school! Analyzing that one fact could produce a good paper.

- Record quotations that spark your interest. Suppose you like and jot down Abe Lincoln's statement that "Most folks are as happy as they make up their minds to be." Later, thinking and writing about that thought could produce a whole paragraph or composition.

- Read through the Quotation Bank at the end of this book, and copy your five favorite quotations into your journal.

PRACTICE 9   Get an 8½-by-11-inch loose-leaf notebook for your journal. Write in it for at least fifteen minutes three times a week.

After the end of each week, reread what you have written, underlining sections or ideas you like and putting a check mark next to subjects you might like to write more about.

PRACTICE 10   Choose one passage in your journal that you would like to rewrite and let others read. Underline the parts you like best. Now rewrite, polish, and improve it.

Unit 2

Discovering the Paragraph

3

The Process of Writing Paragraphs

This chapter will guide you step by step from examining basic paragraphs to writing them. The paragraph makes a good learning model because it is short and yet contains many of the elements found in longer compositions. Therefore, you easily can transfer the skills you gain by writing paragraphs to longer essays, reports, and letters.

In this chapter, you will first look at finished paragraphs and then move through the process of writing paragraphs of your own.

PART A

Defining and Looking at the Paragraph

A **paragraph** is a group of related sentences that develops one main idea. Although there is no definite length for a paragraph, it is often from five to twelve sentences long. A paragraph usually occurs with other paragraphs in a longer piece of writing—an essay, an article, or a letter, for example. Before studying longer compositions, however, we will look at single paragraphs.

A paragraph looks like this on the page:

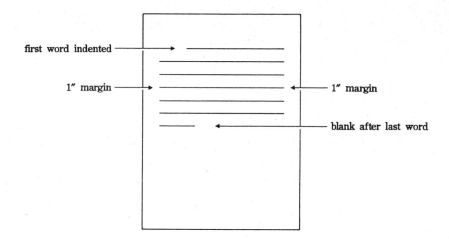

- Clearly **indent** the first word of every paragraph about 1 inch (five spaces on the typewriter or word processor).

- Extend every line of a paragraph to the right-hand margin.

- However, if the last word of the paragraph comes before the end of the line, leave the rest of the line blank.

Topic Sentence and Body

Most paragraphs contain one main idea to which all the sentences relate.

The **topic sentence** states this main idea.

The **body** of the paragraph develops and supports this main idea with particular facts, details, and examples:

> I allow the spiders the run of the house. I figure that any predator that hopes to make a living on whatever smaller creatures might blunder into a four-inch-square bit of space in the corner of the bathroom where the tub meets the floor needs every bit of my support. They catch flies and even field crickets in those webs. Large spiders in barns have been known to trap, wrap, and suck hummingbirds, but there's no danger of that here. I tolerate the webs, only occasionally sweeping away the very dirtiest of them after the spider itself has scrambled to safety. I'm always leaving a bath towel draped over the tub so that the big, haired spiders, who are constantly getting trapped by the tub's smooth sides, can use its rough surface as an exit ramp. Inside the house the spiders have only given me one mild surprise. I washed some dishes and set them to dry over a plastic drainer. Then I wanted a cup of coffee, so I picked from the drainer my mug, which was still warm from the hot rinse water, and across the rim of the mug, strand after strand, was a spider web.
>
> —Annie Dillard, *Pilgrim at Tinker Creek*

■ The first sentence of the paragraph above is the **topic sentence.** It states the main idea of the paragraph: that the spiders are allowed *the run of the house.*

■ The rest of the paragraph, the **body,** fully explains and supports this statement. The writer first gives a reason for her attitude toward spiders and then gives particular examples of her tolerance of spiders.

The topic sentence is more *general* than the other sentences in the paragraph. The other sentences in the paragraph provide specific information relating to the topic sentence. Because the topic sentence tells what the entire paragraph is about, *it is usually the first sentence,* as above. Sometimes the topic sentence occurs elsewhere in the paragraph, for example, as the second sentence after an introduction or as the last sentence. Some paragraphs contain only an implied topic sentence but no stated topic sentence at all.

As you develop your writing skills, however, it is a good idea to write paragraphs that *begin* with the topic sentence. Once you have mastered this pattern, you can try variations.

PRACTICE 1   Find and underline the **topic sentence** in each paragraph below. Look for the sentence that states the **main idea** of the entire paragraph.

Paragraph a: The summer picnic gave ladies a chance to show off their baking hands. On the barbecue pit, chickens and spareribs sputtered in their own fat and in a sauce whose recipe was guarded in the family like a scandalous affair. However, every true baking artist could reveal her prize to the delight and criticism of the town. Orange sponge cakes and dark brown mounds dripping Hershey's chocolate stood layer to layer with ice-white coconuts and light brown caramels. Pound cakes sagged with their buttery weight and small children could no more resist licking the icings than their mothers could avoid slapping the sticky fingers.

—Maya Angelou, *I Know Why the Caged Bird Sings*

Paragraph b: Mental health counselors work with individuals and groups to promote optimum mental health. They help individuals deal with such concerns as addictions and substance abuse, parenting, marital problems, suicide, stress management, problems with self-esteem, issues associated with aging, job and career concerns, educational decisions, and other issues of mental and emotional health. Mental health counselors work closely with other mental health specialists, including psychiatrists, psychologists, clinical social workers, psychiatric nurses, and school counselors.

—Adapted from *Occupational Outlook Handbook,* 1992–93

Paragraph c: Eating sugar can be worse than eating nothing. Refined sugar provides only empty calories. It contributes none of the protein, fat, vitamins or minerals needed for its own metabolism in the body, so these nutrients must be obtained elsewhere. Sugar tends to replace nourishing food in the diet. It is a thief that robs us of nutrients. A dietary emphasis on sugar can deplete the body of nutrients. If adequate nutrients are not supplied by the diet—and they tend not to be in a sugar-rich diet—they must be leached from other body tissues before sugar can be metabolized. For this reason, a U.S. Senate committee labeled sugar as an "antinutrient."

—Janice Fillip, "The Sweet Thief," *Medical Self-Care*

Paragraph d: In just half a century, television has covered the planet. More than 2.5 billion people watch TV—on more than 750 million TV sets, in more than 150 countries. For every child born in the world, a television set is manufactured—a quarter of a million every day. Surprisingly, more people have access to television than to telephones. And there are more than sixty thousand transmitters either on the earth's surface or in orbit over our heads. Because of all this activity, the earth actually gives off more energy at certain low frequencies than the sun does.

—Adapted from Michael Winship, *Television*

PRACTICE 2   Each group of sentences below could be unscrambled and written as a paragraph. Circle the letter of the **topic sentence** in each group of sentences. Remember: the topic sentence should state the main idea of the entire paragraph and should be general enough to include all the ideas in the body.

Example
  a. Rubies were supposed to stimulate circulation and restore lost vitality.
  b. Clear quartz was believed to promote sweet sleep and good dreams.
  ⓒ. For centuries, minerals and precious stones were thought to possess healing powers.
  d. Amethysts were thought to prevent drunkenness.
(Sentence C includes the ideas in all the other sentences.)

1. a. Wayne Gretzky began skating before he was three, belonged to a hockey team when he was six, and scored 378 goals in eighty-five games when he was eleven.
  b. In 1994, he scored his 802nd career goal, passing the legendary Gordie Howe's 801 career goals.
  c. In 1989, not long after he was traded to the Los Angeles Kings, he broke the National Hockey League's record for number of points scored.
  d. An Edmonton Oiler from 1979 to 1988, the fragile-looking Gretzky carried this previously weak team to four Stanley Cup championships.
  e. By 1995, Gretzky held more than 60 NHL records.
  f. Blessed with incredible technique and intellect, Wayne Gretzky is probably the greatest hockey player who has ever lived.

2. a. The better skaters played tag or crack the whip.
   b. Every winter, the lake was the center of activity.
   c. People talked and shoveled snow, exposing the dark, satiny ice.
   d. Children on double runners skated in the center of the cleared area.
   e. Dogs raced and skidded among the skaters.

3. a. Albert Einstein, whose scientific genius awed the world, could not speak until he was four and could not read until he was nine.
   b. Inventor Thomas Edison had such severe problems reading, writing, and spelling that he was called "defective from birth," taken out of school, and taught at home.
   c. Many famous people have suffered from learning disabilities.
   d. Olympic diving champion Greg Louganis was teased and laughed at for his speech delay, stutter, and perceptual problems.

4. a. Here at Kensington College, without our student numbers, we would hardly exist.
   b. We must display our student numbers and IDs just to get onto campus.
   c. We must pencil our student numbers on computer cards in order to register for courses.
   d. When our grades are posted, the *A*'s and *F*'s go not to Felicia Watson and Bill Jenkins, Jr., but to 237–002 and 235–1147.

5. a. Today Americans live longer than ever before.
   b. Statistics show that forcing a person to retire can actually impair his or her emotional and physical health.
   c. Research indicates that workers aged sixty-five to seventy-five perform as well as younger workers in all but heavy physical jobs.
   d. Forced retirement according to age does not make sense when we examine the facts.
   e. Older workers tend to be more stable than younger workers.

6. a. Annie Oakley could riddle a playing card with bullet holes while it was falling from someone's hand to the ground.
   b. From 1869 to 1875, as a poor child in Ohio, she paid off the family's mortgage by hunting and selling wild game.
   c. In her teens, she competed against Frank Butler, a famous marksman who came to town, and beat him by one point.
   d. European kings and queens loved to watch her perform, and she once shot a cigarette from the lips of the future Kaiser Wilhelm II of Germany.
   e. Years later, Annie married Butler and joined Wild Bill's Wild West Show, where she was the star.
   f. Annie Oakley was one of the best sharpshooters of all time.

7. a. In Mexico the folk arts are still thriving.
   b. Beautiful bowls and trays made of papier-mâché are widely available.
   c. Hand-embroidered dresses of pure cotton are common.
   d. Throughout the country, pottery making and the fiber arts are alive and well.
   e. Every town has its market glittering with hand-wrought silver jewelry.

8. a. Maggie throws her head back and slaps her thigh.
   b. The most amazing thing about Maggie is her laughter.
   c. When something strikes her as funny, she first lets out a shriek of surprise.
   d. Then she breaks into loud hoots.
   e. When the laughter stops, she shakes her head from side to side and says, "I just love it!"

9. a. At the University of Michigan, he helped develop a flu vaccine.
   b. He served as a consultant to the World Health Organization, a branch of the United Nations that brings medical help to developing countries.
   c. Dr. Jonas Salk has contributed much to the cure of disease.
   d. After years of research, he finally created the first effective polio vaccine.
   e. Dr. Salk is now racing against time to make an AIDS vaccine.

10. a. Believe it or not, the first contact lens was drawn by Leonardo da Vinci in 1508.
    b. However, not until 1877 was the first thick glass contact actually made by a Swiss doctor.
    c. The journey of contact lenses from an idea to a comfortable, safe reality took nearly five hundred years!
    d. In 1948, smaller, more comfortable plastic lenses were introduced to enthusiastic American eyeglass wearers.
    e. These early glass lenses were enormous, covering the whites of the eyes.
    f. Today, contact lens wearers can choose ultra-thin, colored, or even disposable lenses.

PART B

Narrowing the Topic and Writing the Topic Sentence

A writer can arrive at the goal—a finished paragraph—in several ways. However, before writing a paragraph, most writers go through a process that includes these important steps:

1. Narrowing the topic

2. Writing the topic sentence

3. Generating ideas for the body

4. Selecting and dropping ideas

5. Arranging ideas in a plan or an outline

The rest of this chapter will explain these steps and guide you through the process of writing basic paragraphs.

Narrowing the Topic

As a student, you may be assigned broad writing topics by your instructor—success, drug use in the schools, a description of a person. Your instructor is thereby giving you the chance to cut the topic down to size and to choose one aspect of the topic *that interests you.*

Assume, for example, that your instructor gives this assignment: "Write a paragraph describing a person you know." The challenge is to pick someone you would *like* to write about, someone who interests you and would probably interest your readers.

Giving some thought to your *audience* and *purpose* may help you narrow the topic. In this case, your audience probably will be your instructor and classmates; your purpose is to inform or perhaps entertain them by describing someone.

Now think about the people you know, and freewrite, brainstorm, or ask yourself questions. For example, you might ask yourself, "What person do I love, hate, or admire?" "Is there a family member I would like to write about?" "Who is the funniest, most unusual, or most talented person I know?"

Let's suppose you choose Pete, an unusual person and one about whom you have something to say. But Pete is still too broad a subject for one paragraph; you could probably write pages and pages about him. To narrow the topic further, you might ask yourself, "What is unusual about him? What might interest others?" Pete's room is the messiest place you have ever seen; in fact, Pete's whole life is sloppy, and you decide that you could write a good paragraph about that. You have now narrowed the topic to just one of Pete's qualities: *his sloppiness.*

Writing the Topic Sentence

The next important step is to state your topic clearly *in sentence form.* Writing the topic sentence helps you further narrow your topic by forcing you to make a statement about it. The simplest possible topic sentence about Pete might read *Pete is sloppy,* but you might wish to strengthen it by saying, for instance, *Pete's sloppiness is a terrible habit.*

Writing a good topic sentence is an important step toward an effective paragraph since the topic sentence will determine the direction and scope of the body. The topic sentence should be *complete* and *limited.*

The topic sentence must be a **complete sentence.** It must contain a subject and verb and express a complete thought. Be careful not to confuse a **topic** or **title** with a **topic sentence.** *My last job,* for example, could not be a topic sentence because it is not a complete sentence but a fragment.* However, *My Last Job* could be a title† because topics and titles do not have to be complete sentences.

---

* For more practice in correcting fragments, see Chapter 23, "Avoiding Sentence Errors," Part B.

† For practice in writing titles, see Chapter 19, "The Introduction, the Conclusion, and the Title," Part C.

Below are some possible topic sentences for a paragraph entitled *My Last Job:*

---

1. My last job in the Complaint Department taught me how to calm down angry people.

2. Working in the Complaint Department left me exhausted by the end of the day.

3. Two years in the Complaint Department prepared me to become an assistant manager.

■ Each topic sentence is a *complete sentence* that focuses on one particular aspect of the job.

■ Since there are as many possible topic sentences for any topic as there are writers, creating a topic sentence forces the writer to focus clearly on one aspect of the topic. If you were assigned the topic *my last job,* what would your topic sentence be?

_____

_____

PRACTICE 3   Put a check beside each possible topic sentence below. Remember, a topic sentence must be a grammatically complete thought. Rewrite any fragments into possible topic sentences.

Examples   ✓ Some folk remedies really work.

Rewrite: _____

_____ A four-day work week.

Rewrite: Linear Graphics Company should adopt a four-day work week. _____

1. _____ The worst class I ever had.

Rewrite: _____

_____

2. _____ When it comes to selecting audio equipment, Rupert is a perfectionist.

Rewrite: _____

_____

3. _____ Helping a child learn to read.

Rewrite: _____

_____

4. _____ Police officers who take bribes.

Rewrite: _____

_____

5. _____ The moon cast a silver glow over the empty street.

Rewrite: _____

_____

6. _____ Why I volunteer at a shelter for the homeless.

Rewrite: _____

_____

7. _____ The difficult social life of a single parent.

Rewrite: _____

_____

8. _____ Traveling with a friend.

Rewrite: _____

_____

The topic sentence should be **limited.** It should be carefully worded to express a limited main idea. As a rule, the more limited the topic sentence, the better the paragraph. Which of these topic sentences do you think will produce the best paragraphs?

4. Five wet, bug-filled days at Boy Scout Camp made my son a fan of the great indoors.

5. America today has problems.

6. Norine is a very intelligent basketball player.

■ Topic sentences 4 and 6 are both limited enough to provide the main idea for a good paragraph. Both are carefully worded to suggest clearly what ideas will follow. From topic sentence 4, what do you expect the paragraph to include?

_____

_____

■ What do you expect paragraph 6 to include?

_____

_____

■ Topic sentence 5, on the other hand, is so broad that the paragraph could include almost anything. *Who* or *what* has problems? A school in Topeka? Hospital workers in Chicago? The average consumer? In other words, focus on just one specific problem for an effective paragraph.

PRACTICE 4   Put a check beside each topic sentence that is limited enough to allow you to write a good paragraph. If a topic sentence is too broad, narrow the topic according to your own interests and write a new, limited topic sentence.

Examples

   ✓   Keeping a journal can improve a student's writing.

   Rewrite: _____

   _____   This paper will be about my family.

   Rewrite: _My brother Mark has a unique sense of humor._____

1. _____   Eugene's hot temper causes problems at work.

   Rewrite: _____

   _____

2. _____   This paragraph will discuss study techniques.

   Rewrite: _____

   _____

3. _____   Driving is better today.

   Rewrite: _____

   _____

4. _____ Many beer commercials on TV imply that people need to drink in order to have a good time.

Rewrite: _____

_____

5. _____ Child abuse is something to think about.

Rewrite: _____

_____

6. _____ Tournament prize money in international tennis should be the same for men and women.

Rewrite: _____

_____

7. _____ Learning karate increased my self-confidence.

Rewrite: _____

_____

8. _____ Cooking calms my nerves.

Rewrite: _____

_____

PRACTICE 5   Here is a list of broad topics. Choose three that interest you; then narrow each topic and write a topic sentence. Make sure that each topic sentence is a complete sentence and limited enough for you to write a good paragraph.

Overcoming fears	Youth programs in your community
A supportive mate	Balancing work and play
An experience of success	A person you like or dislike
The value of humor	A time when you were (or were not) in control

1. Topic: _____

Narrowed topic: _____

Topic sentence: _____

_____

_____

2. Topic: _____

Narrowed topic: _____

Topic sentence: _____

_____

_____

3. Topic: _____

Narrowed topic: _____

Topic sentence: _____

_____

_____

PART C

Generating Ideas for the Body

One good way to generate ideas for the body of a paragraph is **brainstorming**—freely jotting down anything that relates to your topic sentence: facts, details, examples, little stories. This step might take just a few minutes, but it is one of the most important elements of the writing process. Brainstorming can provide you with specific ideas to support your topic sentence. Later you can choose from these ideas as you compose your paragraph.

Here, for example, is a possible brainstorm list for the topic sentence *Pete's sloppiness is a terrible habit:*

1. His apartment is carpeted with dirty clothes, books, candy wrappers

2. His favorite candy—M & Ms

3. He is often a latecomer or a no-show

4. He jots time-and-place information for dates and appointments on scraps of paper that are tucked away and forgotten

5. Stacks of old newspapers sit on chair seats

6. Socks bake on lampshades

7. Papers for classes wrinkled and carelessly scrawled

8. I met Pete for the first time in math class

9. His sister is just the opposite, very neat

10. Always late for classes, out of breath

11. He is one messy person

12. Papers stained with Coke or M & Ms

Instead of brainstorming, some writers freewrite or ask themselves questions to generate ideas for their paragraphs. Do what works best for you. If you need more practice in any of these methods, reread Chapter 2, "Generating Ideas."

PRACTICE 6 Choose the topic from Practice 5 (in Part B) that most interests you. Write that topic and your topic sentence here.

Topic: _____

Topic sentence: _____

_____

Now brainstorm. Write anything that comes to you about your topic sentence. Just let your ideas pour onto paper.

1. _____

2. _____

3. _____

4. _____

5. _____

6. _____

7. _____

8. _____

9. _____

10. _____

11. _____

12. _____

13. _____

14. _____

15. _____

and more . . .

Selecting and Dropping Ideas

Next simply read over what you have written, **selecting** those ideas that relate to and support the topic sentence and **dropping** those that do not. That is, keep the facts, examples, or little stories that provide specific information about your topic sentence. Drop ideas that just **repeat** the topic sentence but add nothing new to the paragraph.

If you are not sure which ideas to select or drop, underline the **key word** or **words** of the topic sentence, the ones that indicate the real point of your paragraph. Then make sure that the ideas you select are related to those key words.

Here is the brainstorm list for the topic sentence *Pete's sloppiness is a terrible habit.* The key word in the topic sentence is *sloppiness.* Which ideas would you keep? Why? Which would you drop? Why?

1. His apartment is carpeted with dirty clothes, books, candy wrappers

2. His favorite candy—M & Ms

3. He is often a latecomer or a no-show

4. He jots time-and-place information for dates and appointments on scraps of paper that are tucked away and forgotten

5. Stacks of old newspapers sit on chair seats

6. Socks bake on lampshades

7. Papers for classes wrinkled and carelessly scrawled

8. I met Pete for the first time in math class

9. His sister is just the opposite, very neat

10. Always late for classes, out of breath

11. He is one messy person

12. Papers stained with Coke or M & Ms

You probably dropped ideas 2, 8, and 9 because they do not relate to the topic—Pete's sloppiness. You should also have dropped idea 11 because it merely repeats the topic sentence.

PRACTICE 7   Read through your own brainstorm list in Practice 6 (in Part C). Select the ideas that relate to your topic sentence and cross out those that do not. In addition, cross out any ideas that just repeat your topic sentence. Be prepared to explain why you drop or keep each idea.

PART E

Arranging Ideas in a Plan or an Outline

After you have selected the ideas you wish to include in your paragraph, you can begin to make a plan or an outline. A plan briefly lists and arranges the ideas you wish to present in your paragraph. An outline does the same thing a bit more formally, with letters or numbers indicating the main groupings of ideas.

First, group together ideas that have something in common, that are related or alike in some way. Then order your ideas by choosing which one you want to come first, which one second, and so on.

Below is a plan for a paragraph about Pete's sloppiness:

Topic sentence: Pete's sloppiness is a terrible habit.

His apartment is carpeted with dirty clothes, books, candy wrappers

Stacks of old newspapers sit on chair seats

Socks bake on lampshades

He jots time-and-place information for dates and appointments on scraps of paper that are tucked away and forgotten

He is often a latecomer or a no-show

Always late for classes, out of breath

Papers for classes wrinkled and carelessly scrawled

Papers stained with Coke or M & Ms

■ Do you see the logic in this arrangement? How are the ideas in each group

above related? _____

_____

_____

- Does it make sense to discuss Pete's apartment first, his lateness second, and his written work third? Why? _____

  _____

  _____

- Once you have finished arranging ideas, you should have a clear **plan** from which to write your paragraph.*

PRACTICE 8 On notebook paper, arrange the ideas from your brainstorm list according to some plan or outline. First, group together related ideas; then decide which ideas will come first, which second, and so on.

Keep in mind that there is more than one way to group ideas. Think about what you want to say; then group ideas according to what *your* point is.

PART F

Writing and Revising the Paragraph

Writing the First Draft

The first draft should contain all the ideas you have decided to use in the order you have chosen in your plan. Be sure to start with your topic sentence. Try to write the best, most interesting, or most amusing paragraph you can, but avoid getting stuck on any one word, sentence, or idea. If you are unsure about something, put a check in the margin and come back to it later. Writing on every other line will leave room for later corrections.

Once you have included all of the ideas from your plan, think about adding a concluding sentence that summarizes your main point or adds a final idea. Not all paragraphs need concluding sentences. For example, if you are telling a story, the paragraph can end when the story does. Write a concluding sentence if it will help to bring your thoughts to an end for your reader.

If possible, once you have finished the first draft, set the paper aside for several hours or several days.

Revising

Revising means rethinking and rewriting your first draft and then making whatever additions or corrections are necessary to improve the paragraph. You may cross out and rewrite words or entire sentences. You may add, drop, or rearrange details.

As you revise, keep the *reader* in mind. Ask yourself these questions:

* For more work on order, see Chapter 4, "Achieving Coherence," Part A.

- Is my topic sentence clear?

- Can a reader understand and follow my ideas?

- Does the paragraph follow a logical order and guide the reader from point to point?

- Will the paragraph keep the reader interested?

In addition, check your paragraph for adequate support and unity, characteristics that we'll consider in the following pages.

Revising for Support

As you revise, make sure your paragraph contains excellent **support**—that is, specific facts, details, and examples that fully explain your topic sentence.

Be careful, too, that you have not simply repeated ideas—especially the topic sentence. Even if they are in different words, repeated ideas only make the reader suspect that your paragraph is padded and that you do not have enough facts and details to support your main idea properly.

Which of the following paragraphs contains the most convincing support?

Paragraph a: (1) Our run-down city block was made special by a once-vacant lot called The Community Garden. (2) The lot was planted with all sorts of plants, vegetables, and flowers. (3) There was a path curving through it. (4) We went there to think. (5) The Community Garden made our block special. (6) Though our neighborhood was known as "tough," no one ever vandalized the garden.

Paragraph b: (1) Our run-down city block was made special by a once-vacant lot called The Community Garden. (2) I'm not sure who first had the idea, but the thin soil had been fertilized, raked, and planted with a surprising assortment of vegetables and flowers. (3) Anyone interested in gardening could tend green pepper plants, string beans, fresh herbs, even corn. (4) Others planted flowers, which changed with the seasons—tall red dahlias, white and purple irises, and taxi-yellow marigolds to discourage the insects. (5) A narrow path curved gracefully among the plants, paved with bricks no doubt left over from the building that once stood here. (6) The Community Garden was our pride, the place we went to think and to be still. (7) Though the neighborhood was known as "tough," no one ever vandalized the garden.

- *Paragraph a* contains general statements but little specific information to support the topic sentence.

- *Paragraph a* also contains needless repetition. What is the number of the sentence or sentences that just repeat the topic sentence?

    ■ *Paragraph b,* however, supports the topic sentence with specific details and examples: *thin soil, fertilized, raked and planted, green pepper plants, string beans, fresh herbs, corn, red dahlias.* What other specific support does it give?

_____

_____

_____

_____

_____

_____

PRACTICE 9　　Check the following paragraphs for adequate support. As you read each one, decide which places need more or better support—specific facts, details, and examples. Then rewrite the paragraphs, inventing facts and details whenever necessary and dropping repetitious words and sentences.

    Paragraph a: (1) My uncle can always be counted on when the family faces hardship. (2) Last year, when my mother was very ill, he was there, ready to help in every way. (3) He never has to be called twice. (4) When my parents were in danger of losing their little hardware store because of a huge increase in rent, he helped. (5) Everyone respects him for his willingness to be a real "family man." (6) He is always there for us.

    Paragraph b: (1) Many television talk shows don't really present a discussion of ideas. (2) Some people who appear on these shows don't know what they are talking about; they just like to sound off about something. (3) I don't like these shows at all. (4) Guests shout their opinions out loud but never give any proof for what they say. (5) Guests sometimes expose their most intimate personal and family problems before millions of viewers—I feel embarrassed. (6) I have even heard hosts insult their guests and guests insult them back. (7) Why do people watch this junk? (8) You never learn anything from these dumb shows.

Revising for Unity

It is sometimes easy, in the process of writing, to drift away from the topic under discussion. Guard against doing so by checking your paragraph for **unity**; that is, make sure the topic sentence, every sentence in the body, and the concluding sentence all relate to one main idea.*

* For more work on revising, see Chapter 16, "Putting Your Revision Skills to Work."

This paragraph lacks unity:

> (1) A. Philip Randolph, the great African-American champion of labor and civil rights, led confrontations with three very popular presidents. (2) Mr. Randolph called for a march on Washington by thousands of African-Americans on July 1, 1941, if President Roosevelt would not take action to end discrimination in defense industries during World War II. (3) Mr. Randolph was born in Florida. (4) After much delay, the president met with Randolph and one week later, opened many defense jobs to black workers. (5) A few years later, in 1948, Mr. Randolph threatened mass civil disobedience if President Truman did not end segregation against African-Americans in the military. (6) On July 26, Truman approved the order that integrated the armed services. (7) The last confrontation was with John F. Kennedy, who sought to stop the 1963 civil rights March on Washington. (8) Mr. Randolph led the historic march on August 28; it featured Martin Luther King's unforgettable "I Have a Dream" speech and led to the Civil Rights Bill of 1964.

■ What is the number of the topic sentence in this paragraph?

_____

■ Which sentence in the paragraph does *not* relate to the topic sentence?

_____

This paragraph also lacks unity:

> (1) Quitting smoking was very difficult for me. (2) When I was thirteen, my friend Janice and I smoked in front of a mirror. (3) We practiced holding the cigarette in different ways and tried French inhaling, letting the smoke roll slowly out of our mouths and drawing it back through our noses. (4) I thought this move, when it didn't incite a fit of coughing, was particularly sexy. (5) At first I smoked only to give myself confidence on dates and at parties. (6) Soon, however, I was smoking all the time.

■ Here the topic sentence itself, sentence 1, does not relate to the rest of the paragraph. The main idea in sentence 1, that quitting smoking was difficult, is not developed by the other sentences. Since the rest of the paragraph *is* unified, a more appropriate topic sentence might read, *As a teenager, I developed the bad habit of smoking.*

PRACTICE 10   Check the following paragraphs for **unity.** If a paragraph is unified, write *U* in the blank. If not, write the number of the sentence that does *not* belong. If the topic sentence does not fit the rest of the paragraph, write *T* in the blank and write a more appropriate topic sentence for the paragraph.

Paragraph a: _____ (1) At Paradise Produce, attractive displays of fruit and vegetables caught my eye. (2) On the left, oranges, lemons, and apples were stacked in neat pyramids. (3) In the center of the store, baskets of ripe peaches, plums, and raspberries were grouped in a kind of still life. (4) On the right, the leafy green vegetables had been arranged according to intensity of color: dark green spinach, then romaine lettuce and parsley, next the lighter iceberg lettuce, and finally the nearly white Chinese cabbage. (5) On the wall above the greens hung braided ropes of garlic. (6) Some nutritionists believe that garlic prevents certain diseases.

Paragraph b: _____ (1) Speed and excitement make the Indianapolis 500 one of the world's most popular auto races. (2) Every Memorial Day weekend, thirty-three of the world's fastest cars compete in this 500-mile race around the oval track at the Indianapolis Motor Speedway. (3) Racing cars can be divided into six types. (4) Speeds have increased almost every year since the first Indy 500 was held on May 30, 1911. (5) The winner of that race, Ray Harroun, drove his Marmon Wasp at an average speed of 74.59 miles per hour. (6) In 1994, Al Unser, Jr., won in his Penske-Mercedes car with an average speed of 160.87 miles per hour. (7) However, no one has yet passed Arie Luyendyk's 1990 record; his Lola Chevrolet raced at an average speed of 185.98 miles per hour. (8) Today the Indy 500 draws almost 300,000 fans each year, making it the best-attended sporting event on the planet.

Paragraph c: _____ (1) Turquoise is mined in the Southwest today much as it was mined in prehistoric times. (2) Turquoise was the Native American's bank account. (3) It was given as pawn in exchange for staple items that he or she needed. (4) It was a status symbol. (5) In addition, turquoise was considered a sacred presence and was often a part of religious offerings. (6) Turquoise was an important part of life for Native Americans in the Southwest.

Paragraph d: _____ (1) Dr. Jerome Bach believes that children may play certain roles in the family depending on their birth order. (2) The first child, who usually identifies with the father, takes on the family's more obvious social and career goals. (3) The second child is tuned in to the family's emotional requirements and may act out the hidden needs of others, especially the mother. (4) The behavior of the third child often reflects what is going on between the parents; for instance, if eating is the only thing the parents enjoy doing as a couple, the third child may be overweight. (5) In general, families today have fewer children than in the past.

Writing the Final Draft

Finally, recopy your paper. If you are writing in class, the second draft will usually be the last one. Be sure to include all your corrections. Write neatly and legibly—a carelessly scribbled paper seems to say that you don't care about your own work. When you finish, **proofread** for grammar and spelling. If you are unsure about spelling, check a dictionary. Pointing to each word as you read it will help you catch errors or words you have omitted. Make neat corrections in pen.

Here is the final draft of the paragraph about Pete's sloppiness:

> Pete's sloppiness is a terrible habit. He lives by himself in a one-room apartment carpeted with dirty clothes, books, and crumpled candy wrappers. Stacks of papers cover the chair seats. Socks bake on the lampshades. When Pete makes a date or an appointment, he may jot the time and place on a scrap of paper that is soon tucked into a pocket and forgotten, or—more likely—he doesn't jot down the information at all. As a result, Pete is often a latecomer or completely forgets to appear. His grades have suffered, too, since few instructors will put up with a student who arrives out of breath ten minutes after the class has begun and whose wrinkled, carelessly scrawled papers arrive (late, of course) punctuated with Coca-Cola stains and melted M & Ms. The less Pete controls his sloppiness, the more it seems to control him.

- Note that the paragraph contains good support—specific facts, details, and examples, that explain the topic sentence.

- Note that the paragraph has unity—every idea relates to the topic sentence.

- Note that the final sentence provides a brief conclusion so that the paragraph *feels finished.*

Writing Assignments

The assignments that follow will give you practice in writing basic paragraphs. In each, aim for (1) a clear, complete, and limited topic sentence and (2) a body that fully supports and develops the topic sentence.

Remember to **narrow the topic, write the topic sentence, freewrite or brainstorm, select,** and **arrange ideas** in a plan or an outline before you write. Rethink and **revise** as necessary before composing the final version of the paragraph. As you work, refer to the checklist at the end of this chapter.

Paragraph 1: Discuss an important day in your life. Think back to a day when you learned something important, preferably outside of school. In the topic sentence, tell what you learned. Freewrite or brainstorm to gather ideas. Then describe the lesson in detail, including only the most important steps or events in the learning process. Conclude with an insight.

Paragraph 2: Describe a meeting place. Many towns, neighborhoods, and colleges have a central place where people gather to chat and review the day's experiences—a park, restaurant, and so on. If you know such a place, describe it. Explain who goes there, what they do there, and what they talk about.

Paragraph 3: Interview a classmate about an achievement. Write about a time when your classmate achieved something important, like winning an award for a musical performance, getting an *A* in a difficult course, or helping a friend through a hard time. To gather interesting facts and details, ask your classmate questions like these and take notes: *Is there one accomplishment of which you are very proud? Why was this achievement so important?* Keep asking questions until you feel you can give the reader a vivid sense of your classmate's triumph. In your first sentence, state the person's achievement—for instance, *Being accepted in the honors program improved Gabe's self-esteem.* Then explain specifically why the achievement was so meaningful.

Paragraph 4: Choose an ideal job. Decide what kind of job you are best suited for and, in your topic sentence, tell what this job is. Then give three or four reasons that will convince readers of the wisdom of your choice. Discuss any special qualifications, talents, skills, or attitudes that would make you an excellent _____. Revise your work, checking for support and unity.

Paragraph 5: Discuss a quotation. Look through the quotations in the Quotation Bank before the indexes in this book. Pick a quotation you especially agree or disagree with. In your topic sentence, state how you feel about the quotation. Then explain why you feel the way you do, giving examples from your own experience to support or contradict the quotation. Make sure your reader knows exactly how you feel.

Paragraph 6: Describe your ideal vacation day. Present your ideal vacation day from morning to night. Do *not* tell everything, but highlight the four or five most important moments or activities of the day. As you jot down ideas, look for a pattern. Are the activities you choose all physical and active or lazy and slow? Is your day spent alone, with others, or both? In your topic sentence, state the pattern that includes all the activities or moments discussed in the paragraph.

Paragraph 7: Discuss a childhood experience. Choose an experience that deeply affected you. First tell exactly what happened, giving important details. Then explain the meaning this experience had for you.

Paragraph 8: Describe a portrait. Look closely at this self-portrait by the Mexican painter Frida Kahlo. Notice her mouth, eyes, eyebrows, hair, and other important details. Then write a paragraph in which you describe this picture for a reader who has never seen it. In your topic sentence, state your overall impression of the picture. Support this impression with details.

Checklist: The Process of Writing Basic Paragraphs

_____ 1. Narrow the topic in light of your audience and purpose.

_____ 2. Write a complete and limited topic sentence. If you have trouble, freewrite or brainstorm first; then narrow the topic and write the topic sentence.

_____ 3. Freewrite or brainstorm, generating facts, details, and examples to develop your topic sentence.

_____ 4. Select and drop ideas for the body of the paragraph.

_____ 5. Arrange ideas in a plan or an outline, deciding which ideas will come first, which will come second, and so forth.

_____ 6. Write the best first draft you can.

_____ 7. Conclude. Don't just leave the paragraph hanging.

_____ 8. Revise as necessary, checking your paragraph for support and unity.

_____ 9. Proofread for grammar and spelling errors.

4

Achieving Coherence

PART A   **Coherence Through Order**
PART B   **Coherence Through Related Sentences**

Every composition should have **coherence.** A paragraph *coheres*—holds together—when the sentences are arranged in a clear, logical *order* and when the sentences are *related* like links in a chain.

PART A

Coherence Through Order

An orderly presentation of ideas within the paragraph is easier to follow and more pleasant to read than a jumble. *After* jotting down ideas but *before* writing the paragraph, the writer should decide which ideas to discuss first, which second, which third, and so on, according to a logical order.

There are many possible orders, depending on the subject and the writer's purpose. This section will explain three basic ways of ordering ideas: **time order, space order,** and **order of importance.**

Time Order

One of the most common methods of ordering sentences in a paragraph is **time,** or **chronological, order,** which moves from present to past or past to present. Most stories, histories, and instructions follow the logical order of time.* The following paragraph employs time order:

---

* For work on narrative paragraphs, see Chapter 6, "Narration," and for work on process paragraphs, see Chapter 8, "Process."

(1) It was the most astonishing strikeout the fans had ever seen. (2) It *began* in the top of the seventh inning, when Big Fred Gnocchi came up to bat. (3) He took a few practice swipes to loosen up the power in his shoulders and back. (4) *Then* the catcher signaled, the pitcher nodded, and a steaming fast ball barreled toward Big Fred. (5) He watched it pass. (6) The umpire called a strike. (7) *Next* came a curve ball and another strike as Fred swung and missed. (8) Angry and determined, Fred dug in at the plate, spat, and gritted his teeth. (9) *Again* the pitcher wound up and delivered—a slow ball. (10) Gnocchi swung, realized he had moved too soon, swung again, and missed again. (11) That may have been the first time in baseball history that a batter took four strikes.

- The events in this paragraph are clearly arranged in the order of time. They are presented as they happened, *chronologically.*

- Throughout the paragraph, key words like *began, then, next,* and *again* emphasize time order and guide the reader from event to event.

Careful use of time order helps to avoid confusing writing like this: *Oops, I forgot to mention that before Fred swung and missed the last time, he had already swung and missed, and before that. . . .*

Occasionally, when the sentences in a paragraph follow a very clear time order, the topic sentence is only implied, not stated directly, as in this example:

(1) [Harriet] Tubman was born into slavery, escaped to the North in 1849, and established the "underground railroad" from which she "never lost a single passenger." (2) Tubman led over three hundred men, women, and children from slavery into freedom during the 1850's, risking her freedom nineteen times on her trips into the slave states. (3) Called "Moses," she became a legendary figure, and a reward of forty thousand dollars was offered for her capture. (4) During the Civil War, she worked as a spy, a scout, a nurse, and a commander of both black and white troops for the Union Army. . . . (5) Tubman spread her beliefs in freedom and liberty by speaking, organizing, and inspiring others. (6) In her later years, she attended women's suffrage conventions and helped organize the National Federation of Afro-American Women (1895).

—Judy Chicago, *The Dinner Party:*
A Symbol of Our Heritage

- Time order gives coherence to this paragraph. Sentence 1 tells us the beginning of Harriet Tubman's career as a fighter against slavery. However, it does not express the main idea of the entire paragraph.

- What is the implied topic sentence or main idea developed by the paragraph?

_____

_____

_____

- The implied topic sentence or main idea of the paragraph might read, *Harriet Tubman devoted much of her life to the cause of freedom.*

- Because the writer arranges the paragraph in chronological order, the reader can easily follow the order of events in Tubman's life. What words and phrases indicate time order? Underline them and list them here:

_____

_____

_____

PRACTICE 1   Arrange each set of sentences in logical time order, numbering the sentences 1, 2, 3, and so on, as if you were preparing to write a paragraph. Underline any words and phrases, like *first, next,* and *in 1692,* that give time clues.

1. _____   First, turn off the appliance that caused the fuse to blow.

   _____   Finally, replace with a new fuse of the same amperage.

   _____   To remove the blown fuse, turn it from right to left.

   _____   Changing a fuse is not difficult.

   _____   Then identify the blown fuse by its clouded glass cap.

2. _____   The judge later deeply regretted his part, but this sorry chapter in American history has never been forgotten.

   _____   Two books "proving" that witches existed, by the famous Puritan ministers Increase Mather and his son Cotton Mather, further fanned the hysteria in 1693.

   _____   The stage was set for the terrible Salem witch trials.

   _____   Nineteen so-called "witches and wizards" were hanged, and one was pressed to death.

_____ In 1692, when two girls in Salem Village, Massachusetts, had fits, they blamed the townspeople for bewitching them.

3. _____ She started her new work with the poor by teaching the street children of Calcutta arithmetic and reading.

_____ Mother Teresa has rightly and lovingly been named the "Saint of the Gutters."

_____ After several years at the school, she decided that her calling lay with the poor.

_____ After her efforts in India, she aided relief agencies in Lebanon and Ethiopia, caring for the displaced and the starving.

_____ With help from local authorities, she opened and staffed free clinics in the worst sections of Calcutta.

_____ Soon she realized that what these poor people needed most was adequate medical facilities.

_____ She began her career working at a Catholic school for the wealthy in Calcutta.

Writing Assignment 1

Choose from below one paragraph that you would like to write. Compose a topic sentence, freewrite or brainstorm to generate ideas, and then arrange them *chronologically*. You may wish to use transitional words and phrases like these:*

first	after that
then	soon
next	while
during	moments later
before	finally

Paragraph 1: Narrate the first hour of your average day. Start with when you get up in the morning and continue describing what you do for that first hour. Record your activities, your conversations, if any, and possibly your moods as you go through this hour of the morning. As you revise, make sure that events clearly follow time order.

* For a more complete list, see the section on transitional expressions, pages 61–62.

Paragraph 2: Record an unforgettable event. Choose a moment in sports or in some other activity that you vividly remember, either as a participant or as a spectator. In the topic sentence, tell in a general way what happened. *(It was the most exciting touchdown I have ever seen,* or *Ninety embarrassing seconds marked the end of my brief surfing career.)* Then record the experience, arranging details in time order.

Paragraph 3: Relate an accident or a close call. Focus on just a few critical moments of an accident or a close call that you experienced or witnessed, depicting the most important events in detail. Try to capture your thoughts and perceptions at the time as honestly and exactly as possible. Arrange them in time order.

Space Order

Another useful way to arrange ideas in writing is **space order**—describing a person, a thing, or a place from top to bottom, from left to right, from foreground to background, and so on. Space order is often used in descriptive writing because it moves from detail to detail like a movie camera's eye:*

> (1) We lived on the top floor of a five-story tenement in Williamsburg, facing the BMT elevated train, or as everyone called it, the El. (2) Our floors and windows would vibrate from the El, which shook the house like a giant, roaring as if his eyes were being poked out. (3) When we went down into the street, we played on a checkerboard of sunspots and shadows, which rhymed the railroad ties above our heads. (4) Even the brightest summer day could not lift the darkness and burnt-rubber smell of our street. (5) I would hold my breath when I passed under the El's long shadow. (6) It was the spinal column of my childhood, both oppressor and liberator, the monster who had taken away all our daylight, but on whose back alone one could ride out of the neighborhood into the big broad world.
>
> —Philip Lopate, *Bachelorhood: Tales of the Metropolis*

- This paragraph uses space order.

- Sentence 1 clearly places the scene: on the *top floor* of a tenement, *facing* the elevated train.

- In sentences 3 and 4, the paragraph moves *downstairs,* from the apartment to the street. These sentences describe the pattern made by the sun through the tracks overhead.

* For more work on space order, see Chapter 7, "Description."

- Sentence 5 moves directly *under* the railroad. Note how words and phrases like *on the top floor, facing, down into the street, above our heads,* and *passed under* help locate the action as the paragraph *moves* from place to place.

  Some paragraphs, clearly arranged according to space order, have only an implied topic sentence:

> (1) On my right a woods thickly overgrown with creeper descended the hill's slope to Tinker Creek. (2) On my left was a planting of large shade trees on the ridge of the hill. (3) Before me the grassy hill pitched abruptly and gave way to a large, level field fringed in trees where it bordered the creek. (4) Beyond the creek I could see with effort the vertical sliced rock where men had long ago quarried the mountain under the forest. (5) Beyond that I saw Hollins Pond and all its woods and pastures; then I saw in a blue haze the world poured flat and pale between the mountains.
>
> —Annie Dillard, *Pilgrim at Tinker Creek*

- The main idea of this paragraph is *implied*, not stated by a topic sentence.

  What is the main idea? _____

  _____

- The implied topic sentence or main idea of this paragraph might read, *This is the scene all around me.* Because the paragraph is so clearly arranged according to space order, the reader can easily follow it.

- Transitional phrases like *on my right* and *on my left* guide the reader from sentence to sentence. What phrases in sentences 3, 4, and 5 help

  guide the reader? _____

  _____

PRACTICE 2   Arrange each group of details here according to **space order,** numbering them 1, 2, 3, and so on, as if in preparation for a descriptive paragraph. Be prepared to explain your choices.

1. Describe a science classroom.

   _____ rows of chairs and counters where students are writing

   _____ back wall of shelves with jars containing small animals, a human brain

   _____ on front counter, large plastic model of an eyeball

_____ human skeleton hanging on a pole in front of the jars

_____ professor in white lab coat explaining the parts of the eye

2. Describe a person.

_____ intense brown eyes

_____ faded jeans

_____ broad shoulders

_____ two-inch scar on right cheek

_____ leather Western boots

_____ rumpled sandy-colored hair

3. Describe a car.

_____ painted white

_____ leopard-print upholstery

_____ mangled front bumper

_____ hood ornament, a winged horse

_____ fuzzy dice hanging from rear-view mirror

_____ trunk covered with dents

Writing Assignment 2

Use **space order** to give coherence to each paragraph below. Compose a topic sentence, freewrite or brainstorm for details, and then arrange them in space order. Use transitional words and phrases like these if you wish:*

on the left	above	beside	beyond that
on the right	farther out	behind	next to

Paragraph 1: Describe a classroom scene, a person, or a car. Choose one group of details from Practice 2, formulate a topic sentence that sets the scene for them all, and use them as the basis of a paragraph. Convert the details into complete sentences, adding words if you wish.

* For a more complete list, see the section on transitional expressions, pages 61–62.

Paragraph 2: Describe a room in your home. Describe a room in your home that has special meaning to you—the bedroom, the kitchen, a workroom or den. Write a topic sentence that gives the reader a sense of what the room is like. Then choose details that capture the special feeling or purpose of the room. Before you write the paragraph, arrange your details in space order.

Paragraph 3: Describe a photograph. Describe this unusual beach scene as clearly and exactly as you can. First, jot down the four or five most important details in the scene. Then, before you write your paragraph, arrange these details according to space order—moving from background to foreground, perhaps, or from top to bottom.

Paragraph 4: Describe a public figure. Choose someone you admire or like—for example, a person in the news or a television personality. Working from memory or from a photograph, choose five or six striking details to use as the basis of a paragraph that employs space order. Move from head to toe, from face to hands, but follow a logical plan.

Order of Importance

Ideas in a paragraph can also be arranged in the **order of importance.** You may start with the most important ideas and end with the least, or you may begin with the least important idea and build to a climax with the most important one. If you wish to persuade your reader with arguments or examples, beginning with the most important points impresses the reader with the force of your ideas and persuades him or her to continue reading.*

On essay examinations and in business correspondence, be especially careful to begin with the most important idea. In those situations the reader definitely wants your important points first.

Read the following paragraph and note the order of ideas.

(1) Louis Pasteur is revered as a great scientist for his three major discoveries. (2) Most important, this Frenchman created vaccines that have saved millions of human and animal lives. (3) The vaccines grew out of his discovery that weakened forms of a disease could help the person or animal build up antibodies that would prevent the disease. (4) The vaccines used today to protect children from serious illnesses owe their existence to Pasteur's work. (5) Almost as important was Pasteur's brilliant idea that tiny living beings, not chemical reactions, spoiled beverages. (6) He developed a process, pasteurization, that keeps milk, wine, vinegar, and beer from spoiling. (7) Finally, Pasteur found ways to stop a silkworm disease that threatened to ruin France's profitable silk industry. (8) Many medical researchers regard him as "the father of modern medicine."

■ The ideas in this paragraph are explained in the **order of importance,** from the *most important to the least important:*

What was Pasteur's most important discovery? _____

What was his next most important discovery? _____

What was his least important one? _____

■ Note how the words *most important, almost as important,* and *finally* guide the reader from one idea to another.

* See Chapter 5, "Illustration," and Chapter 12, "Persuasion."

Sometimes, if you wish to add drama and surprise to your paragraphs, you may want to begin with the least important idea and build toward a climax by saving the most important idea for last. This kind of order can help counter the tendency of some writers to state the most important idea first and then let the rest of the paragraph dwindle away.

Read the following paragraph and note the order of ideas.

---

(1) Film director Steven Spielberg has created some of the most spectacular special effects in the history of the movies. (2) When the film *Jaws* was released in 1975, Spielberg's terrifying, lifelike shark was hailed as a special-effects masterpiece. (3) However, *Jaws* was followed by films with even *more* brilliant effects. (4) A sensational scene in the 1977 film *Close Encounters of the Third Kind,* for example, shows dozens of brightly colored UFOs signaling the approach and landing of a gorgeous gigantic starship. (5) And in *E.T.,* made in 1982, Spielberg created an astonishing extraterrestrial that had an aluminum and steel skeleton covered with fiber glass, foam rubber, and plastic to create "muscles." (6) But Spielberg's *most* spectacular special effects appear in his 1993 hit *Jurassic Park.* (7) Four separate special-effects units created the unbelievably realistic dinosaurs. (8) These teams combined animation, miniature photography, electronically controlled models, computer-generated graphics, and full-size models—including a Tyrannosaurus Rex that stood twenty feet tall and weighed over three thousand pounds!

- The special effects that develop the topic sentence in this paragraph are discussed in the **order of importance:** from the *least to the most impressive.*

- The special effects in *E.T.,* for example, are more spectacular than those in *Jaws* or *Close Encounters of the Third Kind.* But the special effects in *Jurassic Park*—the unbelievably realistic dinosaurs—are the most spectacular effects of all.

- Transitional words like *more* and *most* help the reader follow clearly from one set of special effects to the next.

PRACTICE 3   Arrange the ideas that develop each topic sentence in their **order of importance,** numbering them 1, 2, 3, and so on. *Begin with the most important* (or largest, most severe, most surprising) and continue to the *least* important. Or reverse the order if you think that the paragraph would be more dramatic by beginning with the *least* important ideas and building toward a climax, with the most important last.

1. Cynthia Lopez's first year of college brought many unexpected expenses.

   _____ Her English professor wanted her to own a college dictionary.

_____ All those term papers to write required a word processor or at least an electronic typewriter.

_____ She had to spend $90 for textbooks.

_____ Her solid geometry class required various colored pencils and felt-tipped pens.

2. Alcoholic beverages should not be sold at sporting events.

_____ Injuries and even deaths caused by alcohol-induced crowd violence would be eliminated.

_____ Fans could save money by buying soft drinks instead of beer.

_____ Games and matches would be much more pleasant without the yelling, swearing, and rudeness often caused by alcohol.

3. The apartment needed work before the new tenants could move in.

_____ The handles on the kitchen cabinets were loose.

_____ Every room needed plastering and painting.

_____ Grime marred the appearance of the bathroom sink.

_____ Two closet doors hung off the hinges.

Writing Assignment 3

Use **order of importance** to give coherence to the paragraphs that follow. Use transitional words and phrases like these to guide the reader along:

first	even more
another	last
next	least (most) of all

Paragraph 1: Discuss a day in which everything went right (or wrong). Freewrite or brainstorm to generate ideas. Choose three or four of the day's best (or worst) events and write a paragraph in which you present them in order of importance—either from the most to the least important, or from the least to the most important.

Paragraph 2: Describe an unusual person. Choose a person you know whose looks or actions are unusual. Write your topic sentence and generate ideas; choose three to five details about the person's looks or behavior. Arrange the details according to the order of importance—either from the most to the least important or from the least to the most important.

Paragraph 3: Explain a goal. Write a paragraph that begins *I want a college education* (or name some other goal) *for three reasons.* Choose the three reasons that matter most to you and arrange them in the order of importance—either from the most to the least important or from the least to the most important.

PRACTICE 4
Review

Decide how you would develop each of the following topic sentences into a paragraph and choose an appropriate **order** of ideas. In the blanks, state what order you would use and briefly describe your approach.

There are no "right" answers. Some topics can be developed in several ways, depending on the writer.

Example

The fields behind the barn are vibrant with color.

Order: _Space_____   Approach: _Describe the colors of the fields___

_from foreground to background._____

Order: _Time_____   Approach: _Describe the different colors at___

_three different times of day._____

Order: _Importance_____   Approach: _Describe the details of color from__

_most to least striking—or the reverse._____

1. The Pearl Jam performance at Stage Left was a real showstopper.

   Order: _____   Approach: _____

   _____

2. The attic was filled with unusual objects.

   Order: _____   Approach: _____

   _____

3. Three influences formed my decision to major in _____.

   Order: _____   Approach: _____

   _____

4. During my first year at college, I had to make three important changes in my life.

   Order: _____   Approach: _____

   _____

   _____

5. One look at my dog reveals his mixed background.

   Order: _____   Approach: _____

   _____

6. Gregor Mendel, an Austrian monk, performed many experiments before he discovered the laws of heredity.

   Order: _____   Approach: _____

   _____

PART B

Coherence Through Related Sentences

In addition to arranging ideas in a logical order, the writer can ensure paragraph coherence by linking one sentence to the next. This section will present four basic ways to link sentences: **repetition of important words, substitution of pronouns, substitution of synonyms,** and **transitional expressions.**

Repetition of Important Words and Pronouns

Link sentences within a paragraph by *repeating important words and ideas.*

(1) A grand jury is an investigative body composed of members elected from the community. (2) It serves as a buffer between the state and the citizen. (3) The prosecutor, in many cases, brings before the grand jury the evidence gathered on a particular case. (4) The grand jury must then decide if sufficient evidence exists to hand down an indictment—the indictment being a formal charge

> against an accused person written by the prosecutor and submitted to a court by the grand jury. (5) With the indictment issued, the prosecutor can proceed to the arraignment.
>
> —Ronald J. Waldron et al., *The Criminal Justice System: An Introduction*

- What important words are repeated in this paragraph?

- The words *grand jury* are repeated four times, in sentences 1, 3, and 4. The word *indictment,* introduced near the end of the paragraph, is repeated three times, in sentences 4 and 5. The word *prosecutor* is repeated three times, in sentences 3, 4, and 5.

- Repetition of these key words helps the reader follow from sentence to sentence as these terms are defined and the relationships between them are explained.

Although repetition of important words can be effective, it can also become boring if overused.* To avoid *unnecessary* repetition, substitute *pronouns* for words already mentioned in the paragraph, as this author does:

> (1) The technique of coastal whaling spread to the New World, where in the early 1700's *it* underwent a major change. (2) American whalemen gradually extended their range from coastal waters to the open sea. (3) Later *they* transferred their tryworks—furnaces and iron caldrons in which blubber was reduced to oil—from the shore to the ships themselves.
>
> —William Graves, "The Imperiled Giants," *National Geographic*

- The use of *pronouns* in this paragraph avoids unnecessary repetition. In sentence 1, the pronoun *it* refers to its antecedent,[†] *the technique of coastal whaling,* already mentioned in the sentence.

- The pronoun *they* in sentence 3 gives coherence to the paragraph by

referring to what antecedent? _____

Use pronoun substitution together with the repetition of important words for a smooth presentation of ideas.

* For practice in eliminating wordiness (repetition of unimportant words), see Chapter 15, "Revising for Language Awareness," Part B.
† For more work in pronouns and antecedents, see Chapter 28, "Pronouns," Parts A, B, and C.

PRACTICE 5   What important words are repeated in the following paragraph? Underline them. Circle any pronouns that replace them. Notice the varied pattern of repetitions and pronoun replacements.

I have always considered my father a very intelligent person. His intelligence is not the type usually tested in schools; perhaps he would have done well on such tests, but the fact is that he never finished high school. Rather, my father's intelligence is his ability to solve problems creatively as they arise. Once when I was very young, we were driving through the desert at night when the oil line broke. My father improvised a light, squeezed under the car, found the break, and managed to whittle a connection to join the two severed pieces of tubing; then he added more oil and drove us over a hundred miles to the nearest town. Such intelligent solutions to unforeseen problems were typical of him. In fact, my father's brand of brains—accurate insight, followed by creative action—is the kind of intelligence that I admire and most aspire to.

Writing Assignment 4

Paragraph 1: Discuss success. How do you measure *success?* By the money you make, the number or quality of friends you have? Freewrite or brainstorm for ideas. Then answer this question in a thoughtful paragraph. Give the paragraph coherence by repeating important words and using pronouns.

Paragraph 2: Discuss a public figure. Choose a public figure whom you admire—from the arts, politics, media, or sports—and write a paragraph discussing *one quality* that makes that person special. Name the person in your topic sentence. Vary repetition of the person's name with pronouns to give the paragraph coherence.

Synonyms and Substitutions

When you do not wish to repeat a word or use a pronoun, give coherence to your paragraph with a **synonym** or **substitution. Synonyms** are two or more words that mean nearly the same thing. For instance, if you do not wish to repeat the word *car,* you might use the synonym *automobile* or *vehicle.* If you are describing a sky and have already used the word *bright,* try the synonym *radiant.*

Or instead of a synonym, **substitute** other words that describe the subject. If you are writing about José Canseco, for example, refer to him as *this* *powerful slugger* or *this versatile outfielder.* Such substitutions provide a change from constant repetition of a person's name or a single pronoun.*

Use synonyms and substitutions together with repetition and pronouns to give coherence to your writing:

> (1) On September 10, 1990, *the main building of Ellis Island* in New York Harbor reopened as a museum. (2) Restoration of *the huge red brick and limestone structure* took eight years and cost $156 million. (3) From 1900 to 1924, *this famous immigrant station* was the first stop of millions of newcomers to American shores. (4) *The building* was finally abandoned in 1954; by 1980, *it* was in such bad condition that snow and rain fell on its floor. (5) Today, visitors can follow the path of immigrants: from a ferry boat, through the great arched doorway, into the room where the weary travelers left their baggage, up the stairway where doctors kept watch, and into the registry room. (6) Here questions were asked that determined if each immigrant could stay in the United States. (7) *This magnificent monument to the American people* contains exhibits that tell the whole immigration history of the United States.

- This paragraph effectively mixes repetition, pronouns, and substitution. The important word *building* is stated in sentence 1 and repeated in sentence 4.

- Sentence 4 also substitutes the pronoun *it.*

- In sentence 2, *the huge red brick and limestone structure* is substituted for *building,* and a second substitution, *this famous immigrant station,* occurs in sentence 3. Sentence 7 refers to the building as *this magnificent monument to the American people* and concludes the paragraph.

Sometimes the dictionary lists synonyms. For instance, the entry for *smart* might list *clever, witty, intelligent.* An even better source of synonyms is the **thesaurus,** a book of synonyms. For example, if you are describing a city street and cannot think of other words meaning **noisy,** look in the thesaurus. The number of choices will amaze you.

PRACTICE 6   Read each paragraph carefully. Then write on the lines any synonyms and substitutions that the writer has used to replace the word(s) in italics.

Paragraph 1: Rocky Mountain bighorn sheep use their massive horns as percussion instruments. During the fall rutting season, when hormone

---

* For more work on exact language, see Chapter 15, "Revising for Language Awareness," Part A.

changes bring on the breeding urge, 250-pound rams square off in violent, head-butting matches to determine which gains leadership of the herd and pick of the ewes. Duelists rear on hind legs, then drop to all fours and, heads down, charge at full speed.

—*National Geographic*

Rocky Mountain bighorn sheep are also referred to as _____

_____ and _____.

Paragraph 2: Today, over fifty million people chuckle over the *adventures* of Dennis the Menace; they read the comic strip in more than a dozen languages around the world. But it all started one afternoon in 1950 when cartoonist Hank Ketcham heard his wife, Alice, complaining about the pranks of their only child, Dennis, who was then four years old. Dennis had used his nap time to take apart his bedroom—the dresser drawers, the curtain rods, even the bedsprings. Alice told Hank that their son was a menace—and the idea of Dennis the Menace was born. Dennis the Menace's high jinks were the inspiration for the TV series that ran from 1959 to 1963, as well as for the 1993 movie—and for books, clothes, dolls, posters, greeting cards, and more. The mischievous antics of Dennis the Menace seem to have struck a long-lasting chord in people everywhere. Perhaps they keep laughing at his practical jokes because, as someone once observed, everybody knows a Dennis. Most parents have one around the house.

Adventures are also referred to as _____, _____,

_____, and _____.

Paragraph 3: When Lewis and Clark made their way through what is now North Dakota, the Shoshoni Indian woman named *Sacajawea* and her French-Canadian husband joined the team of explorers. Because the expedition was traveling with a Native American, other tribes did not attack the group. In fact, one tribe even supplied horses to help the explorers and their interpreter cross the Rocky Mountains. This invaluable team member taught the men how to find medicine and food in the wilderness and once even saved the records of the journey when a canoe overturned during a storm. Sacajawea reached the Pacific Ocean with Lewis and Clark in 1805. Her fame eventually spread; one of the best-known monuments to her is a statue in Portland, Oregon.

Sacajawea is also referred to as _____,

_____, and _____.

PRACTICE 7   Give coherence to the following paragraphs by thinking of appropriate synonyms or substitutions for the words in italics. Then write them in the blanks.

Paragraph 1: The story of Arnold Schwarzenegger's success exemplifies the American dream. Called the Austrian Oak when he arrived in the United States in 1968, the eighteen-year-old *muscleman* had only twenty dollars and a gym bag. Within a few years, the _____ won five Mr. Universe and seven Mr. Olympia titles, making him the most famous _____ on earth. Then, in the mid-1970's, he was featured in both the book and the movie *Pumping Iron*. Audiences saw that Arnold was not just a _____, but a smart and warm man with a magnetic personality. The _____ soon became the star of a series of thriller films earning him millions of box-office dollars and fans all over the world.

Paragraph 2: Much evidence shows that the urge to take a midafternoon *nap* is natural to humans. Sleep researchers have found that volunteer subjects, kept in underground rooms where they cannot tell the time, need a _____ about twelve hours after the halfway point of their main sleep. For example, if people sleep from midnight till 6:00 A.M., they'll be ready for a _____ at 3:00 the next afternoon. Other studies show that people have less trouble taking a _____ in midafternoon than at any other daylight time. In many countries with warm climates, citizens take their daily _____ in the afternoon. Even stressed Americans take an average of two afternoon naps a week.

Paragraph 3: According to the experts, those who learn about *money* early in life usually make sound financial decisions as adults. How then can parents give children the knowledge and experience they need? Well, even preschoolers can feed _____ into parking meters and pay phones. Young children will become interested in clipping coupons if parents give them the _____ saved off the

regular   prices.   Children   of   seven   and   eight   can   learn   about
_____ by managing an allowance. By the age of ten

or so, kids become fascinated by the idea of having a bank account of their

own and earning interest on their _____. In other

words, parents can provide children with learning experiences about money

at almost every age and stage of their lives. However, if your children won't

accept any gift but stocks for their birthday presents, you may have carried

the concept too far!

Writing Assignment 5

As you do the following assignments, try to achieve paragraph coherence by
using repetition, pronouns, synonyms, and substitutions.

Paragraph 1: Discuss an invention. Pick an invention or product that
intrigues you—a video game, the miniature cassette recorder, the felt-tipped
pen—and discuss the ways in which human beings benefit from its use. Or
you may do a humorous paragraph, showing how frozen pizza or leather
pants have done great things for humankind.

In any case, name the invention in your topic sentence; then give the
paragraph coherence by replacing the name of the product with both
a pronoun and one or two synonyms or substitutions. For example, you
might replace *the miniature cassette recorder* with the pronoun *it*
and with such phrases as *this handy little device* or *this revolutionary
gadget.*

Paragraph 2: Describe your ideal mate. Decide on three or four crucial
qualities that your ideal husband, wife, or friend would possess, and write a
paragraph describing this extraordinary person. Use repetition, pronouns,
and word substitutions to give coherence to the paragraph. For example, *My
ideal husband . . . he . . . my companion.*

Paragraph 3: Choose a quotation from the Quotation Bank before the indexes in this book, one you strongly agree or disagree with. Write a paragraph explaining why you feel that way. As you write, refer to the quotation
as a *wise insight* or a *silly idea*—depending on what you think of it. Use
other substitutions to refer to the quotation without repeating it or calling it
the quotation.

Transitional Expressions

Skill in using transitional expressions is vital to coherent writing. **Transitional expressions** are words and phrases that point out the exact relation between one idea and another, one sentence and another. Words like *therefore, however, for example,* and *finally* are signals that guide the reader from sentence to sentence. Without them, even orderly and well-written paragraphs can be confusing and hard to follow.

The transitional expressions in this paragraph are italicized:

> (1) Zoos in the past often contributed to the disappearance of animal populations. (2) Animals were cheap, and getting new ones was easier than providing the special diet and shelter necessary to keep captive animals alive. (3) *Recently, however,* zoo directors have begun to realize that if zoos themselves are to continue, they must help save many species from extinction. (4) *As a result,* some zoos have begun to redefine themselves as places where endangered species can be protected and even revived. (5) The Basel Zoo in Switzerland, *for example,* selects endangered species and encourages captive breeding. (6) If zoos continue such work, perhaps they can, like Noah's ark, save some of earth's wonderful creatures from extinction.

- Each transitional expression above links, in a precise way, the sentence in which it appears to the sentence before. The paragraph begins by explaining the destructive policies of zoos in the past.

- In sentence 3, two transitional expressions of contrast—*recently* (as opposed to the past) and *however*—introduce the idea that zoo policies have *changed.*

- The phrase *as a result* makes clear that sentence 4 is *a consequence* of events described in the previous sentence(s).

- In sentence 5, *for example* tells us that the Basel Zoo is *one particular illustration* of the previous general statement.

As you write, use various transitional expressions, together with the other linking devices, to connect one sentence to the next. Well-chosen transitional words also help to stress the purpose and order of the paragraph.

Particular groups of transitional expressions are further explained and demonstrated in each chapter of Unit 3. However, here is a combined, partial list for handy reference as you write.

Purpose	*Transitional Expressions*
to add	also, and, and then, as well, besides, beyond that, first (second, third, last, and so on), for one thing, furthermore, in addition, moreover, next, what is more
to compare	also, as well, both (neither), in the same way, likewise, similarly
to contrast	although, be that as it may, but, even though, however, in contrast, nevertheless, on the contrary, on the other hand, whereas, yet
to concede (a point)	certainly, granted that, of course, no doubt, to be sure
to emphasize	above all, especially, indeed, in fact, in particular, most important, surely
to illustrate	as a case in point, as an illustration, for example, for instance, in particular, one such, yet another
to place	above, below, beside, beyond, farther, here, inside, nearby, next to, on the far side, opposite, outside, to the east (south, and so on)
to qualify	perhaps
to give a reason	as, because, for, since
to show a result	and so, as a consequence, as a result, because of this, consequently, for this reason, hence, so, therefore, thus
to summarize	all in all, finally, in brief, in other words, lastly, on the whole, to sum up
to place in time	after a while, afterward, at last, at present, briefly, currently, during, eventually, finally, first (second, and so on), gradually, immediately, in the future, later, meanwhile, next, now, recently, soon, suddenly, then

PRACTICE 8   Carefully determine the *exact relationship* between the sentences in each pair below. Then choose from the list a **transitional expression** that clearly expresses this relationship and write it in the blank. Pay attention to punctuation and capitalize the first word of every sentence.*

* For practice using conjunctions to join ideas, see Chapter 22, "Coordination and Subordination."

1. No one inquired about the money found in the lobby. _____, it was given to charity.

2. First, cut off the outer, fibrous husk of the coconut. _____ poke a hole through one of the dark "eyes" and sip the milk through a straw.

3. The Women's Studies office is on the fifth floor. _____ to it is a small reading room.

4. Some mountains under the sea soar almost as high as those on the land.

   One underwater mountain in the Pacific, _____, is only 500 feet shorter than Mount Everest.

5. All citizens should vote. Many do not, _____.

6. Mrs. Dalworth enjoys shopping in out-of-the-way thrift shops.

   _____, she loves bargaining with the vendors at outdoor flea markets.

7. In 1887, Native Americans owned nearly 138 million acres of land. By

   1932, _____, 90 million of those acres were owned by whites.

8. Kansas corn towered over the fence. _____ the fence, a red tractor stood baking in the sun.

9. Most street crime occurs between 2:00 and 5:00 A.M. _____, do not go out alone during those hours.

10. Dr. Leff took great pride in his work at the clinic. _____, his long hours often left him exhausted.

11. Few scientists have worked so creatively with a single agricultural

    product. _____ peanut oil and peanut butter, George Washington Carver developed literally hundreds of uses for the peanut.

12. We waited in our seats for over an hour. _____ the lights dimmed, and the Fabulous String Band bounded on stage.

PRACTICE 9   Add **transitional expressions** to this paragraph to guide the reader smoothly from sentence to sentence. To do so, consider the relationship between sentences (shown in parentheses). Then write the transitional word or phrase that best expresses this relationship.

Because Dave has been interested in the Internet for months, he will

_____ take steps to join this worldwide computer network.
         (time)

He has spent many enjoyable hours imagining himself using the huge

information highway. He wants, _____, to send electronic
                                    (illustration)

mail to people all over the world, to explore new software games, and to

check library catalogues in other countries. _____, Dave does
                                                    (contrast)

not want to pay high fees or expensive monthly dues. _____,
                                                          (addition)

he needs to learn to find his way around in the system of more than 25,000

computer networks and more than 25 million users. _____,
                                                        (result)

he has been looking for the cheapest and easiest way to get onto the

"Net." He has been learning about many of the access services,

_____ America Online, CompuServe, and Delphi. It may take
   (illustration)

a little time, but Dave _____ will decide how to make his
                            (emphasis)

Internet dream come true.

PRACTICE 10   Most paragraphs achieve coherence through a variety of linking devices:
Review   repetition, pronouns, substitutions, and transitional expressions. Read the
                  following paragraphs with care, noting the kinds of linking devices used by
                  each writer. Answer the questions after each paragraph.

Paragraph 1: (1) The blues is the one truly American music. (2) Born in
the Mississippi Delta, this twelve-bar cry of anguish found its durable, classic form in the searing soliloquies of poor black men and women who used it
to ventilate all the aches and pains of their condition—the great Bessie
Smith, Robert Johnson, Ma Rainey, Lightnin' Hopkins and Son House, Mississippi John Hurt, John Lee Hooker and Blind Lemon Jefferson. (3) And,
ever since, the blues has served as the wellspring of every major movement
in this country's popular music.

—Paul D. Zimmerman with Peter Barnes et al.,
"Rebirth of the Blues," *Newsweek*

1. What important words appear in both the first and the last sentence?

_____

2. In sentence 2, *the blues* is referred to as _____

_____

3. What transitional expressions are used in sentence 3? _____

_____

Paragraph 2: (1) Mrs. Zajac seemed to have a frightening amount of energy. (2) She strode across the room, her arms swinging high and her hands in small fists. (3) Taking her stand in front of the green chalkboard, discussing the rules with her new class, she repeated sentences, and her lips held the shapes of certain words, such as "homework," after she had said them. (4) Her hands kept very busy. (5) They sliced the air and made karate chops to mark off boundaries. (6) They extended straight out like a traffic cop's, halting illegal maneuvers yet to be perpetrated. (7) When they rested momentarily on her hips, her hands looked as if they were in holsters. (8) She told the children, "One thing Mrs. Zajac expects from each of you is that you do *your* best." (9) She said, "Mrs. Zajac gives homework. (10) I'm sure you've all heard. (11) The old meanie gives homework." (12) *Mrs. Zajac.* (13) It was in part a role. (14) She worked her way into it every September.

—Tracy Kidder, *Among Schoolchildren*

1. What important words are repeated in this paragraph? _____

_____

2. What word does *they* in sentences 5 and 6 refer to? _____

_____

Paragraph 3: (1) More important perhaps than the recipes and ideas that flowed into the home through cookbooks and magazines were the conveniences that began more and more to appear in the kitchen. (2) First it was the icebox. (3) Next it was running hot water, along with the cold. (4) Then it was the gas stove, a frightening apparatus for the uninitiated—and then, just as soon as mastery of its dials and heat had been achieved, along came the electric stove to sow confusion again. (5) The icebox gave way to the refrigerator and the freezer. (6) And out of Clarence Birdseye's observation that Eskimos in Labrador froze their meat and fish evolved the quick-freezing of various foodstuffs, a revolution of the first order in American cooking.

—*Foods of the World/American Cooking,*
Time-Life Books Inc.

1. Underline the transitional expressions in this paragraph.

2. What *order* of ideas does the paragraph employ? _____

_____

Unit 3

Developing the Paragraph

5

Illustration

To **illustrate** is to explain a general statement by means of one or more specific *examples*.

Illustration makes what we say more vivid and more exact. Someone might say, "My math professor is always finding crazy ways to get our attention. Just yesterday, for example, he wore a high silk hat to class." The first sentence is a general statement about this professor's unusual ways of getting attention. The second sentence, however, gives a specific example of something he did that *clearly shows* what the writer means.

Writers often use illustration to develop a paragraph. They explain a general topic sentence with one, two, three, or more specific examples. Detailed and well-chosen examples add interest, liveliness, and power to your writing.

Topic Sentence

Here is the topic sentence of a paragraph that is later developed by examples:

> Many famous athletes have overcome severe illness or injury.

- The writer begins an illustration paragraph with a topic sentence that makes a general statement.

- This generalization may be obvious to the writer, but if he or she wishes to convince the reader, some specific examples would be helpful.

Paragraph and Plan

Here is the entire paragraph:

> Many famous athletes have overcome severe illness or injury. For example, basketball great Bernard King suffered a devastating knee injury from which no player had ever come back. After two years of rehabilitation, the Knicks released him, but King would not give up. Signed by the Washington Bullets, he became an All-Star once again. Another inspiring example is power-driving golfer John Daly. He was still in his twenties when alcoholism ended both his career and his marriage, but Daly got sober, changed his life, and went back on the tour, outdriving all challengers. Joan Benoit took up running in order to get back in shape after she broke her leg while skiing. She became America's top female long-distance runner and won many marathon races. Finally, track legend Wilma Rudolph had polio as a child and could not walk without braces until she was eight. Twelve years later, she won three gold medals in the 1960 Olympics, taking the 100- and 200-meter dashes and running on the 400-meter relay team.

▪ How many examples does the writer use to develop the topic sentence?

_____

▪ Who are they?

_____

_____

Before composing this illustration paragraph, the writer probably made an outline or a plan like this:

Topic Sentence: Many famous athletes have overcome serious illness or injury.

Example 1:   Bernard King
        —devastating knee injury
        —Knicks released him after two years
        —signed by Bullets, became an All-Star again

Example 2:   John Daly
        —alcoholism ended golf career and marriage
        —became sober, went back on the tour

Example 3:   Joan Benoit
                    —broke leg and took up running
                    —became top U.S. female long-distance runner
                    —won many marathons

Example 4:   Wilma Rudolph
                    —polio, walked with braces until age eight
                    —three gold medals in 1960 Olympics (100- and
                        200-meter dash and 400-meter relay)

■ Note that each example clearly relates to and supports the topic sentence.

Instead of using three or four examples to support the topic sentence, the writer may prefer instead to discuss one single example:

> Miniaturized versions of many products—from electronic dictionaries to VCRs—are now available to consumers. The pocket television, for instance, is a popular product in the small-scale craze. This tiny TV can be carried in a shirt pocket or purse or worn on a handstrap. Taking up from four to six inches of space, it has a screen the size of a matchbook. It exploits the newest advances in electronics, reproducing images in the same manner as both conventional televisions and digital watches. Although it lacks some of the picture controls of conventional television, the pocket-sized version has all the usual features, including color. Even in noisy public places, it can be heard clearly through its own earphones. With the development of miniature televisions, seasoned travelers may soon automatically pack TVs next to their toothbrushes.

■ What is the general statement? _____

_____

_____

■ What specific example does the writer give to support the general

statement? _____

The single example may also be a **narrative,*** a *story* that illustrates the topic sentence.

_____

* For more on narrative, see Chapter 6, "Narration," and Chapter 18, "Types of Essays,"
    Part B.

> We rarely get tired when we are doing something interesting and exciting. For example, I recently took a vacation in the Canadian Rockies up around Lake Louise. I spent several days trout fishing along Coral Creek, fighting my way through brush higher than my head, stumbling over logs, struggling through fallen timber—yet after eight hours of this, I was not exhausted. Why? Because I was excited, exhilarated. I had a sense of high achievement: six cutthroat trout. But suppose I had been bored by fishing; then how do you think I would have felt? I would have been worn out by such strenuous work at an altitude of seven thousand feet.
>
> —Dale Carnegie, *Banishing Boredom on the Job*

■ What general statement does the trout-fishing story illustrate?

_____

_____

■ Note that this narrative follows time order.*

Transitional Expressions

The simplest way to tell your reader that an example is going to follow is to say so: "*For example*, Bernard King . . ." or "The pocket television, *for instance.* . . ." This partial list should help you vary your use of **transitional expressions** that introduce an illustration:

**Transitional Expressions
for Illustration**

for instance	another instance of
for example	another example of
an illustration of this	another illustration of
a case in point is	here are a few examples
to illustrate	(illustrations, instances)

■ Be careful not to use more than two or three of these transitional expressions in a single paragraph.†

* For more work on time order, see Chapter 4, "Achieving Coherence," Part A.
† For a complete essay developed by illustration, see "Acting to Save Mother Earth," Chapter 18, Part A.

PRACTICE 1   Read each of the following paragraphs of illustration. Underline each topic sentence. Note in the margin how many examples are provided to illustrate each general statement.

Paragraph 1: Random acts of kindness are those little sweet or grand lovely things we do for no reason except that, momentarily, the best of our humanity has sprung . . . into full bloom. When you spontaneously give an old woman the bouquet of red carnations you had meant to take home to your own dinner table, when you give your lunch to the guitar-playing beggar who makes music at the corner between your two subway stops, when you anonymously put coins in someone else's parking meter because you see the red "Expired" medallion signalling to a meter maid—you are doing not what life requires of you, but what the best of your human soul invites you to do.

—Daphne Rose Kingma, *Random Acts of Kindness*

Paragraph 2: There are many quirky variations to lightning. A "bolt from the blue" occurs when a long horizontal flash suddenly turns toward the earth, many miles from the storm. "St. Elmo's Fire," often seen by sailors and mountain climbers, is a pale blue or green light caused by weak electrical discharges that cling to trees, airplanes, and ships' masts. "Pearl lightning" occurs when flashes are broken into segments. "Ball lightning" can be from an inch to several feet in diameter. Pearls and balls are often mistaken for flying saucers or UFOs, and many scientists believe they are only optical illusions.

—Reed McManus, *Sierra Magazine*

PRACTICE 2   Each example in a paragraph of illustration must clearly relate to and support the general statement. Each general statement in this practice is followed by several examples. Circle the letter of any example that does *not* clearly illustrate the generalization. Be prepared to explain your choices.

Example | The museum contains many fascinating examples of African art.
a. It houses a fine collection of Ashanti fertility dolls.
b. Drums and shamans' costumes are displayed on the second floor.
ⓒ The museum building was once the home of Frederick Douglass.
(The fact that the building was once the home of Frederick Douglass is *not an example* of African art.)

1. Amelia Earhart dared to act beyond the limits of what society thought a woman could or should do.
   a. She saw her first plane at the Iowa State Fair.
   b. She became a pilot and mechanic, entering the all-male world of aviation.
   c. She presented her new husband with a marriage contract that gave both partners considerable freedom.

2. Every NBA star has his own way of reacting to success on the court.
   a. After Knicks center Patrick Ewing slam-dunks a rebound, he bumps chests with his teammates.
   b. When "trash talker" Reggie Miller makes a difficult shot, he taunts the player guarding him.
   c. Supersonics star Shawn Kemp beats his chest after a thunderous dunk.
   d. NBA star Dennis Rodman periodically changes his hair color—to white, green, or red—for reasons known only to him.

3. In the Arizona desert, one sees many colorful plants and flowers.
   a. Here and there are patches of pink clover.
   b. Gray-green saguaro cacti rise up like giant candelabra.
   c. Colorful birds dart through the landscape.
   d. Bright yellow Mexican poppies bloom by the road.

4. Many people are lively and creative in old age.
   a. Eighty-seven-year-old Mary Baker Eddy founded *The Christian Science Monitor,* one of the world's great newspapers.
   b. Pablo Picasso was engraving and drawing at ninety.
   c. When she was one hundred years of age, Grandma Moses was still painting.
   d. Madonna's albums still topped the charts when she was 35.

5. My boss seems to go out of his way to make me miserable.
   a. He waits until 4:45 P.M. and then runs to my desk with ten letters that "must be out tonight."
   b. He golfs every weekend.
   c. Last Friday he backed his car into mine and left with my fender.
   d. He allows me vacation time only in the coldest months of the year.

6. Many conveniences of modern life that we take for granted are less than seventy years old.
   a. It was not until 1969 that the Sony Corporation brought out a video recorder with tape in a cassette, causing a revolution in home viewing.
   b. Aluminum foil, introduced by Richard S. Reynolds in 1947, can now be found in almost every home in America.
   c. Hair coloring was first used by the ancient Egyptians.

7. Radio and television personalities sometimes make amusing slips of the tongue when they are on the air.
   a. One radio announcer promoted a cosmetic surgery clinic this way: "If you want to change the way you look, just visit one of the plastered surgeons."
   b. A talk-show host broke for a commercial with "We'll be right back after these words from General Fools."
   c. A slip of the tongue that seems to reveal the speaker's hidden feelings or thoughts is called a Freudian slip.
   d. A radio psychologist told listeners, "The happiest people are always those who wake up every morning with a porpoise."

8. Many months in our calendar take their names from Roman gods or heroes.
   a. Mars, the Roman war god, gave his name to March.
   b. January was named for Janus, the god of doorways, whose two faces looked both forward and back.
   c. August honors Augustus, the first Roman emperor and the second Caesar.
   d. December means "ten" because it was the tenth month in the Roman calendar.

PRACTICE 3   The secret of good illustration lies in well-chosen, well-written examples. Think of one example that illustrates each of the following general statements. Write out the example in sentence form (one to three sentences) as clearly and exactly as possible.

1. Many television commercials exaggerate the effectiveness or quality of the products they sell.

   Example: _____

   _____

   _____

2. In a number of ways, this college makes it easy for working students to attend.

   Example: _____

   _____

   _____

3. Believing in yourself is 90 percent of success.

   Example: _____

   _____

   _____

4. Food prices have risen during the past several years.

   Example: _____

   _____

   _____

5. Our town's health fair features displays about important health issues.

   Example: _____

   _____

   _____

6. Growing up in a large family can teach the value of compromise.

   Example: _____

   _____

   _____

7. Children say surprising things.

   Example: _____

   _____

   _____

8. Sadly, gun violence has affected many Americans.

   Example: _____

   _____

   _____

Checklist: The Process of Writing an Illustration Paragraph

Refer to this checklist of steps as you write an illustration paragraph of your own.

_____ 1. Narrow the topic in light of your audience and purpose.

_____ 2. Compose a topic sentence that can honestly and easily be supported by examples.

_____ 3. Freewrite or brainstorm to find six to eight examples that support the topic sentence. If you wish to use only one example or a narrative, sketch out your idea. (You may want to freewrite or brainstorm before you narrow the topic.)

_____ 4. Select only the best two to four examples and drop any examples that do not relate to or support the topic sentence.

_____ 5. Make a plan or an outline for your paragraph, numbering the examples in the order in which you will present them.

_____ 6. Write a draft of your illustration paragraph, using transitional expressions to show that an example or examples will follow.

_____ 7. Revise as necessary, checking for support, unity, logic, and coherence.

_____ 8. Proofread for errors in grammar, punctuation, sentence structure, spelling, and mechanics.

Suggested Topic Sentences for Illustration Paragraphs

1. A sense of humor can make difficult times easier to bear.

2. In my family, certain traditions (or values or beliefs) are very important.

3. Despite the high divorce rate, a few couples seem to know the secret of a wonderful marriage.

4. Painful experiences sometimes teach valuable lessons.

5. In many ways, women are not yet treated as men's equals in the workplace.

6. Some enjoyable activities in this area are inexpensive or even free.

7. I (do not) perform well under pressure.

8. Many musicians have used their talents to support social causes in recent years.

9. Unfortunately, many great athletes are very poor role models for the young people who look up to them.

10. Some unusual characters live in my neighborhood.

11. Some professors are masters at helping their students learn.

12. The way people dress may reveal their personalities.

13. Films (or television programs) often contain unnecessary violence.

14. Sometimes the best-planned vacations do not work out.

15. Choose one of these sayings (or one of your own favorites). First, state whether you think the saying is true; then use examples from your own experience to support your view.

   a. Beauty is only skin deep.
   b. Honesty is the best policy.
   c. Luck comes to those who earn it.
   d. Necessity is the mother of invention.

6

Narration

To **narrate** is to tell a story that explains what happened, when it happened, and who was involved.

A news report may be a narrative about how Congress voted, what the president did, or how a man was rescued from a burning building. When you read a bedtime story to your children, you are reading them a narrative.

In a letter to a friend, you might want to write a narrative detailing how you were hired for your new job; your narrative could emphasize the fact that your relaxed and confident manner throughout the interview impressed your future employer. Or you might wish to retell what happened on your first skiing trip, when a minor accident proved to you that you prefer tamer recreation.

However, no matter what your narrative is about, it must make a *point:* it must clearly tell what you want your reader to learn or take away from the story.

Topic Sentence

Here is the topic sentence of a **narrative** paragraph:

> Last September, I watched my ten-year-old grandson act like an adult in an emergency.

■ The writer begins a narrative paragraph with a topic sentence that tells the point of the narrative.

- What is the point of this narrative?

_____

_____

Paragraph and Plan

Here is the entire paragraph:

> Last September, I watched my ten-year-old grandson act like an adult in an emergency. While cleaning the living room carpet, I tripped and fell over the vacuum cleaner hose. At first, I was dazed. Soon I realized that my left arm hurt terribly. I called to my grandson Joel, who was the only other person at home. When Joel saw me on the floor, his face went pale. Then he calmly took charge of the situation. He went to the phone and dialed for emergency help. I heard him give our address, exact details of what had happened, and a description of the position I was lying in. I could tell that he was carefully listening to the instructions he was given. Returning to the living room, Joel covered me with a wool blanket and told me that an ambulance was on its way. He sat by my side in the ambulance and stayed with me while the doctor treated me. My sprained arm bothered me for only three weeks, but I will always feel proud of what my grandson did on that day.

- The body of a narrative paragraph is developed according to time, or chronological, order.* That is, the writer explains the narrative—the entire incident—as a series of smaller events or actions in the order in which they occurred. By keeping to strict chronological order, the writer helps the reader follow the story more easily and avoids interrupting the narrative with _But I forgot to mention that before this happened . . ._

- What smaller events make up this narrative?

_____

_____

_____

_____

_____

* For more work on time, see Chapter 4, "Achieving Coherence," Part A.

Before writing this narrative paragraph, the writer probably brainstormed or freewrote to gather ideas and then made an outline or a plan like this:

Topic sentence: Last September, I watched my ten-year-old grandson act like an adult in an emergency.

Event 1:	I tripped and fell. —dazed —left arm hurt
Event 2:	I called to Joel, my grandson.
Event 3:	His face went pale.
Event 4:	He took charge and called for help. —provided information —listened to instructions
Event 5:	He covered me.
Event 6:	He sat by my side in the ambulance.
Event 7:	He stayed with me while I was being treated.

- Note that all of the events occur in chronological order.

- Also note that the first three events provide background information—they tell what led up to the grandson's actions.

- Finally, note that the specific details of certain events (like 1 and 4 above) make the narrative more vivid.

Transitional Expressions

Since narrative paragraphs tell a story in **chronological** or **time order,** transitional expressions that indicate time can be useful.*

Transitional Expressions for Narratives

after	finally	soon
as (soon as)	later	then
before	meanwhile	upon
during	next	when
first	now	while

* For a complete essay developed by narration, see "Maya Lin's Vietnam War Memorial," Chapter 18, "Types of Essays," Part B.

PRACTICE 1: Read the following narrative paragraph carefully and answer the questions.

Walt Disney might be the only filmmaker who claimed to owe his success to a rodent. At first, Disney was an animator who produced a cartoon series called "Oswald the Rabbit." Then he decided to launch out on his own. Realizing that he needed a new animated character, he remembered a friendly mouse from a studio he had once worked in. He decided to name his new character after this old friend, whom he fondly called Mortimer Mouse. Later, he changed the name to Mickey. After only a few cartoons appeared, Mickey Mouse fever swept the nation. Soon, he became an international figure. The French called him "Michel Souris" while the Italians dubbed him "Topolo." During World War II, "Mickey-Mouse" became a secret password in the Allied Command. Disney created many other lovable characters, but none achieved the popularity of that cute little mouse with the white gloves.

▪ What is the point of the narrative? _____

_____

▪ What events make up this narrative paragraph?

List them: _____

_____

_____

_____

_____

_____

_____

PRACTICE 2 Here are three plans for narrative paragraphs. The events in the plans are not in correct chronological order. The plans also contain events that do not belong in each story. Number the events in the proper time sequence and cross out any irrelevant ones.

1. Aesop's fable about a dog and his reflection teaches a lesson about greed.

_____ He thought he saw another dog with another piece of meat in his mouth, so he decided to get that one too.

_____ Now the dog had nothing at all to eat.

_____ A dog was happily carrying a piece of meat in his mouth.

_____ The dog was brown with white spots.

_____ While crossing a bridge, he saw his reflection in the water of a running brook.

_____ When he snapped at the reflection, the meat dropped from his mouth into the water and sank.

2. In 1897, Lena Jordan performed the first triple somersault on the flying trapeze, but for years she did not get credit.

_____ For the next sixty-six years, all the record books listed Clarke as the record holder, not Jordan.

_____ When a second person, a man named Ernest Clarke, managed a triple somersault in 1909, he received national attention.

_____ Only recently did the *Guinness Book of World Records* give Jordan sole credit for the first triple somersault in circus history.

_____ The first free-fall parachute jump from an airplane was also made by a woman.

_____ In 1975, the *Guinness Book of World Records* finally listed Lena Jordan's achievement, but only in addition to Clarke's.

3. The Civil War battle between two iron-covered ships, on March 9, 1862, changed sea warfare forever.

_____ Two hours into the battle, the *Monitor* ran out of ammunition and moved into shallow water to reload.

_____ After four hours, the *Merrimack*, her hull leaking and her smokestack broken, escaped from the scene of battle.

_____ When the *Monitor* returned with guns loaded, the *Merrimack* lured her into deep water and then suddenly swung around and rammed her, leaving barely a dent.

_____ The Civil War lasted from 1861 to 1865.

_____ At the end of the conflict, neither ironclad ship had really won, but the wooden fighting ship was a thing of the past.

_____ At first, the two ships—the North's *Monitor* and the South's *Merrimack*—just circled each other like prehistoric monsters, firing at close range but causing no damage.

PRACTICE 3   Here are topic sentences for three narrative paragraphs. Make a plan for each paragraph, placing the events of the narrative in the proper time sequence.

1. When I was _____, help came from an unexpected source.

   _____

   _____

   _____

   _____

   _____

   _____

2. Sometimes, seemingly unimportant events can prove to be of great importance.

   _____

   _____

   _____

   _____

   _____

   _____

3. Last year, _____ learned something important about himself/herself.

   _____

   _____

   _____

   _____

   _____

   _____

PRACTICE 4 You have been given the photo on the following page and asked to tell the story behind it. That is, you must invent a brief narrative that explains this mysterious picture. What are these people looking at so intently and why? Your narrative can be serious, funny, or otherworldly. First, list the main events and include them in chronological order. State the point of your narrative in the topic sentence, which you may wish to place last rather than first in your paragraph.

Checklist: The Process of Writing a Narrative Paragraph

Refer to this checklist of steps as you write a narrative paragraph of your own.

_____ 1. Narrow the topic in light of your audience and purpose.

_____ 2. Compose a topic sentence that tells the point of the story.

_____ 3. Freewrite or brainstorm for all of the events and details that might be part of the story. (You may want to freewrite or brainstorm before you narrow the topic.)

_____ 4. Select the important events and details; drop any that do not clearly relate to the point in your topic sentence.

_____ 5. Make a plan or an outline for the paragraph, numbering the events in the correct time (chronological) sequence.

_____ 6. Write a draft of your narrative paragraph, using transitional expressions to indicate time sequence.

_____ 7. Revise as necessary, checking for support, unity, logic, and coherence.

_____ 8. Proofread for errors in grammar, punctuation, sentence structure, spelling, and mechanics.

Suggested Topics for Narrative Paragraphs

1. A favorite family story
2. A lesson about life
3. The discovery of a true friend
4. Your or someone else's best (or worst) date
5. An important decision
6. A breakthrough (emotional, physical, spiritual, and so on)
7. A laugh at yourself
8. A typical morning (workday or weekend)
9. A first day at college (or at a new job)
10. A triumphant (or embarrassing) moment
11. One of the first times someone reacted to your writing (positively or negatively)
12. A story that ends with a surprise
13. A strange dream
14. Something you or another person dared to do
15. An incident that made you happy (or proud)

7

Description

To **describe** something—a person, a place, or an object—is to capture it in words so others can imagine it or see it in the mind's eye.

The best way for a writer to help the reader get a clear impression is to use language that appeals to the senses: sight, sound, smell, taste, and touch. For it is through the senses that human beings experience the physical world around them, and it is through the senses that the world is most vividly described.

Imagine, for instance, that you have just gone boating on a lake at sunset. You may not have taken a photograph, yet your friends and family can receive an accurate picture of what you have experienced if you *describe* the pink sky reflected in smooth water, the creak of the wooden boat, the soothing drip of water from the oars, the occasional splash of a large bass jumping, the faint fish smells, the cool and darkening air. Writing down what your senses experience will teach you to see, hear, smell, taste, and touch more acutely than ever before.

Description is useful in English class, the sciences, psychology—anywhere that keen observation is important.

Topic Sentence

Here is the topic sentence of a descriptive paragraph:

> On November 27, 1922, when archaeologist Howard Carter unsealed the door to the ancient Egyptian tomb of King Tut, he stared in amazement at the fantastic objects heaped all around him.

■ The writer begins a descriptive paragraph by pointing out what will be described. What will be described in this paragraph?

- The writer can also give a general impression of this scene, object, or person. What overall impression of the tomb does the writer provide?

_____

_____

Paragraph and Plan

Here is the entire paragraph:

> On November 27, 1922, when archaeologist Howard Carter unsealed the door to the ancient Egyptian tomb of King Tut, he stared in amazement at the fantastic objects heaped all around him. On his left lay the wrecks of at least four golden chariots. Against the wall on his right sat a gorgeous chest brightly painted with hunting and battle scenes. Across from him was a gilded throne with cat-shaped legs, arms like winged serpents, and a back showing King Tut and his queen. Behind the throne rose a tall couch decorated with animal faces that were half hippopotamus and half crocodile. The couch was loaded with more treasures. To the right of the couch, two life-sized statues faced each other like guards. They were black, wore gold skirts and sandals, and had cobras carved on their foreheads. Between them was a second sealed doorway. Carter's heart beat loudly. Would the mummy of King Tut lie beyond it?

- The overall impression given by the topic sentence is that the tomb's many objects were amazing. List three specific details that support this impression.

_____

_____

_____

- Note the importance of words that indicate richness and unusual decoration in helping the reader visualize the scene.* List as many of these words as you can:

_____

_____

_____

* For more work on vivid language, see Chapter 15, "Revising for Language Awareness."

■ This paragraph, like many descriptive paragraphs, is organized according to space order.* The author uses transitional expressions that show where things are. Underline the transitional expressions that indicate place or position.

Before composing this descriptive paragraph, the writer probably brainstormed and freewrote to gather ideas and then made an outline or a plan like this:

Topic sentence: On November 27, 1922, when archaeologist Howard Carter unsealed the door to the ancient Egyptian tomb of King Tut, he stared in amazement at the fantastic objects heaped all around him.

1. **To the left:**	chariots —wrecked —golden
2. **To the right:**	a gorgeous chest —brightly painted with hunting and battle scenes
3. **Across the room:**	a throne —gilded —cat-shaped legs —arms like winged serpents
4. **Behind the throne:**	a couch —decorated with faces that were half hippopotamus and half crocodile
5. **To the right of the couch:**	two life-sized statues —black —gold skirts and sandals —cobras carved on foreheads
6. **Between the two statues:**	a second sealed doorway
7. **Conclusion:**	expectation that King Tut's mummy was beyond the second door

■ Note how each detail supports the topic sentence.

Transitional Expressions

Since space order is often used in description, **transitional expressions** indicating place or position can be useful:

---

* For more work on space order and other kinds of order, see Chapter 4, "Achieving Coherence," Part A.

Transitional Expressions
Indicating Place

next to, near	on top, beneath
close, far	toward, away
up, down, between	left, right, center
above, below	front, back, middle

Of course, other kinds of order are possible. For example, a description of a person might have two parts: details of physical appearance and details of behavior.*

PRACTICE 1   Read the following paragraph carefully and answer the questions.

The woman who met us had an imposing beauty. She was tall and large-boned. Her face was strongly molded, with high cheekbones and skin the color of mahogany. She greeted us politely but did not smile and seemed to hold her head very high, an effect exaggerated by the abundant black hair slicked up and rolled on the top of her head. Her clothing was simple, a black sweater and skirt, and I remember thinking that dressed in showier garments, this woman would have seemed overwhelming.

1. What overall impression does the writer give of the woman?

   _____

   _____

   _____

2. What specific details support this general impression? _____

   _____

   _____

   _____

   _____

3. What kind of order does the writer use? _____

   _____

   _____

* For a complete essay developed by description, see "Disney's Perfect World," Chapter 18, Part C.

PRACTICE 2 It is important that the details in a descriptive paragraph support the overall impression given in the topic sentence. In each of the following plans, one detail has nothing to do with the topic sentence; it is merely a bit of irrelevant information. Find the irrelevant detail and circle the letter.

1. Miami's Calle Ocho Festival, named after S.W. 8th Street in Little Havana, is a giant Latino street party.
   a. as far as the eye can see on S.W. 8th Street, thousands of people stroll, eat, and dance
   b. on the left, vendors sell hot pork sandwiches, *pasteles* (spiced meat pies), and fried sweets dusted with powdered sugar
   c. up close, the press of bare-limbed people, blaring music, and rich smells
   d. during the 1980s, Dominican merengue music hit the dance clubs of New York
   e. on the right, two of many bands play mambo or merengue music

2. In my mind's eye is a plan for the perfect workout room.
   a. complete Nautilus set in center
   b. stationary cycle near the door
   c. on shelf above the bike, a color TV
   d. exercise helps me think more clearly
   e. hot tub with view of woods through one-way glass
   f. spotless blue carpet

3. In the photograph from 1877, Chief Joseph looks sad and dignified.
   a. long hair pulled back, touched with gray
   b. dark eyes gaze off to one side, as if seeing a bleak future
   c. strong mouth frowns at the corners
   d. ceremonial shell necklaces cover his chest
   e. Nez Perce tribe once occupied much of the Pacific Northwest

4. On the plate lay an unappetizing hamburger.
   a. burned bun, black on the edges
   b. burger cost two dollars
   c. fat dripping from the hamburger onto the plate
   d. parts of burger uncooked and partially frozen
   e. sour smell of the meat

5. An illegal dump site has spoiled the field near the edge of town.
   a. fifty or more rusting metal drums, some leaking
   b. pools of green-black liquid on the ground
   c. in the distance, view of the mountains
   d. wildflowers and cottonwood trees dead or dying
   e. large sign reading "Keep Out—Toxic Chemicals"

PRACTICE 3 Here is a list of topic sentences for descriptive paragraphs. Give five specific details that would support the overall impression given in each topic sentence. Appeal to as many of the senses as possible. Be careful not to list irrelevant bits of information.

Example

Stopped in time by the photographer, my mother appears confident.

Details: a. her hair swept up in a sophisticated pompadour

b. a determined look in her young eyes

c. wide, self-assured smile

d. her chin held high

e. well-padded shoulders

(These five details support *confident* in the topic sentence.)

1. This was clearly a music lover's room.

a. _____

_____

b. _____

_____

c. _____

_____

d. _____

_____

e. _____

_____

2. The prizefighter looked tough and fearless.

a. _____

_____

b. _____

_____

c. _____

_____

d. _____

_____

e. _____

_____

3. Spaghetti and meatballs were splattered all over the white kitchen.

   a. _____

   _____

   b. _____

   _____

   c. _____

   _____

   d. _____

   _____

   e. _____

   _____

4. The auto repair shop was alive with activity.

   a. _____

   _____

   b. _____

   _____

   c. _____

   _____

   d. _____

   _____

   e. _____

   _____

5. The buildings on that street look sadly run-down.

   a. _____

   _____

   b. _____

   _____

   c. _____

   _____

d. _____

_____

e. _____

_____

6. The beach on a hot summer day presented a constant show.

a. _____

_____

b. _____

_____

c. _____

_____

d. _____

_____

e. _____

_____

7. During the first week of classes, the college bookstore is wall-to-wall confusion.

a. _____

_____

b. _____

_____

c. _____

_____

d. _____

_____

e. _____

_____

8. The automobile seemed like something from the next century.

a. _____

_____

b. _____

_____

c. _____

_____

d. _____

_____

e. _____

_____

PRACTICE 4   Pick the description you like best from Practice 3. Choose a logical order in which to present the descriptive details and make a plan or an outline for a paragraph.

PRACTICE 5   On pages 95 and 96 are two photographs. Choose the one that most appeals to you. Then describe the photograph as clearly and accurately as you can, so that a reader who has not viewed it can see it in his or her mind's eye. In your topic sentence, state your overall impression of the person or scene in the photograph. Then develop this impression with details. You may wish to use space order to organize these details, moving from left to right, from top to bottom, and so on.

Checklist: The Process of Writing a Descriptive Paragraph

Refer to this checklist of steps as you write a descriptive paragraph of your own.

_____ 1. Narrow the topic in light of your audience and purpose.

_____ 2. Compose a topic sentence that clearly points to what you will describe or gives an overall impression of the person, object, or scene.

_____ 3. Freewrite or brainstorm to find as many specific details as you can to capture your subject in words. Remember to appeal to your readers' senses. (You may want to freewrite or brainstorm before you narrow the topic.)

_____ 4. Select the best details and drop any irrelevant ones.

_____ 5. Make a plan or an outline for the paragraph, numbering the details in the order in which you will present them.

_____ 6. Write a draft of your descriptive paragraph, using transitional expressions wherever they might be helpful.

_____ 7. Revise as necessary, checking for support, unity, logic, and coherence.

_____ 8. Proofread for errors in grammar, punctuation, sentence structure, spelling, and mechanics.

Suggested Topics for Descriptive Paragraphs

1. An unusual man or woman: for example, an athlete, an entertainer, a street person, a food server, or a teacher you won't forget

2. A public place: emergency room, library, fast-food restaurant, town square, or theater lobby

3. The face of a criminal or someone in the news

4. A shop that sells only one item: cheese, soap, Western boots, car parts, flowers

5. An animal, a bird, or an insect you have observed closely

6. A possession you value

7. A photograph of yourself as a child

8. A scene of conflict or a scene of peace

9. A room that reveals something about its owner

10. An intriguing outdoor scene

11. A friend or someone else you know well

12. An interesting person you have seen on campus

13. The ugliest thing you have ever seen

14. A wealthy or a poor neighborhood

15. A bike, car, computer, or piece of machinery

8

Process

Two kinds of **process paragraphs** will be explained in this chapter: the how-to paragraph and the explanation paragraph.

The **how-to paragraph** gives the reader directions on how he or she can do something: how to decorate a room, how to get to the airport, or how to plant a garden. The goals of such directions are the decorated room, the arrival at the airport, or the planted garden. In other words, the reader should be able to do something after he or she has read the paragraph.

The **explanation paragraph,** on the other hand, tells the reader how a particular event occurred or how something works. For example, an explanation paragraph might explain how an internal combustion engine works or how trees reproduce. After reading an explanation paragraph, the reader is not expected to be able to do anything, just to understand how it happened or how it works.

Process writing is useful in history, business, the sciences, sports, and many other areas.

Topic Sentence

Here is the topic sentence of a *how-to paragraph:*

> Learning to make a budget is the key to managing your hard-earned money.

- The writer begins a how-to paragraph with a topic sentence that clearly states the goal of the process—what the reader should be able to do.

- What should the reader be able to do after he or she has read the paragraph following this topic sentence?

_____

Paragraph and Plan

Here is the entire paragraph:

> Learning to make a budget is the key to managing your hard-earned money. First, select your budget period, usually a week or a month. Second, estimate your income for that time period as accurately as you can. Include not only your salary after payroll deductions, but the least you expect to make from any other sources, such as tips, bonuses, and commissions. Third, add up all your expenses for the budget period. Be sure to add in your fixed costs—like rent, utilities, tuition, and taxes—as well as savings. Also include your variable expenses. The most difficult ones to estimate, variable expenses include all your nonfixed living costs, from money for food and transportation to planned events like vacations and less predictable ones like medical and home repair bills. Fourth, subtract your expenses from your income to see whether you need to adjust your budget. If your expenses are greater than your income, look for ways to cut costs—for example, on clothing. If your income is greater than your expenses, you have the luxury of splurging or of saving extra money for that car or trip you have always wanted.

- The body of the how-to paragraph is developed according to time, or chronological, order.* That is, the writer gives directions in the order in which the reader is to complete them. Keeping to a strict chronological order avoids the necessity of saying, *By the way, I forgot to tell you . . .*, or *Whoops, a previous step should have been to . . .*

- How many steps are there in this how-to paragraph and what are they?

_____

_____

_____

_____

_____

Before writing this how-to paragraph, the writer probably brainstormed or freewrote to gather ideas and then made an outline or a plan like the one on page 100.

* For more work on order, see Chapter 4, "Achieving Coherence," Part A.

Topic sentence: Learning to make a budget is the key to managing your hard-earned money.

Step 1:   Select budget period
               —week or month

Step 2:   Estimate income for budget period
               —net salary
               —all other income—tips, bonuses, commissions

Step 3:   Estimate expenses for budget period
               —all fixed costs—rent, utilities, tuition, taxes, savings
               —all variable expenses—food, transportation, medical care, etc.

Step 4:   Subtract expenses from income
               —if short money, cut costs
               —if income left, splurge or save

■ Note that each step clearly relates to the goal stated in the topic sentence.

The second kind of process paragraph, the *explanation paragraph*, tells how something works, how it happens, or how it came to be:

> Many experts believe that recovery from addiction, whether to alcohol or other drugs, has four main stages. The first stage begins when the user finally admits that he or she has a substance abuse problem and wants to quit. At this point, most people seek help from groups like Alcoholics Anonymous or treatment programs because few addicts can "get clean" by themselves. The next stage is withdrawal, when the addict stops using the substance. Withdrawal can be a painful physical and emotional experience, but luckily, it does not last long. After withdrawal comes the most challenging stage—making positive changes in one's life. Recovering addicts have to learn new ways of spending their time, finding pleasure and relaxation, caring for their bodies, and relating to spouses, lovers, family, and friends. The fourth and final stage is staying off drugs. This open-ended part of the process often calls for ongoing support or therapy. For people once defeated by addiction, the rewards of self-esteem and a new life are well worth the effort.

■ What process does the writer explain in this paragraph? _____

_____

■ How many stages or steps are explained in this paragraph? _____

▪ What are they? _____

_____

▪ Make a plan of the paragraph in your notebook.

    Just as the photographs on this page show each stage in the process of a chick hatching, so your process paragraph should clearly describe each step or stage for the reader. Before you write, try to visualize the process as if it were a series of photographs.*

* For a complete essay developed by process, see "How to Prepare for a Final Exam," Chapter 18, Part D, and "Bottle Watching," page 245.

Transitional Expressions

Since process paragraphs rely on **chronological order,** or **time sequence,** words and expressions that locate the steps of the process in time are extremely helpful.

Transitional Expressions for Process			
Beginning a Process	*Continuing a Process*		*Ending a Process*
(at) first	second, third step	when	finally
initially	until	while	at last
begin by	after(ward)	as soon as	
	then	as	
	next	upon	
	later	during	
	before	meanwhile	

PRACTICE 1   Read the following how-to paragraph carefully and answer the questions.

You are sitting in a restaurant quietly having a meal when suddenly a man nearby starts choking on a piece of food lodged in his throat. By using the Heimlich maneuver, you may be able to save this person's life. Your two hands are all you need to perform this lifesaving technique. First, position yourself behind the choking person. Then wrap your arms around the person's midsection, being careful not to apply any pressure to the chest or stomach. Once your arms are around the victim, clench one hand into a fist and cup this fist in the other hand. Now turn the fist so that the clenched thumb points toward the spot between the choker's navel and midsection. Finally, thrust inward at this spot using a quick, sharp motion. If this motion does not dislodge the food, repeat it until the victim can breathe freely.

1. What should you be able to do after reading this paragraph?

   _____

   _____

2. Are any "materials" necessary for this process? _____

   _____

3. How many steps are there in this paragraph? List them.

_____

_____

_____

_____

PRACTICE 2   Here are five plans for process paragraphs. The steps for the plans are not in the correct chronological order. The plans also contain irrelevant details that are not part of the process. Number the steps in the proper time sequence and cross out any irrelevant details.

1. Chewing gum is made entirely by machine.

    _____ Then the warm mass is pressed into thin ribbons by pairs of rollers.

    _____ First, the gum base is melted and pumped through a high-speed spinner that throws out all impurities.

    _____ The gum base makes the gum chewy.

    _____ Huge machines mix the purified gum with sugar, corn syrup, and flavoring, such as spearmint, peppermint, or cinnamon.

    _____ Finally, machines wrap the sticks individually and then package them.

    _____ Knives attached to the last rollers cut the ribbons into sticks.

2. Stress, which is your body's response to physical or mental pressures, occurs in three stages.

    _____ In the resistance stage, your body works hard to resist or handle the threat, but you may become more vulnerable to other stressors, like flu or colds.

    _____ If the stress continues for too long, your body uses up its defenses and enters the exhaustion stage.

    _____ Trying to balance college courses, parenthood, and work is sure to cause stress.

    _____ During the alarm stage (also called *fight or flight*), your body first reacts to a threat by releasing hormones that increase your heart rate and blood pressure, create muscle tension, and supply quick energy.

3. Because turtles are cold-blooded animals, they hibernate during the winter.

_____ After finding the right place, they dig their winter home, bury themselves in the mud, and fall into a deep sleep.

_____ Turtles begin to seek a spot in the mud near a pond to spend the winter, as the weather turns cold.

_____ Contrary to popular opinion, turtles make charming pets.

_____ With the onset of spring, the ice on the pond melts and the thawing mud awakens these buried creatures to new life.

_____ Throughout the winter, their metabolism remains low.

4. Many psychologists claim that marriage is a dynamic process consisting of several phases.

_____ Sooner or later, romance gives way to disappointment as both partners really see each other's faults.

_____ Idealization is the first phase, when two people fall romantically in love, each thinking the other is perfect.

_____ The final phase occurs as the couple face their late years as a twosome once again.

_____ The third phase is sometimes called the productivity period, when two people work at parenting and career development.

_____ Men and women may have different expectations in a marriage.

_____ As the children leave home and careers mature, couples may enter a stage when they rethink their lives and goals.

5. Hard work and ingenuity can help you get a good job, even in a difficult job market.

_____ After you get to know the companies thoroughly, write to request interviews with all three of them.

_____ Next, read everything you can find about each company, its history, and its prospects for the future.

_____ During each interview, stress what you can do for the company rather than what the company can do for you.

_____ Computerized graphic design is a field with many current job opportunities.

_____ Begin by making a survey of companies you might like to work for; then choose three that seem to offer the best opportunities for employment.

_____ Afterward, send a thank-you note to each interviewer, making sure your note is well written and error-free.

PRACTICE 3   Here are topic sentences for five process paragraphs. Make a plan for each paragraph, listing in proper time sequence all the steps that would be necessary to complete the process.

1. Although I'm still not the life of the party, I took these steps to overcome my shyness at parties.

_____

_____

_____

_____

_____

2. Registration was a very complicated (or simple) process this semester.

_____

_____

_____

_____

_____

3. Ted learned _____ in stages over a period of time.

_____

_____

_____

_____

_____

_____

4. Good kids turning bad: it is a process occurring all over the country.

   _____

   _____

   _____

   _____

   _____

   _____

   _____

   _____

5. My morning routine gets me out of the house in twenty minutes.

   _____

   _____

   _____

   _____

   _____

   _____

   _____

Checklist: The Process of Writing a Process Paragraph

Refer to this checklist of steps as you write a process paragraph of your own.

_____ 1. Narrow the topic in light of your audience and purpose.

_____ 2. Compose a topic sentence that clearly states the goal or end result of the process you wish to describe.

_____ 3. Freewrite or brainstorm to generate steps that might be part of the process. (You may want to freewrite or brainstorm before you narrow the topic.)

_____ 4. Drop any irrelevant information or steps that are not really necessary for your explanation of the process.

_____ 5. Make an outline or a plan for your paragraph, numbering the steps in the correct time (chronological) sequence.

_____ 6. Write a draft of your process paragraph, using transitional expressions to indicate time (chronological) sequence.

_____ 7. Revise as necessary, checking for support, unity, logic, and coherence.

_____ 8. Proofread for errors in grammar, punctuation, sentence structure, spelling, and mechanics.

Suggested Topics for Process Paragraphs

1. How to relax
2. How to choose a major
3. How an important discovery was made
4. How to build a child's self-esteem
5. How to use the card catalogue or computer system in the library
6. How to do something you can do well
7. How to get the most from a marriage or relationship
8. How to be a good friend
9. How to appear smarter than you really are
10. How a team won an important game
11. How to break up with someone
12. How to prepare for a test
13. How to give up a bad habit
14. How to prepare your favorite dish
15. How to _____

9
Definition

PART A   Single-Sentence Definitions
PART B   The Definition Paragraph

To **define** is to explain clearly what a word or term means.

As you write, you will sometimes find it necessary to explain words or terms that you suspect your reader may not know. For example, *net profit* is the profit remaining after all deductions have been taken; a *bonsai* is a dwarfed, ornamentally shaped tree. Such terms can often be defined in just a few carefully chosen words. However, other terms—like *courage, racism,* or *a good marriage*—are more difficult to define. They will test your ability to explain them clearly so that your reader knows exactly what you mean when you use them in your writing. They may require an entire paragraph for a complete and thorough definition.

In this chapter, you will learn to write one-sentence definitions and then whole paragraphs of definition. The skill of defining clearly will be useful in such courses as psychology, business, the sciences, history, and English.

PART A

Single-Sentence Definitions

There are many ways to define a word or term. Three basic ways are **definition by synonym, definition by class,** and **definition by negation.**

Definition by Synonym

The simplest way to define a term is to supply a **synonym,** a word that means the same thing. A good synonym definition always uses an easier and more familiar word than the one being defined.

> 1. *Gregarious* means *sociable.*
>
> 2. *To procrastinate* means *to postpone needlessly.*
>
> 3. A *wraith* is a *ghost* or *phantom.*
>
> 4. *Adroitly* means *skillfully.*

Although you may not have known the words *gregarious, procrastination, wraith,* and *adroitly* before, the synonym definitions make it very clear what they mean.

A synonym should usually be the same part of speech as the word being defined, so it could be used as a substitute. *Gregarious* and *sociable* are both adjectives; *to procrastinate* and *to postpone* are verbs; *wraith, ghost,* and *phantom* are nouns; *adroitly* and *skillfully* are adverbs.

> 5. Quarterback Dan Marino *adroitly* moved his team up the field.
>
> 6. Quarterback Dan Marino *skillfully* moved his team up the field.

■ In this sentence *skillfully* can be substituted for *adroitly.*

Unfortunately, it is not always possible to come up with a good synonym definition.

Definition by Class

The **class** definition is the one most often required in college and formal writing—in examinations, papers, and reports.

The class definition has two parts. First, the writer places the word to be defined into the larger **category,** or **class,** to which it belongs.

> 7. *Lemonade* is a *drink* . . .
>
> 8. An *orphan* is a *child* . . .
>
> 9. A *dictatorship* is a *form of government* . . .

Second, the writer provides the **distinguishing characteristics** or **details** that make this person, object, or idea *different* from all others in that category. What the reader wants to know is what *kind* of drink is lemonade? What *specific* type of person is an orphan? What *particular* form of government is a dictatorship?

10. *Lemonade* is a drink *made of lemons, sugar, and water.*

11. An *orphan* is a child *without living parents.*

12. A *dictatorship* is a form of government *in which one person has absolute control over his or her subjects.*

Here is a class definition for the action pictured: A slam-dunk is a basket that is scored when the shooter leaps high, slamming the basketball through the rim from above.

Think of class definitions as if they were in chart form:

Word	Category or Class	Distinguishing Facts or Details
lemonade	drink	made of lemons, sugar, and water
orphan	child	without living parents
dictatorship	form of government	one person has absolute control over his or her subjects

When you write a class definition, be careful not to place the word or term in too broad or vague a category. For instance, saying that lemonade is a *food* or that an orphan is a *person* will make your job of zeroing in on a distinguishing detail more difficult.

Besides making the category or class as limited as possible, be sure to make your distinguishing facts as specific and exact as you can. Saying that lemonade is a drink *made with water* or that an orphan is a child *who has lost family members* is not specific enough to give your reader an accurate definition.

Definition by Negation

A definition by **negation** means that the writer first says what something is not, and then says what it is.

13. A *good parent* does not just feed and clothe a child but loves, accepts, and supports that child for who he or she is.

14. *College* is not just a place to have a good time but a place to grow intellectually and emotionally.

15. *Liberty* does not mean having the right to do whatever you please but carries the obligation to respect the rights of others.

Definitions by negation are extremely helpful when you think that the reader has a preconceived idea about the word you wish to define. You say that *it is not* what the reader thought, but that *it is* something else entirely.

Here is a definition by negation: The grapefruit shield is not just another useless luxury item but a clever device that will allow you to enjoy grapefruit without the mess, sting, and embarrassment of spurting juice.

PRACTICE 1   Write a one-sentence definition by **synonym** for each of the following terms. Remember, the synonym should be more familiar than the term being defined.

1. *irate:* _____

2. *to elude:* _____

3. *pragmatic:* _____

4. *fiasco:* _____

5. *elated:* _____

PRACTICE 2   Here are five **class definitions.** Circle the category and underline the distinguishing characteristics in each. You may find it helpful to make a chart.

1. A *haiku* is a Japanese poem that has seventeen syllables.

2. A *homer* is a referee who unconsciously favors the home team.

3. An *ophthalmologist* is a doctor who specializes in diseases of the eye.

4. A *mentor* is a counselor who guides, teaches, and assists another person.

5. *Plagiarism* is stealing writing or ideas that are not one's own.

PRACTICE 3   Define the following words by **class definition.** You may find it helpful

to use this form: "A _____ is a _____
　　　　　　　　　　　　　(noun)　　　　　　　　　　　(class or category)

that _____."
　　　　　　　　　(distinguishing characteristic)

1. *hamburger:* _____

   _____

   _____

2. *bikini:* _____

   _____

   _____

3. *snob:* _____

   _____

   _____

4. *high tops:* _____

   _____

   _____

5. *adolescence:* _____

   _____

PRACTICE 4   Write a one-sentence definition by **negation** for each of the following terms. First say what each term is not; then say what it is.

1. *hero:* _____

   _____

   _____

2. *final exam:* _____

   _____

   _____

3. *self-esteem:* _____

   _____

   _____

4. *intelligence:* _____

   _____

   _____

5. *freedom of speech:* _____

_____

_____

PART B

The Definition Paragraph

Sometimes a single-sentence definition may not be enough to define a word or term adequately. In such cases, the writer may need an entire paragraph in which he or she develops the definition by means of examples, descriptions, comparisons, contrasts, and so forth.

Topic Sentence

The topic sentence of a definition paragraph is often one of the single-sentence definitions discussed in Part A: definition by synonym, definition by class, definition by negation.

Here is the topic sentence of a definition paragraph:

> *Ambivalence* can be defined as a feeling or attitude that is both positive and negative at the same time.

■ What kind of definition does the topic sentence use?

_____

■ To what larger category or class does *ambivalence* belong?

_____

■ What are the distinguishing details about *ambivalence* that make it different from all other feelings or attitudes?

_____

_____

Paragraph and Plan

Here is the entire paragraph:

> *Ambivalence* can be defined as a feeling or attitude that is both positive and negative at the same time. For instance, a young woman might feel *ambivalent* about motherhood. She may want to have a child yet fears that motherhood will use up energy she would like to spend on her career. Or a Michigan man who is offered a slightly higher salary in Arizona might be ambivalent about moving. He and his family don't want to leave their friends, their schools, and a city they love. On the other hand, they are tempted by a larger income and by Arizona's warm climate and clean air. Finally, two people may have ambivalent feelings about each other, loving and disliking each other at the same time. It hurts to be together, and it hurts to be apart; neither situation makes them happy.

■ One effective way for a writer to develop the body of a definition paragraph is to provide examples.*

■ What three examples does this writer give to develop the definition in the topic sentence?

_____

_____

■ By repeating the word being defined—or a form of it—in the context of each example, the writer helps the reader understand the definition better: A young woman might feel *ambivalent,* a Michigan man might be *ambivalent,* and two people may have *ambivalent* feelings.

Before writing the paragraph, the writer probably brainstormed or freewrote to gather ideas and then made an outline or a plan like this:

Topic sentence: *Ambivalence* can be defined as a feeling or attitude that is both positive and negative at the same time.

Example 1:	A young woman —wants to have a child —yet fears motherhood will use up career energy
Example 2:	Michigan man and his family —don't want to leave friends, schools, city —are tempted by income, climate, clean air
Example 3:	Two people —love each other —also dislike each other

■ Note that each example in the body of the paragraph clearly relates to the definition in the topic sentence.

* For more work on examples, see Chapter 5, "Illustration."

Although examples are an excellent way to develop a definition paragraph, other methods of development are also possible. For instance, you might compare and contrast[†] *love* and *lust, assertiveness* and *aggressiveness,* or *the leader* and *the follower.* You could also combine definition and persuasion.[‡] Such a paragraph might begin *College is a dating service* or *Alcoholism is not a moral weakness, but a disease.* The rest of the paragraph would have to persuade readers that this definition is valid.

There are no transitional expressions used specifically for definition paragraphs. Sometimes phrases like *can be defined as* or *can be considered* or *means that* can help alert the reader that a definition paragraph will follow.[§]

PRACTICE 5   Read the following paragraph carefully and then answer the questions.

A feminist is *not* a man-hater, a masculine woman, a demanding shrew, or someone who dislikes housewives. A feminist is simply a woman or man who believes that women should enjoy the same rights, privileges, opportunities, and pay as men. Because society has deprived women of many equal rights, feminists have fought for equality. For instance, Susan B. Anthony, a famous nineteenth-century feminist, worked to get women the right to vote. Today, feminists want women to receive equal pay for equal work. They support a woman's right to pursue her goals and dreams, whether she wants to be an astronaut, athlete, banker, or mother. On the home front, feminists believe that two partners who work should equally share the housework and child care. Because the term is often misunderstood, some people don't call themselves feminists even though they share feminist values. But courageous feminists of both sexes continue to speak out for equality.

1. The definition here spans two sentences. What kind of definition does the writer use in sentence 1? _____

_____

2. What kind of definition appears in sentence 2? _____

_____

3. The paragraph is developed by describing some key beliefs of feminists. What are these? _____

_____

_____

4. Which point is supported by an example? _____

_____

[†] For more work on contrast, see Chapter 10, "Comparison and Contrast."
[‡] For more work on persuasion, see Chapter 12, "Persuasion."
[§] For an entire essay developed by definition, see "Winning," Chapter 18, Part E.

5. Make a plan or an outline of the paragraph.

_____

_____

_____

_____

_____

_____

_____

_____

_____

_____

PRACTICE 6:   Read the following paragraphs and answer the questions.

Induction is reasoning from particular cases to general principles; that is, the scientific method: you look at a number of examples, then come to a general conclusion based on the evidence. For instance, having known twenty-five people named Glenn, all of whom were men, you might naturally conclude, through induction, that all people named Glenn are men. The problem with inductive reasoning here, however, is Glenn Close, the movie actress.

Deduction is reasoning from the general to the particular. One starts from a statement known or merely assumed to be true and uses it to come to a conclusion about the matter at hand. Once you know that all people have to die sometime and that you are a person, you can logically deduce that you, too, will have to die sometime.

—Judy Jones and William Wilson, "100 Things Every
College Graduate Should Know," *Esquire*

1. What two terms are defined? _____

_____

2. What kind of definition is used in both topic sentences? _____

_____

3. In what larger category do the writers place both induction and deduction?

_____

4. What example of induction do the writers give? _____

_____

5. What example shows the *problem* with induction? _____

_____

6. What example of deduction do the writers give? _____

_____

PRACTICE 7   Here are some topic sentences for definition paragraphs. Choose one that interests you and make a plan for a paragraph, using whatever method of development seems appropriate.

1. An optimist is someone who usually expects the best from life and from people.

2. Prejudice means prejudging people on the basis of race, creed, age, or sex—not on their merits as individuals.

3. A wealthy person does not necessarily have money and possessions, but he or she might possess inner wealth—a loving heart and a creative mind.

4. Registration is a ritual torture that students must go through before they can attend their classes.

5. Bravery and bravado are very different character traits.

PRACTICE 8   The Martians have landed. You have been chosen to answer their questions about several things they have noticed on Earth. Since they can read English but cannot speak it, you must write a clear paragraph defining one of the following: *money, clothes, television, cars, the president of the United States.* Begin with a one-sentence definition; then discuss, giving examples and details that fully define the word or term for your Martian readers.

Checklist: The Process of Writing a Definition Paragraph

Refer to this checklist of steps as you write a definition paragraph of your own.

_____ 1. Narrow the topic in light of your audience and purpose.

_____ 2. Compose a topic sentence that uses one of the three basic methods of definition discussed in this chapter: synonym, class, or negation.

_____ 3. Decide on the method of paragraph development that is best suited to what you want to say.

_____ 4. Freewrite or brainstorm to generate ideas that may be useful in your definition paragraph. (You may want to freewrite or brainstorm before you narrow the topic.)

_____ 5. Select the best ideas and drop any ideas that do not clearly relate to the definition in your topic sentence.

_____ 6. Make a plan or an outline for your paragraph, numbering the ideas in the order in which you will present them.

_____ 7. Write a draft of your definition paragraph, using transitional expressions wherever they might be helpful.

_____ 8. Revise as necessary, checking for support, unity, logic, and coherence.

_____ 9. Proofread for errors in grammar, punctuation, sentence structure, spelling, and mechanics.

Suggested Topics for Definition Paragraphs

1. Success (or failure)

2. The con artist (or loner, dreamer, big mouth, perfectionist, bully, or party pooper)

3. Country and western music (or hard rock, gospel, rap, or some other type of music)

4. Common sense

5. A good marriage (or a good partner, parent, or friend)

6. The racing car (football, fashion, or other) fanatic

7. A dead-end job

8. An interesting term you know from reading (*placebo, acid rain, apartheid, inflation, hubris,* and so forth)

9. Spring break

10. A racist (sexist, feminist, or other *-ist*)

11. The night person (or morning person)

12. An illness you know about (arthritis, alcoholism, diabetes, etc.)

13. A technical term you know from work or a hobby

14. A slang term you or your friends use

15. A word or term from another language that you know (for example, *machismo* or *déjà vu*)

10

Comparison and Contrast

PART A   The Contrast and the Comparison Paragraphs
PART B   The Comparison-Contrast Paragraph

To contrast two persons, places, or things is to examine the ways in which they are different. To compare them is to examine the ways in which they are similar.

When you go shopping, you often compare and contrast. For instance, you might compare and contrast two brands of frozen foods in order to get the most nutritious meals for your family.

Your employer might ask you to write a comparison and contrast report on two computers, two telephone answering services, or two types of packing crates. Your task would be to gather all the relevant information about these products to show in what ways they are similar and in what ways they are different. Your report may then help your employer choose one product or service over another.

Comparison and contrast, then, helps the reader understand one person, place, or thing in relation to another.

PART A

The Contrast and the Comparison Paragraphs

Topic Sentence

Here is the topic sentence of a contrast paragraph:

> Although black bass and striped bass are two familiar fish in the world of salt water fishing, their habits are altogether different.

- The writer begins a contrast paragraph with a topic sentence that clearly states what two persons, things, or ideas will be contrasted.

- What two things will be contrasted?

_____

- What word or words in the topic sentence make it clear that the writer will contrast black bass and striped bass?

_____

Paragraph and Plan

Here is the entire paragraph:

> Although black bass and striped bass are two familiar fish in the world of salt water fishing, their habits are altogether different. The black bass feeds steadily on fiddler crabs, mussels, skimmer, and clams, usually staying in one locale and waiting intently for its victims to pass. Building its home in the rocks that lie along the bottom of the ocean wall, the black bass is well protected from the fisherman, whose line will often snag and break before this fish is taken. Still, the best way to catch the black bass is with a hook and sinker. On the other hand, its cousin, the striped bass, feeds on smaller fish, squid, tin cans, or any glittering and wiggly object. The striped bass remains in constant motion, always searching for its prey. Its home is almost anywhere. This fish is usually caught near the surface of the water or several feet from the bottom. Trolling is the best way to catch the striped bass since this fish doesn't remain in one spot for long. Striped bass and black bass, however, do have one thing in common: both make delicious eating after being caught and then fried in an open pan.
>
> —Paul Gazzola (Student)

- The writer first provides information about (A) black bass and then gives contrasting parallel information about (B) striped bass.

- What information about (A) black bass does the writer provide in the first

half of the paragraph? _____

_____

_____

_____

■ What contrasting parallel information does the writer provide about striped bass in the second half of the paragraph? _____

_____

_____

_____

_____

■ Why do you think the writer chose to present the points of contrast in this order? _____

_____

_____

_____

_____

Before composing the paragraph, the writer probably brainstormed or freewrote to gather ideas and then made an outline or a plan like this:

Topic sentence: Although black bass and striped bass are two familiar fish in the world of salt water fishing, their habits are altogether different.

Points of Contrast	A: Black Bass	B: Striped Bass
1. diet	fiddler crabs, mussels, skimmer, and clams	smaller fish, squid, glittering object, and so on
2. motion	stays in one place	constantly moves
3. home	rocks at bottom	almost anywhere
4. how caught	hook and sinker	trolling

Organized in this manner, the plan for this contrast paragraph helps the writer make sure that the paragraph will be complete. That is, if diet is discussed for black bass, then diet must also be discussed for striped bass, and so on, for all the points of contrast.

Here is another way to write the same contrast paragraph.

Although black bass and striped bass are two familiar fish in the world of salt water fishing, their habits are altogether different. Staying in one locale and waiting intently for its victims to pass, the black bass feeds steadily on fiddler crabs, mussels, skimmer, and clams. Its cousin, the striped bass, however, remains in constant motion, always searching for its prey. The striped bass feeds on smaller fish, squid, tin cans, or any glittering or wiggly object. The black bass builds its home in the rocks that lie along the bottom of the ocean wall; it is well protected from the fisherman, whose line will often snag and break before this fish is taken. On the other hand, the striped bass makes its home almost anywhere; it is usually caught near the surface of the water or several feet from the bottom. The best way to catch the black bass is with a hook and sinker, whereas trolling is the best way to land a striped bass because this fish does not remain in one spot very long. Striped bass and black bass, however, do have one thing in common: both make delicious eating after being caught and then fried in an open pan.

- Instead of giving all the information about the black bass and then going on to the striped bass, this paragraph moves back and forth between the black bass and the striped bass, dealing with *each point of contrast separately.*

Use either one of these two patterns when writing a contrast or a comparison paragraph:

1. Present all the information about **A** and then provide parallel information about **B**:

   First all A: point 1
                          point 2
                          point 3

   Then all B: point 1
                          point 2
                          point 3

- This pattern is good for paragraphs and for short compositions. The reader can easily remember what was said about *A* by the time he or she gets to *B*.

> 2. Move back and forth between **A** and **B**. Present one point about **A** and then go to the parallel point about **B**. Then move to the next point and do the same:
>
> **First A,** point 1;   **then B,** point 1
>
> **First A,** point 2;   **then B,** point 2
>
> **First A,** point 3;   **then B,** point 3

- The second pattern is best for longer papers, where it might be hard for the reader to remember what the writer said about *A* by the time he or she gets to *B* a few paragraphs later. By going back and forth, the writer makes it easier for the reader to keep the contrasts or comparisons in mind.

What you have learned so far about planning a contrast paragraph holds true for a comparison paragraph as well. Just remember that a **contrast** *stresses differences,* whereas a **comparison** *stresses similarities.*

Here is a comparison paragraph:

> "Two birds of a feather," so the family describes my mother and me, and it's true that we have much in common. We share the same honey-colored skin, hazel eyes, and pouting mouth. I like to think I've inherited her creative flair. Though we were poor, she taught me that beauty requires style, not money, and I see her influence in my small apartment, which I have decorated with colorful batiks and my own paintings. One similarity alarms me, however: both my mother and I were battered wives. She believed a woman's place is with her husband, so she stayed with my father despite the abuse. Eventually, he left us. Soon after I married, my husband hit me for the first time. Shocked to think that the secret pain of my mother's life would now be mine, I took the initiative, got counseling, and left him. Two birds of a feather, my mother and I, but not in this.
>
> —Janice Wilson (Student)

- What words in the topic sentence does the writer use to indicate that a

  comparison will follow? _____

  _____

- In what ways are the writer and her mother similar? _____

  _____

  _____

- What transitional words stress the similarities? _____

  _____

- What pattern of presentation does the writer use? _____

  _____

- What one point of *contrast* serves as a strong punch line for the para-

  graph? _____

  _____

- Make a plan or an outline of this comparison paragraph.

Transitional Expressions

Transitional expressions in contrast paragraphs stress opposition and difference:

Transitional Expressions for Contrast	
although	on the other hand
whereas	in contrast
but	while
however	yet
conversely	unlike

Transitional expressions in comparison paragraphs stress similarities:

Transitional Expressions for Comparison	
in the same way	just as ... so
and, also, in addition	similarly
as well as	like
both, neither	too
each of	the same

As you write, avoid using just one or two of these transitional expressions. Learn new ones from the list and practice them in your paragraphs.*

PRACTICE 1   Read the following paragraph carefully and answer the questions.

Two different groups of black musicians evolved in New Orleans. The first of these, the slaves, brought with them the music of Africa and the influences of Caribbean music. Denied education and opportunity by slavery, they improvised, making instruments from gourds, bamboo, and bone. They created songs charged with emotion: work songs, chants, and spirituals. In contrast to the slaves, the "free men of color" were raised as Creoles. Formally educated and sometimes sent to European schools, they were well versed in classical music, and they played classical instruments. During the Reconstruction period, these two groups of musicians were flung together. The brilliant child of this unlikely union was jazz.

1. How can you tell from the topic sentence whether a contrast or a comparison will follow? _____

2. What two groups are being contrasted? _____

   _____

3. What information does the writer provide about the slaves? _____

   _____

   _____

   _____

4. What parallel information does the writer provide about the "free men of color"? _____

   _____

5. What pattern does the writer of this paragraph use to present the contrasts? _____

   _____

   _____

* For an entire essay developed by comparison-contrast, see "Two Childhoods," Chapter 18, Part F.

6. What transitional expression does the writer use to stress the shift from *A* to *B*? _____

PRACTICE 2 The next paragraph is hard to follow because it lacks transitional expressions that emphasize contrast. Revise the paragraph, adding transitional expressions of contrast. Strive for variety.

Mexico City is a fascinating mixture of modern and traditional ways of life. The city boasts sleek skyscrapers, such as the famous Latin America Tower. It proudly displays graceful Spanish colonial palaces and public buildings, many of which are three hundred years old. Glittering stores line the main shopping streets, offering the latest international styles of clothing and home furnishings. Old-fashioned street markets fill the city, from the great food market of the Merced to stalls in small plazas selling such items as piñatas and paper Christmas decorations. Huge modern factories in the northern section turn out most of Mexico's clothing, steel, cement, appliances, and electrical supplies. Craftspeople line the city's streets with their handmade baskets, pottery, metalwork, and textiles.

PRACTICE 3 Below are three plans for contrast paragraphs. The points of contrast in the second column do not follow the same order as the points in the first column. In addition, one detail is missing. First, number the points in the second column to match those in the first. Then fill in the missing detail.

1. **Shopping at a Supermarket**   **Shopping at a Local Grocery**

   1. carries all brands   _____ personal service

   2. lower prices   _____ closed on Sundays

   3. open seven days a week   _____ prices often higher

   4. little personal service   _____ _____

   5. no credit   _____ credit available for steady customers

2. My Son   **My Daughter**

   1. fifteen years old   _____ good at making minor
                                                        household repairs

   2. likes to be alone   _____ likes to be with friends

   3. reads a lot   _____ doesn't like to read

   4. is an excellent cook   _____ expects to attend a technical
                                                        college

   5. wants to go to chef school

                                                        _____ _____

3. Job A   **Job B**

   1. good salary   _____ three-week vacation

   2. office within walking distance   _____ work on a team with others

   3. two-week vacation   _____ one-hour bus ride to office

   4. work alone   _____ health insurance

   5. lots of overtime   _____ no overtime

   6. no health insurance   _____ _____

PRACTICE 4 Here are five topics for either contrast or comparison paragraphs. Compose two topic sentences for each topic, one for a possible contrast paragraph and one for a possible comparison paragraph.

	Topic		**Topic Sentences**
Example	Two members of my family	A.	My brother and sister have different attitudes toward exercise.
		B.	My parents are alike in that they're both easygoing.
	1. Two friends or coworkers	A.	_____
			_____
			_____

B. _____

_____

_____

2. Two kinds of music or dancing   A. _____

_____

_____

B. _____

_____

_____

3. You as a child and you as an adult   A. _____

_____

_____

B. _____

_____

_____

4. Two vacations   A. _____

_____

_____

B. _____

_____

_____

5. Two teachers   A. _____

_____

_____

B. _____

_____

_____

PRACTICE 5   Here are four topic sentences for comparison or contrast paragraphs. Pick just one point of comparison or of contrast that interests you and write a few sentences explaining that particular comparison or contrast. Use a transitional expression wherever you feel it is necessary to show similarities or differences.

1. When it comes to movies (TV shows, books, entertainment), Demetrios and Arlene have totally different tastes.

   _____

   _____

   _____

   _____

2. The average bowl of chili and my family's Texas chili have little in common besides beans.

   _____

   _____

   _____

   _____

3. Although there are obvious differences, the two neighborhoods (blocks, homes) have much in common.

   _____

   _____

   _____

   _____

4. Paying taxes is like having a tooth pulled.*

   _____

   _____

   _____

PRACTICE 6   Choose your favorite of the topic sentences you wrote in Practice 4 and make a plan or an outline for a paragraph. Arrange the points of contrast or comparison in the plan and number them in the order in which you wish to present them to the reader.

* For more work on this kind of comparison, see Chapter 15, "Revising for Language Awareness," Part D.

Writing Assignment 1

Study the three women in this photograph: the bride, the older woman, and the girl. Then write a paragraph *contrasting* the reactions of the older woman and the girl to the bride. Begin by stating your overall impression of the differences between them as they react to the occasion. Then develop your paragraph with details that support your topic sentence—details of facial expression, posture, gesture, and so forth. Remember to conclude your paragraph; don't just stop abruptly.

Checklist: The Process of Writing a Contrast or Comparison Paragraph

Refer to this checklist of steps as you write a contrast or comparison paragraph of your own.

_____ 1. Narrow the topic in light of your audience and purpose.

_____ 2. Compose a topic sentence that clearly states that a contrast or a comparison will follow.

_____ 3. Freewrite or brainstorm to generate as many points of contrast or comparison as you can think of. (You may want to freewrite or brainstorm before you narrow the topic.)

_____ 4. Choose the points you will use, and drop any details that are not really part of the contrast or the comparison.

_____ 5. List parallel points of contrast or of comparison for both *A* and *B*.

_____ 6. Make a plan or an outline, numbering all the points of contrast or comparison in the order in which you will present them in the paragraph.

_____ 7. Write a draft of your contrast or comparison paragraph, using transitional expressions that stress either differences or similarities.

_____ 8. Revise as necessary, checking for support, unity, logic, and coherence.

_____ 9. Proofread for errors in grammar, punctuation, sentence structure, spelling, and mechanics.

Suggested Topics for Contrast or Comparison Paragraphs

1. Compare or contrast two attitudes toward money (the spendthrift and the miser), marriage (the confirmed single and the committed partner), or ambition (the aggressive go-getter and the laid-back person).

2. Compare or contrast two ways of raising children: permissive and strict.

3. Compare or contrast being a full-time worker and a full-time student.

4. Compare or contrast two bosses.

5. Compare or contrast two magazines or newspapers that you read.

6. Compare or contrast two high schools or colleges that you have attended (perhaps one in the United States and one in a different country).

7. Compare or contrast one aspect of life in a big city and life in a small town.

8. Compare or contrast two brands of a product you have purchased or might purchase: TV set, automobile, microwave, down coat.

9. Compare or contrast two TV talk-show hosts.

10. Compare or contrast your best friend and your spouse or partner.

PART B

The Comparison-Contrast Paragraph

Sometimes an assignment will call for you to write a paragraph that both compares and contrasts, one that stresses both similarities and differences. Here is a comparison-contrast paragraph:

> Although contemporary fans would find the game played by the Knickerbockers—the first organized baseball club—similar to modern baseball, they would also note some startling differences. In 1845, as now, the four bases of the playing field were set in a diamond shape, ninety feet from one another. Nine players took the field. The object of the game was to score points by hitting a pitched ball and running around the bases. The teams changed sides after three outs. However, the earlier game was also different. The umpire sat at a table along the third base line instead of standing behind home plate. Unlike the modern game, the players wore no gloves. Rather than firing the ball over the plate at ninety miles an hour, the pitcher gently tossed it underhand to the batter. Since there were no balls and strikes, the batter could wait for the pitch he wanted. The game ended, not when nine innings were completed, but when one team scored twenty-one runs, which were called "aces."

- How are the Knickerbockers' game and modern baseball similar?

  _____

  _____

  _____

- How are these two versions of the game different? _____

  _____

  _____

  _____

  _____

  _____

  _____

  _____

▪ What transitional expressions in the paragraph emphasize similarities

and differences? _____

_____

Before composing this comparison-contrast paragraph, the writer probably brainstormed or freewrote to gather ideas and then made a plan like
this:

Topic Sentence: Although contemporary fans would find the game
played by the Knickerbockers—the first organized baseball club—
similar to modern baseball, they would also note some startling
differences.

Comparisons	Knickerbockers	Modern Game
Point 1	four bases, ninety feet apart, in diamond shape	
Point 2	nine players	
Point 3	scoring points	
Point 4	three outs	
Contrasts		
Point 1	umpire sat at third base line	umpire at home plate
Point 2	no gloves	gloves
Point 3	pitcher gently tossed ball	pitcher fires ball at plate
Point 4	no balls and strikes	balls and strikes
Point 5	twenty-one "aces" to win, no innings	most runs to win, nine innings

▪ A plan such as this makes it easier for the writer to organize a great deal
of material.

▪ The writer begins by listing all the points of comparison—how the
Knickerbockers' game and modern baseball are similar. Then the writer
lists all the points of contrast—how they are different.

PRACTICE 7   Here is a somewhat longer comparison and contrast (two paragraphs). Read
it carefully and answer the questions.

No meal eaten in the Middle East ends without coffee or tea, but coffee
takes precedence most of the time. Coffee is a social beverage, offered to
guests by housewives and to customers by merchants; to refuse it borders

upon insult. There are two distinct but similar ways of preparing it, Turkish and Arabic. Both are served black, in cups the size of a demitasse or smaller. And both are brewed by starting with green beans, roasting them to a chocolate brown color, pulverizing them at once, either with mortar and pestle or in a handsome cylindrical coffee mill of chased brass, and quickly steeping them in boiling water.

The Turkish version is made in a coffee pot that has a long handle to protect the fingers from the fire and a shape narrowing from the bottom to the open neck to intensify the foaming action as the coffee boils up. Water, sugar and coffee are stirred together to your taste; then, at the first bubbling surge, the pot is whisked from the fire. It is returned briefly one or two more times to build up the foamy head, which is poured into each cup in equal amounts, to be followed by the rest of the brew, grounds and all. The dregs soon settle to the bottom, and the rich, brown coffee that covers them is ready to be enjoyed, with more sugar if you like. The Arabs prepare coffee in a single boil; they almost never use sugar; they pour the liquid into a second pot, leaving the sediment in the first, and then add such heady spices as cloves or cardamon seeds.

> —*Foods of the World/Middle Eastern Cooking,*
> Time-Life Books

1. What two things does this writer contrast and compare? _____

   _____

   _____

2. What words indicate that both contrast *and* comparison will follow?

   _____

3. How are Arabic and Turkish coffee similar? _____

   _____

   _____

   _____

   _____

4. How are Arabic and Turkish coffee different? _____

   _____

   _____

   _____

5. On a separate sheet of paper, make a plan or an outline for these paragraphs.

Writing Assignment 2

On this page and the next are photos of two couples. Study closely the details of facial expression, gesture, clothing, and so forth. For a paragraph that both *compares and contrasts* the two couples, jot down possible similarities and differences. Ask yourself, "What is my impression of each pair? How do they seem to be getting along with each other? How are the couples alike and how are they different?" Then plan and write your paragraph.

If you prefer, write a paragraph comparing and contrasting the two women *or* the two men.

Working Through the Comparison-Contrast Paragraph

You can work through the comparison-contrast paragraph in the same way that you do a comparison or a contrast paragraph. Follow the steps in the earlier checklist, but make certain that your paragraph shows both similarities and differences.

Suggested Topics for Comparison-Contrast Paragraphs

1. Compare and contrast two ways to prepare for an examination.

2. Compare and contrast the requirements for two jobs or careers.

3. Compare and contrast your life now with your life five years ago.

4. Compare and contrast two films on similar subjects.

5. Compare and contrast two players of the same sport.

6. Compare and contrast two attitudes toward a subject (sexual activity, education, careers, children, and so forth).

7. Compare and contrast learning something from experience and learning something from books.

8. Compare and contrast two singers or musicians.

9. Compare and contrast styles of party dress or courtship customs in two different cultures.

10. Compare and contrast two popular television programs of the same type (newscasts, situation comedies, talk shows, and so on).

11

Classification

To classify is to gather into types, kinds, or categories according to a single basis of division.

Mailroom personnel, for example, might separate incoming mail into four piles: orders, bills, payments, and inquiries. Once the mail has been divided in this manner—according to which department should receive each pile—it can be efficiently delivered.

The same information can be classified in more than one way. The Census Bureau collects a variety of data about the people living in the United States. One way to classify the data is by age group—the number of people under eighteen, between eighteen and fifty-five, over fifty-five, and over seventy. Such information might be useful in developing programs for college-bound youth or for the elderly. Other ways of dividing the population are by geographic location, occupation, family size, level of education, and so on.

Whether you classify rocks by their origin for a science course or children by their stages of growth for a psychology course, you will be organizing large groups into smaller, more manageable units that can be explained to your reader.

Topic Sentence

Here is the topic sentence for a classification paragraph:

> Houseguests can be classified according to their level of self-sufficiency as independent, semidependent, and completely dependent.

- The writer begins a classification paragraph with a topic sentence that clearly states what group of people or things will be classified.

- What group of people will be classified? _____

- Into how many categories will they be divided? What are the categories?

_____

_____

Paragraph and Plan

Here is the entire paragraph:

> Houseguests can be classified according to their level of self-sufficiency as independent, semidependent, or completely dependent. Independent guests make an effort to fit their routines to yours; they make their own beds, cook breakfast if they get up early, and know how to entertain themselves if you have other things to do. These usually are the guests you want to invite back. Semidependent guests demand more of your attention and companionship; they may want to be driven around town or may urge you to play pool with them even though you hate pool or have a term paper due. Still, the guests in this category may have charming qualities that make their visit worthwhile. Most infuriating are the helplessly dependent guests, who enter your house as if it were a hospital or spa, expecting to be taken care of. My friend George, for example, sprawls on a chair, his feet on my coffee table, complaining about his love life while I cook dinner, set the table, and change the CDs. After two days of waiting on George while I try to solve his problems, I'm exhausted. As these categories show, houseguests are a mixed blessing—some more mixed than others.

- On what basis does the writer classify houseguests?

_____

- What information does the writer provide about the first type, independent houseguests? _____

_____

- What information does the writer provide about the second type, semidependent guests? _____

_____

- What information does the writer provide about the third type, completely dependent guests? _____

_____

■ Giving occasional examples is helpful in a classification. What example of a completely dependent houseguest does the writer provide? _____

_____

■ Why do you think this writer discussed independent guests first, semi-dependent second, and dependent third? _____

_____

Before composing the paragraph, the writer probably brainstormed or freewrote to gather ideas and then made an outline or a plan like this:

Topic sentence: Houseguests can be classified as independent, semi-dependent, or completely dependent, according to their self-sufficiency.

Type 1:   Independent houseguests
               —fit routine to yours
               —example behaviors: make beds, fix breakfast
               —know how to entertain themselves

Type 2:   Semidependent houseguests
               —demand more attention and company
               —example behaviors: may want to be driven around, play
                 pool even if you don't want to
               —may have charming qualities

Type 3:   Completely dependent houseguests
               —are infuriating, expect to be taken care of
               —example: George

Conclusion: Houseguests are a mixed blessing.

■ Note that the body of the paragraph discusses all three types of house-guests mentioned in the topic sentence and does not add any new ones.

This classification paragraph sticks to a single method of classification: *how self-sufficient houseguests are.* If the paragraph had also discussed a fourth category—*left-handed houseguests*—the initial basis of classification would fall apart because *left-handedness* has nothing to do with *how self-sufficient houseguests are.*

There is no set rule about which category to present first, second, or last in a classification paragraph. However, the paragraph should follow some kind of **logical sequence,** such as from the least to the most helpless, from the least to the most expensive, from the largest to the smallest category, and so on.*[†]

* For more work on order, see Chapter 4, "Achieving Coherence," Part A.
[†] For a complete essay developed by classification, see "The Potato Scale," Chapter 18, Part G.

Transitional Expressions

Transitional expressions in classification paragraphs stress divisions and categories:

Transitional Expressions for Classification

can be divided	the first type
can be classified	the second kind
can be categorized	the last category

PRACTICE 1   Read the following paragraph carefully and answer the questions.

Traditional musical instruments can be divided, according to how they produce sound, into three categories: stringed, wind, and percussion. Stringed instruments produce music through the vibration of taut strings that are plucked, strummed, or bowed. The harp, the guitar, the banjo, and the violin are examples of stringed instruments. Wind instruments usually are sounded by the player's breath; this category includes the clarinet, the tuba, the trumpet, and so on. Instead of being bowed or blown, percussion instruments make sounds when they are struck. Obvious examples of percussion instruments are drums, gongs, and cymbals. Surprisingly, the piano is also considered a percussion instrument because, when the player touches a key, a small hammer inside the piano strikes a string.

1. How many categories of traditional musical instruments are there, and what are they?

   _____

2. On what basis does the writer classify musical instruments?

   _____

3. Make a plan or an outline of the paragraph on a separate sheet of paper.

PRACTICE 2   Each group of things or persons below has been divided according to a single basis of classification. However, one item in each group does not belong—it does not fit that single basis of classification.

Read each group of items carefully; then circle the letter of the one item that does *not* belong. Next write the single basis of classification that includes the rest of the group.

Example | shirts
a. cotton
b. suede
ⓒ short-sleeved
d. polyester

material they are made of

1. Shoes
   a. flat heels
   b. 2-inch heels
   c. patent leather heels
   d. 3-inch heels

2. Beds
   a. double
   b. twin
   c. water
   d. king

3. Students
   a. talkative in class
   b. very hard working
   c. goof-offs
   d. moderately hard working

4. Contact lenses
   a. soft
   b. green
   c. brown
   d. lavender

5. Apartments
   a. two-bedroom
   b. three-bedroom
   c. penthouse
   d. studio apartment

6. Dates
   a. very good-looking
   b. sometimes pay
   c. always pay
   d. expect me to pay

7. Plants
   a. full sunlight
   b. shade
   c. sandy soil
   d. moderate light

8. Drivers
   a. obey the speed limit
   b. teenage drivers
   c. speeders
   d. creepers

PRACTICE 3   Any group of persons, things, or ideas can be classified in more than one way. For instance, students in your class can be classified on the basis of height (short, average, tall) or on the basis of class participation (often participate, sometimes participate, never participate). Both of these groupings are valid classifications of the same group of people.

Think of two ways in which each of the following groups could be classified.

Example	Group		Can Be Classified According to
	Bosses	(A)	how demanding they are
		(B)	how generous they are
	1. Members of my family	(A)	_____
		(B)	_____
	2. Vacations	(A)	_____
		(B)	_____
	3. Fans of a certain sport	(A)	_____
		(B)	_____
	4. Dancers	(A)	_____
		(B)	_____
	5. Fitness magazines	(A)	_____
		(B)	_____

PRACTICE 4   Listed below are three groups of people or things. Decide on a single basis of classification for each group and the categories that would develop from your basis of classification. Finally, write a topic sentence for each of your classifications. Answers will vary.

Example	Group	Basis of Classification	Categories
	Professors at Pell College	methods of instruction _____	1. lectures
		_____	2. class discussions
			3. some of both

Topic Sentence: Professors at Pell College can be classified according to their

methods of instructions: those who lecture, those who encourage class discussion,

and those who do both.

Group	Basis of Classification	Categories
1. Car owners	_____	_____
	_____	_____
		_____
		_____

Topic sentence: _____

_____

_____

_____

Group	Basis of Classification	Categories
2. Credit card users	_____	_____
	_____	_____
		_____
		_____

Topic sentence: _____

_____

_____

_____

Group	Basis of Classification	Categories
3. Ways of reacting to crisis	_____	_____
	_____	_____
		_____
		_____

Topic sentence: _____

_____

_____

_____

PRACTICE 5   On a separate sheet of paper, make a plan or an outline for one of the classifications in Practice 4. Be sure that you have listed all the categories that naturally evolve from your basis of classification; remember, every person or thing in the larger group should fit into one of these categories. Then write a brief description of each of the categories in your classification, perhaps including an example of each.

Checklist: The Process of Writing a Classification Paragraph

Refer to this checklist of steps as you write a classification paragraph.

_____ 1. Narrow the topic in light of your audience and purpose. Think in terms of a group of people or things that can easily be classified into types or categories.

_____ 2. Decide on a single basis of classification. This basis will depend on what information you wish to give your audience.

_____ 3. Compose a topic sentence that clearly shows what you are dividing into categories or types. If you wish, your topic sentence can state the basis on which you are making the classification and the types that will be discussed in the paragraph.

_____ 4. List the categories into which the group is being classified. Be sure that your categories cover all the possibilities. Do not add any new categories that are not logically part of your original basis of classification.

_____ 5. Freewrite, cluster, or brainstorm to generate information, details, and examples for each of the categories. (You may want to prewrite before you narrow the topic.)

_____ 6. Select the best details and examples, and drop those that are not relevant to your classification.

_____ 7. Make a plan or an outline for your paragraph, numbering the categories in the order in which you will present them.

_____ 8. Write a draft of your classification paragraph, using transitional expressions wherever they may be helpful.

_____ 9. Revise as necessary, checking for support, unity, logic, and coherence.

_____ 10. Proofread for errors in grammar, punctuation, sentence structure, spelling, and mechanics.

Suggested Topics for Classification Paragraphs

1. Shoppers in a department store
2. Moviegoers
3. Types of friends
4. Students in a particular class
5. Problems facing college freshmen or someone new to a job
6. Women or men you date
7. Clothing in your closet
8. Players of a certain sport
9. College classes or instructors
10. Parents' ways of disciplining their children
11. Coworkers
12. Kinds of success
13. Performers of one type of music
14. Kinds of marriages
15. Brands of athletic shoes (toothbrushes, jeans, backpacks, notebooks, or some other product)

12

Persuasion

To persuade is to convince someone that a particular opinion or point of view is the correct one.

Any time you argue with a friend, you are each trying to persuade, to convince, the other that your opinion is the right one. Commercials on television are another form of persuasion as advertisers attempt to convince viewers that the product they sell—whether a deodorant, soft drink, or automobile—is the best one to purchase.

You will often have to persuade in writing. For instance, if you want a raise, you will have to write a persuasive letter to convince your employer that you deserve one. You will have to back up, or support, your request with proof, listing important projects you have completed, noting new responsibilities you have taken upon yourself, or showing how you have increased sales.

Once you learn how to persuade logically and rationally, you will be less likely to accept the false, misleading, and emotional arguments that you hear and read every day. Persuasion is vital in nearly all college courses and in most careers.

Topic Sentence

Here is the topic sentence of a persuasive paragraph:

> Passengers should refuse to ride in any vehicle driven by someone who has been drinking.

■ The writer begins a persuasive paragraph by stating clearly what he or she is arguing for or against. What will this persuasive paragraph argue against?

_____

_____

■ Words like *should, ought,* and *must* (and the negatives *should not, ought not,* and *must not*) are especially effective in the topic sentence of a persuasive paragraph.

Paragraph and Plan

Here is the entire paragraph:

> Passengers should refuse to ride in any vehicle driven by someone who has been drinking. First and most important, such a refusal could save lives. The National Council on Alcoholism reports that drunk driving causes 25,000 deaths and 50 percent of all traffic accidents each year. Not only the drivers but the passengers who agree to travel with them are responsible. Second, riders might tell themselves that some people drive well even after a few drinks, but this is just not true. Dr. Burton Belloc of the local Alcoholism Treatment Center explains that even one drink can lengthen the reflex time and weaken the judgment needed for safe driving. Other riders might feel foolish to ruin a social occasion or inconvenience themselves or others by speaking up, but risking their lives is even more foolish. Finally, by refusing to ride with a drinker, one passenger could influence other passengers or the driver. Marie Furillo, a student at Central High School, is an example. When three friends who had obviously been drinking offered her a ride home from school, she refused, despite the driver's teasing. Hearing Marie's refusal, two of her friends got out of the car. Until the laws are changed and a vast re-education takes place, the bloodshed on American highways will probably continue. But there is one thing people can do: They can refuse to risk their lives for the sake of a party.

■ The first reason in the argument **predicts the consequence.** If passengers refuse to ride with drinkers, what will the consequence be?

_____

■ The writer also supports this reason with **facts.** What are the facts?

_____

_____

■ The second reason in the argument is really an **answer to the opposition.** That is, the writer anticipates the critics. What point is the writer answering?

_____

_____

- The writer supports this reason by **referring to an authority.** That is, the writer gives the opinion of someone who can provide unbiased and valuable information about the subject. Who is the authority and what does this person say?

  _____

  _____

- The third reason in the argument is that risking your life is foolish. This reason is really another **answer to the opposition.** What point is the writer answering?

  _____

  _____

- The final reason in the argument is that one passenger could influence others. What **example** does the writer supply to back up this reason?

  _____

  _____

- Persuasive paragraphs can begin either with the most important reason and then continue with less important ones, or they can begin with the least important reasons, saving the most important for last.* This paragraph begins with what the author considers *most* important. How can you tell?

  _____

  _____

Before composing this persuasive paragraph, the writer probably brainstormed or freewrote to gather ideas and then made an outline or a plan like this:

Topic sentence: Passengers should refuse to ride in any vehicle driven by someone who has been drinking.

Reason 1:   Refusal could save lives (**predicting a consequence**)
—statistics on deaths and accidents (**facts**)
—passengers are equally responsible

Reason 2:   Riders might say some drinkers drive well; not true (**answering the opposition**)
—Dr. Belloc's explanation (**referring to authority**)

Reason 3:   Others might feel foolish speaking up, but risking lives is more foolish (**answering the opposition**)

* For work on order of importance, see Chapter 4, "Achieving Coherence," Part A.

Reason 4:	One rider might influence other passengers —Marie Furillo (**example**)
Conclusion:	Bloodshed will probably continue, but people can refuse to risk their lives.

■ Note how each reason clearly supports the topic sentence.

Transitional Expressions

The following transitional expressions are helpful in persuasive paragraphs:

Transitional Expressions for Persuasion

Give Reasons	*Answer the Opposition*	*Draw Conclusions*
first (second, third)	of course	therefore
another, next	some may say	thus
last, finally	nevertheless	hence
because, since, for	on the other hand	consequently
	although	

Methods of Persuasion

The drinking-and-driving example showed the basic kinds of support used in persuasive paragraphs: **facts, referring to an authority, examples, predicting the consequences,** and **answering the opposition.** Although you will rarely use all of them in one paragraph, you should be familiar with them all. Here are some more details:

1. **Facts: Facts** are simply statements of *what is.* They should appeal to the reader's mind, not just to the emotions. The source of your facts should be clear to the reader. If you wish to prove that children's eyesight should be checked every year by a doctor, you might look for supporting facts in appropriate books and magazines, or you might ask your eye doctor for information. Your paper might say, "Many people suffer serious visual impairment later in life because they received insufficient or inadequate eye care when they were children, according to an article in *Better Vision.*"

Avoid the vague "everyone knows that" or "it is common knowledge that" or "they all say." Such statements will make your reader justifiably suspicious of your "facts."

2. Referring to an authority: An **authority** is an expert, someone who can be relied on to give unbiased facts and information. If you wish to convince your readers that smoking is a dangerous habit, you might use one of the Surgeon General's warnings that appear on every pack of cigarettes: "Smoking causes lung cancer, heart disease, emphysema, and may complicate pregnancy." The Surgeon General is an excellent and knowledgeable authority whose opinion on medical matters is considered valid and unbiased.

Avoid appealing to "authorities" who are interesting or glamorous but who are not experts. A basketball player certainly knows about sports, but probably knows little about cameras or pantyhose.

3. Examples: An **example** should clearly relate to the argument and should be typical enough to support it.* If you wish to convince your reader that high schools should provide more funds than they do for women's sports, you might say, "Jefferson High School, for instance, has received inquiries from sixty female students who would be willing to join a women's basketball or baseball team if the school could provide the uniforms, the space, and a coach."

Avoid examples that are not typical enough to support your general statement. That your friend was once bitten by a dog does not adequately prove that all dogs are dangerous pets.

4. Predicting the consequence: **Predicting the consequence** helps the reader visualize what will occur if *something does or does not happen.* To convince your readers that a college education should be free to all qualified students, you might say, "If bright but economically deprived students cannot attend college because they cannot afford it, our society will be robbed of their talents."

Avoid exaggerating the consequence. For instance, telling the reader, "If you don't eat fresh fruit every day, you will never be truly healthy," exaggerates the consequences of not eating fresh fruit and makes the reader understandably suspicious.

5. Answering the opposition: **Answering possible critics** shows that you are aware of the opposition's argument and are able to respond to it. If you wish to convince your readers that your candidate is the best on the ballot, you might say, "Some have criticized him for running a low-key campaign, but he feels that the issues and his stand on them should speak for themselves."

Avoid calling the opposition "fools" or "crooks." Attack their ideas, not them.

Considering the Audience

In addition to providing adequate proof for your argument, pay special attention to the **audience** as you write a persuasive paragraph. In general, we assume that our audience is much like us—reasonable and sensible people who wish to learn the truth. Often, however, a persuasive paper should

* For more work on examples, see Chapter 5, "Illustration."

be directed toward a particular audience. It is helpful to consider just *what kind of evidence* this audience would respond to. For instance, if you were attempting to persuade parents to volunteer their time to establish a local Scout troop, you might explain to them the various ways in which their children would benefit from the troop. In other words, show these parents how the troop is important to *them.* You might also say that you realize how much time they already spend on family matters and how little spare time they have. By doing so, you let them know that you understand their resistance to the argument and that you are sympathetic to their doubts. When you take your audience into consideration, you will make your persuasive paragraph more convincing.*†

PRACTICE 1   Read the following persuasive paragraph carefully and answer the questions.

American women should stop buying so-called women's magazines because these publications lower their self-esteem. First of all, publications like *Glamour* and *Cosmo* appeal to women's insecurities and make millions doing it. Topics like "Ten Days to Sexier Cleavage" and "How to Attract Mr. Right" lure women to buy seven million copies a month, reports Donna Kato in *The Miami Herald,* March 8, 1993. The message: women need to be improved. Second, although many people—especially magazine publishers—claim these periodicals build self-esteem, they really do the opposite. One expert in readers' reactions, Deborah Then, says that almost all women, regardless of age or education, feel worse about themselves after reading one of these magazines. Alice, one of the women I spoke with, is a good example: "I flip through pictures of world-class beauties and six-foot-tall skinny women, comparing myself to them. In more ways than one, I come up short." Finally, if women spent the money and time these magazines take on more self-loving activities—studying new subjects, developing mental or physical fitness, setting goals and daring to achieve them—they would really build self-worth. Sisters, seek wisdom, create what you envision, and above all, know that you can.

—Rochelle Revard (Student)

1. What is this paragraph arguing for or against? _____

   _____

2. What audience is the writer addressing? _____

3. Which reason is supported by facts? _____

* For more work on audience, see Chapter 1, "Exploring the Writing Process," Part B.
† For a complete essay developed by persuasion, see "Stopping Youth Violence: An Inside Job," Chapter 18, Part H.

What are the facts, and where did the writer get them? _____

_____

_____

4. Which reason answers the opposition? _____

5. Which reason is supported by an example? _____

   What is the example? _____

   _____

6. Which reason appeals to an authority? _____

   Who is the authority? _____

PRACTICE 2   Read the following carefully and answer the questions.

Automatic fire sprinkler systems should be installed in all public and commercial buildings. First and foremost, sprinklers save lives. As Captain Hornak of the Department of Fire Prevention of Springfield City has noted, "A sprinkler system remains our first defense against a small blaze turning into a major conflagration. Two people needlessly lost their lives at the Springfield City Library fire last year because that sixty-year-old building did not have a sprinkler system." In addition, sprinklers can save property. Fire causes billions of dollars of damage every year to shopping centers, hotels, and office buildings. Sprinklers slow down the rapid spread of small fires, thereby limiting property damage. In states that have enacted stricter sprinkler system requirements—Florida, Hawaii, and Alaska, for instance— the amount of property damage caused by fire has declined. As a related benefit, sprinkler systems allow insurance companies to lower fire insurance rates. These savings can be passed on to consumers in the form of lower prices at department stores, hotels, and other commercial establishments.

1. What is this paragraph arguing for or against? _____

   _____

   _____

2. Which reason appeals to an authority for support? _____

   _____

   Who is the authority? _____

   _____

3. Which reason uses examples for support? _____

_____

What are the examples? _____

_____

4. Which reason predicts the consequences? _____

_____

5. How has the writer ordered the reasons in this paragraph, from most to least important or from least to most important? How do you know?

_____

_____

_____

PRACTICE 3   So far you have learned five basic methods of persuasion: **facts, referring to an authority, examples, predicting the consequence,** and **answering the opposition.** Ten topic sentences for persuasive paragraphs follow. Write one reason in support of each topic sentence, using the method of persuasion indicated.

Facts

1. A stop sign should be placed at the busy intersection of Hoover and Palm streets.

Reason: _____

_____

_____

_____

2. People should not get married until they are at least twenty-five years old.

Reason: _____

_____

_____

_____

Referring to an Authority

(If you cannot think of an authority offhand, name the kind of person who would be an authority on the subject.)

3. These new Sluggo bats will definitely raise your batting average.

   Reason: _____

   _____

   _____

   _____

4. Most people should get at least a half-hour of vigorous exercise every day.

   Reason: _____

   _____

   _____

   _____

Examples

5. Commercials shown during children's television programs can have a negative impact on young viewers.

   Reason: _____

   _____

   _____

   _____

6. High schools must provide young people with adequate sex education because ignorance can be harmful.

   Reason: _____

   _____

   _____

   _____

Predicting the Consequence

7. The military draft should (should not) be brought back.

   Reason: _____

   _____

   _____

   _____

8. The federal government should (should not) prohibit the sale of hand-guns through the mail.

   Reason: _____

   _____

   _____

   _____

Answering the Opposition

(State the opposition's point of view and then refute it.)

9. This college should (should not) drop its required-attendance policy.

   Reason: _____

   _____

   _____

   _____

10. Teenagers should (should not) be required to get their parents' permission before being allowed to have an abortion.

    Reason: _____

    _____

    _____

    _____

PRACTICE 4   Each of the following sentences tells what you are trying to persuade some-one to do. Beneath each sentence are four reasons that attempt to convince the reader that he or she should take this particular course of action. Circle the letter of the reason that seems *irrelevant*, *illogical*, or *untrue*.

1. If you wanted to persuade someone to do holiday shopping earlier, you might say that
   a. shopping earlier saves time.
   b. more gifts will be in stock.
   c. stores will not be overly crowded.
   d. Patti LaBelle shops early.

2. If you wanted to persuade someone to buy a particular brand of cereal, you might say that
   a. it is inexpensive.
   b. it contains vitamins and minerals.
   c. it comes in an attractive box.
   d. it makes a hearty breakfast.

3. If you wanted to persuade someone to move to your town, you might say that
   a. two new companies have made jobs available.
   b. by moving to this town, he or she will become the happiest person in the world.
   c. there is a wide selection of housing.
   d. the area is lovely and still unpolluted.

4. If you wanted to persuade someone to vote for a particular candidate, you might say that
   a. she has always kept her promises to the voters.
   b. she has lived in the district for thirty years.
   c. she has substantial knowledge of the issues.
   d. she dresses very fashionably.

5. If you wanted to persuade someone to learn to read and speak a foreign language, you might say that
   a. knowledge of a foreign language can be helpful in the business world.
   b. he or she may want to travel in the country where the language is spoken.
   c. Jon Secada sings in two languages.
   d. being able to read great literature in the original is a rewarding experience.

6. If you wanted to persuade someone to quit smoking, you might say that
   a. smoking is a major cause of lung cancer.
   b. smoking stains teeth and softens gums.
   c. ashtrays are often hard to find.
   d. this bad habit has become increasingly expensive.

PRACTICE 5 As you write persuasive paragraphs, make sure that your reasons can withstand close examination. Here are some examples of *invalid* arguments. Read them carefully. Decide which method of persuasion is being used and explain why you think the argument is invalid. Refer to the list on pages 150–151.

1. Men make terrible drivers. That one just cut right in front of me without looking.

   Method of persuasion: _____

   Invalid because _____

   _____

2. Many people have become vegetarians during the past ten or fifteen years, but such people have lettuce for brains.

   Method of persuasion: _____

   Invalid because _____

   _____

3. Candy does not really harm children's teeth. Tests made by scientists at the Gooey Candy Company have proved that candy does not cause tooth decay.

   Method of persuasion: _____

   Invalid because _____

   _____

4. Stealing pens and pads from the office is perfectly all right. Everyone does it.

   Method of persuasion: _____

   Invalid because _____

   _____

5. We don't want _____ in our neighborhood. We had a

   _____ family once, and they made a lot of noise.

   Method of persuasion: _____

   Invalid because _____

   _____

6. If our city doesn't build more playgrounds, a crime wave will destroy our homes and businesses.

   Method of persuasion: _____

   Invalid because _____

   _____

7. Studying has nothing to do with grades. My brother never studies and still gets *A*'s all the time.

   Method of persuasion: _____

   Invalid because _____

   _____

8. Women bosses work their employees too hard. I had one once, and she never let me rest for a moment.

   Method of persuasion: _____

   Invalid because _____

   _____

9. The Big Deal Supermarket has the lowest prices in town. This must be true because the manager said on the radio last week, "We have the lowest prices in town."

Method of persuasion: _____

Invalid because _____

_____

10. If little girls are allowed to play with cars and trucks, they will grow up wanting to be men.

Method of persuasion: _____

Invalid because _____

_____

Writing Assignment

To help you take a stand for a persuasive paragraph of your own, try the following exercises on notebook paper:

1. List five things you would like to see changed at your college.

2. List five things you would like to see changed in your home *or* at your job.

3. List five things that annoy you or make you angry. What can be done about them?

4. Imagine yourself giving a speech on national television. What message would you like to convey?

From your lists, pick one topic you would like to write a persuasive paragraph about and write the topic sentence here:

_____

_____

Now make a plan or an outline for a paragraph on a separate sheet of paper. Use at least two of the five methods of persuasion. Arrange your reasons in some logical order.

Checklist: The Process of Writing a Persuasive Paragraph

Refer to this checklist of steps as you write a persuasive paragraph of your own.

_____ 1. Narrow the topic in light of your audience and purpose. Of what do you wish to convince your reader?

_____ 2. Compose a topic sentence that clearly states your position for or against. Use *should, ought, must,* or their negatives.

_____ 3. Freewrite or brainstorm to generate all the reasons you can think of. (You may want to freewrite or brainstorm before you narrow the topic.)

_____ 4. Select the best three or four reasons and drop those that do not relate to your topic sentence.

_____ 5. If you use *facts,* be sure that they are accurate and that the source of your facts is clear. If you use an *example,* be sure that it is a valid one and adequately supports your argument. If you *refer to an authority,* be sure that he or she is really an authority and *not biased.* If one of your reasons *predicts the consequence,* be sure that the consequence flows logically from your statement. If one of your reasons *answers the opposition,* be sure to state the opposition's point of view fairly and refute it adequately.

_____ 6. Make a plan or an outline for the paragraph, numbering the reasons in the order in which you will present them.

_____ 7. Write a draft of your persuasive paragraph, using transitional expressions wherever they may be helpful.

_____ 8. Revise as necessary, checking for support, unity, logic, and coherence.

_____ 9. Proofread for errors in grammar, punctuation, sentence structure, spelling, and mechanics.

Suggested Topics for Persuasive Paragraphs

A list of possible topic sentences for persuasive paragraphs follows. Pick one statement and decide whether you agree or disagree with it. Modify the topic sentence accordingly. Then write a persuasive paragraph that supports your view, explaining and illustrating from your own experience, your observations of others, or your reading.

1. Some rap music encourages violence against women.

2. Occasional arguments are good for friendship.

3. Parents should pay for the damage caused by their delinquent children.

4. TV talk shows trivialize important social issues.

5. Expensive weddings are an obscene waste of money.

6. The elderly in this country face prejudice and disrespect.

7. College basketball (or soccer, football, and so on) emphasizes winning at any cost.

8. People should laugh more because laughter heals.

9. The families of AIDS patients are the hidden victims of AIDS.

10. Condom machines should be permitted on campus.

11. English should be the official language of the United States.

12. Single people should not be allowed to adopt children.

13. To improve academic achievement, this town should create same-sex high schools (all boys, all girls).

14. A required course at this college should be _____ (computer literacy, wilderness survival, public speaking, or another).

15. People convicted of drunk driving should lose their licenses for one year.

16. _____ Company should provide _____ for its employees.

17. To respect all beliefs, including those of nonbelievers, prayer should not be allowed in public schools.

18. _____ is the most _____ (educational, mindless, hilarious, racist) show on television.

19. College students should be required to perform community service activities.

20. _____ (writer, singer, or actor) has a message that more people need to hear.

Unit 4

Improving Your Writing

13

Revising for Consistency and Parallelism

PART A **Consistent Tense**
PART B **Consistent Number and Person**
PART C **Parallelism**
PART D **Consistent Quotations**

All good writing is **consistent.** That is, each sentence and paragraph in the final draft should move along smoothly without confusing shifts in **tense, number,** or **person.** In addition, good writing uses **parallel structure** to balance two or more similar words, phrases, or clauses.

Although you should be aware of consistency and parallelism as you write the first draft of your paragraph or essay, you might find it easier to **revise** for them—that is, to write your first draft and then, as you read it again later, check and rewrite for consistency and parallelism.

PART A

Consistent Tense

Consistency of tense means using the same verb tense whenever possible throughout a sentence or an entire paragraph. Do not shift from one verb tense to another—for example, from present to past or from past to present—unless you really mean to indicate different times.

1. Inconsistent tense:	We *stroll* down Bourbon Street as the jazz bands *began* to play.
2. Consistent tense:	We *strolled* down Bourbon Street as the jazz bands *began* to play.
3. Consistent tense:	We *stroll* down Bourbon Street as the jazz bands *begin* to play.

- Sentence 1 begins in the present tense with the verb *stroll* but then slips into the past tense with the verb *began*. The tenses are inconsistent since both actions (strolling and beginning) occur at the same time.

- Sentence 2 is consistent. Both verbs, *strolled* and *began,* are now in the past tense.

- Sentence 3 is also consistent, using the present tense forms of both verbs, *stroll* and *begin.* The present tense here gives a feeling of immediacy, as if the action is happening now.*

Of course, you should use different verb tenses in a sentence or paragraph if they convey the meaning that you wish to convey:

> 4. Last fall I *took* English 02; now I *am taking* English 13.

- The verbs in this sentence accurately show the time relationship between the two classroom experiences.†

PRACTICE 1   Read the following sentences carefully for meaning. Then correct any inconsistencies of tense by changing the verbs that do not accurately show the time of events.

Example

I took a deep breath and opened the door; there stands a well-dressed man with a large box.

Consistent: I took a deep breath and opened the door; there ~~stands~~ a well- dressed man with a large box. [stood]

or

Consistent: I ~~took~~ a deep breath and ~~opened~~ the door; there stands a well- dressed man with a large box. [take] [open]

1. Two seconds before the buzzer sounded, Mark Price sank a basket from midcourt, and the crowd goes wild.

2. Nestlé introduced instant coffee in 1938; it takes eight years to develop this product.

3. We expand our sales budget, doubled our research, and soon saw positive results.

---

* For more work in spotting verbs, see Chapter 21, "The Simple Sentence," Part C.
† For more work on particular verb tenses and forms, see Chapters 24, 25, and 26.

4. For twenty years, Dr. Dulfano observed animal behavior and seeks clues to explain the increasing violence among human beings.

5. I knew how the system works.

6. I was driving south on Interstate 90 when a truck approaches with its high beams on.

7. Two brown horses graze quietly in the field as the sun rose and the mist disappeared.

8. Lollie had a big grin on her face as she walks over and kicked the Coke machine.

9. Maynard stormed down the hallway, goes right into the boss's office and shouts, "I want curtains in my office!"

10. The nurses quietly paced the halls, making sure their patients rest comfortably.

PRACTICE 2   Inconsistencies of tense are most likely to occur within paragraphs and longer pieces of writing. Therefore, it is important to revise your writing for tense consistency. Read this paragraph for meaning. Then revise, correcting inconsistencies of tense by changing incorrect verbs.

It was 1850. A poor German-born peddler named Levi Strauss came to San Francisco, trying to sell canvas cloth to tentmakers. By chance he met a miner who complained that sturdy work pants are hard to find. Strauss had an idea, measures the man, and makes him a pair of canvas pants. The miner loved his new breeches, and Levi Strauss goes into business. Although he ordered more canvas, what he gets is a brown French cloth called serge de Nimes, which Americans soon called "denim." Strauss liked the cloth but had the next batch dyed blue. He became successful selling work pants to such rugged men as cowboys and lumberjacks. In the 1870s, hearing about a tailor in Nevada adding copper rivets to a pair of the pants to make them stronger, Strauss patents the idea. When he died in 1902, Levi Strauss was famous in California, but the company keeps growing. In the

1930s, when Levi's became popular in the East, both men and women wear them. By the 1990s, people all over the world were buying 85 million pairs of jeans a year.

PRACTICE 3   The following paragraph is written in the past tense. Rewrite it in consistent present tense; make sure all verbs agree with their subjects.*

The tension built as I got into my car. I sat down, breathed deeply, and went through the motions of changing gears, practicing for the race. The seconds crawled by. I heard my heart pound and felt my stomach churning. I stared ahead at the long stretch of road equivalent to a quarter mile. My opponent entered his car, looked at me with a smirk on his face, and gave me the thumbs-down signal. I paid no attention to his teasing but wiped my hands on my shirt. I flexed my fingers and gripped the wheel. The race was about to begin.

_____

_____

_____

_____

_____

_____

_____

_____

PRACTICE 4   The following paragraph is written in the present tense. Rewrite it in consistent past tense.†

At a party in December 1988, an eighteen-year-old aspiring singer and her friend meet Tommy Mottola, the president of Columbia Records. The friend hands him the young singer's demo tape. Speeding home in his limousine, Mottola listens to the soaring seven-octave voice, orders his driver to turn around, and races back to the party in search of the teenager. One week later, she signs her first record deal, and her six million selling debut album, *Mariah Carey*, hits the airwaves in 1990. Over the next four years, Carey releases three more albums—*Emotions, Unplugged*, and *Music Box*—and becomes Tommy Mottola's wife. Some critics compare her

* For more work on agreement, see Chapter 24, "Present Tense (Agreement)."
† For more work on the past tense, see Chapter 25, "Past Tense."

sound to Whitney Houston's as audiences eagerly buy her albums, pushing them all to multiplatinum.

_____

_____

_____

_____

_____

_____

_____

_____

_____

_____

PRACTICE 5   Longer pieces of writing often use both the past tense and the present tense. However, switching correctly from one tense to the other requires care. Read the following essay carefully and note when a switch from one tense to another is logically necessary. Then revise verbs as needed.

A Quick History of Chocolate

Most of us now take solid chocolate—especially candy bars—so much for granted that we find it hard to imagine a time when chocolate didn't exist. However, this delicious food becomes an eating favorite only about one hundred and fifty years ago.

The ancient peoples of Central America began cultivating cacao beans almost three thousand years ago. A cold drink made from the beans is served to Hernando Cortés, the Spanish conqueror, when he arrives at the Aztec court of Montezuma in 1519. The Spaniards took the beverage home to their king. He likes it so much that he kept the formula a secret. For the next one hundred years, hot chocolate was the private drink of the Spanish nobility. Slowly, it makes its way into the fashionable courts of France, England,

and Austria. In 1657, a Frenchman living in London opened a shop where blocks for making the beverage are sold at a high price. Soon chocolate houses appeared in cities throughout Europe. Wealthy clients met in them, sipped chocolate, conducted business, and gossip.

During the 1800s, chocolate became a chewable food. The breakthrough comes in 1828, when cocoa butter was extracted from the bean. Twenty years later, an English firm mixed the butter with chocolate liquor, which results in the first solid chocolate. Milton Hershey's first candy bar come on the scene in 1894, and Tootsie Rolls hit the market two years later. The popularity of chocolate bars soar during World War I when they are given to soldiers for fast energy. M & Ms gave the industry another boost during World War II; soldiers needed candy that wouldn't melt in their hands.

On the average, Americans today eat ten pounds of hard chocolate a year. Their number one choice is Snickers, which sold more than a billion bars every year. However, Americans consume far less chocolate than many Western Europeans. The average Dutch person gobbled up more than fifteen pounds a year, while a Swiss packed away almost twenty pounds. Chocolate is obviously an international favorite.

PART B

Consistent Number and Person

Just as important as verb tense consistency is consistency of **number** and **person**.

Consistency of Number

Consistency of number means avoiding confusing shifts from singular to plural or from plural to singular within a sentence or paragraph. Choose *either* singular *or* plural; then be *consistent*.

1. Inconsistent number:	*The wise jogger* chooses *their* running shoes with care.
2. Consistent number:	*The wise jogger* chooses *his* (or *her*) running shoes with care.
3. Consistent number:	*Wise joggers* choose *their* running shoes with care.

- Since the subject of sentence 1, *the wise jogger,* is singular, use of the plural pronoun *their* is *inconsistent.*

- Sentence 2 is *consistent.* The singular pronoun *his* (or *her*) now clearly refers to the singular *jogger.*

- In sentence 3, the plural number is used *consistently. Their* clearly refers to the plural *joggers.*

If you begin a paragraph by referring to a small-business owner as *she,* continue to refer to *her* in the **third person singular** throughout the paragraph:

The small-business owner . . . .; she . . . . The law may not protect *her* . . . . Therefore, s*he* . . . .

Do not confuse the reader by shifting unnecessarily to *they* or *you.*

PRACTICE 6   Correct any inconsistencies of **number** in the following sentences.* Also make necessary changes in verb agreement.

Example | A singer must protect ~~their~~ voice.
                                    his or her

1. An individual's self-esteem can affect their performance.

2. Jorge started drinking diet sodas only last November, but already he hates the taste of it.

3. The headlines encouraged us, but we feared that it wasn't accurate.

4. The defendant who wishes to do so may ask a higher court to overturn their conviction.

* For more practice in agreement of pronouns and antecedents, see Chapter 28, "Pronouns," Part B.

5. Dreams fascinate me; it is like another world.

6. If a person doesn't know how to write well, they will face limited job opportunities.

7. Oxford University boasts of the great number of ancient manuscripts they own.

8. Always buy corn and tomatoes when it is in season.

9. The average American takes their freedom for granted.

10. Women have more opportunities than ever before. She is freer to go to school, get a job, and choose the kind of life she wants.

Consistency of Person

Consistency of person—closely related to consistency of number—means using the same *person*, or indefinite pronoun form, throughout a sentence or paragraph whenever possible.

First person is the most personal and informal in written work: (singular) *I*, (plural) *we*

Second person speaks directly to the reader: (singular and plural) *you*

Third person is the most formal and most frequently used in college writing: (singular) *he, she, it, one, a person, an individual, a student,* and so on; (plural) *they, people, individuals, students,* and so on

Avoid confusing shifts from one person to another. Choose one, and then be *consistent*. When using a noun in a general way—*a person, the individual, the parent*—be careful not to slip into the second person, *you*, but continue to use the third person, *he* or *she*.

4. Inconsistent person:	A *player* collects $200 when *you* pass "Go."	
5. Consistent person:	A *player* collects $200 when *he* or *she* passes "Go."	
6. Consistent person:	*You* collect $200 when *you* pass "Go."	

- In sentence 4, the person shifts unnecessarily from the third person, *a player*, to the second person, *you*. The result is confusing.

- Sentence 5 maintains consistent third person. *He or she* now clearly refers to the third person subject, *a player*.

- Sentence 6 is also consistent, using the second person, *you*, throughout.

Of course, inconsistencies of person and number often occur together, as shown in the next box.

7. Inconsistent person and number:	Whether *one* enjoys or resents commercials, *we* are bombarded with them every hour of the day.
8. Consistent person and number:	Whether *we* enjoy or resent commercials, *we* are bombarded with them every hour of the day.
9. Consistent person and number:	Whether *one* enjoys or resents commercials, *he* (or *she*, or *one*) is bombarded with them every hour of the day.

- Sentence 7 shifts from the third person singular, *one*, to the first person plural, *we*.

- Sentence 8 uses the first person plural consistently.

- Sentence 9 uses the third person singular consistently.

PRACTICE 7   Correct the shifts in **person** in these sentences. If necessary, change the verbs to make them agree with any new subjects.

Example | One should eliminate saturated fats from ~~your~~ diet.
one's

1. Sooner or later, most addicts realize that you can't just quit when you want to.

2. One problem facing students on this campus is that a person doesn't know when the library will be open and when it will be closed.

3. One should rely on reason, not emotion, when they are forming opinions about such charged issues as abortion.

4. I have reached a time in my life when what others expect is less important than what one really wants to do.

5. Members of the orchestra should meet after the concert and bring your instruments and music.

6. The wise parent knows that she is asking for trouble if you let a small child watch violent television shows.

7. The student who participates in this program will spend six weeks in Spain and Morocco. You will study the art and architecture firsthand, working closely with an instructor.

8. You shouldn't judge a person by the way they dress.

9. If you have been working that hard, one needs a vacation.

10. People who visit the Caribbean for the first time are struck by the lushness of the landscape. The sheer size of the flowers and fruit amazes you.

PRACTICE 8   The following paragraph consistently uses the third person singular—*the salesperson, he or she,* and so on. For practice in revising for consistency, rewrite the paragraph in **consistent third person plural**. Begin by changing *the salesperson* to *salespeople* or *salesclerks.* Then change verbs, nouns, or pronouns as necessary.

The salesperson is crucial to a customer's satisfaction or dissatisfaction with a particular store. In reality, the salesperson acts as the store's representative or ambassador; often he or she is the only contact a customer has with the store. Thousands of dollars may be spent in advertising to woo customers and build a favorable image, only to have this lost by the uncaring salesclerk.

—Robert F. Hartley, *Retailing: Challenge and Opportunity*

_____

_____

_____

_____

_____

_____

_____

PRACTICE 9   Revise the following essay for inconsistencies of person and number. Correct any confusing shifts (changing words if necessary) to make the writing clear and *consistent* throughout.

Immortality in Wax

"Madame Tussaud's. Come and find out who's in. And who's out." That's what English radios advertise to lure visitors to a most unusual show—a display of the rich and famous in the form of lifelike wax statues. Nearly 2.5 million line up each year to rub shoulders with the images of today's and yesterday's celebrities. You make Madame Tussaud's the most popular paid tourist attraction in England.

Visitors are treated to some of Madame Tussaud's original handiwork, as well as to other figures that have been added over the past two hundred years. All told, tourists can see and be photographed with more than three hundred eerily lifelike statues. In the Grand Hall, one can view British royalty standing with other leaders from history. The Chamber of Horrors introduces you to the most infamous criminals of all time. They can walk through a street of Victorian London where scary special effects make you feel as though you are being stalked by Jack the Ripper. The Conservatory houses entertainers, from Marilyn Monroe and Joan Collins to the Beatles and Michael Jackson.

Each month, a committee decides who should be added or taken out of the collection. A celebrity is chosen for your fame, recognizability, and publicity potential. You are invited to sit for moldings, each costing about sixteen thousand dollars. The celebrity usually poses for pictures with their finished statue for the press. Then the figure is put on display. Archbishop Tutu is there, as are Martin Luther King, Jr., Pablo Picasso, Madonna, and Roger Rabbit. Even Princess Diana regularly has her likeness updated for viewing at Madame Tussaud's.

PART C

Parallelism

Parallelism, or **parallel structure,** is an effective way to add smoothness and power to your writing. **Parallelism** is a balance of two or more similar words, phrases, or clauses.

Compare the two versions of each of these sentences:

> 1. She likes dancing, swimming, and to jog.
> 2. She likes *dancing, swimming,* and *jogging.*
> 3. The cable runs across the roof; the north wall is where it runs down.
> 4. The cable runs *across the roof* and *down the north wall.*
> 5. He admires people with strong convictions and who think for themselves.
> 6. He admires people *who have strong convictions* and *who think for themselves.*

- Sentences 2, 4, and 6 use **parallelism** to express parallel ideas.

- In sentence 2, *dancing, swimming,* and *jogging* are parallel; all three are the *-ing* forms of verbs, used here as nouns.

- In sentence 4, *across the roof* and *down the north wall* are parallel prepositional phrases, each consisting of a preposition and its object.

- In sentence 6, *who have strong convictions* and *who think for themselves* are parallel clauses beginning with the word *who.*

Sometimes two entire sentences can be parallel:

> In a democracy we are all equal before the law. In a dictatorship we are all equal before the police.
>
> —Millor Fernandes

- In what ways are these two sentences parallel? _____

_____

Certain special constructions require parallel structure:

> 7. The fruit is *both* tasty *and* fresh.
>
> 8. He *either* loves you *or* hates you.
>
> 9. Yvette *not only* plays golf *but also* swims like a pro.
>
> 10. I would *rather* sing in the chorus *than* perform a solo.

Each of these constructions has two parts:

both . . . and

(n)either . . . (n)or

not only . . . but also

rather . . . than

The words, phrases, or clauses following each part must be parallel:

tasty . . . fresh

loves you . . . hates you

plays golf . . . swims like a pro

sing in the chorus . . . perform a solo

PRACTICE 10   Rewrite each of the following sentences using parallel structure to accent parallel ideas.

Example | The summer in Louisiana is very hot and has high humidity.

The summer in Louisiana is very hot and humid.

1. Teresa is a gifted woman—a chemist, does the carpentry, and she can cook.

    _____

    _____

2. The shape of the rock, how big it was, and its color reminded me of a small elephant.

    _____

    _____

3. Chia, my dog, is overweight and moves clumsily.

    _____

    _____

4. Your job consists of arranging the books, cataloguing new arrivals, and the pamphlets have to be alphabetized.

   _____

   _____

5. A thin film of frost coated the trees; the hedges and shrubs had it also.

   _____

   _____

6. He is an affectionate husband, a thoughtful son, and kind to his kids.

   _____

   _____

7. Marvin was happy to win the chess tournament and he also felt surprised.

   _____

   _____

8. He is a poet of great talent and who is insightful.

   _____

   _____

9. Dr. Tien is the kindest physician I know; she has the most concern of any physician I know.

   _____

   _____

10. Joe would rather work on a farm than spending time in an office.

    _____

    _____

11. Every afternoon in the mountains, it either rains or there is hail.

    _____

    _____

12. _Sesame Street_ teaches children nursery rhymes, songs, how to be courteous, and being kind.

    _____

    _____

13. Alexis would rather give orders than taking them.

_____

_____

14. His writing reveals not only intelligence but also it is humorous.

_____

_____

15. Moving to the United States was frightening, confusing, and it was also thrilling.

_____

_____

PRACTICE 11   Write one sentence that is parallel to each sentence that follows, creating pairs of parallel sentences.

Example   On Friday night, she dressed in silk and sipped champagne.

On Monday morning, she put on her jeans and crammed for a history test.

_____

1. When he was twenty, he worked seven days a week in a fruit store.

_____

_____

2. The child in me wants to run away from problems.

_____

_____

3. The home team charged enthusiastically onto the field.

_____

_____

4. "Work hard and keep your mouth shut" is my mother's formula for success.

_____

_____

5. The men thought the movie was amusing.

_____

_____

PRACTICE 12   Write five sentences of your own using **parallel structure.**

1. _____

2. _____

3. _____

4. _____

5. _____

PRACTICE 13   The following paragraph contains both correct and faulty parallel structures. Revise the faulty parallelism.

During World War II, United States Marines who fought in the Pacific possessed a powerful weapon that was also unbeatable: Navaho Code Talkers. Creating a secret code, Code Talkers sent and were translating vital military information. Four hundred twenty Navahos memorized the code, and it was used by them. It consisted of both common Navaho words and there were also about four hundred invented words. For example, Code Talkers used the Navaho words for _owl, chicken hawk,_ and _swallow_ to describe different kinds of aircraft. Because Navaho is a complex language that is also uncommon, the Japanese military could not break the code. Although Code Talkers helped the Allied Forces win the war, their efforts were not publicly recognized until the code was declassified in 1968. On August 14, 1982, the first Navaho Code Talkers Day honored these heroes, who not only had risked their lives but also been developing one of the few unbroken codes in history.

PRACTICE 14   The following essay contains both correct and faulty parallel structures. Revise the faulty parallelism.

Nellie Bly

As a writer for the *New York World* in the 1880s, Nellie Bly was one of the leading journalists of her time. With determination and courageously, she pioneered what we now call the "media event." Nellie's most renowned exploit was her famous trip that was daring around the world.

Nellie bet her publisher that she could beat the fictional record set by Phineas Fogg in Jules Verne's novel *Around the World in Eighty Days.* Moreover, her telegraphed reports of the trip would boost newspaper sales. Nellie left Jersey City on November 14, 1889, and to travel first to England, France, and the land of Italy. From there, she journeyed over the Mediterranean Sea and the Indian Ocean to Ceylon. After stops in Singapore, Hong Kong, and also in Tokyo, she set sail for San Francisco. During this leg of the journey, she almost lost her bet. First, low winds delayed the sailing; then powerful storms were striking at sea. Adopting the motto "We'll Win or Die for Nellie Bly," the crew managed to get the ship to America. An easy cross-country train trip that was fast returned Nellie Bly to New York on January 25, 1890. Her trip had lasted 72 days, 6 hours, and there were 11 minutes.

Nellie arrived home a great hero and to be a national figure. Cheering crowds greeted her, songs were dedicated to her, toys were named after her, and there were parades that were organized in her honor. She embarked on a national tour, making speeches about her travels and to fascinate crowds with her tales. Nellie had shown the world that a gutsy American woman could travel the world alone, quickly, and with safety.

Consistent Quotations

There are two ways in which a writer can record the words of another person: **direct discourse** and **indirect discourse.**

Direct discourse *records the speaker's exact words inside quotation marks.* Note the punctuation:*

---

1. "Follow me," the guard told us.

2. Phil said, "I've just bought a camcorder."

Indirect discourse *reports what was said without quotation marks but in the writer's words.* Note the punctuation:

---

3. The guard told us to follow him.

4. Phil said that he had just bought a camcorder.

In addition to different punctuation, shifting from direct to indirect or from indirect to direct discourse may require a different verb tense, as in the following:

---

5. "These math problems *are* impossible," Dana complained.

6. Dana complained that the math problems *were* impossible.

- The present tense *are* used in direct discourse must be changed to the past tense *were* in indirect discourse since the problems *were impossible* at the same time that Dana *complained.*

Pronouns may also change when writing shifts between direct and indirect discourse, as in the following:

---

7. Our waitress said, "*I'm* working to finance *my* education."

8. Our waitress said *she* was working to finance *her* education.

---

* For practice in punctuating direct discourse, see Chapter 33, "Mechanics," Part C.

■ The first person pronoun *I* in direct discourse changes to the third person *she* in indirect discourse, and the first person *my* changes to the third person *her*.

Consistency of discourse means using *either* direct *or* indirect discourse within a particular sentence. Do not mix direct and indirect discourse within one sentence, or the inconsistency will confuse the reader:

9. Inconsistent discourse:	Tom growled that he was leaving and don't try to stop me.
10. Consistent discourse: (direct)	Tom growled, "I am leaving. Don't try to stop me."
11. Consistent discourse: (indirect)	Tom growled that he was leaving and we should not try to stop him.

■ The discourse in sentence 9 is inconsistent and incorrect.

■ Notice the differences in punctuation, verb tense, and pronouns between sentences 10 and 11.

12. Inconsistent discourse:	They asked the cashier, "Is the movie over? If he could change a twenty-dollar bill."
13. Consistent discourse: (direct)	They asked the cashier, "Is the movie over? Can you change a twenty-dollar bill?"
14. Consistent discourse: (indirect)	They asked the cashier if the movie was over and if he could change a twenty-dollar bill.

■ Sentence 12 is inconsistent and incorrect.

■ In sentence 13, the two questions *they* asked are shown in direct discourse; therefore, a question mark follows each. Sentence 14, however, states that *they asked if*. . . . Thus no question mark is needed.

PRACTICE 15   Convert each of the following sentences from consistent direct to consistent indirect discourse, making all needed changes in verbs, pronouns, and punctuation. You may change words as long as you do not change the meaning.

Example "Does that blue junk heap belong to you?" the officer asked.

The officer asked whether the blue junk heap belonged to me.

1. The tag states, "This watch is waterproof."

_____

_____

2. Hope asked us, "Do you have any construction paper left?"

_____

_____

3. *"Kakistocracy,"* Professor Davis explained, "means government by the worst."

_____

_____

4. "In a dark time," said Theodore Roethke, "the eye begins to see."

_____

_____

5. "My mind accepts changes months before my emotions do," the psychologist told us.

_____

_____

PRACTICE 16 Convert each sentence below from consistent indirect to consistent direct discourse. Make all necessary changes in punctuation, verbs, and pronouns.

Example The interviewer asked if I had ever written factual reports.

The interviewer asked, "Have you ever written factual reports?"

1. Sharon asked the realtor if any old farmhouses were available.

_____

_____

2. The book advised that a career in law enforcement is not for the squeamish.

_____

_____

3. Charlie said he preferred silent films.

_____

4. The president's press secretary announced that the new tax plan would soon be presented to the nation.

_____

_____

5. My neighbor said he wished I would soundproof my room.

_____

PRACTICE 17   Correct the inconsistent discourse in each of the following sentences. Rewrite each in consistent indirect discourse or consistent direct discourse. Change the wording if necessary but preserve the meaning of the sentence. Punctuate correctly.

Example   John asked did I know who won Saturday's game.

John asked, "Do you know who won Saturday's game?" _____ (direct discourse)

or

John asked me if I knew who won Saturday's game. _____ (indirect discourse)

1. The speaker read a passage from *Animal Farm* and asked did we care to comment?

_____

_____

2. Toni said that "she would drive if we needed extra cars."

_____

_____

3. Don't be alarmed by the noise, they told us, that the boiler was being repaired.

_____

_____

_____

4. He said we could sit on the antique chairs but please don't touch the cut-glass bowls.

_____

_____

_____

5. The poet Kahlil Gibran says, I have learned silence from the talkative, tolerance from the intolerant, and kindness from the unkind. And that he should not be ungrateful to those teachers.

_____

_____

_____

_____

_____

PRACTICE 18 Revise the following sentences for **consistency of discourse.** You may use both direct and indirect discourse in the paragraph, but use _either_ one _or_ the other within each sentence. Write the revised paragraph in the space provided.

Yogi Berra, catcher for the New York Yankees from 1946 to 1963, was almost as famous for his wit as he was for his playing. For instance, when a waitress asked him "if she should cut his pizza into four or eight slices," Yogi replied, "Better make it four. I don't think I can eat eight." Then there was the time that Yogi was asked about a popular restaurant, and he commented "that it's so crowded nobody goes there anymore." On Yogi Berra Day at Yankee Stadium, the former catcher graciously said that I wanted to thank everyone who made today necessary. When asked about a decline in attendance at Yankee games, Yogi offered the following mind-bender: If people don't want to come out to the park, nobody's gonna stop 'em. One day a woman fan told Yogi that he looked cool in spite of the sweltering heat. He returned the compliment by saying, "Thank you, ma'am" that you don't look so hot yourself. A reporter asked Yogi "how he had liked school as a child." Closed was Berra's one-word answer.

_____

_____

_____

_____

_____

14

Revising for Sentence Variety

Good writers pay attention to **sentence variety.** They notice how sentences work together within a paragraph, and they seek a mix of different sentence lengths and types. Experienced writers have a variety of sentence patterns from which to choose. They try not to overuse one pattern.

This chapter will present several techniques for varying your sentences and paragraphs. Some of them you may already know and use, perhaps unconsciously. The purpose of this chapter is to make you more conscious of the **choices** available to you as a writer.

Remember, you achieve sentence variety by practicing, by systematically **revising** your papers and trying out new types of sentences or combinations of sentences.

PART A

Mix Long and Short Sentences

One of the basic ways to achieve sentence variety is to use both long and short sentences. Beginning writers tend to overuse short, simple sentences, which quickly become monotonous. Notice the length of the sentences in the following paragraph:

> (1) There is one positive result of the rising crime rate. (2) This has been the growth of neighborhood crime prevention programs. (3) These programs really work. (4) They teach citizens to patrol their neighborhoods. (5) They teach citizens to work with the police. (6) They have dramatically reduced crime in cities and towns across the country. (7) The idea is catching on.

The sentences in the paragraph above are all nearly the same length, and the effect is choppy and almost childish. Now read this revised version, which contains a variety of sentence lengths.

> (1) One positive result of the rising crime rate has been the growth of neighborhood crime prevention programs. (2) These programs really work. (3) By teaching citizens to patrol their neighborhoods and to work with the police, they have dramatically reduced crime in cities and towns across the country. (4) The idea is catching on.

This paragraph is more effective because it mixes two short sentences, 2 and 4, and two longer sentences, 1 and 3. Although short sentences can be used effectively anywhere in a paragraph or essay, they can be especially useful as introductions or conclusions, like sentence 4 above. Note the powerful effect of short sentences used between longer ones in the paragraph that follows. Underline the short sentences.

> (1) I recall being told, when I first moved to Los Angeles and was living on an isolated beach, that the Indians would throw themselves into the sea when the bad wind blew. (2) I could see why. (3) The Pacific turned ominously glossy during a Santa Ana period, and one woke in the night troubled not only by the peacocks screaming in the olive trees but by the eerie absence of surf. (4) The heat was surreal. (5) The sky had a yellow cast, the kind of light sometimes called "earthquake weather." (6) My only neighbor would not come out of her house for days, and there were no lights at night, and her husband roamed the place with a machete. (7) One day he would tell me that he had heard a trespasser, the next a rattlesnake.
>
> —Joan Didion, *Slouching Towards Bethlehem*

PRACTICE 1   Revise and rewrite the following paragraph in a variety of sentence lengths. Recombine sentences in any way you wish. You may add connecting words or drop words, but do not alter the meaning of the paragraph.

The park is alive with motion today. Joggers pound up and down the boardwalk. Old folks watch them from the benches. Couples row boats across the lake. The boats are green and wooden. Two teenagers hurl a Frisbee back and forth. They yell and leap. A shaggy white dog dashes in from nowhere. He snatches the red disk in his mouth. He bounds away. The teenagers run after him.

_____

_____

_____

_____

_____

_____

_____

_____

PART B

Use a Question, Command, or Exclamation

The most commonly used sentence is the **declarative sentence,** which is a statement. However, an occasional carefully placed **question, command,** or **exclamation** is an effective way to achieve sentence variety.

The Question

> *Why did I become a cab driver?* First, I truly enjoy driving a car and exploring different parts of the city, the classy avenues and the hidden back streets. In addition, I like meeting all kinds of people, from bookmakers to governors, each with a unique story and many willing to talk to the back of my head. Of course, the pay isn't bad and the hours are flexible, but it's the places and the people that I love.

This paragraph begins with a question. The writer does not really expect the reader to answer it. Rather, it is a **rhetorical question,** one that will be answered by the writer in the course of the paragraph. A rhetorical question used as a topic sentence can provide a colorful change from the usual declarative sentences: *Is America really the best-fed nation in the world? What is courage? Why do more young people take drugs today than ever before?*

The Command and the Exclamation

> (1) Try to imagine using failure as a description of an animal's behavior. (2) Consider a dog barking for fifteen minutes, and someone saying, "He really isn't very good at barking, I'd give him a C." (3) How absurd! (4) It is impossible for an animal to fail because there is no provision for evaluating natural behavior. (5) Spiders construct webs, not successful or unsuccessful webs. (6) Cats hunt mice; if they aren't successful in one attempt, they simply go after another. (7) They don't lie there and whine, complaining about the one that got away, or have a nervous breakdown because they failed. (8) Natural behavior simply is! (9) So apply the same logic to your own behavior and rid yourself of the fear of failure.
>
> —Dr. Wayne W. Dyer, *Your Erroneous Zones*

The paragraph above begins and ends with **commands,** or **imperative sentences.** Sentences 1, 2, and 9 address the reader directly and have as their implied subject *you.* They tell the reader to do something: *(You) try to imagine . . . , (you) consider . . . , (you) apply. . . .* Commands are most frequently used in giving directions,* but they can be used occasionally, as in the paragraph above, for sentence variety.

Sentences 3 and 8 in the Dyer paragraph are **exclamations,** sentences that express strong emotion and end with an exclamation point. These should be used very sparingly. In fact, some writers avoid them altogether, striving for words that convey strong emotion instead.

Be careful with the question, the command, and the exclamation as options in your writing. Try them out, but use them—especially the exclamation—sparingly.

Writing Assignment 1

On a separate piece of paper, write a paragraph that begins with a rhetorical question. Choose one of the questions below or compose your own. Be sure that the body of the paragraph really does answer the question.

1. How has college (or anything else) changed me?

2. Is marriage worth the risks?

* For more work on giving directions, see Chapter 8, "Process."

3. Do some MTV videos encourage the mistreatment of women?

4. Is anything safe to eat these days?

5. Should people pamper their pets?

PART C

Vary the Beginnings of Sentences

Begin with an Adverb

Since the first word of many sentences is the subject, one way to achieve sentence variety is by occasionally starting a sentence with a word or words other than the subject.

For instance, you can begin with an **adverb:***

---

1. He *laboriously* dragged the large crate up the stairs.

2. *Laboriously,* he dragged the large crate up the stairs.

3. The contents of the beaker *suddenly* began to foam.

4. *Suddenly,* the contents of the beaker began to foam.

- In sentences 2 and 4, the adverbs *laboriously* and *suddenly* are shifted to the first position. Notice the difference in rhythm that this creates, as well as the slight change in meaning: Sentence 2 emphasizes *how* he dragged the crate—*laboriously;* sentence 4 emphasizes the *suddenness* of what happened.

- A comma usually follows an adverb that introduces a sentence; however, adverbs of time—*often, now, always*—do not always require a comma. As a general rule, use a comma if you want the reader to pause briefly.

PRACTICE 2   Rewrite the following sentences by shifting the adverbs to the beginning. Punctuate correctly.

Example | He skillfully prepared the engine for the race.

> Skillfully, he prepared the engine for the race.

1. Two deer moved silently across the clearing.

---

* For more work on adverbs, see Chapter 30, "Adjectives and Adverbs."

2. The chief of the research division occasionally visits the lab.

_____

3. Proofread your writing always.

_____

4. Children of alcoholics often marry alcoholics.

_____

5. Jake foolishly lied to his supervisor.

_____

PRACTICE 3   Begin each of the following sentences with an appropriate adverb. Punctuate correctly.

1. _____ the detective approached the ticking suitcase.

2. _____ Steffi Graf powered a forehand past her opponent.

3. _____ she received her check for $25,000 from the state lottery.

4. _____ he left the beach.

5. _____ the submarine sank out of sight.

PRACTICE 4   Write five sentences of your own that begin with adverbs. Use different adverbs from those in Practices 1 and 2; if you wish, use _graciously, absentmindedly, cheerfully, furiously, sometimes._ Punctuate correctly.

1. _____

2. _____

3. _____

4. _____

5. _____

Begin with a Prepositional Phrase

A **prepositional phrase** is a group of words containing a **preposition** and its **object** (a noun or pronoun). _To you, in the evening,_ and _under the old bridge_ are prepositional phrases.*

* For work on spotting prepositional phrases, see Chapter 29, "Prepositions."

Preposition	Object
to	you
in	the evening
under	the old bridge

Here is a partial list of prepositions:

Common Prepositions

about	beneath	into	throughout
above	beside	near	to
across	between	of	toward
against	by	on	under
among	except	onto	up
at	for	out	upon
behind	from	over	with
below	in	through	without

For variety in your writing, begin an occasional sentence with a prepositional phrase:

5. Charles left the room *without a word.*

6. *Without a word,* Charles left the room.

7. A fat yellow cat lay sleeping *on the narrow sill.*

8. *On the narrow sill,* a fat yellow cat lay sleeping.

■ In sentences 6 and 8, the prepositional phrases have been shifted to the beginning. Note the slight shift in emphasis that results. Sentence 6 stresses that Charles left the room *without a word,* and 8 stresses the location of the cat, *on the narrow sill.*

■ Prepositional phrases that begin sentences are usually followed by commas. However, short prepositional phrases need not be.

Prepositional phrases are not always movable; rely on the meaning of the sentence to determine whether or not they are movable:

9. The dress *in the picture* is the one I want.

10. Joelle bought a bottle *of white wine for dinner.*

■ *In the picture* in sentence 9 is a part of the subject and cannot be
   moved. *In the picture the dress is the one I want* makes no sense.

■ Sentence 10 has two prepositional phrases. Which one *cannot* be moved to
   the beginning of the sentence? Why?

   _____

   _____

PRACTICE 5   Underline the prepositional phrases in each sentence. Some sentences con-
               tain more than one prepositional phrase. Rewrite each sentence by shifting a
               prepositional phrase to the beginning. Punctuate correctly.

Example   A large owl with gray feathers watched us from the oak tree.

               From the oak tree, a large owl with gray feathers watched us.

   1. The coffee maker turned itself on at seven o'clock sharp.

      _____

      _____

   2. A growling Doberman paced behind the chain link fence.

      _____

      _____

   3. A man and a woman held hands under the street lamp.

      _____

      _____

   4. They have sold nothing except athletic shoes for years.

      _____

      _____

5. A group of men played checkers and drank iced tea beside the small shop.

_____

_____

PRACTICE 6 Begin each of the following sentences with a different prepositional phrase. Refer to the list and be creative. Punctuate correctly.

1. _____ we ordered potato skins, salad, and beer.

2. _____ a woman in horn-rimmed glasses balanced her checkbook.

3. _____ everyone congratulated Jim on his promotion.

4. _____ one can see huge sculptures in wood, metal, and stone.

5. _____ three large helium-filled balloons drifted.

PRACTICE 7 Write five sentences of your own that begin with prepositional phrases. Use these phrases if you wish: _in the dentist's office, between them, at my wedding, under that stack of books, behind his friendly smile._ Punctuate correctly.

1. _____

2. _____

3. _____

4. _____

5. _____

PART D

Vary Methods of Joining Ideas*

Join Ideas with a Compound Predicate

A sentence with a **compound predicate** contains more than one verb, but the subject is *not* repeated before the second verb. Such a sentence is really composed of two simple sentences with the same subject:

---

1. The nurse entered.

2. The nurse quickly closed the door.

3. The nurse *entered* and quickly *closed* the door.

- *The nurse* is the subject of sentence 1 and *entered* is the verb; *the nurse* is also the subject of sentence 2 and *closed* is the verb.

- When these sentences are combined with a compound predicate in sentence 3, *the nurse* is the subject of both *entered* and *closed* but is not repeated before the second verb.

- No comma is necessary when the conjunctions *and, but, or,* and *yet* join the verbs in a compound predicate.

  A compound predicate is useful in combining short, choppy sentences:

---

4. He serves elaborate meals.

5. He never uses a recipe.

6. He serves elaborate meals yet never uses a recipe.

7. Aviators rarely get nosebleeds.

8. They often suffer from backaches.

9. Aviators rarely get nosebleeds but often suffer from backaches.

- Sentences 4 and 5 are joined by *yet;* no comma precedes *yet.*

- Sentences 7 and 8 are joined by *but;* no comma precedes *but.*

* For work on joining ideas with coordination and subordination, see Chapter 22, "Coordination and Subordination."

PRACTICE 8   Combine each pair of short sentences into one sentence with a compound predicate. Use *and, but, or,* and *yet.* Punctuate correctly.

Example | Toby smeared peanut butter on a thick slice of white bread.

He devoured the treat in thirty seconds.

Toby smeared peanut butter on a thick slice of white bread and devoured the treat

in thirty seconds.

1. Americans eat more than 800 million pounds of peanut butter.

   They spend more than $1 billion on the product each year.

   _____

   _____

2. Peanut butter was first concocted in the 1890s.

   It did not become the food we know for thirty years.

   _____

   _____

3. George Washington Carver did not discover peanut butter.

   He published many recipes for pastes much like it.

   _____

   _____

   _____

4. The average American becomes a peanut butter lover in childhood.

   He or she loses enthusiasm for it later on.

   _____

   _____

   _____

5. Older adults regain their passion for peanut butter.

   They consume great quantities of the delicious stuff.

   _____

   _____

   _____

PRACTICE 9   Complete the following compound predicates. *Do not repeat* the subjects.

1. Three Korean writers visited the campus and _____

_____.

2. The singer breathed heavily into the microphone but _____

_____.

3. Take these cans to the recycling center or _____

_____.

4. The newspaper printed the story yet _____

_____.

5. Three men burst into the back room and _____

_____.

PRACTICE 10   Write five sentences with compound predicates. Be careful to punctuate correctly.

1. _____

2. _____

3. _____

4. _____

5. _____

Join Ideas with an *-ing* Modifier

An excellent way to achieve sentence variety is by occasionally combining two sentences with an *-ing* modifier.

10. He peered through the microscope.

11. He discovered a squiggly creature.

12. *Peering through the microscope,* he discovered a squiggly creature.

■ Sentence 10 has been converted to an *-ing* modifier by changing the verb *peered* to *peering* and dropping the subject *he*. *Peering through the microscope* now introduces the main clause, *he discovered a squiggly creature*.

■ A comma sets off the *-ing* modifier from the word it refers to, *he*. To avoid confusion, the word referred to must immediately follow the *-ing* modifier.

An *-ing* modifier indicates that two actions are occurring at the same time. The main idea of the sentence should be contained in the main clause, not in the *-ing* modifier. In the preceding example, the discovery of the creature is the main idea, not the fact that someone peered through a microscope.

Be careful: misplaced *-ing* modifiers can result in confusing sentences: *He discovered a squiggly creature peering through the microscope.* (Was the creature looking through the microscope?)

Convert sentence 13 into an *-ing* modifier and write it in the blank:

> 13. We drove down Tompkins Road.
>
> 14. We were surprised by the number of "for sale" signs.
>
> 15. _Driving down Tompkins Road_____, we were surprised by the number of "for sale" signs.

■ The new *-ing* modifier is followed directly by the word to which it refers, *we*.

PRACTICE 11   Combine the following pairs of sentences by converting the first sentence into an *-ing* modifier. Make sure the subject of the main clause directly follows the *-ing* modifier. Punctuate correctly.

Example | Jake searched for his needle-nose pliers.

He completely emptied the tool chest.

Searching for his needle-nose pliers, Jake completely emptied the tool chest.

1. She installed the air conditioner.

   She saved herself $50 in labor.

   _____

   _____

2. The surgeons raced against time.

   The surgeons performed a liver transplant on the child.

   _____

   _____

3. They conducted a survey of Jackson Heights residents.

   They found that most opposed construction of the airport.

   _____

   _____

4. Three flares spiraled upward from the little boat.

   They exploded against the night sky.

   _____

   _____

5. Virgil danced in the Pennsylvania Ballet.

   Virgil learned discipline and self-control.

   _____

   _____

6. The hen squawked loudly.

   The hen fluttered out of our path.

   _____

   _____

7. The engineer made a routine check of the blueprints.

   He discovered a flaw in the design.

   _____

   _____

8. Dr. Jackson opened commencement exercises with a humorous story.

   He put everyone at ease.

   _____

   _____

PRACTICE 12   Add either an introductory *-ing* modifier *or* a main clause to each sentence. Make sure that each *-ing* modifier refers clearly to the subject of the main clause.

Examples   Reading a book a week _____, Jeff increased his vocabulary.

Exercising every day, I lost five pounds _____.

1. _____, she felt a sense of accomplishment.

2. Growing up in Hollywood, _____

_____.

3. _____, the father and son were reconciled.

4. Interviewing his relatives, _____

_____.

5. _____, the wrecking ball swung through the air and smashed into the brick wall.

PRACTICE 13   Write five sentences of your own that begin with *-ing* modifiers. Make sure that the subject of the sentence follows the modifier and be careful of the punctuation.

1. _____

_____

2. _____

_____

3. _____

_____

4. _____

_____

5. _____

_____

Join Ideas with a Past Participial Modifier

Some sentences can be joined with a **past participial modifier**. A sentence that contains a *to be* verb and a **past participle*** can be changed into a past participial modifier:

---

16. Judith *is alarmed* by the increase in meat prices.

17. Judith has become a vegetarian.

18. *Alarmed by the increase in meat prices,* Judith has become a vegetarian.

- Sentence 16 has been made into a past participial modifier by dropping the helping verb *is* and the subject *Judith*. The past participle *alarmed* now introduces the new sentence.

- A comma sets off the past participial modifier from the word it modifies, *Judith*. To avoid confusion, the word referred to must directly follow the modifier.

  Be careful: misplaced past participial modifiers can result in confusing sentences: *Packed in dry ice, Steve brought us some ice cream.* (Was Steve packed in dry ice?)

  Sometimes two or more past participles can be used to introduce a sentence:

---

19. The term paper was *revised* and *rewritten*.

20. It received an *A*.

21. *Revised and rewritten,* the term paper received an *A*.

- The past participles *revised* and *rewritten* become a modifier that introduces sentence 21. What word(s) do they refer to?

PRACTICE 14   Combine each pair of sentences into one sentence that begins with a past participial modifier. Convert the sentence containing a form of *to be* plus a **past participle** into a past participial modifier that introduces the new sentence.

* For more work on past participles, see Chapter 26, "The Past Participle."

Example | Duffy was surprised by the interruption.

He lost his train of thought.

Surprised by the interruption, Duffy lost his train of thought.
_____

1. My mother was married at the age of sixteen.

   My mother never finished high school.

   _____

   _____

2. The 2:30 flight was delayed by an electrical storm.

   It arrived in Lexington three hours late.

   _____

   _____

3. The old car was waxed and polished.

   It shone in the sun.

   _____

   _____

4. The house was built by Frank Lloyd Wright.

   It is famous.

   _____

   _____

5. The Nineteenth Amendment was ratified in 1920.

   It gave women the right to vote.

   _____

   _____

6. The manuscript is very hard to read.

   It is written in longhand.

   _____

   _____

7. Dr. Bentley will address the premed students.

   He has been recognized for his contributions in the field of immunology.

   _____

   _____

8. Mrs. Witherspoon was exhausted by night classes.

She declined the chance to work overtime.

_____

_____

PRACTICE 15 Complete each sentence by filling in *either* the past participial modifier *or* the main clause. Remember, the past participial modifier must clearly refer to the subject of the main clause.

Example Wrapped in blue paper and tied with string, _the gift arrived._____ .

_Chosen to represent the team_____, Phil proudly accepted the trophy.

1. Made of gold and set with precious stones, _____

_____.

2. Overwhelmed by the response to her ad in *The Star,* _____

_____.

3. _____, Tom left no forwarding address.

4. _____, we found a huge basket of fresh fruit on the steps.

5. Astonished by the scene before her, _____

_____.

PRACTICE 16 Write five sentences of your own that begin with past participial modifiers. If you wish, use participles from this list:

thrilled	moved	seen	honored
shocked	dressed	hidden	bent
awakened	lost	stuffed	examined
annoyed	found	pinched	rewired

Make sure that the subject of the sentence clearly follows the modifier.

1. _____

_____

2. _____

   _____

3. _____

   _____

4. _____

   _____

5. _____

   _____

Join Ideas with an Appositive

A fine way to add variety to your writing is to combine two choppy sentences with an appositive. An **appositive** is a word or group of words that renames or describes a noun or pronoun:

> 22. Carlos is the new wrestling champion.
>
> 23. He is a native of Argentina.
>
> 24. Carlos, *a native of Argentina,* is the new wrestling champion.

- *A native of Argentina* in sentence 24 is an appositive. It renames the noun *Carlos.*

- An appositive must be placed either directly *after* the word it refers to, as in sentence 24, or directly *before* it, as follows:

> 25. *A native of Argentina,* Carlos is the new wrestling champion.

- Note that an appositive is set off by commas.

Appositives can add versatility to your writing because they can be placed at the beginning, in the middle, or at the end of a sentence. When you join two ideas with an appositive, place the idea you wish to stress in the main clause and make the less important idea the appositive:

26. Naomi wants to become a fashion model.

27. She is the daughter of an actress.

28. *The daughter of an actress,* Naomi wants to become a fashion model.

29. FACT made headlines for the first time in 1995.

30. FACT is now a powerful consumer group.

31. FACT, *now a powerful consumer group,* made headlines for the first time in 1995.

32. Watch out for Smithers.

33. He is a dangerous man.

34. Watch out for Smithers, *a dangerous man.*

Using an appositive to combine sentences eliminates unimportant words and creates longer, more fact-filled sentences.

PRACTICE 17   Combine the following pairs of sentences by making the *second sentence* an appositive. Punctuate correctly.

These appositives should occur at the *beginning* of the sentences.

Example | My uncle taught me to use watercolors.

He is a well-known artist.

A well-known artist, my uncle taught me to use watercolors.

1. Dan has saved many lives.

   He is a dedicated fire fighter.

   _____

   _____

2. Acupuncture is becoming popular in the United States.

   It is an ancient Chinese healing system.

   _____

   _____

   _____

3. The Cromwell Hotel was built in 1806.

    It is an elegant example of Mexican architecture.

    _____

    _____

These appositives should occur in the *middle* of the sentences. Punctuate correctly.

Example | His African-American literature course is always popular with students.

It is an introductory survey.

His African-American literature course, an introductory survey, is always popular

with students.

4. The Korean Ping-Pong champion won ten games in a row.

    She is a small and wiry athlete.

    _____

    _____

5. The pituitary is located below the brain.

    It is the body's master gland.

    _____

    _____

6. The elevator shudders violently and begins to rise.

    It is an ancient box of wood and hope.

    _____

    _____

These appositives should occur at the *end* of the sentences. Punctuate correctly.

Example | I hate fried asparagus.

It is a vile dish.

I hate fried asparagus, a vile dish.

7. Jennifer flaunted her new camera.

   It was a Nikon with a telephoto lens.

   _____

   _____

8. At the intersection stood a hitchhiker.

   He was a young man dressed in a tuxedo.

   _____

   _____

9. We met for pancakes at the Cosmic Cafe.

   It was a greasy diner on the corner of 10th and Vine.

   _____

   _____

PRACTICE 18   Write six sentences using appositives. In two sentences, place the appositive at the beginning; in two sentences, place the appositive in the middle; and in two sentences, place it at the end.

1. _____

   _____

2. _____

   _____

3. _____

   _____

4. _____

   _____

5. _____

   _____

6. _____

   _____

Join Ideas with a Relative Clause

Relative clauses can add sophistication to your writing. A **relative clause** begins with *who, which,* or *that* and describes a noun or pronoun. It can join two simple sentences in a longer, more complex sentence:

---

35. Jack just won a scholarship from the Arts Council.

36. He makes wire sculpture.

37. Jack, *who makes wire sculpture,* just won a scholarship from the Arts Council.

- In sentence 37, *who makes wire sculpture* is a relative clause, created by replacing the subject *he* of sentence 36 with the relative pronoun *who.*

- *Who* now introduces the subordinate relative clause and connects it to the rest of the sentence. Note that *who* directly follows the word it refers to, *Jack.*

    The idea that the writer wishes to stress is placed in the main clause, and the subordinate idea is placed in the relative clause. Study the combinations in sentences 38–40 and 41–43.

---

38. Carrots grow in cool climates.

39. They are high in vitamin A.

40. Carrots, *which* are high in vitamin A, grow in cool climates.

41. He finally submitted the term paper.

42. It was due six months ago.

43. He finally submitted the term paper *that* was due six months ago.

- In sentence 40, *which are high in vitamin A* is a relative clause, created by replacing *they* with *which.* What word in sentence 40 does *which* refer to?

_____

- What is the relative clause in sentence 43?

_____

- What word does *that* refer to?

_____

Punctuating relative clauses can be tricky; therefore, you will have to be careful:*

---

44. Claude, *who grew up in Haiti,* speaks fluent French.

- *Who grew up in Haiti* is set off by commas because it adds information about Claude that is not essential to the meaning of the sentence. In other words, the sentence would make sense without it: *Claude speaks fluent French.*

- *Who grew up in Haiti* is called a **nonrestrictive clause.** It does not restrict or provide vital information about the word it modifies.

---

45. People *who crackle paper in theaters* annoy me.

- *Who crackle paper in theaters* is not set off by commas because it is vital to the meaning of the sentence. Without it, the sentence would read, *People annoy me;* yet the point of the sentence is that people *who crackle paper in theaters* annoy me, not all people.

- *Who crackle paper in theaters* is called a **restrictive clause** because it restricts the meaning of the word it refers to, *people.*

Note that *which* usually begins a nonrestrictive clause and *that* usually begins a restrictive clause.

PRACTICE 19 Combine each pair of sentences by changing the second sentence into a relative clause introduced by *who, which,* or *that.* Remember, *who* refers to persons, *that* refers to persons or things, and *which* refers to things.

These sentences require **nonrestrictive relative clauses.** Punctuate correctly.

Example My cousin will spend the summer hiking in the Rockies.

She lives in Indiana.

My cousin, who lives in Indiana, will spend the summer hiking in the

Rockies.

* For more practice in punctuating relative clauses, see Chapter 32, "The Comma," Part D.

1. Scrabble has greatly increased my vocabulary.

   It is my favorite game.

   _____

   _____

2. Contestants on game shows often make fools of themselves.

   They may travel thousands of miles to play.

   _____

   _____

3. Arabic is a difficult language to learn.

   It has a complicated verb system.

   _____

   _____

   The next sentences require **restrictive relative clauses.** Punctuate correctly.

Example | He described a state of mind.

I have experienced it.

He described a state of mind that I have experienced.

4. The house is for sale.

   I was born in it.

   _____

   _____

5. My boss likes reports.

   They are clear and to the point.

   _____

   _____

6. People know how intelligent birds are.

   They have owned a bird.

   _____

   _____

PRACTICE 20   Combine each pair of sentences by changing one into a relative clause introduced by *who, which,* or *that.* Remember, *who* refers to persons, *that* refers
to persons or things, and *which* refers to things.
    Be careful of the punctuation. (Hint: *Which* clauses are usually set off by
commas and *that* clauses are usually not.)

1. Her grandfather enjoys scuba diving.

   He is seventy-seven years old.

   _____

   _____

2. The Xerox machine earned millions for Chester Carlson.

   It had been rejected by RCA, IBM, and G.E.

   _____

   _____

3. You just dropped an antique pitcher.

   It is worth two thousand dollars.

   _____

   _____

4. Parenthood has taught me acceptance, forgiveness, and love.

   It used to terrify me.

   _____

   _____

5. James Fenimore Cooper was expelled from college.

   He later became a famous American novelist.

   _____

   _____

6. The verb *to hector* means "to bully someone."

   It derives from a character in Greek literature.

   _____

   _____

PRACTICE 21   Write six sentences with relative clauses. Make three relative clauses restrictive and three nonrestrictive. Be careful of the punctuation.

1. _____

_____

2. _____

_____

3. _____

_____

4. _____

_____

5. _____

_____

6. _____

_____

PART E

Review and Practice

Before practicing some of the techniques of sentence variety discussed in this chapter, review them briefly:

1. Mix long and short sentences.

2. Add an occasional question, command, or exclamation.

3. Begin with an adverb: *Unfortunately,* the outfielder dropped the fly ball.

4. Begin with a prepositional phrase: *With great style,* the pitcher delivered a curve.

5. Join ideas with a compound predicate: The fans *roared and banged* their seats.

6. Mix coordination and subordination.*

Coordination
{
The fans hissed, *but* the umpire paid no attention.
The fans hissed; the umpire paid no attention.
The fans hissed; *however,* the umpire paid no attention.
}

Subordination
{
The umpire paid no attention *although* the fans hissed.
Although the fans hissed, the umpire paid no attention.
}

* For more work, see Chapter 22, "Coordination and Subordination."

7. Join ideas with an *-ing* modifier: *Diving chin first onto the grass,* Johnson caught the ball.

8. Join ideas with a past participial modifier: *Frustrated by the call,* the batter kicked dirt onto home plate.

9. Join ideas with an appositive: Beer, *the cause of much rowdiness,* should not be sold at games.

10. Join ideas with a relative clause: Box seats, *which are hard to get for important games,* are frequently bought up by corporations.

Of course, the secret of achieving sentence variety is practice. Chose one, two, or three of these techniques to focus on and try them out in your writing. Revise your paragraphs and essays with an eye to sentence variety.

PRACTICE 22   Revise and then rewrite this essay, aiming for sentence variety. Vary the length and pattern of the sentences. Vary the beginnings of some sentences. Join two sentences in any way you wish, adding appropriate connecting words or dropping unnecessary words. Punctuate correctly.

Little Richard, the King of Rock 'n' Roll

With "A-Wop-Bop-A-Loo-Bop-A-Lop-Bam-Boom," Little Richard hit the American music scene on September 14, 1955. It has never been the same since. He had almost insane energy. He wore flamboyant clothes. He defined the rebellious behavior at the heart of rock 'n' roll. He has influenced countless performers. These performers include the Beatles, Mick Jagger and the Rolling Stones, David Bowie, and Prince.

Richard Wayne Penniman was born on December 5, 1932, in Macon, Georgia. He was the third of thirteen children. He and his siblings sang gospel music. They were called the Penniman Singers. Richard was a wild and independent child. He left home at fourteen. During his teens, he traveled throughout Georgia with musical shows of all kinds. These included "Dr. Hudson's Medicine Show" and the "Tidy Jolly Steppers." He appeared in "Sugarfoot Sam from Alabam." Here he played "Princess Lavonne" and wore a dress. He sang with B. Brown and his orchestra. He was called "Little Richard" for the first time.

By 1955, Richard had developed his own musical style. It combined gospel with rhythm and blues. At its center was a wild scream of pure joy. He had developed a stage style as well. It combined outrageous costumes, a mile-high pompadour, thick mascara, manic piano-playing, and uninhibited hip-swinging. "Tutti Frutti" made him an overnight sensation. Over the next two years, he produced one hit after another. Fans will never forget such classics as "Long Tall Sally," "Slippin' and Slidin'," "Rip It Up," "Lucille," and "Good Golly Miss Molly."

Richard had a five-year lull. He resurfaced in 1962. He became a cult figure for the next thirteen years. He was called "The Prince of Clowns" and "The King of Rock 'n' Roll." His behavior on and off the stage became more and more outrageous. In one show, he would dress as Queen Elizabeth. In the next show, he would dress as the pope. He once wore a suit covered with small mirrors. It prevented him from sitting in a car. His followers treated him royally. He was seated on a throne and crowned with jewels. He was carried into restaurants like a king.

Between 1957 and 1962, and then again in 1975, Little Richard had a spiritual awakening. The demon of rock 'n' roll dropped alcohol, drugs, and sexual promiscuity. He took on a devout lifestyle. He became an evangelist. He went to work for a Bible company. During these times, he returned to singing the gospel music of his youth.

Richard's life continues to be filled with extremes. In 1985, he drove his sports car into a telephone pole. He survived with 36 pins in his leg. At Bill Clinton's inaugural party in 1993, Little Richard led the festivities. He is now in his sixties. He is still going strong.

Little Richard, the King of Rock 'n' Roll

_____

_____

_____

_____

_____

_____

_____

_____

_____

_____

_____

_____

_____

_____

_____

_____

_____

_____

Writing Assignment 2

Study this photograph of an abandoned mission or church; then write a paragraph describing it. What mood or feeling does the photograph convey to you? In your topic sentence, state this mood or feeling. Then describe the scene, choosing details that help create this mood.

Next, revise your paragraph, paying special attention to sentence variety. Aim for a variety of sentence lengths and types.

15

Revising for Language Awareness

PART A   Exact Language: Avoiding Vagueness
PART B   Concise Language: Avoiding Wordiness
PART C   Fresh Language: Avoiding Triteness
PART D   Figurative Language: Similes and Metaphors

Although it is important to write grammatically correct English, good writing is more than just correct writing. Good writing has life, excitement, and power. It captures the attention of the reader and compels him or her to read further.

The purpose of this chapter is to increase your awareness of the power of words and your skill at making them work for you. The secret of powerful writing is **revision.** *Do not settle* for the first words that come to you, but go back over what you have written, replacing dull or confusing language with language that is exact, concise, fresh, and possibly figurative.

PART A

Exact Language: Avoiding Vagueness

Good writers express their ideas as *exactly* as possible, choosing *specific, concrete,* and *vivid* words and phrases. They do not settle for vague terms and confusing generalities.

Which sentence in each of the following pairs gives the more *exact* information? That is, which uses specific and precise language? What words in these sentences make them sharper and more vivid?

1. A car went around the corner.

2. A battered blue Dodge careened around the corner.

3. Janet quickly ate the main course.

4. Janet devoured the plate of ribs in two and a half minutes.

5. The president did things that caused problems.

6. The president's military spending increased the budget deficit.

- Sentences 2, 4, and 6 contain language that is *exact*.

- Sentence 2 is more exact than sentence 1 because *battered blue Dodge* gives more specific information than the general term *car*. The verb *careened* describes precisely how the car went around the corner, fast and recklessly.

- What specific words does sentence 4 substitute for the more general words *ate, main course,* and *quickly* in sentence 3?

- _____ , _____ , and

  _____

  Why are these terms more exact than those in sentence 3?

  _____

  _____

- What words in sentence 6 make it more exact and clearer than sentence 5?

  _____

  _____

Concrete and detailed writing is usually exciting as well and makes us want to read on, as does this passage by Toni Morrison, who won the Nobel Prize for literature:

> It is called the suburbs now, but when black people lived there it was called the Bottom. One road, shaded by beeches, oaks, maples, and chestnuts, connected it to the valley. The beeches are gone now, and so are the pear trees where children sat and yelled down through the blossoms at passersby. Generous funds have been allotted to level the stripped and faded buildings that clutter the road from Medallion up to the golf course. They are going to raze the Time and a Half Pool Hall, where feet in long tan shoes once pointed down from chair rungs. A steel ball will knock to dust Irene's Palace of Cosmetology, where women used to lean their heads back on sink trays and doze while Irene lathered Nu Nile into their hair. Men in khaki work clothes will pry loose the slats of Reba's Grill, where the owner cooked in her hat because she couldn't remember the ingredients without it.
>
> —Toni Morrison, *Sula*

Now compare a similar account written in general and inexact language:

> It is called the suburbs now, but when black people lived there it was called the Bottom. One road, shaded by big trees, connected it to the valley. Many of the trees are gone now. Generous funds have been allotted to level the buildings on the road from Medallion up to the golf course. They are going to knock down the pool hall, the beauty parlor, and the restaurant.

You do not need a large vocabulary to write exactly and well, but you do need to work at finding the right words to fit each sentence. As you revise, cross out vague or dull words and phrases and replace them with more exact terms. When you are tempted to write *I feel good,* ask yourself exactly what *good* means in that sentence: *relaxed? proud? thin? in love?* When people walk by, do they *flounce, stride, lurch, wiggle,* or *sneak?* When they speak to you, do people *stammer, announce, babble, murmur,* or *coo?* Question yourself as you revise; then choose the right words to fit that particular sentence.

PRACTICE 1   Lively verbs are a great asset to any writer. The following sentences contain four overused general verbs—*to walk, to see, to eat,* and *to be.* In each case, replace the general verb in parentheses with a more exact verb *chosen to fit the context of the sentence.* Use a different verb in every sentence. Consult a dictionary or thesaurus* if you wish.

* A thesaurus is a book of *synonyms*—words that have the same or similar meanings.

Examples | In no particular hurry, we ___strolled___ (walked) through the botanical gardens.

Jane ___fidgets___ (is) at her desk and watches the clock.

1. With guns drawn, three police officers _____ (walked) toward the door of the warehouse.

2. As we stared in fascination, an orange lizard _____ (walked) up the wall.

3. The four-year-old _____ (walked) onto the patio in her mother's high-heeled shoes.

4. A furious customer _____ (walked) into the manager's office.

5. Two people who _____ (saw) the accident must testify in court.

6. We crouched for hours in the underbrush just to _____ (see) a rare white fox.

7. Three makeshift wooden rafts were _____ (seen) off the coast this morning.

8. For two years, the zoologist _____ (saw) the behavior of bears in the wild.

9. There was the cat, delicately _____ (eating) my fern!

10. Senator Gorman astounded the guests by loudly _____ (eating) his soup.

11. All through the movie, she _____ (ate) hard candies in the back row.

12. Within seconds, Dan had bought two tacos from a street vendor and

_____ (eaten) them both.

13. During rush hour, the temperature hit 98 degrees, and dozens of cars

_____ (were) on the highway.

14. A young man _____ (is) on a stretcher in the emergency room.

15. Workers who _____ (are) at desks all day should make special efforts to exercise.

16. Professor Nuzzo _____ (was) in front of the blackboard, excited about this new solution to the math problem.

PRACTICE 2   The sentences that follow contain vague and inexact language. Write at least
one specific and vivid revision for each sentence. Use vivid verbs and adjectives whenever possible.

Examples   A dog lies down in the shade.

A mangy collie flops down in the shade of a parked car.

My head hurts.

My head throbs.

I have shooting pains in the left side of my head.

1. Everything about the man looked mean.

   _____

   _____

2. I feel good today for several reasons.

   _____

   _____

3. A woman in unusual clothes went down the street.

   _____

   _____

4. The sunlight made the yard look pretty.

   _____

   _____

5. What the company did bothered the townspeople.

   _____

   _____

6. The pediatrician's waiting room was crowded.

   _____

   _____

7. As soon as he gets home from work, he hears the voice of his pet asking
   for dinner.

   _____

   _____

8. The noises of construction filled the street.

_____

_____

9. When I was sick, you were helpful.

_____

_____

10. This college does things that make the students feel bad.

_____

_____

PRACTICE 3   A word that works effectively in one sentence might not work in another sentence. In searching for the right word, always consider the **context** of the sentence into which the word must fit. Read each of the following sentences for meaning. Then circle the word in parentheses that *most exactly fits* the context of the sentence.

Example | The alchemist cautiously (threw, dripped, held) the liquid mercury onto copper in order to make it look like gold.

1. Alchemy, an early form of chemistry, was a (course, way, science) that flourished from ancient times until around 1700.

2. It was based on the (knowledge, belief, fact) that a metal could be converted into another ore.

3. Alchemists considered gold the (perfect, nicest, shiniest) metal.

4. Therefore, their goal was to (transform, redo, make) base metals, like lead, into gold.

5. They searched (eagerly, high and low, lots) for the "philosopher's stone," the formula that would make this change possible.

6. All "philosopher's stones" consisted of sulphur and mercury; the trick was to discover the proper way to (combine, destroy, mix up) the two.

7. Over time, alchemy incorporated various (aspects, things, stuff) of astrology and magic.

8. For example, certain metals were (the same as, equated with, sort of like) specific heavenly bodies—gold with the sun or silver with the moon.

9. One famous alchemist proudly (said, muttered, boasted) that he could magically transform winter into summer.

10. Many alchemists went to work for greedy princes and kings, who always (liked, lusted for, thought about) more gold.

11. It was dangerous work though; more than one alchemist was (done away with, executed, knocked off) because he could not produce gold.

12. In their search for gold, however, some alchemists (foolishly, hopefully, accidentally) made valid scientific discoveries that led to the development of modern chemistry.

PRACTICE 4   The following paragraph is the beginning of a horror story. Revise the paragraph, making it as exact and exciting as possible. Then finish the story yourself; be careful to avoid vague language.

The weather was bad, and I was all alone in this old place. I had a bad feeling and decided to leave. When I looked up, I saw someone coming after me. He was very big and had weird stuff all over him. I quickly went out the door and headed for what looked like a bridge over a river; but when I got closer, I saw it was not a bridge at all, but something else, something horrible.

_____

_____

_____

_____

_____

_____

_____

_____

_____

PART B

Concise Language: Avoiding Wordiness

Concise writing comes quickly to the point. It avoids **wordiness**—unnecessary and repetitious words that add nothing to the meaning.

Which sentence in each of the following pairs is more *concise?* That is, which does *not* contain unnecessary words?

1. Because of the fact that the watch was inexpensive in price, he bought it.

2. Because the watch was inexpensive, he bought it.

3. In my opinion I think that the financial aid system at Ellensville Junior College is in need of reform.

4. The financial aid system at Ellensville Junior College needs reform.

5. On October 10, in the fall of 1995, we learned the true facts about the robbery.

6. On October 10, 1995, we learned the facts about the robbery.

■ Sentences 2, 4, and 6 are *concise* whereas sentences 1, 3, and 5 are *wordy*.

■ In sentence 1, *because of the fact that* is really a *wordy* way of saying *because. In price* simply repeats information already given by the word *inexpensive*.

■ The writer of sentence 3 undercuts the point with the wordy apology of *in my opinion I think*. As a general rule, leave out such qualifiers and simply state the opinion; but if you do use them, use either *in my opinion* or *I think*, not both! Sentence 4 replaces *is in need of* with one direct verb, *needs*.

■ *In the fall of* in sentence 5 is *redundant*; it repeats information already given by what word?

_____

■ Why is the word *true* also eliminated in sentence 6?

_____

Concise writing avoids wordiness, unnecessary repetition, and padding. Of course, conciseness *does not mean* writing short, bare sentences, but simply cutting out all deadwood and never using fifteen words when ten will do.

PRACTICE 5   The following sentences are *wordy*. Make them more *concise* by crossing out or replacing unnecessary words or by combining two sentences into one concise sentence. Rewrite each new sentence on the lines beneath, capitalizing and punctuating correctly.

Examples   The U.S. Census uncovers many interesting facts that have a lot of truth to them.

The U.S. Census uncovers many interesting facts.

_____

In the year 1810, Philadelphia was called the cigar capital of the United States. The reason why was because the census reported that the city produced 16 million cigars each year.

In 1810, Philadelphia was called the cigar capital of the United States because the

census reported that the city produced 16 million cigars each year.

1. The Constitution requires and says that the federal government of the United States must take a national census every ten years.

_____

_____

2. At first, the original function of the census was to ensure fair taxation and representation.

_____

_____

3. Since the first count in 1790, the census has become controversial. There are at least two main reasons why it has become controversial.

_____

_____

4. One reason why is because there are always some people who aren't included.

_____

_____

5. In the 1990 census, for example, many homeless people with no place to live were not counted.

_____

_____

6. Another reason is due to the fact that many people think the census is too personal.

_____

_____

7. Many citizens were angry in 1800 when the census first began asking women the question of what their age was.

_____

_____

8. People were also offended when they were asked to tell the answer to another question. The question was whether they had indoor or outdoor toilets.

   _____

   _____

9. In my opinion, I think that even in this day and age of today certain information should be private.

   _____

   _____

10. Despite controversy, the U.S. census still continues to serve beneficial functions that are for the good of our country.

    _____

    _____

PRACTICE 6 Rewrite this essay *concisely*, cutting out all unnecessary words. Reword or combine sentences if you wish, but do not alter the meaning.

Dr. Alice Hamilton, Medical Pioneer

At the age of forty years old, Dr. Alice Hamilton became a pioneer in the field of industrial medicine. In 1910, the governor of Illinois appointed her to investigate rumors that people who were doing the work in Chicago's paint factories were dying from lead poisoning. The result of her investigation was the first state law that was passed to protect workers.

The following year, the U.S. Department of Labor hired this woman, Dr. Hamilton, to study industrial illness throughout the country of the United States. In the next decade, she researched and studied many occupational diseases, including tuberculosis among quarry workers and silicosis—clogged lungs—among sandblasters. To gather information, Dr. Hamilton went to the workplace—deep in mines, quarries, and underwater tunnels. She also spoke to the workers in their homes where they lived.

With great zeal, Dr. Hamilton spread her message about poor health conditions on the job. What happened with her reports is that they led to

new safety regulations, workmen's compensation insurance, and improved
working conditions in many industries. She wrote many popular articles and
spoke to groups of interested citizens. In the year of 1919, she became the
first woman to hold courses and teach at Harvard University. Her textbook
which she wrote, *Industrial Poisons in the U.S.*, became the standard book
on the subject. By the time she died in 1970—she was 101—she had done
much to improve the plight of many working people. The reason why she is
remembered today is because she cared at a time when many others seemed
not to care at all.

PART C

Fresh Language: Avoiding Triteness

Fresh writing uses original and lively words. It avoids **clichés,** those tired
and trite expressions that have lost their power from overuse.
    Which sentence in each pair that follows contains fewer expressions that
you have heard or read many times before?

> 1. Some people can relate to the hustle and bustle of city life.
>
> 2. Some people thrive on the energy and motion of city life.
>
> 3. This book is worth its weight in gold to the car owner.
>
> 4. This book can save the car owner hundreds of dollars a year in
>   repairs.

■ You probably found that sentences 2 and 4 contained fresher language.
What words and phrases in sentences 1 and 3 have you heard or seen before, in conversation, on TV, or in magazines and newspapers? List them:

_____

_____

    Clichés and trite expressions like the following have become so familiar
that they have almost no impact on the reader. Avoid them. Say what you
mean in your own words:

Cliché: She is pretty as a picture.

Fresh: Her amber eyes and wild red hair are striking.

Or occasionally, play with a cliché and turn it into fresh language:

Cliché: . . . as American as apple pie.

Fresh: . . . as American as a Big Mac.

Cliché: The grass is always greener on the other side of the fence.

Fresh: "The grass is always greener over the septic tank."
            —Erma Bombeck

The following is a partial list of trite expressions to avoid. Add to it any others that you overuse in your writing.

Trite Expressions

at a loss for words	last but not least
at this point in time	like there's no tomorrow
better late than never	living hand to mouth
cold cruel world	one in a million
cool, hot	out of this world
cry your eyes out	red as a rose
easier said than done	sad but true
free as a bird	tried and true
green with envy	under the weather
I can relate to that	where he/she is coming from
in this day and age	work like a dog

PRACTICE 7   Cross out clichés and trite expressions in the following sentences and replace them with fresh and exact language of your own.

1. In 1929, toy dealer Edwin S. Lowe came across people having more fun than a barrel of monkeys while playing a game at a carnival in rural Georgia.

2. A leader called out each and every number, and the players used beans to cover the matching numbers on their cards.

3. The winners yelled "Beano!" at the top of their lungs when they had filled in a row of numbers.

4. According to the carnival owner, a stranger had brought the game from Europe, so it went without saying that no one owned the game.

5. Quick as a wink, Lowe saw the game was a winner.

6. As soon as he returned home, the businessman, who was as sharp as a tack, began testing beano out on friends.

7. One night, instead of "Beano!" a guest who was beside himself with excitement shouted out, "Bingo!"

8. Lowe went on to market the game as Bingo, and it sold like crazy.

9. Soon many nonprofit organizations were holding bingo tournaments as a tried and true method of raising funds.

10. Because Lowe had produced only twenty-four different cards, too many people were cleaning up.

11. Therefore, Lowe paid a mathematics professor an awesome amount to develop six thousand cards, each with a different combination of numbers.

12. By 1934, hundreds of thousands of Americans were playing bingo like there was no tomorrow.

PART D

Figurative Language: Similes and Metaphors

One way to add sparkle and exactness to your writing is to use an occasional simile or metaphor. A **simile** is a comparison of two things using the word *like* or *as*:

"He was *as ugly as* a wart."   —Anne Sexton

"The frozen twigs of the huge tulip poplar next to the hill clack in the cold *like* tinsnips."   —Annie Dillard

A **metaphor** is a similar comparison without the word *like* or *as:*

> "My soul is a dark forest." —D. H. Lawrence
>
> Love is a virus.

■ The power of similes and metaphors comes partly from the surprise of comparing two apparently unlike things. A well-chosen simile or metaphor can convey a lot of information in very few words.

■ To compare a person to a wart, as Sexton does, lets us know quickly just how ugly that person is. And to say that *twigs clack like tinsnips* describes the sound so precisely that we can almost hear it.

■ What do you think D. H. Lawrence means by his metaphor? In what ways is a person's soul like a *dark forest?*

_____

_____

■ The statement *love is a virus* tells us something about the writer's attitude toward love. What is it? In what ways is love like a virus?

_____

_____

_____

Similes and metaphors should not be overused; however, once in a while, they can be a delightful addition to a paper that is also exact, concise, and fresh.

PRACTICE 8 The author of the following paragraph contrasts a fat priest and his thin parishioners. He uses at least one simile and two metaphors in his description. Underline the simile and circle the metaphors.

He was a large, juicy man, soft and sappy as a melon, and this sweet roundness made him appear spoiled and self-indulgent, especially when contrasted with the small, spare, sticklike peons* who comprised his parish. . . . Everything about them, the peons, was withered and bone-dry. Everything about him was full and fleshy and wet. They were mummies. He was a whale, beached upon the desert sands, draped in black to mourn his predicament.

—Bill Porterfield, *Texas Rhapsody*

* Peons: farm workers or laborers of Latin America.

PRACTICE 9   Think of several similes to complete each sentence that follows. Be creative! Then underline your favorite simile, the one that best completes each sentence.

Example | My English class is like an orchestra.
                                     the Everglades.
                                     an action movie.
                                     a vegetable garden.

1. Job hunting is like _____   2. Writing well is like _____

   _____   _____

   _____   _____

   _____   _____

3. My room looks like _____   4. Marriage is like _____

   _____   _____

   _____   _____

   _____   _____

PRACTICE 10   Think of several metaphors to complete each sentence that follows. Jot down three or four ideas, and then underline the metaphor that best completes each sentence.

Example | Love is a blood transfusion.
                    a sunrise.
                    a magic mirror.
                    a roller coaster ride.

1. Television is _____   2. My car is _____

   _____   _____

   _____   _____

   _____   _____

3. Registration is _____   4. Courage is _____

   _____   _____

   _____   _____

   _____   _____

Writing Assignments

1. Good writing can be done on almost any subject if the writer approaches the subject with openness and with "new eyes." Take a piece of fruit or a vegetable—a lemon, a green pepper, a cherry tomato. Examine it as if for the first time. Feel its texture and parts, smell it, weigh it in your palm.

Now capture your experience of the fruit or vegetable in words. First jot down words and ideas, or freewrite, aiming for the most *exact* description possible. Don't settle for the first words you think of. Keep writing. Then go back over what you have written, underlining the most exact and powerful writing. Compose a topic sentence and draft a paragraph that conveys your unique experience of the fruit or vegetable.

2. In the paragraph that follows, Annie Dillard describes a "small" event in such rich, exact detail that it becomes amazing and intriguing to the reader as well. Read her paragraph, underlining language that strikes you as especially *exact and fresh.* Can you spot the two **similes?** Notice her forceful and varied verbs.

One night a moth flew into the candle, was caught, burnt dry, and held. I must have been staring at the candle, or maybe I looked up when a shadow crossed my page; at any rate, I saw it all. A golden female moth, a biggish one with a two-inch wingspan, flapped into the fire, dropped her abdomen into the wet wax, stuck, flamed, frazzled and fried in a second. Her moving wings ignited like tissue paper, enlarging the circle of light in the clearing and creating out of the darkness the sudden blue sleeves of my sweater, the green leaves of jewelweed by my side, the ragged red trunk of a pine. At once the light contracted again and the moth's wings vanished in a fine, foul smoke. At the same time her six legs clawed, curled, blackened, and ceased, disappearing utterly. And her head jerked in spasms, making a spattering of noise; her antennae crisped and burned away and her heaving mouth parts crackled like pistol fire. When it was all over, her head was, so far as I could determine, gone, gone the long way of her wings and legs. Had she been new, or old? Had she mated and laid her eggs, had she done her work? All that was left was the glowing horn shell of her abdomen and thorax—a fraying, partially collapsed gold tube jammed upright in the candle's round pool.

—Annie Dillard, *Holy the Firm*

Write a paragraph in which you also describe a brief but interesting event that caught your attention. As you freewrite or brainstorm, try to capture the most precise and minute details of what happened. Revise the paragraph, making the language as *exact, concise,* and *fresh* as you can.

3. The photo above shows a painting by the artist Magritte. Look closely at the figure Magritte has created, noting the birdcage where the chest should be, the positions of the two birds, and other details. Then write a two-paragraph composition discussing this painting. First, describe the painting very exactly, pointing out important details. Then discuss what you think Magritte is trying to say by creating such a figure.

As you revise, make your writing as exact, concise, and fresh as possible so that a reader who has not seen Magritte's painting can visualize and experience it as you have.

16

Putting Your Revision Skills to Work

In Unit 2 of this book, you learned to **revise** basic paragraphs—to rethink and rewrite them with such questions as the following in mind:

Can a reader understand and follow my ideas?

Is my topic sentence clear?

Have I fully supported my topic sentence with details and facts?

Does my paragraph have unity? That is, does every sentence relate to the main idea?

Does my paragraph have coherence? That is, does it follow a logical order and guide the reader from point to point?

Of course, the more writing techniques you learn, the more options you have as you revise. Unit 4 has moved beyond the basics to matters of style: consistency and parallelism, sentence variety, and clear, exact language. This chapter will guide you again through the revision process, adding questions like the following to your list:

Are my verb tenses and pronouns consistent?

Have I used parallel structure to highlight parallel ideas?

Have I varied the length and type of my sentences?

Is my language exact, concise, and fresh?

Many writers first revise and rewrite with questions like these in mind. They do *not* worry about grammar and minor errors at this stage. Then in a separate, final process, they proofread* for spelling and grammatical errors.

Here are two sample paragraphs by students, showing the first draft, the revisions made by the student, and the revised draft of each. Each revision has been numbered and explained to give you a clear idea of the thinking process involved.

---

* For practice proofreading for particular errors, see individual chapters in Unit 6.

Writing Sample 1

First Draft

I like to give my best performance. I must relax completely before a show. I often know ahead of time what choreography I will use and what I'll sing, so I can concentrate on relaxing completely. I usually do this by reading, etc. I always know my parts perfectly. Occasionally I look through the curtain to watch the people come in. This can make you feel faint, but I reassure myself and say I know everything will be okay.

Revisions

① In order

~~I like~~ to give my best performance, I must relax completely before a

② and vocals   Add 6 here

show. I often know ahead of time what choreography I will use, and ~~what~~

③ during that long, last hour before curtain,   ④

~~I'll sing;~~ so I can concentrate on relaxing ~~completely.~~ I usually do this by

⑤ an action-packed mystery, but sometimes I joke with the
other performers or just walk around backstage.

reading, ~~etc.~~ ⟨I always know my parts perfectly,⟩ Occasionally I ~~look~~

⑦ peek

⑥   audience file   ⑧ me

through the curtain to watch the ~~people come~~ in. This can make ~~you~~ feel

⑨ "Vickie," I say, "the minute you're out there
singing to the people, everything will be okay."

faint, but I reassure myself ~~and say I know everything will be okay.~~

Reasons for Revisions

1. Combine two short sentences. (sentence variety)

2. Make *choreography* and *vocals* parallel and omit unnecessary words. (parallelism)

3. Make time order clear: First discuss what I've done during the days before the performance, and then discuss the hour before performance. (time order)

4. Drop *completely,* which repeats the word used in the first sentence. (avoid wordiness)

5. This is important! Drop *etc.,* add more details, and give examples. (add examples)

6. This idea belongs earlier in the paragraph—with what I've done during the days before the performance. (order)

7. Use more specific and interesting language in this sentence. (exact language)

8. Use the first person singular pronouns *I* and *me* consistently throughout the paragraph. (consistent person)

9. Dull—use a direct quotation, the actual words I say to myself. (exact language, sentence variety)

Revised Draft

In order to give my best performance, I must relax completely before a show. I often know ahead of time what choreography and vocals I will use, and I always know my parts perfectly, so during that long, last hour before curtain, I can concentrate on relaxing. I usually do this by reading an action-packed mystery, but sometimes I joke with the other performers or just walk around backstage. Occasionally I peek through the curtain to watch the audience file in. This can make me feel faint, but I reassure myself. "Vickie," I say, "the minute you're out there singing to the people, everything will be okay."

—Victoria DeWindt (Student)

Writing Sample 2

First Draft

My grandparents' house contained whole rooms that my parents' house did not (pantry, a parlor, a den where Grandpa kept his loot). The furniture and things always fascinated me. Best of all was the lake behind the house. Grandpa said that Evergreen Lake had grown old just like Grandma and him, that the game fish are gone and only a few bluegills remained. But one day he let me fish. No one thought I'd catch anything, but I caught a foot-long goldfish! Grandpa said it was a goddam carp, but it was a goldfish to me and I nearly fainted with ecstasy.

Revisions

① Visiting my grandparents at Evergreen Lake was always an exotic adventure.
② Their cavernous ③
~~My grandparents'~~ house contained whole rooms that my parents' house

④ —a pantry,   with a big black grand piano, and   ⑤ The rooms
did not ~~(pantry, a parlor,~~ a den where Grandpa kept his loot). ~~The furniture~~

were furnished with musty deer heads, hand-painted candlesticks, and velvet drapes.
~~and things always fascinated me.~~ Best of all was the lake behind the house.

Grandpa said that Evergreen Lake had grown old just like Grandma and

⑥ were
him, that the game fish ~~are~~ gone and only a few bluegills remained. ~~But one~~

⑦ Add new section below*
~~day he let me fish. No one thought I'd catch anything, but I caught a foot-~~

B
~~long goldfish. Grandpa said it was a goddam carp,~~ but it was a goldfish to me,

⑧
and I nearly fainted with ecstasy.

> *Add: But one day he rigged up a pole for me and tossed my line into the water. I sat motionless for several hours, waiting for a miracle. Suddenly I felt a tug on my line. I screeched and yanked upward. By the time Grandpa arrived on the dock, there on the surface lazily moving its fins was the biggest goldfish I had ever seen, nearly a foot long! Grandpa reached down with the net and scooped the huge orange fish out of the water. "Bring down the pail," he shouted. "It's a goddam carp."

Reasons for Revisions

1. No topic sentence; add one. (topic sentence)

2. Now *grandparents* repeats the first sentence; use *their.* (pronoun substitution)

3. Add a good descriptive word to give the feeling of the house. (exact language)

4. Expand this; add more details. (details, exact language)

5. More details and examples needed for support! Try to capture the "exotic" feeling of the house. (details, exact language)

6. Verb shifts to present tense; use past tense consistently. (consistent tense)

7. This section is weak. Tell the story of the goldfish; try to create the sense of adventure this had for me as a kid. Quote Grandpa? (details, exact language, direct quotation)

8. Revised paragraph is getting long. Consider breaking into two paragraphs, one on the house and one on the lake.

Revised Draft

Visiting my grandparents at Evergreen Lake was always an exotic adventure. Their cavernous house contained whole rooms that my parents' house did not—a pantry, a parlor with a big black grand piano, and a den where Grandpa kept his loot. The rooms were furnished with musty deer heads, hand-painted candlesticks, and velvet drapes.

Best of all was the lake behind the house. Grandpa said that Evergreen Lake had grown old just like Grandma and him, that the game fish were gone and only a few bluegills remained. But one day he rigged up a pole for me and tossed my line into the water. I sat motionless for several hours, waiting for a miracle. Suddenly I felt a tug on my line. I screeched and yanked upward. By the time Grandpa arrived on the dock, there on the surface lazily moving its fins was the biggest goldfish I had ever seen, nearly a foot long! Grandpa reached down with the net and scooped the huge orange fish out of the water. "Bring down the pail," he shouted. "It's a goddam carp." But it was a goldfish to me, and I nearly fainted with ecstasy.

PRACTICE   Because revising, like writing, is a personal process, the best practice is to revise your own paragraphs and essays. Nevertheless, we include below a first draft that needs revision.

Revise this essay *as if you had written it.* Use and build on the good parts, but rewrite unclear or awkward sentences, drop unnecessary words, add details, perhaps reorder parts. Especially, ask yourself these questions: Are my verb tenses and pronouns consistent? Have I used parallel structure? Have I varied the length and type of my sentences? Is my language exact, concise, and fresh? Then write the revised draft on the lines below.

Breaking the Yo-Yo Syndrome

For years, I was a yo-yo dieter. I bounced from fad diets to eating binges when I ate a lot. This leaves you tired and with depression. Along the way, though, I have learned a few things. As a result, I personally will never go on a weight-loss diet again for the rest of my life.

I have learned that all weight-loss diets are short-term. I lose about ten pounds. I wind up gaining more weight than I originally lost. I get sick and tired of the restricted diet. On one diet, I ate six grapefruits and ten hard-boiled eggs a day. After two weeks, I never want to see another grapefruit or egg again. I also ended up craving all the foods I am not supposed to eat. Nutritionists say that the craving occurs because of the reason that weight-loss diets are nutritionally unbalanced. The body needs fat, and if the dieter takes in too little fat, you are constantly hungry. Moreover, in the short term, all one loses is water; you cannot lose body fat—the real factor in weight loss—unless you reduce regularly and at a steady rate over a long period of time.

The main reason why I will not diet again is because diets are unhealthy even in the short term. For instance, many low-carbohydrate diets have appeared over the years. Some are high in fat, and accumulating fat through meat, eggs, and the eating of cheese can raise blood levels of cholesterol and led to artery and heart disease. Other diets are too high in protein and can cause kidney ailments, and other things can go wrong with your body too. Most diets also leave you deficient in essential vitamins and minerals that are necessary to health, such as calcium and iron.

In place of weight-loss dieting, I now follow a long-range plan. It is sensible, exciting, and improved my health. I eat three well-balanced meals, exercise daily, and meeting regularly with my support group for weight control. I am much happier and don't weigh as much.

_____

_____

_____

_____

_____

_____

_____

_____

_____

_____

_____

_____

_____

_____

_____

_____

_____

_____

_____

Unit 5

Writing the Essay

17

The Process of Writing an Essay

Although writing effective paragraphs will help you complete short-answer exams and do brief writing assignments, much of the time—in college and in the business world—you will be required to write essays and reports several paragraphs long. Essays are longer and contain more ideas than the single paragraphs you have practiced so far, but they require many of the same skills that paragraphs do.

This chapter will help you apply the skills of paragraph writing to the writing of short essays. It will guide you from a look at the essay and its parts through the planning and writing of essays.

PART A

Looking at the Essay

The **essay** is a group of paragraphs about one subject. In many ways, an essay is like a paragraph in extended, fuller form. Just as the paragraph has a topic sentence, body, and conclusion, so too the essay has an introduction, body, and conclusion.

The **introduction*** begins the essay and prepares the reader for what will follow. The introduction contains the **thesis statement,** which sets forth the main idea of the entire essay.

The **body** of the essay, like the body of a paragraph, is the longest part. Every paragraph in the body of the essay must support and explain the thesis statement.

* For more work on introductions, see Chapter 19, "The Introduction, the Conclusion, and the Title."

The **conclusion*** signals the end of the essay and leaves the reader with a final thought.

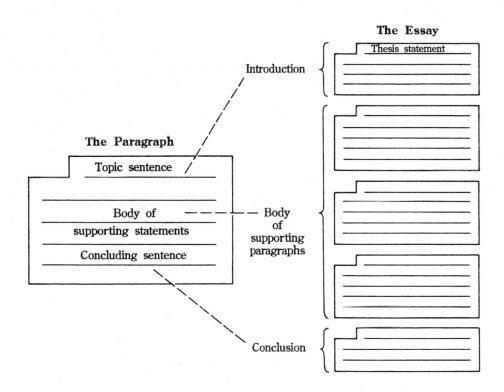

Here is a student essay:

Making a Difference

The Community Service Office at Westlake College offers placement opportunities for students who wish to do volunteer work. For a number of reasons, students who have the time should consider volunteering to help out their neighbors in the community.

Most important, volunteers can do much to improve the quality of life in Westlake. A sophomore named Annie Blakely, for instance, volunteered with a crew of other students to spruce up the neglected Stevenson Park. Because budget cuts had reduced the number of caretakers, some of its gardens had become overgrown. Supervised by the Parks Department, the crew cleared weeds, trimmed bushes, and planted several colorful flowerbeds. They also painted the park benches a bright red, a welcome change from their former drab and faded gray. For six Saturday afternoons, Annie and the other volunteers worked their magic. Thanks to them, the park is certainly prettier and more inviting than it had been.

* For more work on conclusions, see Chapter 19, "The Introduction, the Conclusion, and the Title."

While helping out, volunteers can also develop a deeper understanding and appreciation of others. Last year, another student, Bob Hairston, worked for a few hours each week at the Westlake Home for the Aged. He began with many preconceptions about the elderly; however, his work with them convinced him how wrong he had been. For example, he assumed that the residents, because they lived in the home, had lost contact with the rest of the world. While playing chess or chatting with them, he realized that they avidly watched the news on TV, read newspapers, and were well informed about local, national, and world affairs. Also a surprise to Bob, their opinions were often similar to his own. These seventy-year-olds were not as "old-fashioned" as he had thought. Bob Hairston, the person, owes his respect for the elderly and his open-mindedness to Bob Hairston, the volunteer.

Finally, volunteers can often learn new skills. Margo Rosa, a whiz in mathematics, volunteered to tutor Sandy Lewin, a junior high school student struggling with her math homework. Aspiring to become a teacher, Margo hoped this assignment would give her a head start on her future career. At first, she had trouble understanding why Sandy found fractions so confusing or decimals so difficult. Soon, however, Margo saw where and why Sandy got stuck and thought of creative ways to help. She also increased her patience, a necessary trait for any good teacher. By the end of the semester, when Sandy's grades had improved, Margo was certain that she would become a first-rate teacher.

Community service not only benefits the community but also rewards the volunteer. Signing up can make a big difference in many lives.

- The last sentence in the introduction (the first paragraph) of this essay is the *thesis statement*. Just as the topic sentence sets forth the main idea of a paragraph, so the thesis statement sets forth the main idea of the entire essay. This means that the thesis statement *must be general enough to include every topic sentence in the body:*

1. INTRODUCTION and
   Thesis statement: For a number of reasons, students who have the time should consider volunteering to help out their neighbors in the community.

2. Topic sentence: Most important, volunteers can do much to improve the quality of life in Westlake.

3. Topic sentence: While helping out, volunteers can also develop a deeper understanding and appreciation of others.

4. Topic sentence: Finally, volunteers can often learn new skills.

5. CONCLUSION

■ Note that *every topic sentence supports the thesis statement.* Every paragraph in the body discusses one *reason* for students to consider volunteering. Each paragraph also provides an *example* to back up that reason.

PRACTICE 1   Read this student essay carefully and then answer the questions.

Bottle Watching

(1) Every time I see a beer bottle, I feel grateful. This reaction has nothing to do with beer. The sight reminds me of the year I spent inspecting bottles at a brewery. That was the most boring and painful job I've ever had, but it motivated me to change my life.

(2) My job consisted of sitting on a stool and watching empty bottles pass by. A glaring light behind the conveyor belt helped me to spot cracked bottles or bottles with something extra—a dead grasshopper, for example, or a mouse foot. I was supposed to grab such bottles with my hooked cane and break them before they went into the washer. For eight or nine hours a day that was all I did. I got dizzy and sore in the eyes. I longed to fall asleep. I prayed that the conveyor would break down so the bottles would stop.

(3) After a while, to put some excitement into the job, I began inventing little games. I would count the number of minutes that passed before a broken bottle would come by, and I would compete against my own past record. Or I would see how many broken bottles I could spot in one minute. Once, I organized a contest for all the bottle watchers with a prize for the best dead insect or animal found in a bottle—anything to break the monotony of the job.

(4) After six months at the brewery, I began to think hard about my goals for the future. Did I want to spend the rest of my life looking in beer bottles? I realized that I wanted a job I could believe in. I wanted to use my mind for better things than planning contests for bleary-eyed bottle watchers. I knew I had to hand in my hook and go back to school.

(5) Today I feel grateful to that terrible job because it motivated me to attend college.

—Pat Barnum (Student)

1. Underline the **thesis statement** in the essay above.

2. What is the topic sentence of paragraph 2? _____

_____

What is the topic sentence of paragraph 3? _____

_____

What is the topic of paragraph 4? _____

_____

3. Does every paragraph in the body support the thesis statement?

_____

4. Does the thesis statement include the main idea of every paragraph in

the body? _____

Writing the Thesis Statement

The steps in the essay-writing process are the same as those in the paragraph-writing process: **narrow the topic, write the thesis statement, develop ideas for the body,** and **organize them.** However, in essay writing, planning on paper and prewriting are especially important because an essay is longer than a paragraph and more difficult to organize.

Narrowing the Topic

The essay writer usually starts with a broad subject and then narrows it to a manageable size. An essay is longer than a paragraph and gives the writer more room to develop ideas; nevertheless, the best essays, like the best paragraphs, are often quite specific. For example, if you are assigned a three-hundred-word essay entitled "A Trip I Won't Forget," a description of your recent trip to Florida would be too broad a subject. You would need to *narrow* the topic to just one aspect of the trip. Many writers list possible narrowed subjects on paper:

1. huge job of packing was more tiring than the trip

2. how to pack for a trip with the children without exhausting yourself

3. Disney World, more fun for adults than for children

4. our afternoon of deep-sea fishing: highlight of the trip

5. terrible weather upset many of my sightseeing plans

Any one of these topics is narrow enough and specific enough to be the subject of a short essay. If you had written this list, you would now consider each narrowed topic and perhaps freewrite or brainstorm possible ways to support it. Keeping your audience and purpose in mind may also help you narrow your topic. Your audience here might be a friend or more likely your instructor and classmates; your purpose might be to inform (by giving tips about packing) or to entertain (by narrating a funny or a dramatic incident). Having considered your topic, audience, and purpose, you would then choose the topic that you could best develop into a good essay.

If you have difficulty with this step, reread Chapter 2, "Gathering Ideas."

Writing the Thesis Statement

The thesis statement—like the topic sentence in a paragraph—further focuses the subject because it must clearly state, in sentence form, the writer's **central point**: the main idea or opinion that the rest of the essay will support and discuss.

The thesis statement should be as **specific** as possible. By writing a specific thesis statement, you focus on your subject and give yourself and your reader a clearer idea of what will follow in the body of the essay.

There are many ways to make a vague thesis statement more specific. As a general rule, replace vague words with more exact words* and replace vague ideas with more complete information:

Vague thesis statement:	My recent trip to Florida was really bad.
Revised thesis statement:	My recent trip to Florida was disappointing because the weather upset my sightseeing plans.

- The first thesis statement above is vague because of the inexact words *really bad*. This thesis statement gives no indication of why the trip was bad or just what the rest of the essay will discuss.

- The second thesis statement is more specific. The words *really bad* are replaced by the more exact word *disappointing*. In addition, the writer has added more complete information about why the trip was disappointing. From this thesis statement, it is clear that the essay will discuss the ways in which the weather upset the writer's plans.

It is sometimes possible to make a thesis statement more specific by stating the natural divisions of the subject. Done thoughtfully, this approach can set up an outline for the entire essay:

Vague thesis statement:	The movie *Southern Smoke* seemed phony.
Revised thesis statement:	The costumes, the dialogue, and the plot of the movie *Southern Smoke* all seemed phony.

* For more practice in choosing exact language, see Chapter 15, "Revising for Language Awareness," Part A.

- The first thesis statement above gives little specific direction to the writer or the reader.

- The second thesis statement, however, actually sets up a plan for the whole essay. The writer has divided the subject into three parts—the costumes, the dialogue, and the plot—and he or she will probably devote one paragraph to discussing the "phoniness" of each one. This writer probably first "thought on paper" to get ideas.

PRACTICE 2   Revise each vague thesis statement, making it more specific. Remember, a specific thesis statement should give the reader a clear idea of what the essay will discuss.

Example | Watching TV has its good points.

Watching news and public affairs programs on TV can make one a more informed

and responsible citizen.

1. The library at this college is bad.

     _____

     _____

2. Some workers should not be allowed to strike.

     _____

     _____

3. There are many nice people in my family.

     _____

     _____

4. Marriage is a good idea.

     _____

     _____

5. I work at a great place.

     _____

     _____

6. Professors should teach better.

     _____

     _____

7. You can learn a lot by observing children.

_____

_____

8. Sketching caricatures is a great hobby.

_____

_____

PRACTICE 3   Eight possible topics for short essays follow. Pick three that interest you and **narrow** the topic to just one aspect that you would like to write about. Then, keeping in mind your audience and purpose, compose a specific thesis statement for each of the three essays.

a time you surprised yourself	why sports fans get violent
ways to start (or stop) an argument	something that angers you at work
unusual relatives	handling disappointment
a neighborhood problem	falling in (or out) of love

1. Subject: _____

   Thesis statement: _____

   _____

   _____

2. Subject: _____

   Thesis statement: _____

   _____

   _____

3. Subject: _____

   Thesis statement: _____

   _____

   _____

PART C

Generating Ideas for the Body

The thesis statement sets forth the main idea of the entire essay, but it is the **body** of the essay that must fully support and discuss that thesis statement. In composing the thesis statement, the writer should already have given some thought to what the body will contain. Now he or she should make a **plan** or an **outline** that includes the following:

1. Two to four main ideas to support the thesis statement

2. Two to four topic sentences stating these ideas

3. A plan for each paragraph in the body (developed in any of the ways explained earlier in this book)

4. A logical order in which to present these paragraphs

Different writers create such plans in different ways. Some writers brainstorm or freewrite ideas and then find paragraph groups. Others first write topic sentences and then plan paragraphs.

1. Brainstorm ideas and then find paragraph groups. Having written the thesis statement, some writers brainstorm—they jot down any ideas that develop the thesis statement, including main ideas, specific details, and examples, all jumbled together. Only after creating a long list do they go back over it, drop any ideas that do not support the thesis statement, and then look for "paragraph groups."

Suppose, for instance, that you have written this thesis statement: *Although people often react to stress in harmful ways, there are many positive ways to handle stress.* By brainstorming and then dropping ideas that do not relate, you would eventually produce a list like this:

work out

dig weeds or rake leaves

call a friend

talking out problems relieves stress

jogging

many sports ease tension

go to the beach

take a walk

taking breaks, long or short, relieves stress

talk to a shrink if the problem is really bad

escape into a hobby—photography, bird watching

go to a movie

talk to a counselor at the college

talk to a minister, priest, rabbi, etc.

many people harm themselves trying to relieve stress

they overeat or smoke

drinking too much, other addictions

do vigorous household chores—scrub a floor, beat the rugs, pound pillows

doing something physical relieves stress

some diseases are caused by stress

take a nap

some people blow up to help tension, but this hurts their relationships

Now read over the list, looking for groups of ideas that could become paragraphs. Some ideas might become topic sentences; others might be used to support a topic sentence. How many possible paragraphs can you find in this list?

PRACTICE 4   From the list, make a **plan** or an **outline** for an essay that supports the thesis statement *Although people often react to stress in harmful ways, there are many positive ways to handle stress.*

Plan four paragraphs for the body of the essay. Find four paragraph groups in the list and determine the main idea of each paragraph; then write a topic sentence stating this main idea.

Now arrange the topic sentences in an order that makes sense. Under each topic sentence, list supporting examples or details.

1. INTRODUCTION and
    Thesis statement: Although people often react to stress in
                                         harmful ways, there are many positive ways
                                         to handle stress.

2. Topic sentence: _____

   _____

   (examples) _____

   _____

3. Topic sentence: _____

   _____

(examples) _____

_____

4. Topic sentence: _____

_____

(examples) _____

_____

5. Topic sentence: _____

_____

(examples) _____

_____

6. CONCLUSION: _____

_____

_____

_____

■ Does every topic sentence support the thesis statement?

■ Have you arranged the paragraphs in a logical order?

   2. Write topic sentences and then plan paragraphs. Sometimes a writer can compose topic sentences directly from the thesis statement without extensive jotting first. This is especially true if the thesis statement itself shows how the body will be divided or organized. Such a thesis statement makes the work of planning paragraphs easy because the writer has already broken down the subject into supporting ideas or parts:

Thesis statement:	Because of the student cafeteria's many problems, the college should hire a new administrator to see that it is properly managed in the future.

■ This thesis statement contains two main ideas: (1) that the cafeteria has many problems and (2) that a new administrator should be hired. The first idea states the problem and the second offers a solution.

From this thesis statement, a writer could logically plan a two-paragraph body, with one paragraph explaining each idea in detail. He or she might compose two topic sentences as follows:

Thesis statement:	Because of the student cafeteria's many problems, the college should hire a new administrator to see that it is properly managed in the future.
Topic sentence:	Foremost among the cafeteria's problems are the unappetizing food, the slow service, and the high prices.
Topic sentence:	A new administrator could do much to improve these terrible conditions.

These topic sentences might need to be revised later, but they will serve as guides while the writer further develops each paragraph.

The writer might develop the first paragraph in the body by giving **examples**[*] of the unappetizing foods, the slow service, and the high prices.

He or she could develop the second paragraph through **process,**[†] by describing the **steps** that the new administrator could take to solve the cafeteria's problems. The completed essay **plan** might look like this:

1. INTRODUCTION and
   Thesis statement: Because of the student cafeteria's many problems, the college should hire a new administrator to see that it is properly managed in the future.

2. Topic sentence: Foremost among the cafeteria's problems are the unappetizing food, the slow service, and the high prices.

   Problem 1: Food is unappetizing

   —sandwiches with tough meat, stale bread
   —salads with wilted lettuce, tasteless tomatoes
   —hot meals often either overcooked or undercooked

   Problem 2: Service is slow

   —students wait 30 minutes for sandwiches
   —students wait 15 minutes just for a cup of coffee
   —have to gulp meals to get to class on time

   Problem 3: Prices too high

   —sandwiches overpriced
   —coffee or tea costs eighty-five cents

[*] For more work on developing paragraphs with examples, see Chapter 5, "Illustration."
[†] For more work on developing paragraphs by process, see Chapter 8, "Process."

3. Topic sentence: A new administrator could do much to improve these terrible conditions.

Step 1. Set minimum quality standards

—personally oversee purchase of healthful food
—set and enforce rules about how long food can be left out
—set cooking times for hot meals

Step 2. Reorganize service lines

—study which lines are busiest at different times of the day
—shift cooks and cashiers to those lines
—create a separate beverage line

Step 3. Lower prices

—better food and faster service would attract more student customers
—cafeteria could then lower prices

4. CONCLUSION

Note that the order of paragraphs logically follows the order in the thesis statement, discussing first the problem and then the solution.

The writer now has a clear plan from which to write the first draft of the essay.

PRACTICE 5   Write from two to four topic sentences to support *three* of the thesis statements that follow. (First you may wish to brainstorm or freewrite on scratch paper.) Make sure that every topic sentence really supports the thesis statement and that every one could be developed into a good paragraph. Then arrange your topic sentences in a **plan** in the space provided.

Example   Before you buy a VCR, do these three things.

Topic sentence: Decide how much you can spend, and determine your

price range.

Topic sentence: Examine the models that are within your price range.

Topic sentence: Shop around; do not assume that all electronics stores are

created equal.

1. I vividly recall the sights, smells, and tastes of the baking table at the county fair.

   Topic sentence: _____

   _____

   Topic sentence: _____

   _____

   Topic sentence: _____

   _____

   Topic sentence: _____

   _____

2. Living alone has both advantages and disadvantages.

   Topic sentence: _____

   _____

   Topic sentence: _____

   _____

   Topic sentence: _____

   _____

   Topic sentence: _____

   _____

3. Doing well at a job interview requires careful planning.

   Topic sentence: _____

   _____

   Topic sentence: _____

   _____

   Topic sentence: _____

   _____

   Topic sentence: _____

   _____

4. _____ is a fascinating and profitable hobby.

   Topic sentence: _____

   _____

   Topic sentence: _____

   _____

   Topic sentence: _____

   _____

   Topic sentence: _____

   _____

5. My three children have individual techniques for avoiding housework.

   Topic sentence: _____

   _____

   Topic sentence: _____

   _____

   Topic sentence: _____

   _____

   Topic sentence: _____

   _____

PRACTICE 6   Choose *one* thesis statement that you wrote for Practice 3, and develop the plan for an essay of your own. Your plan should include your thesis sentence, two to four topic sentences, supporting details, examples, and so forth. Brainstorm or freewrite every time you need ideas; rewrite the thesis and topic sentences until they are sharp and clear.

PART D

Ordering and Linking Paragraphs in the Essay

An essay, like a paragraph, should have **coherence**. That is, the paragraphs in an essay should be arranged in a clear, logical order and should follow one another like links in a chain.

Ordering Paragraphs

It is important that the paragraphs in your plan, and later in your essay, follow a **logical order.** The rule for writers is this: Use your common sense and plan ahead. *Do not* leave the order of your paragraphs to chance.

The types of order often used in single paragraphs—**time order, space order,** and **order of importance***—can sometimes be used to arrange paragraphs within an essay. Essays about subjects that can be broken into stages or steps, with each step discussed in one paragraph, should be arranged according to *time. Space order* is used occasionally in descriptive essays. A writer who wishes to save the most important or convincing paragraph for last would use *order of importance.* Or he or she might wish to reverse this order and put the most important paragraph first.

Very often, however, the writer simply arranges paragraphs in whatever order makes sense in the particular essay. Suppose, for example, that you have written the thesis statement *Laura and Janet have much in common,* and you plan three paragraphs with these topic sentences:

They have the same taste in clothes.

They have similar career goals.

People tell them that they look alike.

Since taste in clothes and looks are both *physical* similarities, it would be logical to arrange these two paragraphs one after the other. Furthermore, it makes sense to begin rather than end the essay with a physical description so that the reader can visualize the two women while reading more about them. A logical order of paragraphs, then, would be the following:

1. INTRODUCTION and
   Thesis statement: Laura and Janet have much in common.
2. Topic sentence: People tell them that they look alike.
3. Topic sentence: They have the same taste in clothes.
4. Topic sentence: They have similar career goals.
5. CONCLUSION

Finally, if your thesis statement is divided into two, three, or four parts, the paragraphs in the body should follow the order in the thesis; otherwise the reader will be confused. Assume, for instance, that you are planning three paragraphs to develop the thesis statement *My first flight on a 747 was frightening, exciting, and educational.*

---

* For more work on time order, space order, and order of importance, see Chapter 4, "Achieving Coherence," Part A.

Paragraph 2 should discuss _____

Paragraph 3 should discuss _____

Paragraph 4 should discuss _____

PRACTICE 7   Plans for three essays follow, each containing a thesis statement and several topic sentences in scrambled order. Number the topic sentences in each group according to an *order that makes sense*. Be prepared to explain your choices.

1. Thesis statement: The new computer is fast, versatile, and small.

   Topic sentences: _____ The compact size of this computer sets it apart.

   _____ The computer processes information in a matter of seconds.

   _____ It can handle a useful variety of software programs.

2. Thesis statement: The history of European contact with the Karaja Indians of Brazil is one of violence and exploitation.

   Topic sentences: _____ The Karaja, exposed to European diseases during the nineteenth century, were reduced in numbers by 90 percent!

   _____ During the eighteenth century, the *bandeirantes* led attacks on Karaja villages to get slaves.

   _____ Since the turn of the twentieth century, Brazilian pioneers have increasingly used Indian territory as grazing land.

3. Thesis statement: Although "convenience" foods offer short-term ease to the modern cook, they may result in long-term health hazards.

   Topic sentences: _____ The health hazards these foods pose, when used consistently, may be serious.

   _____ By "convenience" foods, I refer to canned, frozen, and boxed dinners.

   _____ For the busy cook, convenience foods offer several advantages.

PRACTICE 8   Now, go over the essay plan that you developed in Practice 6 and decide which paragraphs should come first, which second, and so forth. Does time order, space order, or order of importance seem appropriate to your subject? Number your paragraphs accordingly.

Linking Paragraphs

Just as the sentences within a paragraph should flow smoothly, the paragraphs within an essay should be clearly **linked** one to the next. As you write your essay, do not make illogical jumps from one paragraph to another. Instead, guide your reader. Link the first sentence of each new paragraph to the thesis statement or to the paragraph before. Here are four ways to link paragraphs:

1. Repeat key words or ideas from the thesis statement.

2. Refer to words or ideas from the preceding paragraph.

3. Use transitional expressions.

4. Use transitional sentences.

    1. Repeat key words or ideas from the thesis statement.* The topic sentences in the essay plan below repeat key words from the thesis statement.

Thesis statement:	Many films show the glamour but not the pain of street life.
Topic sentence:	These films portray drugs and gangs as glamorous and exciting.
Topic sentence:	These movies do not show the pain of wasted lives.

- In the first topic sentence, the words *these films* and *glamorous* repeat, in slightly altered form, words from the thesis statement.

- What words in the second topic sentence repeat key words from the thesis statement?

_____

_____

* For more work on repetition of key words, see Chapter 4, "Achieving Coherence," Part B. See also "Synonyms and Substitutions" in the same section.

2. Refer to words or ideas from the preceding paragraph. Link the first sentence of a new paragraph to the paragraph before, especially by referring to words or ideas near the end of the paragraph. Note how one writer links two paragraphs in the following passage:

---

(1) No wonder a newborn baby cries. It is hungry, naked and—if it is an American—already owes the government $12,010.57, its approximate share of the U.S. national debt.

(2) But if that baby happens to be, like mine, the American-born child of recent immigrant parents from Asia or Africa, it has all the more reason to cry, because its parents must face the genuine problem of whether to give the child a name from their old country or their new.

—Richard Crasta, "What's in a Name?"
The Indian American

- What two phrases in paragraph 2 clearly refer to paragraph 1?

---

3. Use transitional expressions.* Transitional expressions—words like *for example, therefore,* and *later on*—are used within a paragraph to show the relationship between sentences. Transitional expressions can also be used within an essay to show the relationships between paragraphs:

---

(1) The house where I grew up was worn out and run-down. The yard was mostly mud, rock hard for nine months of the year but wet and swampy for the other three. Our nearest neighbors were 40 miles away, so it got pretty lonely. Inside, the house was shabby. The living room furniture was covered in stiff, nubby material that had lost its color over the years and become a dirty brown. Upstairs in my bedroom, the wooden floor sagged a little further west every year.

(2) *Nevertheless,* I love the place for what it taught me. There I learned to thrive in solitude. During the hours I spent alone, when school was over and the chores were done, I learned to play the guitar and sing. Wandering in the fields around the house or poking under stones in the creek bed, I grew to love the natural world. Most of all, I learned to see and to appreciate small wonders.

---

* For a complete list of transitional expressions, see Chapter 4, "Achieving Coherence," Part B. See also the chapters in Unit 3 for ways to use transitional expressions in each paragraph and essay pattern.

- The first paragraph describes some of the negative details about the writer's early home. The second paragraph *contrasts* the writer's attitude, which is positive. The transitional expression *nevertheless* eases the reader from one paragraph to the next by pointing out the exact relationship between the paragraphs.

- Transitional expressions can also highlight the *order* in which paragraphs are arranged.* Three paragraphs arranged in time order might begin: *First . . . , Next . . . , Finally . . .* Three paragraphs arranged in order of importance might begin: *First . . . , More important . . . , Most important . . .* Use transitional expressions alone or together with other linking devices.

4. Use transitional sentences. From time to time, you may need to write an entire sentence of transition to link one paragraph to the next, as shown in this passage:

> (1) With his restaurant forced to close because of a new highway, Sanders took five frozen frying-chickens, a special cooker, and some flour and spices, and attempted to interest restaurant managers in his method of high temperature cooking. Acceptance was slow. He gave franchises away; he leased cookers; he supplied at cost paper, napkins, and buckets with his picture and the Kentucky Fried Chicken name.
>
> (2) *After three years he finally made some headway.* Then the idea caught on. In eight years he had sold over 500 franchises. Receiving 5 cents for each chicken sold by these restaurants, he made over $2.3 million. In 1962, then seventy-two years of age, he expanded the business to include take-home sales. In 1964 he sold the entire business for $2 million. By 1968 sales were over $250 million and there were over 1,500 outlets. His age when all this began? Sixty-five years.
>
> —Robert F. Hartley, *Retailing: Challenge and Opportunity*

- In the first paragraph above, Sanders is a struggling businessman. In the second paragraph, he makes it big. The topic sentence of paragraph 2 is the second sentence: *Then the idea caught on.*

- The first sentence of paragraph 2 is actually a **sentence of transition** that eases the reader from failure to success. (Note that it includes a transitional expression of time, *after three years.*)

Use all four methods of linking paragraphs as you write your essays.

* For more work on transitional expressions of time, space, and importance, see Chapter 4, "Achieving Coherence," Part A.

PRACTICE 9   Read the essay that follows, noting the paragraph-to-paragraph *links*. Then answer the questions.

Banking in Computer Wonderland

(1) Although computer banking is clearly here to stay, I for one wish it were not. Now I know that a computer counts much faster than some human with a pencil and that it frees up the bank personnel to spend more time with the customers and that it gives me money on the weekends. I am a reasonable woman. These arguments should convince me.

(2) However, it is not admiration for technology I feel as I stick my plastic card into the slot and push my secret code number (my shirt size plus my shoe size with a three in between for good luck). "Hello," say the lighted green dots, brainlessly reporting the time right down to the second. "How can I assist you?" Conversing with a machine gives me the creeps. Soon, I imagine, it will be calling me "Susan" and noticing my outfit. Worse, if someone steals my plastic card, will I spend my life in prison?

(3) This fear is firmly based on past experience. "Sorry," the green dots told me recently. "I am unable to give you cash at this time. Your current balance is minus $10,303.00." Isn't that strange, I thought: the computer is making a mistake. Only later did I learn that computers never make mistakes. Therefore, I was told, I *must* have overdrawn my account by $10,303.00. It took four hours of my time and a year off my life to fix up that minor error.

(4) The bank employees are little help in situations like this. First of all, they have to spend a lot of time protecting the reputation of the computer, reminding the customers that it never makes mistakes. Second, they are allowed to tell me only what the computer tells them, and often, the computer isn't talking. I demand an explanation. I am told that the information is "in the computer" and cannot be reached for comment. "In the computer," I have learned, is much worse than "lost under the porch" or "fallen down the drain in the bathtub." There is nothing to be done. "But that's crazy," I shout and am coolly informed that it is I who am irrational.

(5) In spite of all this, I feel sorry for the bank personnel. It must be pretty depressing to be bested by a computer all day long and then yelled at besides. It is my theory that bank employees begin to feel ashamed that they are only human and that they *do* make mistakes. After a while, some of them start to pretend that they, too, are error-proof. A story will illustrate. I know a young woman whose computerized bank statement reported one day that she had $24,132.00 in her checking account, instead of $132.00. A moral person, she brought this bonanza to the attention of a bank officer. He insisted that, since the computer doesn't make mistakes, it had to be true. Perhaps she had forgotten having made the deposit. "Do you mean to tell me I could withdraw this money right now and it would all belong to me?" she asked. "Of course," he said. And that is what she did. Rather than give up his faith in computers or take the rap, he gave away $24,000.

(6) Meanwhile, my bank becomes more and more computerized. White modular hoods with digital screens swivel on the computer tops. The surveillance equipment is computerized; the doors and windows are computerized. The vault boasts a computerized lock, and along the walls gleam

computerized banking terminals. And what of the people in this computer wonderland? From one side of the bank to the other, the tellers and officers, freed up to spend more time with people, are fighting with the customers about all the computer's mistakes.

1. What transitional expressions does this writer use to link paragraphs? (Find at least three.)

   _____

   _____

2. How does the writer link paragraphs 2 and 3?

   _____

   _____

3. How does the writer link paragraphs 3 and 4?

   _____

   _____

PART E

Writing and Revising Short Essays

Writing the First Draft

Make sure you have a clear plan or outline from which to write your first draft. This plan should include your thesis statement, two to four topic sentences that support it, details and facts to develop each paragraph, and a logical order. Write on every other line to leave room for later corrections, including all your ideas and paragraphs in the order you have chosen to present them. Explain your ideas fully, but avoid getting stuck on a particular word or sentence. When you have finished the draft, set it aside, if possible, for several hours or several days.

PRACTICE 10   Write a first draft of the essay you have been working on in Practices 6 and 8.

Revising

Revising an essay involves the same principles as revising a paragraph.* Read your first draft slowly and carefully to yourself—aloud if possible. Imagine you are a reader who has never seen the paper before. As you read,

---

* For more work on revising, see Chapter 3, "The Process of Writing Paragraphs," Part F, and Chapter 16, "Putting Your Revision Skills to Work."

underline trouble spots, draw arrows, and write in the margins, if necessary, to straighten out problems.

Here are some questions to keep in mind as you revise:

1. Is my thesis statement clear?

2. Does the body of the essay fully support my thesis statement?

3. Does the essay have unity; does every paragraph relate to the thesis statement?

4. Does the essay have coherence; do the paragraphs follow a logical order?

5. Are my topic sentences clear?

6. Does each paragraph provide good details, well-chosen examples, and so on?

7. Is the language exact, concise, and fresh?

8. Are my sentences varied in length and type?

9. Does the essay conclude, not just leave off?

If possible, ask a "peer reviewer"—a trusted classmate or friend—to read your paper and give you feedback. Of course, this person should not rewrite or correct the essay but should simply tell you what parts are clear and what parts are confusing.

To guide your peer reviewer, you might ask him or her to answer these questions in writing:

1. What do you like about this piece of writing?

2. What seems to be the main point?

3. What parts could be improved (meaning unclear sentences, supporting points missing, order mixed up, writing not lively, and so forth)? Please be specific.

4. What one change would most improve this essay?

Proofreading and Writing the Final Draft

Next, carefully **proofread** the draft for grammar and spelling. Check especially for those errors you often make: verb errors, comma splices, and so forth.* If you are unsure about the spelling of a word, check a dictionary.

Finally, recopy your essay. Type or write neatly on 8½-by-11-inch paper, using one side only. When you finish, proofread the final copy.

The following sample essay by a student shows his first draft, the revisions he made, and the revised draft. Each revision has been numbered and explained to give you a clear idea of the thinking process involved.

* For practice proofreading for individual errors, see chapters in Unit 6.

First Draft

Portrait of a Bike Fanatic

(1) I first realized how serious Diane was when I joined her on a long trip one Sunday afternoon. Her bike looked new, so I asked her if it was. When she told me she had bought it three years ago, I asked her how she kept it looking so good. She showed me how she took good care of it.

(2) Diane had just about every kind of equipment I've ever seen. She put on her white crash helmet and attached a tiny rearview mirror on it—the kind the dentist uses to check out the backs of your teeth. She put a warning light on her left leg. She carried a whole bag full of tools. When I looked into it, I couldn't believe how much stuff was in there (wrenches, inner tubes, etc.)—tools to meet every emergency. I was tempted to see if it had a false bottom.

(3) I had no idea she was such a bike nut. We rode thirty miles and I was exhausted. Her equipment was something else, but useful because she had a flat and was able to fix it, saving our trip.

(4) She doesn't look like a bike fanatic, just a normal person. You'd never guess that her bike has more than 10,000 miles on it.

(5) As we rode, Diane told me about her travels throughout the Northeast (Cape Cod, Vermont, Penn., New York). Riding to work saved her money, kept her in shape. Her goal for the next summer was a cross-country tour over the Rockies!

(6) Our trip was no big deal to her but to me it was something. I might consider biking to work because it keeps you in shape. But basically I'm lazy. I drive a car or take the bus. I do like to walk though.

Revisions

Portrait of a Bike Fanatic

① Add intro and thesis   ② about bicycling

I first realized how serious Diane was when I

③ thirty-mile

joined her on a ~~long~~ trip one Sunday afternoon. Her

bike looked new, so I asked her if it was. When she

told me she had bought it three years ago, I asked

④ Describe in detail

her how she kept it looking so good. ~~She showed me~~

~~how she took good care of it.~~

Diane had just about every kind of equipment

⑤ For example,

I've ever seen. She put on her white crash helmet and

attached a tiny rearview mirror on it—the kind the

⑥ examine

dentist uses to ~~check out~~ the backs of your teeth. She

⑦ strapped   to   , just below the knee

put a warning light ~~on~~ her leg.

⑧ Mention trip
location

> She carried a whole bag full of tools. When I looked into it, I couldn't believe how much stuff was in there (wrenches, inner tubes, etc.)—tools to meet every emergency. I was tempted to see if it had a false bottom.

⑨ New ¶ on tools,
flat tire

⑩ ~~I had no idea she was such a bike nut. We rode thirty miles and I was exhausted.~~ Her equipment was something else, but useful because she had a flat and was able to fix it, saving our trip.

⑪ Combine into one ¶
on tools

⑫ Move to intro.?

She doesn't look like a bike fanatic, just a normal person. You'd never guess that her bike has more than 10,000 miles on it.

As we rode, Diane told me about her travels throughout the Northeast (Cape Cod, Vermont, Penn., New York). Riding to work saved her money, kept her in shape. Her goal for the next summer was a cross-country tour over the Rockies!

⑬ Describe in detail.
Make interesting!

⑭ Better conclusion
needed

Our trip was no big deal to her, but to me it was something. ~~I might consider biking to work because it keeps you in shape. But basically I'm lazy. I drive a car or take the bus. I do like to walk though.~~

⑮ Drop. Irrelevant

Reasons for Revisions

1. No thesis statement. Add catchy introduction. (introduction and thesis statement)

2. Add *bicycling*. What she is serious *about* is not clear. (exact language)

3. Tell *how* long! (exact language)

4. Expand this; more details needed. (support, exact language)

5. Add transition. (transitional expression)

6. Wrong tone for college essay. (exact language)

7. Find more active verb; be more specific. (exact language)

8. Conclude paragraph; stress time order. (order)

9. This section is weak. Add one paragraph on tools. Tell story of flat tire? (paragraphs, support)

10. Drop! Repeats thesis. Not really a paragraph. (unity, paragraphs)

11. Put this in tools paragraph. Order is mixed up. (order)

12. Put this in introduction? (order)

13. Add details; make this interesting! (support, exact language)

14. Write a better conclusion. (conclusion)

15. Drop! Essay is about Diane and biking, not my bad exercise habits. (unity)

Final Draft

Portrait of a Bike Fanatic

(1) You'd never guess that the powder-blue ten-speed Raleigh had more than 10,000 miles on it. And you'd never guess that the tiny woman with the swept-back hair and the suntanned forearms had ridden those miles over the last two years, making trips through eleven states. But Diane is a bicycle fanatic.

(2) I first realized how serious Diane was about bicycling when I joined her on a thirty-mile trip one Sunday afternoon. Her bike looked new, so I asked her if it was. When she told me she had bought it three years ago, I asked her how she kept it looking so good. From her saddlebag she took the soft cloth that she wiped the bike down with after every long ride and the plastic drop cloth that she put over it every time she parked it outdoors overnight.

(3) Diane had just about every kind of bike equipment I've ever seen. For example, she put on her white crash helmet and attached a tiny rearview mirror to it—the kind the dentist uses to examine the backs of your teeth. She strapped a warning light to her left leg, just below the knee. Then we set off on our trip, starting at Walden Pond in Concord and planning to go to the Wayside Inn in Sudbury and back again before the sun set.

(4) We were still in Concord when Diane signaled me to stop. "I think I have a flat," she said. I cursed under my breath. I was sure that would mean the end of our trip; we'd have to walk her bike back to the car and she'd have to take it to the shop the next day. But she reached into her saddlebag again, and out came a wrench and a new tube. Before I knew it, she took the rear wheel off the bike, installed the new tube, and put the wheel back on. I began to wonder what else was in that saddlebag. When I asked, she showed me

two sets of wrenches, another spare inner tube, two brake pads, a can of lubricating oil, two screwdrivers, a roll of reflective tape, extra bulbs for her headlight and taillight, and an extra chain. She had so much in the bag, I was tempted to see if it had a false bottom. Diane is one of those bicyclists who have tools to meet any emergency and know how to use them.

(5) As we rode along, Diane told me about her travels throughout the Northeast. She had taken her bike on summer vacations on Cape Cod and fall foliage tours in Vermont. She had ridden all over Pennsylvania and upstate New York, covering as much as seventy miles in a single day. She also rode to and from work every day, which she said saved money, kept her in shape, and helped her start each day feeling good. Her goal for the next summer, she said, was a cross-country tour. "All the way?" I asked. "What about the Rockies?" "I know," she said. "What a challenge!"

(6) Our trip took a little less than three hours, but I'm sure Diane was slowing down to let me keep up with her. When we got back to the parked car, I was breathing hard and had worked up quite a sweat. Diane was already there waiting for me, looking as if she did this every day—which she does. For Diane, riding a bike is as easy and natural as walking is for most people. Look out, Rockies.

PRACTICE 11   Now, carefully read over the first draft of your essay from Practice 10 and **revise** it, referring to the checklist of questions. Take your time and write the best essay you can. Once you are satisfied, **proofread** your essay for grammar and spelling errors. Neatly write the final draft.

Writing Assignments

The assignments that follow will give you practice in writing short essays. In each, concentrate on writing a clear thesis statement and a full, well-organized body. Because introductions and conclusions are not discussed until Chapter 19, you may wish to begin your essay with the thesis statement and conclude as simply as possible.

Before you write, make a plan or an outline that includes

- a clear thesis statement

- two to four topic sentences that support the thesis statement

- details, facts, and examples to develop each paragraph

- a logical order of paragraphs

1. Many people assume that aging is a negative process. Set out to prove the opposite. Discuss some of the positive aspects of growing older, some of the benefits: physical, emotional, financial, spiritual. What changes in self-knowledge and self-confidence go along with aging? Do relationships with others change for the better? Choose one main idea to write about.

Consider using examples from your experience to back up your thesis statement.

2. Do you feel that certain television programs show stereotypical women, African Americans, Hispanics, or members of any other group instead of believable people? Examine and discuss just one such program and one group of people. What situations, words, and actions by the TV characters are stereotypical, not real? Focus your subject, make a plan, and write a well-organized essay.

   You might wish to construct a thesis statement divided in this way: On the television program _____(name show)_____, _____(name group)_____ are often portrayed as being _(name stereotype)_.

3. Interview a classmate (or, if you do this assignment at home, someone with an unusual skill). As you talk to the person, look for a thesis: ask questions, take notes. What stands out about the person? Is there an overall impression or idea that can structure your essay? Use your descriptive powers. Notice the person's looks, clothes, typical expressions, and gestures. Later, formulate a thesis statement about the person, organize your ideas, and write.

4. Give advice to the weary job hunter. Describe the most creative job-hunting strategies you have ever tried or heard about. Support your thesis statement with examples, or consider using time order to show a successful job-hunting day in the life of the expert, you.

5. For better or worse, sex education begins at home—whether or not parents speak about the subject, whether parents' words reinforce or contradict the message of their own behavior. How do you think a parent should handle this responsibility? Be as specific as possible, including details from your own and your friends' experiences to make your point.

6. Have you ever had a close call with death? Describe the experience and its effect, if any, on your attitudes and actions since. If it has had little or no effect on you, try to explain why. Be sure to unify your essay with a clear thesis statement.

7. One marriage out of every two in America now ends in divorce. Think about this fact, its causes and implications. Are people less loyal? More free? Is marriage changing, or should it change? Are you or do you plan to be married in spite of the odds? Why? Focus on one aspect of the subject that you can discuss fully in a short essay.

Checklist: The Process of Writing an Essay

_____ 1. Narrow the topic in light of your audience and purpose. Be sure you can discuss this topic fully in a short essay.

2. Write a clear thesis statement. If you have trouble, freewrite or brainstorm first; then narrow the topic and write the thesis statement.

_____ 3. Freewrite or brainstorm, generating facts, details, and examples to support your thesis statement.

_____ 4. Plan or outline your essay, choosing from two to four main ideas to support the thesis statement.

_____ 5. Write a topic sentence that expresses each main idea.

_____ 6. Decide on a logical order in which to present the paragraphs.

_____ 7. Plan the body of each paragraph, using all you have learned about paragraph development in Unit 2 of this book.

_____ 8. Write the first draft of your essay.

_____ 9. Revise as necessary, checking your essay for support, unity, and coherence. Refer to the list of revision questions on page 264.

_____ 10. Proofread carefully for grammar, punctuation, sentence structure, spelling, and mechanics.

Suggested Topics for Essays

1. My Community's Worst Problem (propose a solution)
2. The Phone Call I Hated to Make
3. The Best (or Worst) Teacher I Ever Had
4. Portrait of a Special (or Unusual) Person
5. Parenting: Basic Rules for Raising Children
6. The Career for Which I Am Best Suited
7. How to Resolve a Disagreement Peacefully
8. Self-Discipline
9. Family Ties
10. What My Future Holds
11. Someone Who Changed My Life (tell how he or she changed it)
12. What This College Needs
13. Crime Does (Does Not) Pay
14. How to Get a Raise

15. Changing Bad Habits

16. What I Never Told Anyone

17. A Moving Film (Magazine, Program)

18. Portrait of a (Sports, Clothes, Neatness, Homework, or other) Fanatic

19. How to Shop on a Budget

20. Should Courts Require a One-Year "Cooling Off" Period Before a Divorce?

18

Types of Essays

Because an essay is like an expanded paragraph, the methods for developing a paragraph that you learned in Unit 3—illustration, process, and so forth—can also be used to develop an entire essay. The rest of this chapter will show you how.

PART A

The Illustration Essay

The **illustration** essay is one of the most frequently used in college writing and in business. For papers and exams in history, psychology, health, English, and other subjects, you will often be asked to develop a main point with examples. In a letter of job application, you might wish to give examples of achievements that demonstrate your special skills.

Here is an illustration essay:

Acting to Save Mother Earth

(1) Every day we hear more bad news about our planet. Reports tell us that wildlife and forests are disappearing at an alarming rate. Newscasts give the latest word on how quickly Earth is losing its protective shield and warming up. Newspapers lament the pollution of our air, water, and soil. What can we do in the face of such widespread gloom? In fact, we do not have to feel helpless. We can each learn practical ways to better our environment.

(2) For example, saving and recycling newspapers has a number of positive results. First, recycling newspaper saves trees. The average American consumes about 120 pounds of newsprint a year—enough to use up one tree. That means close to 250 million trees each year are destroyed for paper in this country alone. If we recycled only one-tenth of our newspaper, we would save 25 million trees a year. Second, making new paper from old paper uses up much less energy than making paper from trees. Finally, this process also reduces the air pollution of paper making by 95 percent.

(3) Another Earth-saving habit is "precycling" waste. This means buying food and other products packaged only in materials that will decay naturally or that can be recycled. The idea is to prevent unrecyclable materials from even entering the home. For instance, 60 of the 190 pounds of plastic—especially styrofoam—each American uses a year are thrown out as soon as packages are opened. Be kind to your planet by buying eggs, fast food, and other products in cardboard instead of styrofoam cartons. Buy beverages in recyclable glass, aluminum, or plastic containers. Buy in bulk to reduce the amount of packaging; you will save money too. Finally, when you can, buy products whose packaging shows the "recycled" logo. Materials that have been recycled once can be recycled again.

(4) Wise management of hazardous household wastes is yet another way of taking action for the planet. Hazardous wastes include paint, old car batteries, oven and drain cleaners, mothballs, floor and furniture polish, pesticides, and even toilet bowl cleaners. First of all, we should store hazardous materials properly by keeping them in their original containers, making sure they are clearly labeled, and keeping them in a cool, dry place that is out of the reach of children. Second, we can reduce our use of these products by buying only what we need and by sharing anything that might be left over. Third, we should take great care of disposing of hazardous wastes. Certain wastes such as old car batteries and motor oil can be refined and reused, and in some cities they can be turned in for special burning. However, local authorities have to be contacted because disposal practices vary so much from place to place.

(5) These personal actions may not *seem* important. At the very least, though, they can relieve some of the helplessness we all feel when faced with threats of global disaster. If carried out on a larger scale by millions of individuals, they could greatly improve our environment and lives.

- The **thesis statement** of an illustration essay states the writer's central point—a general statement that the rest of the essay will develop with examples.

- Which sentence in the introductory paragraph is the thesis statement?

  _____

  _____

- How many examples does the writer use to develop the thesis statement? What are they?

  _____

  _____

- Underline the topic sentence of each supporting paragraph.

- The thesis statement and topic sentences setting forth the three examples create a **plan** for this essay. The writer no doubt made such a plan or an outline before she wrote the first draft.

Before writing an illustration essay, you may wish to reread Chapter 5, "Illustration." As you pick a topic and plan your illustration essay, make sure your thesis statement can be richly developed by examples. Then brainstorm or freewrite, jotting down as many possible examples as you can think of; choose the best two or three examples. If you devote one paragraph to each example, each topic sentence should introduce the example to be developed. As you revise, make sure you have fully discussed each example, including all necessary details and facts.

PRACTICE 1   Choose a topic from the following list or one that you or your instructor has chosen. Write an illustration essay, referring to the essay checklist at the end of Chapter 17.

Suggested Topics: The Illustration Essay

1. Interesting ways in which people choose their jobs or professions

2. TV programs that present the elderly (or another group) in a positive or negative light

3. Ways in which people dress to attract attention

4. Odd places to get married or have parties

5. People who have overcome handicaps, poverty, prejudice, and so on

6. Sexual harassment in the workplace

PART B

The Narrative Essay

The narrative essay is used frequently in college writing. For instance, in a history course you might be assigned a paper on the major battles of World War I or be given an essay examination on the story of women's struggle to gain the right to vote. An English teacher may ask you to write a composition in which you retell a meaningful incident or personal experience. In all of these instances, your ability to organize facts and details in clear chronological or time order—to tell a story well—will be a crucial factor in the success of your paper.

Here is a narrative essay.

Maya Lin's Vietnam War Memorial

(1) The Vietnam War, which lasted from 1965 until 1975, was the longest war in United States history. It was also the most controversial, leaving a deep wound in the nation's conscience. The creation of the Vietnam War Memorial—despite disagreements about its design—helped this wound to heal.

(2) In 1980, when the call went out for designs for a Vietnam War Memorial, no one could have predicted that as many as 14,000 entries would be submitted. The rules were clear. The memorial had to be contemplative, harmonize with its surroundings, list the names of those dead or missing, and—most important—make no political statement about the war. When the judges, all well-known architects and sculptors, met in April 1981, they unanimously chose entry number 1026. The winner was Maya Lin, a twenty-one-year-old Asian-American architecture student who, ironically, was too young to have had any direct experience of the war.

(3) Lin envisioned shiny black granite slabs embedded in a long V-shaped trench, with one end pointing toward the Lincoln Memorial and the other toward the Washington Monument. She defined the trench as a cut in the earth, "an initial violence that in time would heal." Names would be carved into the granite in the order of the dates on which the soldiers had died or disappeared. Lin felt that finding a name on the memorial with the help of a directory would be like finding a body on a battlefield.

(4) Although her design satisfied all the contest criteria and was the judges' clear favorite, it aroused much controversy. Some critics called it a "black gash of shame and sorrow," labeling it unpatriotic, unheroic, and morbid. They were upset that the memorial contained no flags, no statues of soldiers, and no inscription other than the names. Privately, some complained that Lin was too young to win the contest—and that she was female besides. She fought back. She claimed that a flag would make the green area around the memorial look like a golf course and that a traditional statue on her modern structure would be like a mustache drawn on someone else's portrait. At last, a compromise was reached: A flag and a statue were added to the memorial, and the critics withdrew their complaints. On Veterans Day, November 11, 1982, the Vietnam War Memorial was finally dedicated.

(5) Since then, the memorial has become the most popular site in Washington, D.C. Some visit to see the monument and pay tribute to those who died in the war. Others come to locate and touch the names of loved ones. As they stand before the wall, they also learn the names of those who served and died with their relatives and friends. When the rain falls, all the names seem to disappear. Visitors often leave memorials of their own—flowers, notes to the departed, bits of old uniforms. A place of national mourning and of love, Maya Lin's monument has helped to heal the wounds of the Vietnam War.

- The **thesis statement** of a narrative essay gives the point of the essay.

- What is the thesis statement of the essay?

_____

_____

- Paragraphs 2, 4, and 5 of this essay tell in chronological order the incidents of the narrative.

- What are the incidents?

  _____

  _____

- What is the main idea of paragraph 3?

  _____

- Paragraph 1 provides background information that helps the reader understand the narrative.

- What background material is given in this paragraph?

  _____

  _____

Before writing a narrative essay, you may wish to reread Chapter 6, "Narration." Make sure that your thesis statement clearly states the point of your narrative. Organize all the incidents and details in chronological or time order, in general beginning with the earliest event and ending with the latest. Be sure to supply any necessary background information. As you plan your essay, pay careful attention to paragraphing; if your narrative consists of just a few major incidents, you may wish to devote one paragraph to each one. Use transitional expressions that indicate time order to help your reader follow the narrative easily.

PRACTICE 2   Choose a topic from the following list or one that you or your instructor has chosen. Write a narrative essay, referring to the essay checklist at the end of Chapter 17.

Suggested Topics: The Narrative Essay

1. A family event that changed your view of yourself

2. An incident in which you or someone you know acted with courage or cowardice

3. Your "man or woman of the year" and what he or she did to merit that award

4. A successful struggle to achieve something by someone you admire

5. An amazing real-life incident you have witnessed

6. A plot line for a movie or TV show you would like to produce

PART C

The Descriptive Essay

Although paragraphs of **description** are more common than whole essays, you will sometimes need to write a descriptive essay. In science labs, you may need to describe accurately cells under a microscope or a certain kind of rock. In business, you might have to describe a product or piece of equipment. Travel writers frequently use description, and personal letters often call on your descriptive powers.

Here is a descriptive essay:

Disney's Perfect World

(1) Disney World in Orlando, Florida, is America's best-known, busiest, and most profitable tourist attraction. Of all Disney World's wonders, the Magic Kingdom draws the most visitors. Tourists can step into the past, ride a sleek spaceship into the future, or dance with a mouse. The Magic Kingdom certainly delivers the fantasy it promises. However, for me, its most fantastic aspect is that everything seems so perfect—or almost everything.

(2) Every building, object, and decoration is sparkling clean. Take Main Street, for example, Disney's re-creation of small-town America in 1900. Visitors walking from Town Square toward Cinderella's Castle cannot help but notice the gleaming paint on every well-kept building. Right down to their gold signs and gingerbread moldings, such shops as the Emporium and the House of Magic are freshly painted several times a year. Every window, street lamp, and display is free of smudges. In fact, white-suited maintenance workers rush to pick up any litter, including droppings left by the horses that pull the shiny trolley cars along Main Street. Each night, all of Main Street is hosed down and scrubbed.

(3) The people of the Magic Kingdom are equally flawless. As a marching band drums in the distance, cartoon characters like Goofy and Snow White stop mingling with the tourists and begin to usher them to the sides of Main Street for a parade. This parade differs from any other you have seen, however. Here no one is drunk, sloppy, or unusual; no band member trips on a shoelace or toots a wrong note. Dressed in spotless uniforms, the fit, attractive band members hold their instruments at the perfect angle. The shapely twirlers always catch their batons. All strut in unison, only to reappear like clockwork in an hour. At nighttime parades, spectacular fireworks are electronically detonated in sync with the announcer's pleasant, perfectly modulated voice.

(4) Only the all-too-human visitors, thousands of us who come to gape and marvel, bring reality into this paradise. We grumble and fidget in endless lines, and then jam into attractions like the Haunted Mansion in Liberty Square and the Space Mountain roller coaster in Tomorrowland. We dribble chili on our shirts, cut ahead of each other, shout at our crying children, and glare suspiciously if a stranger jostles our pocketbook. I watched one couple dressed in cute Mickey Mouse hats plop themselves down at the end of an empty row at the Hall of Presidents show, and then hiss obscenities at everyone who was forced to climb over them. Of course, we visitors are not all

young or beautiful either. I am a case in point, a balding, hefty gent who neither dresses nor carries himself very well.

(5) At Disney World, it occurred to me that I like imperfection. As the lights dimmed right on cue for yet another precision performance, I noted a mist of dandruff on the shoulders of the woman in front of me, and I felt fine.

—Angus Fletcher (Student)

■ The **thesis statement** of a descriptive essay says what will be described and sometimes gives an overall impression of it.

■ Which sentence in the introductory paragraph is the thesis statement?

_____

_____

■ Each paragraph in the body of this essay describes one scene or aspect of the topic. How many scenes or aspects are described and what are they?

_____

_____

■ What kind of **order** does the writer follow in organizing paragraph 2?

_____

_____

■ Note that the thesis statement and topic sentences make a **plan** for the whole essay.

Before writing an essay of description, you may wish to reread Chapter 7, "Description." Make sure that your thesis statement clearly sets forth the precise subject your essay will describe. Use your senses—sight, smell, hearing, taste, and touch—as you jot down ideas for the body. As you plan, pay special attention to organizing details and observations; space order is often the best way to organize a description. As you revise, pay special attention to the richness and exactness of your language and details; these are what make good descriptions come alive.

PRACTICE 3   Choose a topic from the following list or one that you or your instructor has chosen. Write an essay of description, referring to the essay checklist at the end of Chapter 17.

Suggested Topics: The Descriptive Essay

1. Life in the twenty-first century

2. The most interesting spot in your neighborhood or hometown

3. A person or animal you have closely observed

4. A place you know from your travels or from reading

5. An appliance or machine

6. A health club, park, or other place where people pursue fitness

PART D

The Process Essay

The **process** essay is frequently used in college and business. In psychology, for example, you might describe the stages of personality development. In history, you might explain the process of electing a president or how a battle was won or lost, while in business, you might set forth the steps of an advertising campaign. In science labs, you will often have to record the stages of an experiment.

Here is a process essay:

How to Prepare for a Final Exam

(1) At the end of my first semester at college, I postponed thinking about final examinations, desperately crammed the night before, drank enough coffee to keep the city of Cincinnati awake, and then got C's and D's. I have since realized that the students who got A's on their finals weren't just lucky; they knew how to *prepare*. There are many different ways to prepare for a final examination, and each individual must perfect his or her own style, but over the years, I have developed a method that works for me.

(2) First, when your professor announces the date, time, and place of the final—usually at least two weeks before—ask questions and take careful notes on the answers. What chapters will be covered? What kinds of questions will the test contain? What materials and topics are most important? The information you gather will help you study more effectively.

(3) Next, survey all the textbook chapters the test will cover, using a highlighter or colored pen to mark important ideas and sections to be studied later. Many textbooks emphasize key ideas with boldface titles or headlines; others are written so that key ideas appear in the topic sentences at the beginning of each paragraph. Pay attention to these guides as you read.

(4) Third, survey your class notes in the same fashion, marking important ideas. If your notes are messy or disorganized, you might want to rewrite them for easy reference later.

(5) Fourth, decide approximately how many hours you will need to study. Get a calendar and clearly mark off the hours each week that you will devote to in-depth studying. If possible, set aside specific times: Thursday from 1 to 2 p.m., Friday from 6 to 8 p.m., and so on. If you have trouble committing yourself, schedule study time with a friend; but pick someone as serious as you are about getting good grades.

(6) Fifth, begin studying systematically, choosing a quiet place free from distractions in which to work—the library, a dorm room, whatever helps you concentrate. One of my friends can study only in his attic, another, in her car. As you review the textbook and your notes, ask yourself questions based on your reading. From class discussions, try to spot the professor's priorities

and to guess what questions might appear on the exam. Be creative; one friend of mine puts important study material on cassette tapes, which he plays walking to and from school.

(7) Finally, at least three days before the exam, start reviewing. At the least opportunity, refer to your notes, even if you are not prepared to digest all the material. Use the moments when you are drinking your orange juice or riding the bus; just looking at the material can promote learning. By the night before the exam, you should know everything you want to know—and allow for a good night's sleep!

(8) By following these simple procedures, you may find, as I do, that you are the most prepared person in the exam room, confident that you studied thoroughly enough to do well on the exam.

—Mark Reyes (Student)

- The **thesis statement** in a process essay tells the reader what process the rest of the essay will describe.

- What is the thesis statement in this essay?

  _____

  _____

  _____

- What process will be described?

  _____

- How many steps make up this process and what are they?

  _____

  _____

  _____

- What kind of order does the writer use to organize his essay?

  _____

Before writing a process essay, you may wish to reread Chapter 8, "Process." The thesis statement should clearly set forth the process you intend to describe. As you plan your essay, make sure you jot down all the necessary steps or stages and put them in logical order. As you revise, make sure you have fully and clearly explained each step so that a reader who may not be familiar with the subject matter can follow easily. Clear language and logical organization are the keys to good process writing. Pay special attention to paragraphing; if the process consists of just three or four steps, you may wish to devote one paragraph to each step. If the steps are short or numerous, you will probably wish to combine two or three steps in each paragraph.

PRACTICE 4   Choose a topic from the list below or one that you or your instructor has chosen. Write a process essay, referring to the essay checklist at the end of Chapter 17.

Suggested Topics: The Process Essay

1. How someone became a success

2. How to impress the boss

3. How to plan a great party

4. How to toilet train your child (or teach your child some task or skill)

5. How to get an *A*

6. How to prepare for a backpacking trip, vacation, and so on

---

PART E

The Definition Essay

Although paragraphs of **definition** are more common in college writing than essays are, you may at some time have to write a definition essay. In a computer course, for example, you might be called on to define *disk operating system*. In psychology, you might need to define the *Oedipus complex*, or in biology, the term *DNA*.

Here is a definition essay:

Winning

(1) The dictionary defines winning as "achieving victory over others in a competition, receiving a prize or reward for achievement." Yet some of the most meaningful wins of my life were victories over no other person, and I can remember winning when there was no prize for performance. To me, winning means overcoming obstacles.

(2) My first experience of winning occurred in elementary school gym. Nearly every day, after the preparatory pushups and squat-thrusts, we had to run relays. Although I had asthma as a child, I won many races. My chest would burn terribly for a few minutes, but it was worth it to feel so proud—not because I'd beaten others or won a prize, but because I'd overcome a handicap. (By the way, I "outgrew" my asthma by age eleven.)

(3) In high school, I had another experience of winning. Although I loved reading about biology, I could not bring myself to dissect a frog in lab. I hated the smell of the dead animals, and the idea of cutting them open disgusted me. Every time I tried, my hands would shake and my stomach would turn. Worst of all, my biology teacher reacted to my futile attempts with contempt. After an upsetting couple of weeks, I decided to get hold of myself. I realized that I was overreacting. "The animals are already dead," I told myself. With determination, I swept into my next lab period, walked up

to the table, and with one swift stroke, slit open a frog. After that, I excelled in biology. I had won again.

(4) I consider the fact that I am now attending college winning. To get here, I had to surmount many obstacles, both outside and inside myself. College costs money, and I don't have much of it. College takes time, and I don't have much of that either with a little son to care for. But I overcame these obstacles and a bigger one still—lack of confidence in myself. I had to keep saying, "I won't give up." And here I am, winning!

(5) These examples should clarify what winning means to me. I don't trust anything that comes too easily. In fact, I expect the road to be rocky, and I appreciate a win more if I have to work, sacrifice, and overcome. This is a positive drive for me, the very spirit of winning.

—Audrey Holmes (Student)

- The **thesis statement** of a definition essay tells the reader what term will be defined and usually defines it as well.

- Which sentence in the introductory paragraph is the thesis statement?

  _____

  _____

- What is the writer's definition of *winning?*

  _____

  _____

- Underline the topic sentences of paragraphs 2, 3, and 4.

- How do paragraphs 2, 3, and 4 develop the thesis statement?

  _____

  _____

- What order does the writer follow in paragraphs 2, 3, and 4?

  _____

  _____

Before writing a definition essay, you may wish to reread Chapter 9, "Definition." Choose a word or term that truly interests you, one about which you have something to say. Decide what type of definition you will use and write the thesis statement, which should state and define your term. Then brainstorm ideas to explain your definition. Consider using two or three examples to develop the term—the way the writer does in the preceding essay—devoting one paragraph to each example. As you revise, make sure your writing is very clear, so the reader knows exactly what you mean.

PRACTICE 5   Choose a topic from the following list or one that you or your instructor has chosen. Write a definition essay, referring to the essay checklist at the end of Chapter 17.

Suggested Topics: The Definition Essay

1. A true friend

2. A good student (or a good teacher)

3. A slang term in current use

4. A term you know from sports, science, art, psychology, or some other field

5. Courage

6. A happy marriage (or good relationship)

PART F

The Comparison or Contrast Essay

Essays of **comparison** or **contrast** are frequently called for in college courses. In an English or drama class, you might be asked to contrast two of Shakespeare's villains—perhaps Iago and Claudius. In psychology, you might have to contrast the training of the clinical psychologist and that of the psychiatrist, or in history, to compare ancient Greek and Roman religions.

Does the following essay compare or contrast?

Two Childhoods

(1) When I was young, my mother told me stories about her childhood. I loved her tales and still think of them. It was intriguing to hear about life thirty years before mine began. What fascinated me most, however, were the differences between her youth and mine.

(2) My mother grew up in the country. She spent most of her young years on a farm in South Carolina, surrounded by animals, orchards, cane fields, and agricultural machinery. By the time she was six, she was a walking agricultural textbook. Hers was a simple, serene, and comfortable life within a close-knit, neighborly environment. My mother's days were filled with swimming in nearby rivers and lakes, climbing and falling off trees, scooter riding down country lanes, playing marbles with siblings and friends, bird watching and mending of wings, and building fences and tree houses.

(3) My childhood, on the other hand, was spent in New York City, without animals, scenic surroundings, or close-knit neighbors. Mine was a lifestyle of fast activity crammed into a tight schedule. Nature was replaced by shops and businesses, trees by tall buildings. My knowledge was not based on the simple things at hand, but on expensive toys, the latest clothes, and the newest sneakers. Compared to my mother's country existence, my city childhood seems humdrum—a constant series of trips to the park or movies,

visits to the grocery store or shopping center, picnics at the amusement park or beach, and a few birthday parties thrown in.

(4) Just as our lifestyles differed, so too did our personalities. Relatives say that my mother was a loving, caring child who was always willing to help. She was praised for being clever and vibrant, levelheaded and respectful to others. My mother was strong willed and spoke her mind when she saw fit, but she placed few demands on her parents for toys or fancy clothes. Somehow her environment, which had instilled in her an appreciation of nature and living things, was enough.

(5) I, on the other hand, was considered a bit too extroverted, selfish, and stubborn. I reveled in being petulant, pigheaded, demanding, and unstable. Although I could be loving, I cleverly used this trait to my advantage in an attempt to manipulate my parents and get the beautiful toys and clothes I wanted. After all, these gave me all the aesthetic appreciation I needed. In fact, I was a brazenfaced brat.

(6) Looking back, I think it would have been wonderful as a child to have fallen off a few trees or driven a scooter at maniacal speeds or even milked a cow or crushed some coffee beans in a mortar. Yes, that would have been wonderful. It really would have been.

—Cheryl Parris (Student)

- The **thesis statement** of a comparison or contrast essay tells what two persons or things will be compared or contrasted.

- What is the thesis statement of this essay?

  _____

  _____

- Will this essay compare or contrast the two people? What word or words in the thesis indicate this?

  _____

- Does the writer discuss all points about A and then all points about B, or skip back and forth from A to B?

  _____

- Note that the thesis statement and topic sentences make a **plan** for this essay.

Before you plan or outline your essay, you may wish to reread Chapter 10, "Comparison and Contrast." Bear in mind, as you choose a subject, that the most interesting essays usually compare two things that are different or contrast two things that are similar. Otherwise, you run the risk of saying the obvious ("Cats and dogs are two different animals.").

Here are a few tips to keep in mind as you write your thesis statement: Don't just say that A and B are similar or different; instead, say *in what way* A and B are similar or different, as the writer does above. You may wish to use this form for a contrast thesis: *Although A and B have this similarity, they are different in these ways.* And for a comparison: *Although A and B are unlike in this way, they are similar in these ways.*

As you plan the body of your essay, you may wish to make a chart of all your points of comparison or contrast. In any case, if you discuss the food, service, price, and atmosphere of Restaurant A, you must discuss the food, service, price, and atmosphere of Restaurant B as well.

In your essay, you can first discuss A (one paragraph), then discuss B (one paragraph), or you can skip back and forth between A and B (one paragraph on point one, A and B, one paragraph on point two, A and B, and one paragraph on point three, A and B). Refer to the charts in Chapter 10, pages 123–124.

PRACTICE 6   Choose a topic from the list below or one that you or your instructor has chosen. Write either a comparison or a contrast essay, referring to the essay checklist at the end of Chapter 17.

Suggested Topics: The Comparison or Contrast Essay

1. Two athletes, entertainers, philosophers, political figures, or other public figures

2. Two restaurants, street corners, movie theaters, or rooms

3. Your mother's or father's childhood and your own

4. Challenging classes and mediocre classes

5. Two cars, computers, or other complex machines

6. A current and a past attitude or state of mind

PART G

The Classification Essay

The **classification** essay is useful in college and business. In music, for example, you might have to classify Mozart's compositions according to the musical periods of his life. A retail business might classify items in stock according to popularity—how frequently they must be reordered.

While the classification essay is usually serious, the pattern can make a good humorous essay, as this essay shows:

The Potato Scale

(1) Television has become the great American pastime. Nearly every household has at least one TV, which means that people are spending time watching it, unless, of course, they bought it to serve as a plant stand. Television viewers can be grouped in many ways—by the type of shows they watch (but there is no accounting for taste) or by hours per week of watching (but that seems unfair since a working, twelve-hour-a-week viewer could

conceivably become a fifty-hour-a-week viewer if he or she were out of a job). So I have developed the Potato Scale. The four major categories of the Potato Scale rank TV viewers on a combination of leisure time spent watching, intensity of watching, and the desire to watch versus the desire to engage in other activities.

(2) First, we have the True Couch Potatoes. They are diehard viewers who, when home, will be found in front of their televisions. They no longer eat in the dining room, and if you visit them, the television stays on. The *TV Guide* is their Bible. They will plan other activities and chores around their viewing time, always hoping to accomplish these tasks in front of the tube. If a presidential address is on every channel but one, and they dislike the president, they will tune in that one channel, be it Bugs Bunny or Polynesian barge cooking. These potatoes would never consider turning off the box.

(3) The second group consists of the Pseudo Couch Potatoes. These are scheduled potatoes. They have outside interests and actually eat at the table, but for a certain period of time (let's say from 7 to 11 in the evening), they will take on the characteristics of True Couch Potatoes. Another difference between True and Pseudo Potatoes deserves note. The True Potato must be forced by someone else to shut off the television and do something different; however, if the Pseudo Potato has flipped through all the channels and found only garbage, he or she still has the capacity to think of other things to do.

(4) Third, we have the Selective Potatoes. These more discriminating potatoes enjoy many activities, and TV is just one of them. They might have a few shows they enjoy watching regularly, but missing one episode is not a world-class crisis. After all, the show will be on next week. They don't live by the *TV Guide*, but use it to check for interesting specials. If they find themselves staring at an awful movie or show, they will gladly, and without a second thought, turn it off.

(5) The fourth group consists of Last Resort Potatoes. These people actually prefer reading, going to the theater, playing pickup basketball, walking in the woods, and many other activities to watching television. Only after they have exhausted all other possibilities or are dog tired or shivering with the flu, will they click on the tube. These potatoes are either excessively choosy or almost indifferent to what's on, hoping it will bore them to sleep.

(6) These are the principal categories of the Potato Scale, from the truly vegetable to the usually human. What type of potato are you?

—Helen Petruzzelli (Student)

■ The **thesis statement** in a classification essay tells the reader what group will be classified and on what basis.

■ This entire essay **classifies** people on the basis of their television viewing habits. Which sentence is the thesis statement?

_____

_____

- Into how many categories are TV viewers divided?

  _____

- Each paragraph in the body of the essay discusses one of four categories, which the writer names. What are they?

  1: _____

  2: _____

  3. _____

  4: _____

- The thesis statement and the topic sentences setting forth the four categories create a **plan** for the essay. The writer no doubt made the plan before she wrote the first draft.

- Can you see the logic in the writer's *order* of paragraphs? That is, why does she present True Couch Potatoes first, Pseudo Potatoes second, Selective Potatoes third, and Last Resort Potatoes last?

  _____

  _____

Before writing your classification essay, you may wish to reread Chapter 11, "Classification." Choose a topic that lends itself to classification. Your thesis statement should state clearly the group you will classify and your basis of classification. As you plan, make sure that all your categories (three or four is a good number) reflect that basis of classification. Discuss one category per paragraph, including enough examples, details, and facts that the reader completely understands your ideas.

PRACTICE 7   Choose a topic from the following list or one that you or your instructor has chosen. Write a classification essay, referring to the essay checklist at the end of Chapter 17.

Suggested Topics: The Classification Essay

1. Members of your family

2. Music systems

3. Riders on the subway, bus, or train

4. People studying in the library

5. Houseplants

6. Cars, computers, or some other machines

PART H

The Persuasive Essay

Persuasive essays are perhaps the essay type most frequently called for in college and business. That is, you will often be asked to take a stand on an issue—legalized abortion, capital punishment, whether a company should invest in on-site child care—and then try to persuade others to agree with you. Examination questions asking you to "agree or disagree" are really asking you to take a stand and make a persuasive case for that stand—for example, "World War II was basically a continuation of World War I. Agree or disagree." You are asked to muster factual evidence to support your stand.

Here is a persuasive essay:

Stopping Youth Violence: An Inside Job

(1) Every year, nearly a million 12- to 19-year-olds are murdered, robbed, or assaulted—many by their peers—and the number of teens arrested for murder has increased a shocking 85 percent since 1987, reports Barbara Kantrowitz in "Wild in the Streets," *Newsweek's* cover story for August 2, 1993. Although the growing problem of youth violence is far too complex for any one solution, teaching young people conflict resolution skills—that is, nonviolent techniques for resolving disputes—seems to help. To reduce youth violence, conflict resolution skills should be taught to all children before they reach junior high school.

(2) First and most important, young people need to learn nonviolent ways of dealing with conflict. In a dangerous society where guns are readily available, many youngsters feel they have no choice but to respond to an insult or an argument with violence. If they have grown up seeing family members and neighbors react to stress with verbal or physical violence, they may not know that other choices exist. Robert Steinback, a *Miami Herald* columnist who works with at-risk youth in Miami, writes that behavior like carrying a weapon or refusing to back down gives young people "the illusion of control," but what they desperately need is to learn real control—for example, when provoked, to walk away from a fight.

(3) Next, conflict resolution programs have been shown to reduce violent incidents and empower young people in a healthy way. Many programs and courses around the country are teaching preteens and teens to work through disagreements without violence. Tools include calmly telling one's own side of the story and listening to the other person without interrupting or blaming— skills that many adults don't have! Conflict Busters, a Los Angeles public school program, starts in the third grade; it trains students to be mediators, helping peers find their own solutions to conflicts ranging from "sandbox fights to interracial gang disputes," according to *Newsweek*. Schools in Claremont, Connecticut, run a conflict resolution course written by Dr. Luz Rivera, who said in a phone interview that fewer violent school incidents have been reported since the course began. Although conflict resolution is useful at any age, experts agree that students should first be exposed before they are hit by the double jolts of hormones and junior high school.

(4) Finally, although opponents claim that this is a "Band-Aid" solution that does not address the root causes of teen violence—poverty, troubled families, bad schools, and drugs, to name a few—in fact, conflict resolution training saves lives now. The larger social issues must be addressed, but they will take years to solve, whereas teaching students new attitudes and "people skills" will empower them immediately and serve them for a lifetime. For instance, fourteen-year-old Verna, who once called herself Vee Sinister, says that Ms. Rivera's course has changed her life: "I learned to stop and think before my big mouth gets me in trouble. I use the tools with my mother, and guess what? No more screaming at home."

(5) The violence devastating Verna's generation threatens everyone's future. One proven way to help youngsters protect themselves from violence is conflict resolution training that begins early. Although it is just one solution among many, this solution taps into great power: the hearts, minds, and characters of young people.

- The **thesis statement** in a persuasive essay clearly states the issue to be discussed and the writer's position on it. What is the thesis statement?

_____

_____

_____

- This introduction includes *facts*. What is the source of these facts and why does the writer include them here?

_____

_____

_____

- Sometimes a writer needs to define terms he or she is using. What term does the writer define?

_____

- How many reasons does this writer give to back up the thesis statement?

_____

- Notice that the writer presents one reason per paragraph.
- Which reasons refer to an *authority*?

_____

- Who are these authorities?

_____

_____

_____

- How is the second reason supported?

  _____

- Which reason is really an *answer to the opposition*?

  _____

- This reason also uses an *example*. What or who is the example?

  _____

- Note that the thesis statement and topic sentences make up a **plan** or **outline** for the whole essay.

  Before writing an essay of persuasion, reread Chapter 12, "Persuasion." Make sure your thesis statement takes a clear stand. Devote one paragraph to each reason, developing each paragraph fully with facts and discussion. Try to use some of the methods of persuasion discussed in Chapter 12. Revise for clarity and support; remember, ample factual support is the key to successful persuasion.

PRACTICE 8   Choose a topic from the list below or one that you or your instructor has chosen. Write a persuasive essay, referring to the essay checklist at the end of Chapter 17.

Suggested Topics: The Persuasive Essay

1. A college education is (not) worth the time and money
2. Sexually explicit magazines should (not) be sold at newsstands
3. Only minority police should patrol minority neighborhoods
4. Gay couples should (not) be allowed to adopt children
5. Illegal aliens in the United States should be entitled to basic health services
6. Suicides of teenagers should (not) be reported in national media

19

The Introduction, the Conclusion, and the Title

PART A   **The Introduction**
PART B   **The Conclusion**
PART C   **The Title**

PART A

The Introduction

An **introduction** has two functions in an essay. First, it contains the **thesis statement** and, therefore, tells the reader what central idea will be developed in the rest of the paper. Since the reader should be able to spot the thesis sentence easily, it should be given a prominent place—for example, the first or the last sentence in the introduction. Second, the introduction has to interest the reader enough that he or she will want to continue reading the paper.

Sometimes the process of writing the essay will help clarify your ideas about how best to introduce it. So once you have completed your essay, you may wish to revise and rewrite the introduction, making sure that it clearly introduces the essay's main idea.

There is no best way to introduce an essay, but you should certainly avoid beginning your work with "I'm going to discuss" or "This paper is about." You needn't tell the reader you are about to begin; just begin!

Below are six basic methods for beginning your composition effectively. In each example, the thesis statement is italicized.

1. Begin with a single-sentence thesis statement. A single-sentence thesis statement can be effective because it quickly and forcefully states the main idea of the essay:

> *Time management should be a required course at this college.*

- Note how quickly and clearly a one-sentence thesis statement can inform the reader about what will follow in the rest of the essay.

2. Begin with a general idea and then narrow to a specific thesis statement. The general idea gives the reader background information or sets the scene. Then the topic narrows to one specific idea—the thesis statement. The effect is like a funnel, from wide to narrow.

> Few Americans stay put for a lifetime. We move from town to city to suburb, from high school to college in a different state, from a job in one region to a better job elsewhere, from the home where we raise our children to the home where we plan to live in retirement. *With each move we are forever making new friends, who become part of our new life at that time.*
>
> —Margaret Mead and Rhoda Metraux, "On Friendship," in *A Way of Seeing*

- What general idea precedes the thesis statement and then leads the reader to focus on the specific main point of the essay?

_____

_____

3. Begin with an illustration. One or more brief illustrations in the introduction of an essay make the thesis statement more concrete and vivid:

> One day in 1946, Percy Spencer stuck a chocolate bar in his pocket and went to work. Later, standing next to the radar machine he was working on, he noticed that his chocolate bar had melted. Almost immediately, Spencer saw the possibilities, sent for unpopped popcorn, and invented the first microwave oven—marketed the following year as the "radar range." *The microwave is just one of many important inventions created out of the interaction of two factors: a lucky accident and the presence of a trained person who understood what that accident meant.*

- What example does the writer provide to make the thesis statement more concrete?

_____

_____

4. Begin with a surprising fact or idea. A surprising fact or idea arouses the reader's curiosity about how you will support this initial startling statement.

> *Millions of law-abiding Americans are physically addicted to caffeine—and most of them don't even know it.* Caffeine is a powerful central nervous system stimulant with substantial addiction potential. When deprived of their caffeine, addicts experience often severe withdrawal symptoms, which may include a throbbing headache, disorientation, constipation, nausea, sluggishness, depression, and irritability. As with other addictive drugs, heavy users develop a tolerance and require higher doses to obtain the expected effect.
>
> —Tom Ferguson and Joe Graedon, "Caffeine," *Medical Self-Care*

▪ Why are the facts in this introduction likely to startle or surprise the reader?

_____

_____

5. Begin with a contradiction. In this type of introduction, your thesis statement contradicts what many or most people believe. In other words, your essay will contrast your opinion with the widely held view.

> Everybody in America is tough on crime. Parents, teachers, cops, judges, rich people, poor people, ditch diggers, brain surgeons—just ask them.
>
> So, listen: How come there is so much crime in America? How is it that we no longer possess our basic civil liberty from which all others flow—freedom to walk our streets without fear?
>
> Squirm, duck, run—there is no hiding place from the answer. *We Americans are not tough on crime at all. We are pudgily soft, with great rolls of fat hanging from our bellies and brains.*
>
> —A. M. Rosenthal, "Pudgy on Crime," *New York Times*

▪ This writer's introduction consists of three short paragraphs. What widely held view does he present?

_____

_____

- How does he contradict this idea?

_____

_____

- What will the rest of the essay discuss?

_____

_____

6. Begin with a direct quotation. A direct quotation is likely to catch your reader's attention and to show that you have explored what others have to say about the subject. You can then proceed to agree or to disagree with the direct quotation.

> "Music is the speech of angels," wrote Thomas Carlyle over a hundred years ago. Today, growing numbers of scientists might agree. Soothing music has been shown to lower the blood pressure of heart patients, reduce pain after surgery, and help premature babies gain weight. _In fact, research studies show that music has the power to heal and to work medical miracles._

- Does the author agree or disagree with the statement by Thomas Carlyle?

_____

_____

Of course, definitions, comparisons, or any of the other kinds of devices you have already studied can also make good introductions. Just make sure that the reader knows exactly which sentence is your thesis statement.

Writing Assignment 1

Here are five statements. Pick three that you would like to write about and compose an introduction for each one. Use any of the methods for beginning compositions discussed above.

1. Sometimes, you should look before you leap.

2. Noise is definitely a form of pollution.

3. Serious illness—our own or a loved one's—sometimes can bring surprising blessings.

4. Studying with someone else can pay off in better grades.

5. My college should offer a three-day course in "How to _____ ."

PART B

The Conclusion

A conclusion signals the end of the essay and leaves the reader with a final thought. As with the introduction, you may wish to revise and rewrite the conclusion once you have completed your essay. Be certain your conclusion flows logically from the body of the essay.

Like introductions, conclusions can take many forms, and the right one for your essay depends on how you wish to complete your paper—with what thought you wish to leave the reader. However, never conclude your paper with "As I said in the beginning," and try to avoid the overused "In conclusion" or "In summary." Don't end by saying you are going to end; just end!

Here are three ways to conclude an essay.

1. End with a call to action. The call to action says that, in view of the facts and ideas presented in this essay, the reader should *do something*.

> Thus, if race relations in this country are to improve, something must change; *we* must change. E. M. Forster has written that asking all people to love one another is probably asking too much, but that asking them to tolerate each other just might be achievable. I agree that tolerance is a more realistic goal. Today, if you and I make a sincere effort to tolerate others, the world will be a slightly different, and better, place.

■ What does the writer want the reader to do?

_____

_____

2. End with a final point. The final point can tie together all the other ideas in the essay; it provides the reader with the sense that the entire essay has been leading up to this one final point.

> Students who follow their hearts in choosing majors will most likely end up laboring at what they love. They're the ones who will put in the long hours and intense effort that achievement requires. And they're the ones who will find the sense of purpose that underlies most human happiness.
>
> —Lynne V. Cheney, "Students of Success,"
> *Newsweek*

■ With what final point does Cheney end her article?

_____

_____

3. End with a question. By ending with a question, you leave the reader with a final problem that you wish him or her to think about.

> Illness related to chemical dumping is increasing in Larkstown, yet only a handful of citizens have joined the campaign to clean up the chemical dump on the edge of town and to stop further dumping. Many people say that they don't want to get involved, but with their lives and their children's futures at stake, can they afford not to?

■ What problem does the writer's final question point to?

_____

Writing Assignment 2

Review two or three essays that you have written recently. Do the conclusions bring the essays to clear ends? Are they interesting? How could they be improved? Using one of the three strategies taught in this section, write a new conclusion for one of the essays.

PART C

The Title

If you are writing just one paragraph, chances are that you will not be required to give it a title, but if you are writing a multiparagraph essay, a title is definitely in order.

The title is centered on the page above the body of the composition and separated from it by several blank lines (about 1 inch of space), as shown on the following page.

> Title
> about 1½"
> about 1"
>
> If you are writing just one paragraph, chances are that you will not be required to give it a title, but if you are writing a multiparagraph theme, a title is definitely in order.
>
> The title is centered on the page above the body of the theme and separated from it by several blank lines (about 1 inch of space).

- *Do not* put quotation marks around the title of your own paper.

- *Do not* underline the title of your own paper.

- Remember, unlike the topic sentence, the title is not part of the first paragraph; in fact, it is usually only four to five words long and is rarely an entire sentence.

A good title has two functions: to suggest the subject of the essay and to spark the reader's interest. Although the title is the first part of your essay the reader sees, the most effective titles are usually written *after* the essay has been completed.

To create a title, reread your essay, paying special attention to the **thesis statement** and the **conclusion.** Try to come up with a few words that express the main point of your paper.

Here are some basic kinds of titles.

1. The most common title used in college writing is the no-nonsense descriptive title. In writing such a title, stress key words and ideas developed in the essay:

> The Search for Identity in *The Bluest Eye*
>
> Advantages and Disadvantages of Buying on Credit
>
> The Role of Chlorophyll in Photosynthesis

2. Two-part titles are also effective; write one or two words stating the general subject, and then add several words that narrow the topic:

Legal Gambling: Pro and Con

AIDS: A Tragedy of Governmental Neglect

Mother Teresa: A Life Lived for Others

3. Write the title as a rhetorical question. Then answer the question in your theme:

What Can Be Done About Child Abuse?

Should Students Grade Their Teachers?

4. Relate the title to the method of development used in the essay (see Unit 3 and Chapter 18):

Illustration:	Democracy in Action Three Roles I Play
Narration:	The Development of Rap Music Sandra Cisneros: The Making of a Storyteller
Description:	Portrait of a Farm Worker A Waterfront Scene
Process:	How to Get Organized How to Get in Shape Fast
Definition:	What It Means to Be Unemployed A Definition of Love
Comparison:	Two Country Stars Who Crossed Over Michael Douglas: In His Father's Footsteps
Contrast:	Pleasures and Problems of Owning a Home Montreal: City of Contrasts

Classification: Three Types of Soap Operas
                    What Kind of Risk Taker Are You?

Persuasion: Pornography Should Be Banned
                    The Need for Metal Detectors in Our Schools

Use this list the next time you title a paper.

Writing Assignment 3

Review two or three essays that you have written recently. Are the titles clear and interesting? Applying what you've learned in this chapter, write a better title for at least one paper.

20

The Essay Question and the Summary

PART A   The Essay Test: Budgeting Your Time
PART B   Reading and Understanding the Essay Question
PART C   Choosing the Correct Paragraph or Essay Pattern
PART D   Writing the Topic Sentence or the Thesis Statement
PART E   Preparing a Summary

This chapter will help you master two important writing tasks: responding to an **essay question** and writing a **summary**. Throughout your college career, you will have to take essay examinations; in fact, the placement test you took before enrolling in your first English class may have included an essay, and you may be asked to take an exit examination to show whether you have mastered good writing skills. Clearly, it is crucial that you learn how to do your best on essay examinations.

An **essay question** requires the same skills that a student uses in writing a paragraph or essay. Like it or not, how well you do on an essay test depends partly on how well you write; however, many students, under the pressure of a test, forget or fail to apply what they know about good writing. This chapter should improve your ability to take essay tests. Many of the sample questions on the following pages are questions from real college examinations.

Summary writing, which requires you to condense information and present it clearly, is a skill that will help you both in college and on the job. Part E of this chapter will help you write effective summaries.

PART A

The Essay Test: Budgeting Your Time

To do well on an essay test, it is not enough to know the material. You must also be able to call forth what you know, organize it, and present it in writing—all under pressure in a limited time.

Since most essay examinations are timed, it is important that you learn how to **budget** your time effectively so that you can devote adequate time to each question *and* finish the test. The following five tips will help you budget your time well.

1. **Make sure you know exactly how long the examination lasts.** A one-hour examination may really be only fifty minutes; a two-hour examination may last only one hour and forty-five minutes.

2. **Note the point value of all questions and allot time accordingly to each question.** That is, allot the most time to questions that are worth the most points and less time to ones that are worth fewer.

3. **Decide on an order in which to answer the questions.** You do not have to begin with the first question on the examination and work, in order, to the last. Instead, you may start with the questions worth the most points. Some students prefer to begin with the questions they feel they can answer most easily, thereby guaranteeing points toward the final grade on the examination. Others combine the two methods. No matter which system you use, be sure to allot enough time to the questions that are worth the most points—whether you do them first or last.

4. **Time yourself.** As you begin a particular question, calculate when you must be finished with that question in order to complete the examination, and note that time in the margin. As you write, check the clock every five minutes so that you remain on schedule.

5. **Finally, do not count on having enough time to recopy your essay.** Skip lines and write carefully so that the instructor can easily read your writing as well as any neat corrections you might make.

PRACTICE 1   Imagine that you are about to take the two-hour history test shown below. Read the test carefully, noting the point value of each question, and then answer the questions that follow the examination.

Part I   Answer both questions. 15 points each.

1. Do you think that the Versailles Peace Treaty was a "harsh" one? Be specific.

2. List the basic principles of Karl Marx. Analyze them in terms of Marx's claim that they are scientific.

Part II   Answer two of the following questions. 25 points each.

3. Describe the origins of, the philosophies behind, and the chief policies of either Communist Russia or Fascist Italy. Be specific.

---

4. What were the causes of Nelson Mandela's presidential victory in South Africa in 1994?

5. European history of the nineteenth and twentieth centuries has been increasingly related to that of the rest of the world. Why? How? With what consequences for Europe?

Part III   Briefly identify ten of the following. 2 points each.

a. John Locke
b. Franco-Prussian War
c. Stalingrad
d. Cavour
e. Manchuria, 1931
f. Entente Cordiale
g. Existentialism

h. Jacobins
i. The Opium Wars
j. Social Darwinism
k. The Reform Bill of 1832
l. The most interesting reading you have done this term (from the course list)

1. Which part would you do first and why? _____

_____

_____

How much time would you allot to the questions in this part and why?

_____

_____

2. Which part would you do second and why? _____

_____

_____

How much time would you allot to the questions in this part and why?

_____

_____

_____

3. What part would you do last and why? _____

_____

_____

How much time would you allot to the questions in this part and why?

_____

_____

_____

PART B

Reading and Understanding the Essay Question

Before you begin writing, carefully examine each question to decide exactly what your purpose is; that is, what the instructor expects you to do.

> *Question:*   Using either Communist China or Nazi Germany as a model, (a) describe the characteristics of a totalitarian state, and (b) explain how such a state was created.

- This question contains three sets of instructions.
- First, you must use "either Communist China or Nazi Germany as a model." That is, you must **choose** *one or the other* as a model.
- Second, you must **describe** and, third, you must **explain.**
- Your answer should consist of two written parts, a **description** and an **explanation.**

   It is often helpful to underline the important words, as shown in the box above, to make sure you understand the entire question and have noted all its parts.

> | *The student must* | (1) *choose* to write about *either* Communist China or Nazi Germany, not both; (2) *describe* the totalitarian state; (3) *explain* how such a state was created. |

PRACTICE 2   Read each essay question and underline key words. Then, on the lines beneath the question, describe in your own words exactly what the question requires: (1) What directions does the student have to follow? (2) How many parts will the answer contain?

Example | What were the <u>causes</u> of the Cold War? What were its chief <u>episodes</u>? <u>Why</u> has there <u>not</u> been a "hot" war?

Student must ___(1) tell what caused the Cold War (two or more causes), (2) mention___

main events of Cold War, (3) give reasons why we haven't had a full-scale war. The

essay will have three parts: causes, main events, and reasons.

1. State Newton's First Law and give examples from your own experience.

    Student must _____

    _____

    _____

    _____

2. Choose one of the following terms. Define it, give an example of it, and then show how it affects *your* life: (a) freedom of speech, (b) justice for all, (c) equal opportunity.

    Student must _____

    _____

    _____

    _____

3. Shiism and Sunni are the two great branches of Islam. Discuss the religious beliefs and the politics of each branch.

    Student must _____

    _____

    _____

    _____

4. Name and explain four types of savings institutions. What are three factors that influence one's choice of a savings institution?

   Student must _____

   _____

   _____

   _____

5. Steroids: the athlete's "unfair advantage." Discuss.

   Student must _____

   _____

   _____

   _____

6. Since the 1970s, increasing numbers of women have received undergraduate and graduate degrees in business. Discuss this change, suggesting reasons and consequences.

   Student must _____

   _____

   _____

   _____

7. Define the Monroe Doctrine of the early nineteenth century and weigh the arguments for and against it.

   Student must _____

   _____

   _____

   _____

8. The sixteenth century is known for the Renaissance, the Reformation, and the Commercial Revolution. Discuss each event, showing why it was important to the history of Western civilization.

   Student must _____

   _____

   _____

   _____

9. Erik Erikson has theorized that adult actions toward children may produce either (a) trust or mistrust, (b) autonomy or self-doubt, (c) initiative or guilt. Choose one of the pairs above and give examples of the kinds of adult behavior that might create these responses in a child.

Student must _____

_____

_____

_____

_____

_____

10. Simón Bolívar may not have been as great a hero as he was believed to be. Agree or disagree.

Student must _____

_____

_____

_____

_____

_____

_____

PART C

Choosing the Correct Paragraph or Essay Pattern

Throughout this book, you have learned how to write various types of paragraphs and compositions. Many examinations will require you simply to **illustrate, define, compare,** and so forth. How well you answer questions may depend partly on how well you understand these terms.

1. *Illustrate* "behavior modification."
2. *Define* "continental drift."
3. *Compare* Agee and Nin as diarists.

- The key words in these questions are *illustrate, define,* and *compare*—
  instruction words that tell you what you are supposed to do and what
  form your answer should take.

Here is a review list of some common instruction words used in college
examinations:

1. **Classify:** Gather into categories, types, or kinds according to a single basis of division (see Chapter 11).

2. **Compare:** Point out similarities (see Chapter 10). Instructors often use *compare* to mean point out both *similarities* and *differences*.

3. **Contrast:** Point out differences (see Chapter 10).

4. **Define:** State clearly and exactly the meaning of a word or term (see Chapter 9). You may be required to write a single-sentence definition or a full paragraph. Instructors may use *identify* as a synonym for *define* when they want a short definition.

5. **Discuss:**
   (analyze, describe, or explain) Often an instructor uses these terms to mean "thoughtfully examine a subject, approaching it from different angles." These terms allow the writer more freedom of approach than many of the others.

6. **Evaluate:** Weigh the pros and cons, advantages and disadvantages (see Chapters 10 and 12).

7. **Identify:** Give a capsule who-what-when-where-why answer. Sometimes *identify* is a synonym for *define.*

8. **Illustrate:** Give one or more examples (see Chapter 5).

9. **Narrate:**
   (trace) Follow the development of something through time, event by event (see Chapters 6 and 8).

10. **Summarize:** Write the substance of a longer work in condensed form (see Chapter 20, Part E).

PRACTICE 3   You should have no trouble deciding what kind of paragraph or composition
to use if the question uses one of the terms just defined—*contrast, trace,
classify,* and so on. However, questions are often worded in such a way that
you have to discover what kind of paragraph or essay is required. What kind
of paragraph or essay is required by each of the following questions?

Example   What is *schizophrenia?* Write a
paragraph to   define _____

1. In one concise paragraph, give the main ideas of Simone de Beauvoir's famous book *The Second Sex.*

   _____

2. What is the difference between debit and credit?

   _____

3. Follow the development of Miles Davis's musical style.

   _____

4. How do jet- and propeller-driven planes differ?

   _____

5. Who or what is each of the following: the Gang of Four, Ho Chi Minh, Tiananmen Square.

   _____

6. Explain the causes of the American Civil War.

   _____

7. Explain what is meant by *inertia.*

   _____

8. Take a stand for or against legalizing drugs in this country. Give reasons to support your stand.

   _____

9. Give two instances of the way in which demand in one industry affects demand in another industry.

   _____

10. Divide into groups the different kinds of television programs that are aired on a typical day.

    _____

PART D

Writing the Topic Sentence or the Thesis Statement

A good way to ensure that your answer truly addresses itself to the question is to compose a topic sentence or thesis statement that contains the key words of the question.

> *Question:* How do savings banks and commercial banks differ?

- The key words in this question are *savings banks, commercial banks,* and *differ.*
- What kind of paragraph or essay would be appropriate for this question?

_____

_____

> *Topic Sentence* or *Thesis Statement of Answer:* Savings banks and commercial banks differ in three basic ways.

- The answer repeats the key words of the question: *savings banks, commercial banks,* and *differ.*

PRACTICE 4   Here are eight examination questions. Write a topic sentence or thesis statement for each question by using the question as part of the answer. Even though you may not know anything about the subjects, you should be able to formulate a topic sentence or thesis statement based on the question.

1. Do you think the Dawes Allotment Act was fair to Native Americans?

   Topic sentence or thesis statement: _____

   _____

   _____

2. Contrast high school requirements in Jamaica with those in the United States.

   Topic sentence or thesis statement: _____

   _____

   _____

3. What steps can a busy person take to reduce the destructive impact of stress in his or her life?

   Topic sentence or thesis statement: _____

   _____

   _____

4. Gay couples should be allowed to adopt children. Agree or disagree with this statement.

   Topic sentence or thesis statement: _____

   _____

   _____

5. Assume that you manage a small shop that sells men's apparel. What activities would you undertake to promote the sale of sportswear?

   Topic sentence or thesis statement: _____

   _____

   _____

6. The U.S. government should cover the medical costs of AIDS. Agree or disagree with this statement.

   Topic sentence or thesis statement: _____

   _____

   _____

7. The state should subsidize students in medical school because the country needs more doctors. Agree or disagree with this statement.

   Topic sentence or thesis statement: _____

   _____

   _____

8. Does religion play a more vital role in people's lives today than it did in your parents' generation?

   Topic sentence or thesis statement: _____

   _____

   _____

PRACTICE 5
Review

This practice asks you to apply what you've learned in this chapter as you answer an essay question by following the steps listed.

1. Here is a question that might appear on a history examination. Read the question carefully, underlining important words:

   Several events in the year 1963 confirmed Martin Luther King, Jr., as the most important leader to date in the struggle for civil rights for blacks. Name at least three of these events, and tell how they demonstrated King's effectiveness and advanced his cause.

2. Decide how many parts the answer should contain.

    _____

    _____

3. Choose the paragraph or essay pattern that would best develop an answer to the question.

    _____

4. Write a topic sentence that repeats the key words of the question. Use the information provided in step 5.

    _____

    _____

    _____

    _____

5. Quickly jot down ideas on scrap paper. Select the ideas you wish to use in your answer and drop those that are irrelevant or repetitious. Here are some facts and ideas you may find helpful. Use this information to write a topic sentence (step 4) and cross out any information you do not need for your answer.

    - August '63: Marches on Washington with 250,000 people to demand passage of a civil rights law ("I have a dream" speech).
    - Important—meets with President Kennedy immediately after march on Washington; Kennedy enthusiastic.
    - December '64: Wins Nobel Prize for Peace.
    - April '68: Assassinated in Memphis, Tenn.
    - November '63: Kennedy assassinated in Dallas.
    - April–May '63: Leads nonviolent direct action in Birmingham, Ala., to fight segregation in public places. Boycotts, marches, police with attack dogs and fire hoses. King arrested.
    - April '63: Writes "Letter from a Birmingham Jail," explaining why he & his followers disobey unjust laws, why they act now. ("Freedom is never voluntarily given by the oppressor; it must be demanded by the oppressed.") Published in several magazines, and more than 1 million copies circulated in churches.
    - May '63: Leads children's marches in Birmingham. Some police refuse orders to turn fire hoses on crowds of black children.
    - May '63: Birmingham merchants agree to desegregate stores, hire some blacks.
    - June '63: After Birmingham, at MLK's urging, Kennedy submits civil rights bill to Congress. (Passed June '64.)
    - June '63: Medgar Evers assassinated in Mississippi.

6. Decide on a logical order in which to present your ideas, numbering the ideas on your list. Using the information in step 5, create a plan of the information you wish to present, in the order in which you wish to present it.

7. Using your numbered list of facts and ideas, write the clearest and best answer you can on a separate sheet of paper.

8. Now proofread your answer, correcting any grammatical errors or misspelled words.

Checklist: The Process of Writing the Essay Question

_____ 1. Survey the test and budget your time.

_____ 2. Read each question carefully, underlining important words.

_____ 3. Determine how many parts the answer should contain.

_____ 4. Considering your audience (usually the teacher) and purpose, choose the paragraph or essay pattern that would best answer the question.

_____ 5. Write a topic sentence or thesis statement that repeats the key words of the question.

_____ 6. Quickly freewrite or brainstorm ideas on scrap paper, and arrange them in a logical order, making a scratch outline or plan.

_____ 7. Write your paragraph or essay neatly, skipping lines so you will have enough room to make corrections.

_____ 8. Revise your paper and proofread it carefully, making corrections above the lines.

PART E

Preparing a Summary

A **summary** presents the main idea and supporting points of a longer work in very brief form. It might be one sentence, one paragraph, or several paragraphs long, depending on the length of the original and the nature of your assignment.

Summarizing is a useful ability both in college and at work. You might be asked, for example, to prepare a written summary of a book, an article, a report, or even the plot of a film—that is, to condense it, presenting only the highlights, *in your own words*.

Here is a one-paragraph summary of the essay in Chapter 18, Part F, of this book:

> (1) In "Two Childhoods" (Susan Fawcett and Alvin Sandberg, *Evergreen*, Fifth Edition, Houghton Mifflin Company, 1996), student Cheryl Parris contrasts her mother's childhood on a farm in South Carolina with her own childhood in New York City. (2) As a child, the writer's mother enjoyed simple, slow-paced country activities like swimming in rivers and mending birds' wings, while Ms. Parris's fast-paced youth was crammed with such urban activities as moviegoing, parties, and shopping. (3) Their personalities differed as much as—and perhaps because of—their lifestyles. (4) As a girl, the mother was known as caring, respectful, and content with nature and invented games. (5) Ms. Parris, however, describes herself as having been "petulant, pigheaded, demanding, and unstable"—very focused on material possessions. (6) Now, however, she seems to have examined her values, and she wishes her childhood had been more like her mother's.

- Notice that sentence 1 tells the title and the writer of the original essay, as well as the authors, title, publisher, and publication date of the book in which the essay appears. Sentence 1 also states the main idea of "Two Childhoods." What is its main idea?

_____

_____

- What points support this idea?

_____

_____

_____

- If you read the original essay, you will see that the writer above has summarized it *in his own words*. Only one sentence quotes Ms. Parris directly. How is this shown?

_____

_____

Preparing to Write a Summary

The secret of writing a good summary is to understand the original clearly and thoroughly. If you doubt this, try to summarize out loud for someone the highlights of last night's football game or Chapter 3 of your biology book; to summarize well, you have to know the subject matter.

Before you summarize a piece of writing, notice the title and the subtitle, if there is one; these often state the main idea. Now carefully read the work, underlining or jotting notes for yourself. What is the author's thesis? What ideas does he or she offer in support? Be careful to distinguish between the most and the least important points; your summary should include only the most important.

To help yourself understand what the author thinks is important, read with special care the first and last paragraphs of the work and the topic sentence of every paragraph. If you are summarizing a magazine article or textbook chapter, notice how the subheads (often in boldface type) point out important ideas.

Writing a Summary

A good summary includes the following:

1. the author, title, and source of the original piece of writing

2. the main idea or thesis of the original, *written in your own words*

3. the most important supporting ideas or points of the original, *written in your own words*

Try to present the ideas in your summary in proportion to those in the original. For instance, if the author devotes one paragraph to each of four ideas, you might give one sentence to each idea.

PRACTICE 6   Carefully read either "How to Prepare for a Final Exam," on pages 279–280 of this book, or "Stopping Youth Violence: An Inside Job," pages 288–289. Then, in one paragraph, summarize the essay you have chosen. As you compose your summary, refer to the checklist.

PRACTICE 7   Flip through a current copy of a magazine that attracts you: *Newsweek*, *People*, *Essence*, or another. Pick an article that interests you, read it carefully, and write a one- to three-paragraph summary of the article. Refer to the checklist that follows.

Checklist: The Process of Writing a Summary

_____ 1. Read the title and subtitle of the original; do these state its main idea?

_____ 2. Carefully read the original, underlining and jotting notes for yourself.

_____ 3. Determine the author's thesis or main idea.

_____ 4. Find the author's main supporting points. Subheads (if any), topic sentences, and the first and last paragraphs of the original may help you locate key points.

_____ 5. Now write your topic sentence, stating the author's thesis and giving the title, source, and publication date of the original.

_____ 6. In your own words, jot the author's most important supporting points, following his or her order. Use the same proportion of coverage as the original.

_____ 7. Write your summary, skipping lines so that you will have room to make corrections.

_____ 8. Now revise, asking yourself, "Will my summary convey to someone who has never read the original the author's main idea and key supporting points?"

_____ 9. Proofread, making neat corrections above the lines.

Unit 6

Reviewing the Basics

21

The Simple Sentence

PART A   Defining and Spotting Subjects
PART B   Spotting Prepositional Phrases
PART C   Defining and Spotting Verbs

Defining and Spotting Subjects

Every sentence must contain two basic elements: a **subject** and a **verb.**

A subject is the *who* or *what* word that performs the action or the *who* or *what* word about which a statement is made:

> 1. Three *hunters* tramped through the woods.
>
> 2. The blue *truck* belongs to Ralph.

- In sentence 1, *hunters,* the *who* word, performs the action—"tramped through the woods."

- In sentence 2, *truck* is the *what* word about which a statement is made—"belongs to Ralph."

- Some sentences have more than one subject, joined by *and:*

> 3. Her *aunt and uncle* love country music.

- In sentence 3, *aunt and uncle,* the *who* words, perform the action—they "love country music."

- *Aunt and uncle* is called a **compound subject.**

Sometimes an *-ing* word can be the subject of a sentence:

318

> 4. *Reading* strains my eyes.

- *Reading* is the *what* word that performs the action—"strains my eyes."

PRACTICE 1   Circle the subjects in these sentences.

1. Do you know the origin and customs of Kwanzaa?
2. This African-American holiday celebrates black heritage and lasts for seven days—from December 26 through January 1.
3. Maulana Karenga introduced Kwanzaa to America in 1966.
4. In Swahili, Kwanzaa means "first fruits of the harvest."
5. During the holiday, families share simple meals of foods from the Caribbean, Africa, South America, and the American South.
6. Specific foods have special meanings.
7. For instance, certain fruits and vegetables represent the products of group effort.
8. Another important symbol is corn, which stands for children.
9. At each dinner, celebrants light a black, red, or green candle and discuss one of the seven principles of Kwanzaa.
10. These seven principles are unity, self-determination, collective work and responsibility, cooperative economics, purpose, creativity, and faith.

PART B

Spotting Prepositional Phrases

One group of words that may confuse you as you look for subjects is the prepositional phrase. A **prepositional phrase** contains a **preposition** (a word like *at, in, of, from,* and so forth) and its **object.**

Preposition	Object
at	the beach
on	time
of	the students

The object of a preposition *cannot be* the subject of a sentence. Therefore, spotting and crossing out the prepositional phrases will help you find the subject.

---

1. The sweaters in the window look handmade.

2. The sweaters ~~in the window~~ look handmade.

3. ~~On Tuesday,~~ a carton ~~of oranges~~ was left ~~on the porch.~~

▪ In sentence 1, you might have trouble finding the subject. But once the prepositional phrase is crossed out in sentence 2, the subject, *sweaters,* is easy to spot.

▪ In sentence 3, once the prepositional phrases are crossed out, the subject, *carton,* is easy to spot.

Here are some common prepositions that you should know:

Common Prepositions

about	before	in	through
above	behind	into	to
across	between	like	toward
after	by	near	under
along	during	of	until
among	for	on	up
at	from	over	with

PRACTICE 2   Cross out the prepositional phrases in each sentence. Then circle the subject of the sentence.

1. From 6 A.M. until 10 A.M., Angel works out.

2. Local buses for Newark leave every hour.

3. Three of my friends take singing lessons.

4. That man between Ralph and Cynthia is the famous actor Hank the Hunk.

5. Near the door, a pile of laundry sits in a basket.

6. Toward evening, the houses across the river disappear in the thick fog.

7. Before class, Helena and I meet for coffee.

8. In one corner of the lab, beakers of colored liquid bubbled and boiled.

PART C

Defining and Spotting Verbs

Action Verbs

In order to be complete, every sentence must contain a **verb.** One kind of verb, called an **action verb,** expresses the action that the subject is performing:

> 1. The star quarterback *fumbled.*
>
> 2. The carpenters *worked* all day, but the bricklayers *went* home early.

- In sentence 1, the action verb is *fumbled.*

- In sentence 2, the action verbs are *worked* and *went.**

Linking Verbs

Another kind of verb, called a **linking verb,** links the subject to words that describe or identify it:

> 3. Don *is* a fine mathematician.
>
> 4. This fabric *feels* rough and scratchy.

- In sentence 3, the verb *is* links the subject *Don* with the noun *mathematician.*

- In sentence 4, the verb *feels* links the subject *fabric* with the adjectives *rough* and *scratchy.*

Here are some common linking verbs:

*For work on compound predicates, see Chapter 14, "Revising for Sentence Variety," Part D.

Common Linking Verbs

appear	feel
be (am, is, are, was, were, has been, have been, had been . . .)	look
become	seem

Verbs of More Than One Word—Helping Verbs

So far you have dealt with verbs of only one word—*fumbled, worked, is, feels,* and so on. But many verbs consist of more than one word:

---

5. He *should have taken* the train home.

6. *Are* Tanya and Joe *practicing* the piano?

7. The lounge *was painted* last week.

- In sentence 5, *taken* is the main verb; *should* and *have* are the **helping verbs.**

- In sentence 6, *practicing* is the main verb; *are* is the helping verb.

- In sentence 7, *painted* is the main verb; *was* is the helping verb.*

PRACTICE 3   Underline the verbs in these sentences.

1. Daphne blushed.

2. This sheepskin coat looks warm.

3. You should have seen Karen at her first golf lesson.

4. Is he a magician?

5. Professor Avery was humming the latest hit.

6. Shall we visit Dime Box, Texas?

7. The wedding presents will be delivered tonight.

8. Those uninvited guests have finally left.

9. Al and Leon are writing a script for a documentary about jazz.

10. At midnight my roommate closed his books, but I studied until 2 A.M.

*For more work on verbs in the passive voice, see Chapter 26, "The Past Participle," Part E.

PRACTICE 4 Circle the subjects and underline the verbs in the following sentences. First, cross out any prepositional phrases.

1. Do you think of baseball as America's oldest team sport?

2. In fact, lacrosse takes that honor.

3. Native Americans were playing the sport long before the arrival of Europeans.

4. In order to score, one team must throw a ball into the opposing team's goal.

5. The goal is ferociously guarded by a goalie.

6. Each player uses a curved racket with a mesh basket at its end.

7. Algonquin tribes in the valley of the St. Lawrence River invented the game.

8. The Hurons and Iroquois soon learned this demanding sport.

9. By 1500, the rough and tumble game was played by dozens of tribes in Canada and the United States.

10. Sometimes matches would require hundreds of players and might last for days.

11. Playing lacrosse trained young warriors for battle.

12. With this in mind, the Cherokees named lacrosse "little brother of war."

13. However, tribes often settled their differences peaceably with a lacrosse match.

14. French missionaries saw a resemblance between the racket and a bishop's cross.

15. They changed the name of the game from *boggotaway,* the native word, to *lacrosse,* a French word for *cross.*

22

Coordination and Subordination

PART A   Coordination
PART B   Subordination
PART C   Semicolons
PART D   Conjunctive Adverbs
PART E   Review

PART A

Coordination

A **clause** is a group of words that contains a subject and a verb. If a clause can stand alone as a complete idea, it is an **independent clause** and can be written as a **simple sentence.***

Here are two independent clauses written as simple sentences:

> 1. The dog barked all night.
>
> 2. The neighbors didn't complain.

You can join two clauses together by placing a comma and a **coordinating conjunction** between them:

> 3. The dog barked all night, *but* the neighbors didn't complain.
>
> 4. Let's go to the beach today, *for* it is too hot to do anything else.

- The coordinating conjunctions *but* and *for* join together two clauses.

- Note that *a comma precedes each coordinating conjunction.*

* For more work on simple sentences, see Chapter 21, "The Simple Sentence."

Here is a list of the most common coordinating conjunctions:

> **Coordinating Conjunctions**
>
> and   for   or   yet
>
> but   nor   so

Be sure to choose the coordinating conjunction that best expresses the *relationship* between the two clauses in a sentence:

> 5. It was late, *so* I decided to take a bus home.
>
> 6. It was late, *yet* I decided to take a bus home.

- The *so* in sentence 5 means that the lateness of the hour caused me to take the bus. (The trains don't run after midnight.)

- The *yet* in sentence 6 means that despite the late hour I still decided to take a bus home. (I knew I might have to wait two hours at the bus stop.)

- Note that a comma precedes the coordinating conjunction.

PRACTICE 1   Read the following sentences for meaning. Then fill in the coordinating conjunction that *best* expresses the relationship between the two clauses. Don't forget to add the comma.

1. Diners still dot the highways of the United States _____ they are not as popular as they once were.

2. In 1872, Walter Scott of Providence, Rhode Island, decided to make prepared and cooked food easier to buy _____ he started selling sandwiches and pies from a large horse-drawn wagon.

3. Customers flocked to this first "diner" _____ the food was delicious, plentiful, and inexpensive.

4. Many did not like standing outside to eat _____ another businessman, Sam Jones, redecorated the wagon and invited customers inside to dine.

5. In order to widen the appeal of their diners, some owners installed stained-glass windows _____ other proprietors added elegant decorations.

6. In the 1920s, narrow booths began to replace stools _____ diners were fixed permanently on the ground.

7. Stainless steel, efficient-looking diners were everywhere by the 1940s

   _____ even this style gave way to the fancy colonial and Mediterranean designs of the 1960s.

8. Diners are not as common as they were twenty years ago _____ can they compete with fast food take-out chains like McDonald's and Wendy's.

9. Nonetheless, customers do have a choice; they can stand in line and wait

   for a quick hamburger _____ they can sit and be waited on in a diner.

10. Most choose fast food _____ the more leisurely diner still has its charm.

PRACTICE 2   Combine these simple sentences with a coordinating conjunction. Punctuate correctly.

1. My daughter wants to be a mechanic. She spends every spare minute at the garage.

   _____

   _____

2. Ron dared not look over the edge. Heights made him dizzy.

   _____

   _____

3. Tasha's living room is cozy. Her guests always gather in the kitchen.

   _____

   _____

4. Meet me by the bicycle rack. Meet me at Lulu's Nut Shop.

   _____

   _____

5. In 1969, the first manned spaceship landed on the moon. Most Americans felt proud.

   _____

   _____

PART B

Subordination

Two clauses can also be joined with a **subordinating conjunction.** The clause following a subordinating conjunction is called a **subordinate** or **dependent clause** because it depends on an independent clause to complete its meaning:

---

1. We will light the candles *when Flora arrives.*

- *When Flora arrives* is a subordinate or dependent clause introduced by the subordinating conjunction *when.*

- By itself, *when Flora arrives* is incomplete; it depends on the independent clause to complete its meaning.*

Note that sentence 1 can also be written this way:

---

2. *When Flora arrives,* we will light the candles.

- The meaning of sentences 1 and 2 is the same, but the punctuation is different.

- In sentence 1, because the subordinate clause *follows* the independent clause, *no comma* is needed.

- In sentence 2, however, because the subordinate clause *begins* the sentence, it is followed by a *comma.*

Here is a partial list of subordinating conjunctions:

Subordinating Conjunctions			
after	because	since	when(ever)
although	before	unless	whereas
as (if)	if	until	while

---

* For more work on incomplete sentences, or fragments, see Chapter 23, "Avoiding Sentence Errors," Part B.

Be sure to choose the subordinating conjunction that *best expresses the relationship* between the two clauses in a sentence:

> 3. This course was excellent *because* Professor Green taught it.
>
> 4. This course was excellent *although* Professor Green taught it.

- Sentence 3 says that the course was excellent *because* Professor Green, a great teacher, gave it.

- Sentence 4 says that the course was excellent *despite the fact that* Professor Green, apparently a bad teacher, gave it.

PRACTICE 3 Read the following sentences for meaning. Then fill in the subordinating conjunction that *best* expresses the relationship between the two clauses.

1. We could see very clearly last night _____ the moon was so bright.

2. Violet read *Sports Illustrated* _____ Daisy walked in the woods.

3. _____ it is cold outside, our new wood-burning Franklin stove keeps us warm.

4. The students buzzed with excitement _____ Professor Hargrave announced that classes would be held at the zoo.

5. _____ his shoulder loosens up a bit, Ron will stay on the bench.

PRACTICE 4 Punctuate the following sentences by adding a comma where necessary. Put a *C* after any correct sentences.

1. Carmen worked on her sculpture until the studio closed at 11 P.M.

2. Whenever Hank and Reggie get together they argue about computers.

3. I admire Thomas Edison because he dedicated his life to developing useful inventions.

4. Since you are very good at mathematics why don't you consider a career in accounting?

5. Although few people realize it the planet Pluto was discovered only about sixty years ago.

PRACTICE 5   Combine each pair of ideas below by using a subordinating conjunction. Write each combination twice, once with the subordinating conjunction at the beginning of the sentence and once with the subordinating conjunction in the middle of the sentence. Punctuate correctly.

Example   We stayed on the beach.

The sun went down.

We stayed on the beach until the sun went down.

Until the sun went down, we stayed on the beach.

1. The wilderness inspires him.

2. He hopes to settle in northern Ontario.

_____

_____

_____

_____

3. Hilda breaks out in a rash.

4. Ragweed blooms in the back yard.

_____

_____

_____

_____

5. I had known you were coming.

6. I would have vacuumed the guest room.

_____

_____

_____

_____

7. He was the first person to eat a slice of meat between two pieces of bread.

8. The sandwich was named after the Earl of Sandwich.

_____

_____

_____

_____

_____

9. Peter was about to answer the final question.

10. The buzzer sounded.

_____

_____

_____

_____

11. Few soap operas remain on the radio.

12. Daytime television is filled with them.

_____

_____

_____

_____

13. The snow stopped.

14. People with sleds and toboggans headed for White Knuckle Hill.

_____

_____

_____

_____

15. The chimney spewed black smoke and soot.

16. Nobody complained to the local environmental agency.

_____

_____

_____

_____

_____

PART C

Semicolons

You can join two independent clauses by placing a **semicolon** between them. The semicolon takes the place of a conjunction:

---

1. She hopes to receive good grades this semester; her scholarship depends on her maintaining a 3.5 index.

2. Tony is a careless driver; he has had three minor accidents this year alone.

- Each of the sentences above could also be made into two *separate sentences* by replacing the semicolon with a period.

- Note that the first word after a semicolon is *not* capitalized.

PRACTICE 6   Combine each pair of independent clauses by placing a semicolon between them.

1. Rush-hour traffic was worse than usual no one seemed to mind.

2. The senator appeared ill at ease at the news conference he seemed afraid of saying the wrong thing.

3. The new seed catalogue, a fifteen-hundred-page volume, was misplaced the volume weighed ten pounds.

4. On Thursday evening, Stuart decided to go camping on Friday morning, he packed his bags and left.

5. In the early 1960s, the Beatles burst on the rock scene rock music has never been the same.

6. Ron Jackson has been promoted he will be an effective manager.

7. This stream is full of trout every spring men and women with waders and fly rods arrive on its banks.

8. Not a single store was open at that hour not a soul walked the streets.

PRACTICE 7   Each independent clause that follows is the first half of a sentence. Add a semicolon and a second independent clause. Make sure your second thought is also independent and can stand alone.

1. At 2 A.M. I stumbled toward the ringing telephone _____

   _____

2. Toby rented a VCR on Thursday _____

   _____

3. The police officer lobbed tear gas through the warehouse window _____

   _____

4. Faulkner's stories often depict life in the South _____

   _____

5. His mud-covered boots looked like antiques _____

   _____

6. During the Great Depression, millions of workers were unemployed _____

   _____

7. Cameras are not permitted in the museum _____

   _____

8. Employees objected to the drug tests _____

   _____

PART D

Conjunctive Adverbs

A **conjunctive adverb** placed after the semicolon can help clarify the relationship between two clauses:

---

1. I like the sound of that stereo; *however,* the price is too high.

2. They have not seen that film; *moreover,* they have not been to a theater for three years.

- Note that a comma follows the conjunctive adverb.

Here is a partial list of conjunctive adverbs.

Conjunctive Adverbs

consequently	in fact	nevertheless
furthermore	indeed	then
however	moreover	therefore

PRACTICE 8   Punctuate each sentence correctly by adding a semicolon, a comma, or both, where necessary. Put a *C* after any correct sentences.

1. I hate to wash my car windows nevertheless it's a job that must be done.

2. Sonia doesn't know how to play chess however she would like to learn.

3. Dean Fader is very funny in fact he could be a professional comedian.

4. Deep water makes Maurice nervous therefore he does not want to row to the middle of the lake.

5. I like this painting; the soft tones of peach and blue remind me of tropical sunsets.

6. The faculty approved of the new trimester system; furthermore, the students liked it too.

7. Bill has a cassette player plugged into his ear all day consequently he misses a lot of good conversations.

8. We toured the darkroom then we watched the models pose for the photographer.

PRACTICE 9   Combine each pair of independent clauses by placing a semicolon and a conjunctive adverb between them. Punctuate correctly.

1. The lake is quite long we rowed from one end of it to the other.

2. I can still see the streaks under the fresh white paint we will have to give the room another coat.

3. Mr. Farrington loves bluegrass music he plays with a local bluegrass band every Saturday night.

4. Jay, a tall boy, has poor eyesight he was turned down for the basketball team.

5. Yesterday, hikers from the Nature-Walkers' Club made real progress in blazing a trail they managed to get as far as the foot of Mt. Lookout.

6. By midnight Tien had finished tuning his engine he still had enough time for a short nap before the race.

7. An arthroscope helps doctors examine the inside of an injured knee the use of this instrument can prevent unnecessary surgery.

8. Rhinoceroses live in protected animal preserves poachers still manage to kill a few of these magnificent beasts each year.

PART E

Review

In this chapter, you have combined simple sentences by means of a **coordinating conjunction,** a **subordinating conjunction,** a **semicolon,** and a **semicolon** and **conjunctive adverb.** Here is a review chart of the sentence patterns discussed in this chapter.*

* For more ways to combine sentences, see Chapter 14, "Revising for Sentence Variety," Part D.

Coordination

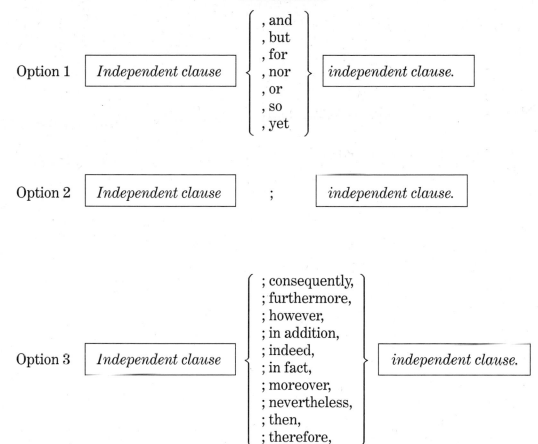

Option 1 — Independent clause { , and / , but / , for / , nor / , or / , so / , yet } independent clause.

Option 2 — Independent clause   ;   independent clause.

Option 3 — Independent clause { ; consequently, / ; furthermore, / ; however, / ; in addition, / ; indeed, / ; in fact, / ; moreover, / ; nevertheless, / ; then, / ; therefore, } independent clause.

Subordination

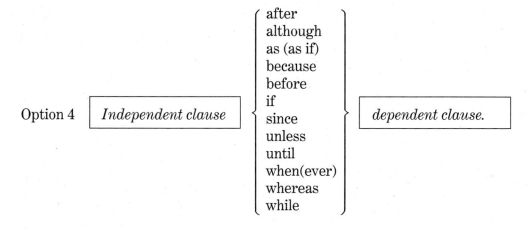

Option 4 — Independent clause { after / although / as (as if) / because / before / if / since / unless / until / when(ever) / whereas / while } dependent clause.

Option 5 {
After
Although
As (as if)
Because
Before
If
Since
Unless
Until
When(ever)
Whereas
While
}

> *dependent clause, independent clause.*

PRACTICE 10   Read each pair of simple sentences to determine the relationship between them. Then join each pair in three different ways, using the conjunctions or conjunctive adverbs in parentheses at the left. Punctuate correctly.

Example   The company picnic was canceled.

Rain started to fall in torrents.

(for)   The company picnic was canceled, for the rain started to fall in torrents.

(because)   Because the rain started to fall in torrents, the company picnic was canceled.

(therefore)   The rain started to fall in torrents; therefore, the company picnic was canceled.

1. This rug costs a great deal.

   It is hand-loomed.

   (for) _____

   _____

   (because) _____

   _____

   (therefore) _____

   _____

2. We just put in four hours paving the driveway.

   We need a long break and a cold drink.

   (since) _____

   _____

(because) _____

_____

(consequently) _____

_____

_____

3. The fishermen trolled in the bay for hours.

They caught nothing.

(but) _____

_____

(although) _____

_____

(however) _____

_____

4. Don is an expert mechanic.

He intends to open a service center.

(and) _____

_____

(since) _____

_____

(furthermore) _____

_____

5. We haven't heard from her.

We haven't given up hope.

(but) _____

_____

(although) _____

_____

(nevertheless) _____

_____

PRACTICE 11   In your writing, aim for variety by mixing coordination, subordination, and simple sentences.* Rewrite the following paragraphs to eliminate monotonous simple sentences. First, read the paragraph to determine the relationships between ideas; then choose the conjunctions that best express these relationships. Punctuate correctly.

Adam rewrite only one,

Paragraph a: Difficult situations sometimes bring out the best in people. A blizzard struck our city last week. I huddled on a corner, shivering and grumbling. The bus arrived. It was crowded and cold on board. The mood was cheery, almost partylike. The driver was a kind and patient man. His pleasantness seemed to spread to the passengers. He allowed them to alight at unscheduled stops. They didn't have to walk a block or two out of their way. People were fighting the wind on their way to the bus stop. He would wait for them. The passengers were very grateful. One woman bowed to the bus driver. She got off. She exclaimed not simply, "Thank you" or "Have a good evening," but "Have a good life!"

_____

_____

_____

_____

_____

_____

_____

_____

_____

_____

_____

_____

Paragraph b: A great star blazed in the sky. Paiea was born in Hawaii in 1758. Seers had foretold that this son of a chieftain would defeat his enemies and govern a united Hawaii. A jealous former ruler ordered the baby killed. Sympathetic courtiers hid the noble infant in a cave. There he was renamed Kamehameha. This name means "The Lonely One" or "The One Set Apart." In time, it was safe for young Kamehameha to leave the cave. He was very strong and agile. He excelled in war games. James Cook, an English sea captain, landed in Hawaii in 1778. Kamehameha had already become the most

* For more work on sentence variety, see Chapter 14, "Revising for Sentence Variety."

important chieftain. He gained even more power by conquering one independent island after another. With the help of English sailors, he successfully invaded Maui. Eventually, the rest of the Hawaiian islands came under his control. By 1810, this shrewd and powerful king ruled a united country. A lover of his native culture, he continued many ancient traditions of his homeland. He also borrowed many ideas from the Europeans. The prophecies at his birth had come true. He had defeated his enemies and become the sole ruler of a united Hawaii.

_____

_____

_____

_____

_____

_____

_____

_____

_____

_____

_____

_____

_____

23

Avoiding Sentence Errors

PART A   Avoiding Run-Ons and Comma Splices
PART B   Avoiding Fragments

Avoiding Run-Ons and Comma Splices

Be careful to avoid **run-ons** and **comma splices.**

A **run-on sentence** incorrectly runs together two independent clauses without a conjunction or punctuation. This error confuses the reader, who cannot tell where one thought stops and the next begins:

> 1. Run-on: My neighbor Mr. Hoffman is seventy-five years old he plays tennis every Saturday afternoon.

A **comma splice** incorrectly joins two independent clauses with a comma but no conjunction:

> 2. Comma splice: My neighbor Mr. Hoffman is seventy-five years old, he plays tennis every Saturday afternoon.

The run-on and the comma splice can be corrected in five ways:

340

Use two separate sentences.	My neighbor Mr. Hoffman is seventy-five years old. He plays tennis every Saturday afternoon.
Use a coordinating conjunction. (See Chapter 22, Part A.)	My neighbor Mr. Hoffman is seventy-five years old, but he plays tennis every Saturday afternoon.
Use a subordinating conjunction. (See Chapter 22, Part B.)	Although my neighbor Mr. Hoffman is seventy-five years old, he plays tennis every Saturday afternoon.
Use a semicolon. (See Chapter 22, Part C.)	My neighbor Mr. Hoffman is seventy-five years old; he plays tennis every Saturday afternoon.
Use a semicolon and a conjunctive adverb. (See Chapter 22, Part D.)	My neighbor Mr. Hoffman is seventy-five years old; however, he plays tennis every Saturday afternoon.

PRACTICE 1 Some of these sentences contain run-ons or comma splices; others are correct. Put a *C* next to the correct sentences. Revise the run-ons and comma splices in any way you choose. Be careful of punctuation.

1. Ms. Jones took the Concorde to Paris the flight lasted just three hours.

   Revised: _____

   _____

2. These new sneakers hurt my daughter's feet they'll have to be returned.

   Revised: _____

   _____

3. Ken started wearing a hairpiece, everyone complimented him on how young he looked.

   Revised: _____

   _____

4. Most successful people don't fear failure, they know that mistakes are good teachers.

   Revised: _____

   _____

5. Either of those roads will lead you to the center of town take your pick.

   Revised: _____

   _____

6. The movie will not begin for two hours let's window-shop.

   Revised: _____

   _____

7. The hot-air balloon rose off the ground the crowd gasped.

   Revised: _____

   _____

8. Solar energy can become the fuel of the future the government has to invest more funds for research.

   Revised: _____

   _____

9. When I first moved into this house, I never dreamed I would live here for fifteen years.

   Revised: _____

   _____

10. Students applying to the Fashion Institute of Technology must show creative talent only one student in six gets accepted.

    Revised: _____

    _____

PRACTICE 2 Proofread the following essay for run-ons and comma splices. Correct them in any way you choose, writing your revised essay on a separate sheet of paper. Be careful of the punctuation.

Will K. Kellogg, Least Likely to Succeed

(1) Will Kellogg was an unlikely candidate for fame and fortune, he became one of America's great successes.

(2) The two Kellogg boys could not have been more different. (3) Will was a slow learner with few friends and interests. (4) His father pulled him from school at the age of thirteen he made Will a traveling broom salesman for the family company. (5) Eight years older than Will, John Harvey Kellogg was the family genius. (6) He became a noted surgeon and head of an exclusive health resort. (7) He treated his patients with exercise and a strict vegetarian diet he, wrote best-selling books about healthful living.

(8) In 1880, Will was twenty years old, Dr. John hired him to work at the resort. (9) For the next twenty-five years, Will served as his brother's flunky. (10) According to rumor, he shaved Dr. John every day and shined his shoes. (11) John bicycled to work, Will jogged alongside getting his daily work orders. (12) Dr. John was a wealthy man, he never paid Will more than eighty-seven dollars a month.

(13) One of the special foods at the resort was pressed wheat. (14) The brothers boiled wheat dough then they pressed it through rollers into thin sheets. (15) One night, they left the boiled dough out. (16) When they pressed it, it turned into flakes instead of forming sheets. (17) Will suggested that they toast the flakes. (18) Resort guests loved the new cereal, former guests ordered it from their homes. (19) To meet the demand, the brothers opened a mail-order business, however, the snobbish Dr. John refused to sell the flakes to grocery stores.

(20) In 1906, Will finally bought out John's share of the cereal patents, struck out on his own. (21) Will turned out to be a business genius. (22) He invented advertising techniques that made his new product,

Kellogg's Corn Flakes, a household word. (23) Will K. Kellogg quickly became one of the richest persons in America.

(24) Sadly, the two brothers never reconciled. (25) In 1943, ninety-one-year-old Dr. John wrote Will an apology John died before the letter reached his younger brother.

PART B

Avoiding Fragments

Another error to avoid is the **sentence fragment**. A **sentence** must contain a subject and a verb and must be able to stand alone as a complete idea. A **sentence fragment,** therefore, can be defined in terms of what it lacks: either a subject or a verb, or both—it cannot stand alone as a complete idea.

Here are some common kinds of sentence fragments and ways to correct them:

Complete sentence:	1. Kirk decided to major in psychology.
Fragment:	2. Since human behavior had always fascinated him.

- Example 1 is a complete simple sentence.

- Example 2 is a fragment because it is a dependent clause beginning with the subordinating conjunction *since.* Furthermore, it is not a complete idea.

This fragment can be corrected in two ways:

Corrected:	3. Kirk decided to major in psychology since human behavior had always fascinated him.
	4. Kirk decided to major in psychology. Human behavior had always fascinated him.

- In sentence 3, the fragment is combined with the sentence before it.

- In sentence 4, the fragment is changed into a complete sentence.

Fragment:	5. A fine pianist.
Complete sentence:	6. Marsha won a scholarship to Juilliard.

- Example 5 is a fragment because it lacks a verb and is not a complete idea.
- Example 6 is a complete sentence.

This fragment can be corrected in two ways:

Corrected:	7. A fine pianist, Marsha won a scholarship to Juilliard.
	8. Marsha won a scholarship to Juilliard. She is a fine pianist.

- In sentence 7, the fragment is combined with the sentence after it.
- In sentence 8, the fragment is changed into a complete sentence by the addition of a verb, *is*, and a subject, *she*.

Complete sentence:	9. Daniel can always be seen on the track in the morning.
Fragment:	10. Running a mile or two before breakfast.

- Example 9 is a complete sentence.
- Example 10 is a fragment because it lacks a subject and because an *-ing* verb cannot stand alone without a helping verb.*

This fragment can be corrected in two ways:

Corrected:	11. Daniel can always be seen on the track in the morning, running a mile or two before breakfast.
	12. Daniel can always be seen on the track in the morning. He runs a mile or two before breakfast.

* For work on joining ideas with an *-ing* modifier, see Chapter 14, "Revising for Sentence Variety," Part D.

- In sentence 11, the fragment is combined with the sentence before it.

- In sentence 12, the fragment is changed into a complete sentence.

Complete sentence:	13. Luz is a chemistry teacher who never runs out of creative ideas.
Fragment:	14. Who has the ability to keep her classes involved throughout the lesson.

- Example 13 is a complete sentence.

- Example 14 is a fragment because it is a relative clause beginning with *who.**

The fragment in example 14 can be corrected in two ways, as shown below:

Corrected:	15. Luz is a chemistry teacher who never runs out of creative ideas and who has the ability to keep her classes involved throughout the lesson.
	16. Luz is a chemistry teacher who never runs out of creative ideas. She has the ability to keep her classes involved throughout the lesson.

- In sentence 15, the fragment is combined with the sentence before it.

- In sentence 16, the fragment is changed into a complete sentence.

Complete sentence:	17. Laura has always wanted to become a travel agent.
Fragment:	18. To tell people about exotic countries that they might visit.

- Example 17 is a complete sentence.

- Example 18 is a fragment because it lacks a subject and contains only the infinitive form of the verb—*to* plus the simple form of the verb *tell.*

* For more work on relative clauses, see Chapter 14, "Revising for Sentence Variety," Part D, and Chapter 24, "Present Tense (Agreement)," Part G.

This fragment can be corrected in two ways:

> Corrected: 19. Laura has always wanted to become a travel agent and to tell people about exotic countries that they might visit.
>
> 20. Laura has always wanted to become a travel agent. She would find it exciting to tell people about exotic countries that they might visit.

- In sentence 19, the fragment is combined with the sentence before it.
- In sentence 20, the fragment is changed into a complete sentence.

PRACTICE 3   Some of these examples are fragments; others are complete sentences. Put a *C* next to the complete sentences. Revise the fragments in any way you choose.

Example | Leaping into the air.

Revised | Leaping into the air, she shouted, "I won, I won!" _____

1. Interviewing divorced people for her research project.

   Revised: _____

   _____

2. Since we live near the Colorado River.

   Revised: _____

   _____

3. Couldn't find the group's new album.

   Revised: _____

   _____

4. A tall, thin man with bushy eyebrows.

   Revised: _____

   _____

5. To earn money for college.

   Revised: _____

   _____

6. Ten minutes after they won the Super Bowl.

   Revised: _____

   _____

7. She has patented three of her inventions.

   Revised: _____

   _____

8. Frantically flipping through the pages of the dictionary.

   Revised: _____

   _____

9. Someone who loves to take risks.

   Revised: _____

   _____

10. Although I usually ask my friends for advice.

    Revised: _____

    _____

PRACTICE 4   Proofread this essay for fragments. Correct them in any way you choose, either adding the fragments to other sentences or making them into complete sentences. Write your revised essay on a separate piece of paper. Be careful of punctuation.

The Regent Diamond

(1) Throughout its exciting history. (2) The Regent diamond has been one of the world's most desired jewels.

(3) In 1701, the 410-carat gem was discovered in an Indian mine by a slave. (4) Who risked his life to smuggle it out. (5) Slashing his leg. (6) He stuffed the huge diamond into the wound and headed for the seacoast. (7) A shifty sea captain offered to sail him to freedom for half the value of the jewel. (8) When at sea, the captain stole the stone. (9) And threw

the slave overboard. (10) He then sold the precious rock to a powerful diamond merchant.

(11) The merchant had difficulty unloading the diamond. (12) Because it was so large and because it was stolen. (13) He finally sold it to Robert Pitt, a young Englishman. (14) Who had come to India seeking his fortune. (15) By the time this shrewd adventurer returned home. (16) The English had nicknamed him "Diamond" Pitt and christened the stone "the Pitt."

(17) Few people believed Pitt had come by the diamond honestly. (18) So he also had trouble selling it. (19) Pitt was terrified of being robbed and murdered. (20) Whenever he carried the stone. (21) He disguised himself and would not sleep in the same place for more than two nights. (22) If someone recognized him. (23) He would deny that he carried the stone with him. (24) It took years. (25) But he finally sold his diamond in 1717 for an enormous sum to the Duke of Orleans. (26) The Regent of France.

(27) Now called the Regent diamond. (28) The fabulous stone was the most valuable French crown jewel. (29) In 1792, during the French Revolution. (30) It disappeared, only to be found in a ditch in the middle of Paris. (31) Upon becoming emperor. (32) Napoleon had the diamond set into the hilt of his ceremonial sword. (33) In 1887 when the last French monarchy fell and the jewel collection was auctioned. (34) The Regent diamond was placed in the Louvre, the famous museum in Paris. (35) Where it still glitters today.

PRACTICE 5 Review   Proofread these two essays for run-ons, comma splices, and fragments. Correct the errors in any way you choose, writing the revised draft on a separate piece of paper.

Words for the Wise

(1) Everyone knows that Scrabble is America's favorite word game. (2) It was invented by Alfred Butts. (3) An architect who wanted to create

a word game that required both luck and skill. (4) In 1938, Butts produced a board with 225 squares and 100 tiles with letters on them. (5) Each letter was worth a certain number of points, depending on how easy it was to use that letter in a word.

(6) Butts made fifty Scrabble sets by hand he gave them to his friends (7) Who loved playing Scrabble. (8) Strangely enough, Butts could not interest a manufacturer in the game. (9) A friend of his, James Brunot, asked Butts for permission to manufacture and sell the game. (10) However, Brunot also had little success. (11) Selling only a few sets a year. (12) Then suddenly, in 1953, Scrabble caught on a million sets were sold that year.

(13) Butts and Brunot couldn't keep up with the demand, they sold the rights to a game manufacturer. (14) The rest is history today Scrabble is produced in half a dozen foreign languages it is also used as a learning tool. (15) To teach children spelling and vocabulary.

A Royal Refreshment

(1) The simple marmalade that many people spread on toast each morning has a long, distinguished history. (2) The preferred food of kings and queens. (3) Marmalade the favorite food of Henry VIII, King of England. (4) Mary, Queen of Scots, believed that marmalade cured seasickness she ate some on her long Channel crossings. (5) The table at Queen Elizabeth I's court always included a serving of marmalade.

(6) Served for hundreds of years as a dessert. (7) Marmalade finally became a breakfast food in the 1700s. (8) Because it was an aid to digestion, people ate it for their first meal of the day it tasted delicious on a cold morning. (9) No longer just a royal treat, it very popular.

(10) There are many recipes for marmalade. (11) Which is prepared all over the world. (12) British cooks use bitter Seville oranges from Spain. (13) To make a thick jelly filled with shredded orange peel. (14) Some recipes

call for quince,* others use lemons or grapefruit. (15) Boiling these fruits and their peels. (16) The chefs of many countries create their own special versions of marmalade.

---

* Quince: a fruit that resembles an apple.

24

Present Tense (Agreement)

PART A

Defining Subject-Verb Agreement

Subjects and verbs in the present tense must **agree** in number; that is, singular subjects take verbs with singular endings, and plural subjects take verbs with plural endings.

Verbs in the Present Tense
Sample Verb: To Leap

	Singular		*Plural*	
	If the subject is	*the verb is*	*If the subject is*	*the verb is*
1st person:	I	leap	we	leap
2nd person:	you	leap	you	leap
3rd person:	he she it	leaps	they	leap

- Use an *-s* or *-es* ending on the verb only when the subject is *he, she,* or *it* or the equivalent of *he, she,* or *it.*

The subjects and verbs in the following sentences agree:

---

1. He *bicycles* to the steel mills every morning.

2. They *bicycle* to the steel mills every morning.

3. This student *hopes* to go to social work school.

4. The planets *revolve* around the sun.

- In sentence 1, the singular subject, *he,* takes the singular form of the verb, *bicycles. Bicycles* agrees with *he.*

- In sentence 2, the plural subject, *they,* takes the plural form of the verb, *bicycle. Bicycle* agrees with *they.*

- In sentence 3, the subject, *student,* is equivalent to *he* or *she* and takes the singular form of the verb, *hopes.*

- In sentence 4, the subject, *planets,* is equivalent to *they* and takes the plural form of the verb, *revolve.*

Subjects joined by the conjunction *and* usually take a plural verb:

---

5. Kirk and Quincy *attend* a pottery class at the Y.

- The subject, *Kirk and Quincy,* is plural, the equivalent of *they.*

- *Attend* agrees with the plural subject.*

PRACTICE 1 Underline the subject and circle the correct present tense verb.

1. Many Americans (thinks, think) of Seattle, Washington, as the ideal city.

2. They (praises, praise) it for many reasons, including a relaxed lifestyle, cultural diversity, and spectacular natural scenery.

3. Puget Sound and Lake Washington (surrounds, surround) most of Seattle.

4. Beyond the water, mountains (looms, loom) on the horizon, Mount Rainier the tallest of all.

5. Seattle Center, the site of the 1962 World's Fair, (symbolizes, symbolize) the city's energy.

* For work on consistent verb tense, see Chapter 13, "Revising for Consistency and Parallelism," Part A.

6. The Space Needle tower (rises, rise) 605 feet above the center.

7. At its top, a revolving restaurant (treats, treat) diners to a stunning view.

8. To learn the city's history, visitors (explores, explore) such areas as the Water Front and Pioneer Square.

9. Seattle's East Asian community, the third largest in the country, (congregates, congregate) in the International District.

10. Splashing fountains and sculpture (lines, line) the streets and other public areas.

11. The city also (boasts, boast) an extensive park system, complete with an aquarium and a zoo.

12. Running and hiking trails (lures, lure) athletes.

13. Some people (complains, complain) about the amount of rain that falls on Seattle.

14. However, thousands (flocks, flock) to this vibrant city each year to live and vacation.

15. Can you (blames, blame) them?

PART B

Three Troublesome Verbs in the Present Tense: To Be, To Have, To Do

Choosing the correct verb form of *to be,* *to have,* and *to do* can be tricky. Study these charts:

Reference Chart—*To Be*
Present Tense

	Singular		*Plural*	
	If the subject is	the verb is	If the subject is	the verb is
1st person:	I	am	we	are
2nd person:	you	are	you	are
3rd person:	he she it	is	they	are

Reference Chart—*To Have*
Present Tense

	Singular		*Plural*	
	If the subject is	*the verb is*	*If the subject is*	*the verb is*
1st person:	I	have	we	have
2nd person:	you	have	you	have
3rd person:	he she } it	has	they	have

Reference Chart—*To Do*
Present Tense

	Singular		*Plural*	
	If the subject is	*the verb is*	*If the subject is*	*the verb is*
1st person:	I	do	we	do
2nd person:	you	do	you	do
3rd person:	he she } it	does	they	do

PRACTICE 2   Write the correct present tense form of the verb in the space at the right of the pronoun.

To be	*To have*	*To do*
I _____	we _____	it _____
we _____	she _____	they _____
he _____	he _____	she _____
you _____	they _____	you _____
it _____	I _____	he _____
they _____	it _____	we _____
she _____	you _____	I _____

PRACTICE 3   Fill in the correct present tense form of the verb in parentheses.

1. She _____ (to have) a wonderful habit of sticking to her principles.

2. The old churchyard _____ (to be) a wonderful place to think.

3. You always _____ (to do) well in statistics.

4. To save money, Angel and she _____ (to be) bringing their own lunch to the office.

5. Tyrone _____ (to have) a large collection of Bruins photos.

6. _____ (to do) he always act so pleased with himself?

7. These felt-tip pens _____ (to be) useful for highlighting important ideas in books and magazines.

8. This apartment _____ (to have) a view of the river; those

   apartments _____ (to have) views of Euclid Avenue.

9. Mr. Weston _____ (to be) an excellent photographer; you

   _____ (to have) to see his show at the museum.

10. The employment agency _____ (to have) a number of jobs available in dental hygiene and home repair.

11. The ferret and the goldfish _____ (to be) Mr. Caproni's favorite pets.

12. The electric fans _____ (to be) turning at full speed; unfor-

    tunately, the room _____ (to be) still warm.

13. As soon as Leslie and Bob _____ (to be) ready, we _____ (to have) to be on our way.

14. The judges _____ (to have) doubts about the suspect's chances

    of getting a fair trial, but it _____ (to do) seem that the case will go to court anyway.

15. The all-terrain vehicle and the tractor _____ (to be) in decent

    condition, but the pickup truck _____ (to do) need work.

PART C

Special Singular Constructions

Each of these constructions takes a **singular** verb:

Special Singular Constructions

| either (of) . . . | each (of) . . . | every one (of) . . . |
| neither (of) . . . | one (of) . . . | which one (of) . . . |

---

1. *Neither* of the birds *has* feathers yet.
2. *Each* of the solutions *presents* difficulties.

- In sentence 1, *neither* means *neither one. Neither* is a singular subject and requires the singular verb *has*.

- In sentence 2, *each* means *each one. Each* is a singular subject and requires the singular verb *presents*.

However, an exception to this general rule is the case in which two subjects are joined by *(n)either . . . (n)or . . .* Here, the verb agrees with the subject closer to it:

---

3. Neither the teacher nor the *pupils want* the semester shortened.
4. Either the graphs or the *map has* to be changed.

- In sentence 3, *pupils* is the subject closer to the verb. The subject *pupils* takes the verb *want*.

- In sentence 4, *map* is the subject closer to the verb. The subject *map* takes the verb *has*.

PRACTICE 4   Underline the subject and circle the correct verb in each sentence.

1. Each of these ferns (needs, need) special care.
2. One of the customers always (forget, forgets) his or her umbrella.

3. Which one of the flights (goes, go) nonstop to Dallas?

4. Every one of those cameras (costs, cost) more than I can afford.

5. Either you or Doris (is, are) correct.

6. Either of these computer diskettes (contain, contains) the information you need.

7. Do you really believe that one of these oysters (holds, hold) a pearl?

8. Neither of the twins (resembles, resemble) his parents.

9. One of the scientists (believes, believe) he can cure baldness.

10. Each of these inventions (has, have) had an effect on how we spend our leisure time.

PART D

Separation of Subject and Verb

Sometimes a phrase or clause separates the subject from the verb. First, look for the subject; then make sure that the verb agrees with the subject.

---

1. The economist's *ideas* on this matter *seem* well thought out.

2. *Radios* that were made in the 1930s *are* now collector's items.

- In sentence 1, the *ideas* are well thought out. The prepositional phrase *on this matter* separates the subject *ideas* from the verb *seem*.*

- In sentence 2, *radios* are now collector's items. The relative clause *that were made in the 1930s* separates the subject *radios* from the verb *are*.

PRACTICE 5   Read each sentence carefully for meaning. Cross out any phrase or clause that separates the subject from the verb. Underline the subject and circle the correct verb.

1. The plums in that bowl (tastes, taste) sweet.

2. The instructions on the package (is, are) in French and Japanese.

3. Our new community center, which has a swimming pool and tennis courts, (keeps, keep) everyone happy.

4. The lampshades that are made of stained glass (looks, look) beautiful at night.

* For more work on prepositional phrases, see Chapter 21, "The Simple Sentence," Part B.

5. All the CD players on that shelf (comes, come) with a remote control.

6. A movie that lasts more than three hours usually (puts, put) me to sleep.

7. The man with the dark sunglasses (looks, look) like a typical movie villain.

8. The two nurses who check blood pressure (enjoys, enjoy) chatting with the patients.

9. The function of these metal racks (remains, remain) a mystery to me.

10. The green lizard on the wall (hasn't, haven't) moved for hours.

PART E

Sentences Beginning with *There* and *Here*

In sentences that begin with **there** or **here,** the subject usually follows the verb:

---

1. There *seem* to be two *flies* in my soup.

2. Here *is* my *prediction* for the coming year.

- In sentence 1, the plural subject *flies* takes the plural verb *seem.*

- In sentence 2, the singular subject *prediction* takes the singular verb *is.*

You can often determine what the verb should be by reversing the word order: *two flies seem . . .* or *my prediction is . . .*

PRACTICE 6 Underline the subject and circle the correct verb in each sentence.

1. There (goes, go) Tom Cruise.

2. There (is, are) only a few seconds left in the game.

3. Here (is, are) a terrific way to save money—make a budget and stick to it!

4. There (has, have) been robberies in the neighborhood lately.

5. Here (is, are) the plantains you ordered.

6. Here (comes, come) Johnny, the television talk-show host.

7. There (is, are) no direct route to Black Creek from here.

8. There (seems, seem) to be something wrong with the doorbell.

9. Here (is, are) the teapot and sugar bowl I've been looking for.

10. There (is, are) six reporters in the hall waiting for an interview.

PART F

Agreement in Questions

In questions, the subject usually follows the verb:

1. What *is* the *secret* of your success?

2. Where *are* the *copies* of the review?

- In sentence 1, the subject *secret* takes the singular verb *is*.
- In sentence 2, the subject *copies* takes the plural verb *are*.

You can often determine what the verb should be by reversing the word order: *the secret of your success is . . .* or *the copies are . . .*

PRACTICE 7   Underline the subject and circle the correct verb in each sentence.

1. How (does, do) the combustion engine actually work?

2. Why (is, are) Robert and Charity so suspicious?

3. Where (is, are) the beach chairs?

4. (Have, Has) the grades for the biology final been posted yet?

5. (Are, Is) Dianne and Bill starting a mail-order business?

6. What (seems, seem) to be the problem here?

7. Why (is, are) all his ties so ugly?

8. (Is, Are) the mattress factory really going to close in June?

9. How (does, do) you feel about their replacing this orchard with a shopping mall?

10. Who (is, are) those people on the fire escape?

PART G

Agreement in Relative Clauses

A **relative clause** is a subordinate clause that begins with *who, which,* or *that.* The verb in the relative clause must agree with the antecedent of the *who, which,* or *that.**

> 1. People *who have a good sense of humor* make good neighbors.
> 2. Be careful of a scheme *that promises you a lot of money fast.*

- In sentence 1, the antecedent of *who* is *people. People* takes the verb *have.*
- In sentence 2, the antecedent of *that* is *scheme. Scheme* takes the verb *promises.*

PRACTICE 8   Underline the antecedent of the *who, which,* or *that.* Then circle the correct verb.

1. Most patients prefer doctors who (spends, spend) time talking with them.

2. The gnarled oak that (shades, shade) the garden is my favorite tree.

3. Laptop computers, which (has, have) become very popular recently, are still fairly expensive.

4. My neighbor, who (swims, swim) at least one hour a day, is seventy years old.

5. Listing things to do, which (saves, save) hours of wasted time, is a good way to manage time effectively.

6. Employers often appreciate employees who (asks, ask) intelligent questions.

7. This air conditioner, which now (costs, cost) eight hundred dollars, rarely breaks down.

8. Everyone admires her because she is someone who always (sees, see) the bright side of a bad situation.

9. He is the man who (creates, create) furniture from scraps of walnut, cherry, and birch.

10. Foods that (contains, contain) artificial sweeteners may be hazardous to your health.

* For more work on relative clauses, see Chapter 14, "Revising for Sentence Variety," Part D.

PRACTICE 9 Proofread the following essay for verb agreement errors. Correct any
Review errors by writing above the lines.

Chimp Smarts

(1) Chimpanzees sometimes seem uncannily human, especially in their use of tools and language. (2) Neither the gorilla nor the orangutan, both close relatives of the chimp, exhibit such behavior.

(3) Chimps employs a number of tools in their everyday lives. (4) They dine by inserting sticks into insect nests and then licking their utensils clean. (5) Each of these intelligent animals also crack fruit and nuts with stones. (6) What's more, chimpanzees creates their own tools. (7) They make their eating sticks by cleaning leaves from branches. (8) They even attaches small sticks together to make longer rods for getting at hard-to-reach insects. (9) Some of the other tools chimps make is fly-whisks, sponges of chewed bark, and leaf-rags to clean themselves with. (10) Scientists on safari has observed infant chimps imitating their parents' use of these tools.

(11) Recent experiments indicate that chimpanzees probably also understands language though they lack the physical ability to speak. (12) There are little doubt that they can comprehend individual words. (13) Using sign language and keyboards, some chimps in captivity use nearly two hundred words. (14) This vocabulary include nouns, verbs, and prepositions. (15) Hunger and affection is needs that they have expressed by punching keyboard symbols. (16) Do chimps has the ability to string words into sentences? (17) Intriguingly, one chimp named Lucy has shown that she understand the difference between such statements as "Roger tickles Lucy" and "Lucy tickles Roger."

(18) Scientists still argue about just how much language a chimpanzee truly comprehend. (19) However, no one who have watched them closely doubt the intelligence of these remarkable beings.

25

Past Tense

PART A   Regular Verbs in the Past Tense
PART B   Irregular Verbs in the Past Tense
PART C   A Troublesome Verb in the Past Tense: *To Be*
PART D   Troublesome Pairs in the Past Tense: *Can/Could,*
**   *Will/Would***

Regular Verbs in the Past Tense

Regular verbs in the past tense take an *-ed* or *-d* ending:

---

1. The captain *hoisted* the flag.

2. They *purchased* lawn furniture yesterday.

3. We *deposited* a quarter in the meter.

- *Hoisted, purchased,* and *deposited* are regular verbs in the past tense.

- Each verb ends in *-ed* or *-d*.

PRACTICE 1   Fill in the past tense of the regular verbs in parentheses.*

1. On December 28, 1958, more than 64,000 people _____
   (pack) Yankee Stadium in New York City to witness one of the most
   exciting football games of all time.

2. The Baltimore Colts _____ (battle) the New York
   Giants for the National Football League Championship.

* If you have questions about spelling, see Chapter 34, "Spelling," Parts C, D, and E.

3. In the first quarter, the Giants _____ (score) a field goal; however, the Colts _____ (earn) two touchdowns during the second quarter.

4. At halftime, the scoreboard _____ (flash) 14 to 3 in favor of the Colts.

5. Early in the third quarter, Frank Gifford, the Giants' halfback, _____ (snatch) a 15-yard touchdown pass from quarterback Charlie Conerly.

6. Later in the quarter, Conerly _____ (pass) to left end Kyle Rote, who _____ (dodge) down the field and then _____ (fumble) at the 25-yard line.

7. Alex Webster _____ (recover) the ball, leading the Giants to another touchdown.

8. Going into the final quarter, the Colts _____ (trail) 17 to 14, but Johnny Unitas, their quarterback, soon _____ (change) all that as he _____ (maneuver) the team down the field.

9. The Colts _____ (reach) the Giants' 13-yard line with only eight seconds remaining in the game.

10. Steve Myrha _____ (boot) a perfect field goal and _____ (tie) the score, 17 to 17.

11. For the first time ever, a regular league game _____ (extend) into sudden-death overtime.

12. The Giants just _____ (miss) a first down by inches.

13. Then, the great Unitas _____ (complete) four of six passes, driving the Colts eighty yards in thirteen plays.

14. At the Giants' 1-yard line, Johnny Unitas _____ (hand) off the ball to "Horse" Ameche, who _____ (plunge) across the goal line.

15. In 8 minutes, 15 seconds of overtime, the Colts _____ (prevail), winning the game 23 to 17.

Irregular Verbs in the Past Tense

Irregular verbs do not take an *-ed* or *-d* ending in the past but change internally:

---

1. I *wrote* that letter in ten minutes.

2. Although the orange cat *fell* from a high branch, she escaped unharmed.

3. The play *began* on time but ended fairly late.

- *Wrote* is the past tense of *write.*

- *Fell* is the past tense of *fall.*

- *Began* is the past tense of *begin.*

Here is a partial list of irregular verbs.

Reference Chart
Irregular Verbs in the Past Tense

Simple Form	Past Tense	Simple Form	Past Tense
be	was, were	draw	drew
become	became	drink	drank
begin	began	drive	drove
blow	blew	eat	ate
break	broke	fall	fell
bring	brought	feed	fed
build	built	feel	felt
buy	bought	fight	fought
catch	caught	find	found
choose	chose	fly	flew
come	came	forbid	forbade
cut	cut	forget	forgot
deal	dealt	forgive	forgave
dig	dug	freeze	froze
dive	dove (dived)	get	got
do	did	give	gave

(continued)

Reference Chart
Irregular Verbs in the Past Tense
(continued)

Simple Form	*Past Tense*	*Simple Form*	*Past Tense*
go	went	sell	sold
grow	grew	send	sent
have	had	shake	shook
hear	heard	shine	shone (shined)
hide	hid	sing	sang
hold	held	sit	sat
hurt	hurt	sleep	slept
keep	kept	speak	spoke
know	knew	spend	spent
lay	laid	split	split
lead	led	spring	sprang
leave	left	stand	stood
let	let	steal	stole
lie	lay	stink	stank
lose	lost	swim	swam
make	made	take	took
mean	meant	teach	taught
meet	met	tear	tore
pay	paid	tell	told
quit	quit	think	thought
read	read	throw	threw
ride	rode	understand	understood
rise	rose	wake	woke (waked)
run	ran	wear	wore
say	said	win	won
see	saw	write	wrote
seek	sought		

PRACTICE 2   Fill in the past tense of the regular and irregular verbs in parentheses. If you are not sure of the past tense, use the chart. Do not guess.

The Tragic Fate of Port Royal

(1) In its heyday, Port Royal _____ (have) a reputation as the most wicked city in the world. (2) Situated on a beautiful bay, the Jamaican port _____ (welcome) English pirates like Henry Morgan, who _____ (prey) on

Spanish galleons loaded with gold from Mexico and Peru. (3) Port Royal _____ (bustle) with the immoral activities of the unsavory characters who _____ (swagger) down its crowded streets. (4) Suddenly, in three minutes on June 7, 1692, this thriving city _____ (meet) its untimely end.

(5) At 11:40 A.M., the first of three earth tremors _____ (shake) the city. (6) Citizens _____ (flee) from their homes and _____ (take) to the streets. (7) Before they _____ (recover), a second, more powerful shock _____ (knock) them to the ground. (8) As they _____ (lie) there, the worst tremor of all _____ (topple) most of the town's buildings. (9) People _____ (fall) into gaping holes. (10) Later shocks actually _____ (belch) a few lucky ones back up. (11) As the quakes _____ (hit), water _____ (withdraw) from the harbor and then _____ (tumble) back to shore in monstrous waves, flooding half the city. (12) The harbor area _____ (slide) into the sea. (13) Ships either _____ (capsize) or _____ (run) aground far into town. (14) Close to half the city's population _____ (die) instantly.

(15) Some _____ (think) the city _____ (deserve) its terrible fate. (16) Others _____ (mourn) the town's bad luck. (17) Thirty years after the earthquake, a fierce hurricane _____ (wipe) out the little that _____ (remain) of Port Royal. (18) For more than one hundred years, sailors _____ (say) that complete houses, bright and perfect, still _____ (stand) beneath the sea.

PART C

A Troublesome Verb in the Past Tense: *To Be*

To be is the only verb that in the past tense has different forms for different persons. Be careful of subject-verb agreement:

	Reference Chart—To Be			
	Past Tense			
	Singular		*Plural*	
	If the subject is	*the verb is*	*If the subject is*	*the verb is*
1st person:	I	was	we	were
2nd person:	you	were	you	were
3rd person:	he she it	was	they	were

- Note that the form for the first-person singular and the third-person singular is the same—*was.*

Be especially careful of agreement when adding *not* to *was* or *were* to make a contraction:

> was + not = wasn't
>
> were + not = weren't

PRACTICE 3   Circle the correct form of the verb *to be* in the past tense. Do not guess. If you are not sure of the correct form, use the chart.

1. Edward (was, were) curious about how bees communicate.

2. The pop fly (was, were) easily caught by the shortstop.

3. Camping and sports cars (was, were) his passions.

4. The play (was, were) well acted, but the staging and the music (was, were) weak.

5. (Wasn't, Weren't) you honored at graduation?

6. Cynthia and Lou (was, were) partners in the hardware store.

7. How (was, were) the sweet potato fries? They (wasn't, weren't) good the last time we (was, were) here.

8. We (was, were) where the action (was, were).

9. (Wasn't, Weren't) you born in Sweden?

10. I (was, were) fascinated by those blue and gold tropical fish in your tank.

11. (Was, Were) the results of the vote exactly what you had expected?

12. Tom and Roberta (wasn't, weren't) together for more than a month before they broke up again.

13. (Was, Were) all these trees blown down by the hurricane?

14. I (was, were) confused at first, but Bill (was, were) able to answer my questions.

15. My cousin (was, were) a famous violinist when she (was, were) a child; her fans (was, were) always happy to listen to her perform. Those (was, were) the days!

PART D

Troublesome Pairs in the Past Tense: *Can/Could, Will/Would*

Use **could** as the past tense of **can.**

> 1. Maria is extraordinary because she *can* remember what happened to her when she was three years old.
>
> 2. When I was in high school, I *could* do two sit-ups in an hour.

- In sentence 1, *can* shows the action is in the present.

- In sentence 2, *could* shows the action occurred in the past.

PRACTICE 4   Fill in either the present tense *can* or the past tense *could.*

1. Tom is so talented that he _____ play most music on the piano by ear.

2. He _____ leave the hospital as soon as he feels stronger.

3. Last week we _____ not find fresh strawberries.

4. When we were in Spain last summer, we _____ see all of Madrid from our hotel balcony.

5. As a child, I _____ perform easily in public, but I _____ no longer do it.

6. Anything you _____ do, he _____ do better.

7. Nobody _____ find the guard after the robbery yesterday.

8. These days, Fred _____ usually predict the weather from the condition of his bunions.

Use **would** as the past tense of **will.**

> 3. Roberta says that she *will* arrive with her camera in ten minutes.
>
> 4. Roberta said that she *would* arrive with her camera in ten minutes.

- In sentence 3, *will* points to the future from the present.
- In sentence 4, *would* points to the future from the past.

PRACTICE 5   Fill in either the present tense *will* or the past tense *would.*

1. He hoped that he _____ succeed in his new career.

2. He hopes that he _____ succeed in his new career.

3. I said what I liked and didn't like about my friend's essay, but I _____ not rewrite it for her.

4. The guests promised that they _____ help clean up the messy kitchen.

5. The guests promise that they _____ help clean up the messy kitchen.

6. Robert thinks that he _____ enroll in a swimming course next semester.

7. The customer stood by the door, but she _____ not leave.

8. The customer stands by the door, but she _____ not leave.

PRACTICE 6
Review Proofread the following essay for past tense errors. Then write the correct past tense form above the line.

The Warrior Queen of Jhansi

(1) The British cursed her as a devil; the people of India revered her almost as a god. (2) All agreed, however, that the Indian queen, Lakshmi Bai, were a powerful and daring woman.

(3) Before the ruler of Jhansi died in 1853, he willed his land and title to his five-year-old son. (4) He told his young wife, Lakshmi Bai, to rule until their child come of age. (5) Despite the young queen's ability and popularity, the British declared the will illegal and seize the kingdom. (6) Lakshmi Bai swallowed the insult and remained loyal to the British.

(7) However, throughout India, discontent against the British grew until rebellion broken out in 1857. (8) In Jhansi, rebels taked the British fort and then massacred the British women and children living in the city. (9) Though the queen do not support this bloodshed, the British held her responsible. (10) For a while in late 1857, in the absence of the British, the queen gotten her chance to rule. (11) Rising at 3:00 A.M., she spent her days first attending to matters of state, then riding and training with arms, and later meditating and praying.

(12) Finally, in early 1858, the British maked the queen an outlaw and lay siege to Jhansi for more than two weeks. (13) The queen heroically fighted for her city from a high tower where her people and the enemy can clearly see her. (14) As the city prepared for defeat, the queen, an expert

horsewoman, fleed. (15) After riding for four days, she at last formally join the rebelling forces.

(16) The queen lead the defense at Gwalior, the last rebel stronghold. (17) Leading her men in hand-to-hand combat, she wore trousers, a silk blouse, and a red silk cap with a loose turban around it. (18) A pearl necklace that were one of the treasures of India hang around her neck. (19) Mortally wounded in this battle, she immediately become a beloved hero of the Indian nationalist movement.

Present Tense	Past Tense	Helping Verb plus Past Participle
1. We *sing*.	1. We *sang*.	1. We *have sung*.
2. Bill *writes*.	2. Bill *wrote*.	2. Bill *has written*.
3. I *think*.	3. I *thought*.	3. I *have thought*.

- Irregular verbs change from present to past to past participle in unusual ways.

- *Sung, written,* and *thought* are all past participles of irregular verbs.

- Note that the past tense and past participle of *think* are the same—*thought*.

Reference Chart
Irregular Verbs, Past and Past Participle

Simple Form	Past Tense	Past Participle
be	was, were	been
become	became	become
begin	began	begun
blow	blew	blown
break	broke	broken
bring	brought	brought
build	built	built
buy	bought	bought
catch	caught	caught
choose	chose	chosen
come	came	come
cut	cut	cut
dive	dove (dived)	dived
do	did	done
draw	drew	drawn
drink	drank	drunk
drive	drove	driven
eat	ate	eaten
fall	fell	fallen
feed	fed	fed
feel	felt	felt
fight	fought	fought
find	found	found

(continued)

Reference Chart
Irregular Verbs, Past and Past Participle
(continued)

Simple Form	*Past Tense*	*Past Participle*
fly	flew	flown
forget	forgot	forgotten
forgive	forgave	forgiven
freeze	froze	frozen
get	got	got (gotten)
give	gave	given
go	went	gone
grow	grew	grown
have	had	had
hear	heard	heard
hide	hid	hidden
hold	held	held
hurt	hurt	hurt
keep	kept	kept
know	knew	known
lay	laid	laid
lead	led	led
leave	left	left
let	let	let
lie	lay	lain
lose	lost	lost
make	made	made
meet	met	met
pay	paid	paid
quit	quit	quit
read	read	read
ride	rode	ridden
rise	rose	risen
run	ran	run
say	said	said
see	saw	seen
sell	sold	sold
send	sent	sent
shake	shook	shaken
shine	shone (shined)	shone (shined)
sing	sang	sung
sit	sat	sat
sleep	slept	slept
speak	spoke	spoken
spend	spent	spent
spring	sprang	sprung

(continued)

Reference Chart
Irregular Verbs, Past and Past Participle
(*continued*)

Simple Form	Past Tense	Past Participle
stand	stood	stood
steal	stole	stolen
stink	stank	stunk
swim	swam	swum
take	took	taken
teach	taught	taught
tear	tore	torn
tell	told	told
think	thought	thought
throw	threw	thrown
understand	understood	understood
wake	woke (waked)	woken (waked)
wear	wore	worn
win	won	won
write	wrote	written

PRACTICE 2 The first sentence of each pair that follows contains an irregular verb in the past tense. Fill in *have* or *has* plus the past participle of the same verb to complete the second sentence.

1. Sean took plenty of time buying the groceries.

   Sean _____ _____ plenty of time buying the groceries.

2. We sent our latest budget to the mayor.

   We _____ _____ our latest budget to the mayor.

3. My daughter hid her diary.

   My daughter _____ _____ her diary.

4. The jockey rode all day in the hot sun.

   The jockey _____ _____ all day in the hot sun.

5. Hershey, Pennsylvania, became a great tourist attraction.

   Hershey, Pennsylvania, _____ _____ a great tourist attraction.

6. The company's managers knew about these hazards for two years.

   The company's managers _____ _____ about these hazards for two years.

7. Carrie floated down the river on an inner tube.

   Carrie _____ _____ down the river on an inner tube.

8. At last, our team won the bowling tournament.

   At last, our team _____ _____ the bowling tournament.

9. Larry and Marsha broke their long silence.

   Larry and Marsha _____ _____ their long silence.

10. Science fiction films were very popular this past year.

    Science fiction films _____ _____ very popular this past year.

PRACTICE 3   Complete each sentence by filling in *have* or *has* plus the past participle of the verb in parentheses. Some verbs are regular, some irregular.

1. Recently, soccer _____ _____ (gain) in popularity in the United States.

2. Traditionally, North Americans _____ _____ (consider) soccer much less exciting than basketball, football, or hockey.

3. Moreover, North American players _____ _____ (find) it very difficult to compete at the highest levels of the game.

4. In the 1990 World Cup, for example, the United States lost all three

   of its games, a defeat that _____ _____ (haunt) many soccer fans.

5. However, North American interest in soccer _____ _____ (grow) ever since the 1994 World Cup, which was held in the United States.

6. Sports fans _____ _____ (saw) the enormous enthusiasm and passionate emotion that soccer arouses in such countries as Brazil, Argentina, Italy, and Portugal.

7. The United States also _____ _____ (demonstrate) that it is able to win games in the biggest soccer competition in the world.

8. The Federation Internationale de Football Association (FIFA) and other organizations _____ _____ (turn) their attention to the next World Cup.

9. However, the FIFA _____ _____ (show) strong support for soccer in the United States.

10. It _____ _____ (promise) to establish a new North American soccer league by the year 2000.

PART C

Using the Present Perfect Tense

The **present perfect tense** is composed of the present tense of *to have* plus the past participle. The present perfect tense shows that an action has begun in the past and is continuing into the present.

1. Past tense:	Beatrice *taught* English for ten years.
2. Present perfect tense:	Beatrice *has taught* English for ten years.

- In sentence 1, Beatrice *taught* English in the past, but she no longer does so. Note the use of the simple past tense, *taught*.

- In sentence 2, Beatrice *has taught* for ten years and is still teaching English *now. Has taught* implies that the action is continuing.

PRACTICE 4   Read these sentences carefully for meaning. Then circle the correct verb—either the **past tense** or the **present perfect tense.**

1. He (directed, has directed) traffic for many years now.

2. Emilio lifted the rug and (has swept, swept) the dust under it.

3. Kenneth (worked, has worked) on that coin collection for years; it's worth at least $5,000.

4. She (went, has gone) to the library last night.

5. The coffee maker gurgled so loudly that the noise (awakened, has awakened) me at 6 A.M.

6. For the past four years, I (enrolled, have enrolled) in summer school every summer.

7. We (talked, have talked) about the problem of your lateness for three days; it's time for you to do something about it.

8. While I was in Mexico, I (took, have taken) many photographs of Aztec ruins.

9. She (won, has won) that contest ten years ago.

10. The boxers (fought, have fought) for an hour, and they look very tired.

11. He (applied, has applied) to three colleges and attended the one with the best engineering department.

12. Raymond looked at the revised plans for his new house and (decided, has decided) he could afford to build.

13. These useless tools (have been, were) here for quite a while, but no one wants to throw them out.

14. The most exciting moment of the game (occurred, has occurred) during the sudden death overtime.

15. The coauthors (worked, have worked) together for eight years and are now planning a new book.

PART D

Using the Past Perfect Tense

The **past perfect tense** is composed of the past tense of *to have* plus the past participle. The past perfect tense shows that an action occurred further back in the past than other past action.

1. Past tense:	Rhonda *left* for the movies.
2. Past perfect tense:	Rhonda *had* already *left* for the movies by the time we *arrived*.

- In sentence 1, *left* is the simple past.

- In sentence 2, the past perfect *had left* shows that this action occurred even before another action in the past, *arrived*.

PRACTICE 5   Read these sentences carefully for meaning. Then circle the correct verb—either the **past tense** or the **past perfect tense**.

1. Tony came to the office with a cane last week because he (sprained, had sprained) his ankle a month ago.

2. As Jay (piled, had piled) the apples into a pyramid, he thought, "I should become an architect."

3. Celia (finished, had finished) her gardening by the time I (drove, had driven) up in my new convertible.

4. Bonnie (operated, had operated) a drill press for years before she became a welder.

5. The man nervously (looked, had looked) at his watch and then walked a bit faster.

6. Last year Ming bought a compact disc player; he (wanted, had wanted) one for years.

7. Roberto told us that he (decided, had decided) to enlist in the Marines.

8. I (worked, had worked) on that essay for a week before I handed it in.

9. The caller asked whether we (received, had received) our free toaster yet.

10. Dianne (completed, had completed) college before her younger brother was old enough for the first grade.

11. Last week he told me that he (forgot, had forgotten) to mail the rent check.

12. As the curtain went down, everyone (rose, had risen) and applauded the African dance troupe.

13. Scott (closed, had closed) his books and went to the movies.

14. Brad missed the rehearsal on Saturday because no one (notified, had notified) him earlier in the week.

15. The prosecutor proved that the defendant was lying; until then I (believed, had believed) he was innocent.

PART E

Using the Passive Voice (*To Be* and the Past Participle)

The **passive voice** is composed of the past participle with some form of *to be* (*am, is, are, was, were, has been, have been,* or *had been*). In the passive voice, the subject does not act but is *acted upon.*

Compare the passive voice with the active voice in the following pairs of sentences.

> 1. Passive voice: This newspaper *is written* by journalism students.
>
> 2. Active voice: Journalism students *write* this newspaper.
>
> 3. Passive voice: My garden *was devoured* by rabbits.
>
> 4. Active voice: Rabbits *devoured* my garden.

- In sentence 1, the subject, *this newspaper,* is passive; it is acted upon. In sentence 2, the subject, *students,* is active; it performs the action.

- Note the difference between the passive verb *is written* and the active verb *write.*

- However, both verbs (*is written* and *write*) are in the *present tense.*

- The verbs in sentences 3 and 4 are both in the *past tense: was devoured* (passive) and *devoured* (active).

Use the passive voice sparingly. Write in the passive voice when you want to emphasize the receiver of the action rather than the doer.

PRACTICE 6 Fill in the correct **past participle** form of the verb in parentheses. If you are not sure, check the chart.

1. The barn was _____ (build) by friends of the family.

2. Who was _____ (choose) to represent us at the union meeting?

3. These ruby slippers were _____ (give) to me by my grandmother.

4. These jeans are _____ (sell) in three sizes.

5. On their weekend camping trip, Sheila and Una were constantly _____ (bite) by mosquitoes and gnats.

6. It was _____ (decide) that Bill would work the night shift.

7. The getaway car is always _____ (drive) by a man in a gray fedora.

8. Her articles have been _____ (publish) in the *Texas Monthly.*

9. Harold was _____ (see) sneaking out the back door.

10. A faint inscription is _____ (etch) on the back of the old gold watch.

PRACTICE 7   Rewrite each sentence, changing the verb into the **passive** voice. Make all necessary verb and subject changes. Be sure to keep the sentence in the original tense.

Example   My father wore this silk hat.

This silk hat was worn by my father. _____

1. The goalie blocked the shot.

_____

2. The lifeguard taught us to swim.

_____

3. The usher warned the noisy group.

_____

4. Her rudeness hurt her reputation.

_____

5. The campers folded up the tent.

_____

6. The judges declared the match a draw.

_____

7. The conductor punched my ticket full of holes.

_____

8. The interviewer asked too many personal questions.

_____

PART F

Using the Past Participle as an Adjective

The **past participle** form of the verb can be used as an **adjective** after a linking verb:

> 1. The window is *broken*.

■ The adjective *broken* describes the subject *window*.

The **past participle** form of the verb can sometimes be used as an adjective before a noun or a pronoun.

> 2. This *fried* chicken tastes wonderful.

■ The adjective *fried* describes the noun *chicken*.

PRACTICE 8   Use the past participle form of the verb in parentheses as an adjective in each sentence.

1. My _____ (use) car was a great bargain at only $700.

2. The _____ (hide) scrolls were discovered accidentally.

3. Bob is highly _____ (qualify) to install a water heater.

4. The _____ (air-condition) room was making everyone shiver.

5. A raise was granted to the _____ (overwork) maintenance staff.

6. The _____ (break) video games were moved to the basement.

7. It is a widely _____ (know) fact that Laura is an avid hockey fan.

8. Were you _____ (surprise) to hear about my raise?

9. This car is carefully ____ _____ (design) for safety.

10. He feels _____ (depress) on rainy days.

11. The newly _____ (rise) cinnamon bread smelled wonderful.

12. In the tiny office, Wilfred felt like a _____ (forget) man.

13. She knows the power of the _____ (write) word.

14. I love that old shirt even though it is _____ (tear).

15. The _____ (steal) wallet was returned to its owner.

16. My gym teacher seems _____ (prejudice) against short people.

17. Funny, you don't act like a _____ (marry) man.

18. Don't be _____ (annoy) by my loud voice; I can't help it.

19. The _____ (embarrass) child pulled her jacket over her head.

20. We ordered _____ (toss) salad, _____ (broil) chicken, _____ (mash) potatoes, and _____ (bake) apples.

PRACTICE 9
Review

Proofread the following essay for past participle errors. Correct the errors by writing above the lines.

The Man of a Thousand Faces

(1) Lon Chaney, who was knowed as "the man of a thousand faces," was born in Colorado in 1883. (2) Both his parents were unable to hear or speak, and as a child, Chaney communicated with them through gestures and facial expressions. (3) Later, his astonishing ability to express himself in pantomime was often credit to his childhood experiences with his parents.

(4) In the most famous of his many silent-film roles, Chaney played repulsive-appearing characters who made the audience feel both disgust and pity. (5) In *The Hunchback of Notre Dame*, which was maked in 1923, Chaney played Quasimodo, a grotesquely deformed man who nevertheless aroused compassion. (6) In *The Phantom of the Opera*, which was bringed out two years later, Chaney played a hideous-looking composer who haunted the sewers under the Paris Opera; again he was able to make people see the man behind the ugliness.

(7) Chaney is also celebrate for his use of makeup and extraordinary disguises. (8) In *The Hunchback of Notre Dame,* for example, he wore a forty-pound rubber hump, which was attach to a thirty-pound breastplate. (9) A hairy rubber skin was then stretch over everything. (10) His crooked nose and mismatch eyes were molded onto his face with wax.

(11) Chaney's great talents as an actor, as well as his use of those creative, if sometimes painful, disguises, have gave him a distinguish place in the history of film. (12) Ironically, Chaney died of throat cancer when he was only forty-seven; in his last days he was force once again to pantomime what he wanted to communicate.

27

Nouns

PART A   **Defining Singular and Plural**
PART B   **Signal Words: Singular and Plural**
PART C   **Signal Words with _Of_**

PART A

Defining Singular and Plural

Nouns are words that refer to people, places, or things. They can be either singular or plural. **Singular** means one. **Plural** means more than one.

Singular	Plural
the glass	the glasses
a lamp	lamps
a lesson	lessons

■ As you can see, nouns usually add _-s_ or _-es_ to form the plural.

Some nouns form their plurals in other ways; here are a few examples:

Singular	Plural	
child	children	
crisis	crises	
criterion	criteria	
foot	feet	_(continued)_

387

(continued)	Singular	Plural
	goose	geese
	man	men
	medium	media
	memorandum	memoranda (memorandums)
	phenomenon	phenomena
	tooth	teeth
	woman	women

These nouns ending in *-f* or *-fe* change endings to *-ves* in the plural:

Singular	Plural
half	halves
knife	knives
life	lives
scarf	scarves
shelf	shelves
wife	wives
wolf	wolves

Hyphenated nouns form plurals by adding *-s* or *-es* to the main word:

Singular	Plural
brother-in-law	brothers-in-law
maid-of-honor	maids-of-honor
inspector-general	inspectors-general

Others do not change at all to form the plural; here are a few examples:

Singular	Plural
deer	deer
fish	fish
moose	moose
sheep	sheep

If you are unsure about the plural of a noun, check a dictionary. For example, if you look up the noun *woman* in the dictionary, you may see an entry like this:

woman, women

The first word listed, *woman,* is the singular form of the noun; the second word, *women,* is the plural.

Some dictionaries list the plural form of a noun only if the plural is unusual. If no plural is listed, that noun probably adds *-s* or *-es.** Remember:* Do not add an *-s* to words that form plurals by changing an internal letter. For example, the plural of *man* is *men,* not *mens;* the plural of *woman* is *women,* not *womens;* the plural of *foot* is *feet,* not *feets.*

PRACTICE 1   Make these singular nouns plural.

1. man _____
2. half _____
3. foot _____
4. son-in-law _____
5. moose _____
6. life _____
7. tooth _____
8. medium _____
9. woman _____
10. crisis _____
11. passer-by _____
12. criterion _____
13. shelf _____
14. mouse _____
15. child _____
16. father-in-law _____
17. knife _____
18. deer _____
19. secretary _____
20. goose _____

* For more work on spelling plurals, see Chapter 34, "Spelling," Part G.

PART B

Signal Words: Singular and Plural

A **signal word** tells you whether a singular or a plural noun usually follows.

■ These signal words tell you that a singular noun usually follows:

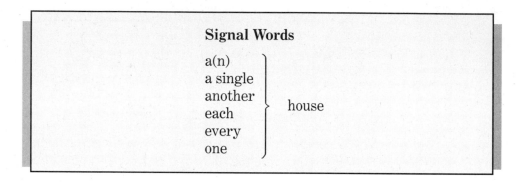

Signal Words

a(n)
a single
another
each   } house
every
one

■ These signal words tell you that a plural noun usually follows:

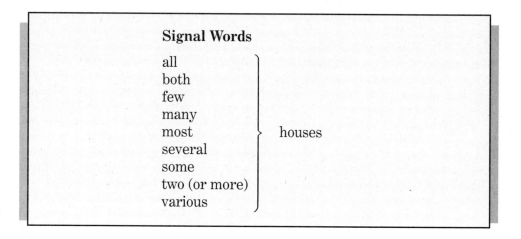

Signal Words

all
both
few
many
most   } houses
several
some
two (or more)
various

PRACTICE 2   Some of the following sentences contain incorrect singulars and plurals. Correct the errors. Put a *C* after correct sentences.

1. For many American, Chinese food used to mean only Chinese-American dishes like chow mein or chop suey.

2. In 1958, however, Joyce Chen opened a restaurant in Cambridge, Massachusetts, that would change all our idea about Chinese cuisine.

3. To introduce Mandarin food, Chen established a buffet with various Mandarin dish.

4. At first, several customer at Chen's restaurant wanted American items like bread or steak.

5. So that every individuals would be happy, she even included a large roast turkey on the menu.

6. Within a few week, however, people were ignoring the turkey and eating only authentic Chinese food.

7. Two dishes that Joyce Chen made popular are Peking duck and hot and sour soup.

8. Chen also wrote one very popular cookbooks and hosted the television program *Joyce Chen Cooks.*

9. By the time she died in 1994, few American cities were without at least one Chinese restaurant.

10. Most American man and woman who now like authentic Chinese food do so because of the efforts of Joyce Chen.

PART C

Signal Words with *Of*

Many signal words are followed by *of* . . . or *of the* . . . Usually, these signal words are followed by a **plural** noun (or a collective noun) because they really refer to one or more from a larger group.

one of the each of the	pictures is . . .
many of the a few of the lots of the	pictures are . . .

- *Be careful:* The signal words *one of the* . . . and *each of the* . . . are followed by a **plural** noun, but the verb is **singular** because only the signal word (*one* or *each*) is the real subject.*

* For more work on this type of construction, see Chapter 24, "Present Tense (Agreement)," Part C.

> *One* of the coats *is* on sale.
>
> *Each* of the flowers *smells* sweet.

PRACTICE 3   Fill in your own nouns in the following sentences. Use a different noun in each sentence.

1. Since Jacob wrote each of his _____ with care, the *A*'s came as no surprise.

2. You are one of the few _____ I know who can listen to the radio and watch television at the same time.

3. Naomi liked several of the new _____ but remained faithful to her long-time favorites.

4. Many of the _____ on the beach carried picnic baskets.

5. Determined to win the Salesperson of the Year award, Clyde called on all

   of his _____ two or three times a month.

6. One of the _____ was wearing a down jacket.

7. Before spring, each of these old _____ will have to be demolished.

PRACTICE 4   Proofread the following essay for errors in singular and plural nouns.
Review   Correct the errors above the lines.

Hot off the Press

(1) Although it was certainly not the *New York Times* or the *Washington Post*, the first newspaper was a media not all that different from the ones we read today.

(2) In 59 B.C., the Roman government began to publish *Action Journal*, which carried many story of social events and political activities. (3) Roman men and woman could read about the births of childrens, as well as the marriages and deaths of other citizen. (4) The trials of thiefs and other lawless persons—and their executions—were also described. (5) In addition,

this early newspaper reviewed the many spectacular show presented at the Colosseum.

(6) Several century later, on another continents, the Chinese government began publishing a news sheet. (7) Each government officials could read about social and political occurrences, as well as about court intrigues and gossip. (8) Many diplomat also found out about natural phenomenons— like eclipses and meteors—which they believed were good or bad omens. (9) This court chronicle was the first printed newspaper. (10) It lasted for almost 1,200 year until the Chinese Empire fell in 1911.

(11) The main difference between both of these newspaper and today's American press is that they were state run and controlled. (12) Roman and Chinese authoritys applied strict criterions of censorship to every articles. (13) In contrast, the modern press, freely written and circulated, was begun by Dutch merchants in the two city of Antwerp and Venice during the seventeenth century.

28

Pronouns

PART A

Defining Pronouns and Antecedents

Pronouns take the place of or refer to nouns, other pronouns, or phrases. The word that the pronoun refers to is called the **antecedent** of the pronoun.

> 1. *Eric* ordered *baked chicken* because *it* is *his* favorite dish.
>
> 2. *Simone and Lee* painted *their* room.
>
> 3. *I* like *camping in the woods* because *it* gives *me* a chance to be alone with *my* thoughts.

- In sentence 1, *it* refers to the antecedent *baked chicken,* and *his* refers to the antecedent *Eric.*

- In sentence 2, *their* refers to the plural antecedent *Simone and Lee.*

- In sentence 3, *it* refers to the antecedent *camping in the woods.* This antecedent is a whole phrase. *Me* and *my* refer to the pronoun antecedent *I.*

PRACTICE 1   In each sentence, a pronoun is circled. Write the pronoun first and then its antecedent, as shown in the example.

394

Example | Have you ever wondered why we exchange rings in (our) wedding ceremonies?   *our*   *we*

1. When a man buys a wedding ring, he follows an age-old tradition. _____

2. Rich Egyptian grooms gave their brides gold rings five thousand years ago. _____

3. To Egyptian couples, the ring represented eternal love; it was a circle without beginning or end. _____

4. By Roman times, gold rings had become more affordable, so ordinary people could also buy them. _____

5. Still, many a Roman youth had to scrimp to buy his bride a ring. _____

6. The first bride to slip a diamond ring on her finger lived in Venice about five hundred years ago. _____

7. The Venetians knew that setting a diamond in a ring was an excellent way of displaying its beauty. _____

8. Nowadays, a man and a woman exchange rings to symbolize the equality of their relationship. _____

PART B

Making Pronouns and Antecedents Agree

A pronoun must *agree* with its antecedent in number and person.*

---

1. When *Tom* couldn't find *his* pen, *he* asked to borrow mine.

2. The three *sisters* wanted to start *their* own business.

---

* For more work on pronoun agreement, see Chapter 13, "Revising for Consistency and Parallelism," Part B.

■ In sentence 1, *Tom* is the antecedent of *his* and *he*. Since *Tom* is singular and masculine, the pronouns referring to *Tom* are also singular and masculine.

■ In sentence 2, *sisters* is the antecedent of *their*. Since *sisters* is plural, the pronoun referring to *sisters* must also be plural.

As you can see from these examples, making pronouns agree with their antecedents is usually easy. However, three special cases can be tricky.

1. Indefinite Pronouns

anybody
anyone
everybody
everyone   Each of these words is **singular.** Any pronoun that
nobody   refers to one of them must also be singular: *he, him,*
no one   *his, she,* or *her.*
one
somebody
someone

---

3. *Anyone* can quit smoking if *he* or *she* wants to.

4. *Everybody* should do *his* or *her* best to keep the reception area uncluttered.

■ *Anyone* and *everybody* require the singular pronouns *he, she, his,* and *her.*

In the past, writers used *he* or *him* to refer to both men and women. Now, however, many writers use *he or she, his or her,* or *him or her.* Of course, if *everyone* or *someone* is a woman, use *she* or *her;* if *everyone* or *someone* is a man, use *he* or *him.* For example:

---

5. *Someone* left *her* bracelet on the sofa.

6. *Everyone* is wearing *his* new tie.

PRACTICE 2   Fill in the correct pronoun and circle its antecedent. Make sure each pronoun agrees in number and person with its antecedent.

1. Anyone can become a good cook if _____ tries.

2. Someone dropped _____ lipstick behind the bookcase.

3. No one in the mixed doubles let _____ guard down for a minute.

4. Everybody wants _____ career to be rewarding.

5. Everyone is entitled to _____ full pension.

6. Mr. Hernow will soon be here, so please get _____ contract ready.

7. One should wear a necktie that doesn't clash with _____ suit.

8. The movie theater was so cold that nobody took off _____ coat.

2. Special Singular Antecedents

each (of) . . .
either (of) . . .
neither (of) . . .   Each of these constructions is **singular.** Any
every one (of) . . .   pronoun that refers to one of them must also be
one (of) . . .   singular.*

> 7. *Neither* of the two men paid for *his* ticket to the wrestling match.
>
> 8. *Each* of the houses has *its* own special charm.

- The subject of sentence 7 is the singular *neither*, not *men*; therefore, the singular masculine pronoun *his* is required.

- The subject of sentence 8 is the singular *each,* not the plural *houses;* therefore, the singular pronoun *its* is required.

PRACTICE 3   Fill in the correct pronoun and circle its antecedent. Make sure each pronoun agrees in number and person with its antecedent.

1. Each of the men wanted to be _____ own boss.

2. One of the saleswomen left _____ sample case on the counter.

3. Every one of the colts has a white star on _____ forehead.

4. Neither of the actors knew _____ lines by heart.

* For more work on prepositional phrases, see Chapter 21, "The Simple Sentence," Part B.

5. Neither of the dentists had _____ office remodeled.

6. Each of these arguments has _____ flaws and _____ strengths.

7. Every one of the jazz bands had _____ own distinctive style.

8. Either of these telephone answering machines will work very well if _____ is properly cared for.

3. Collective Nouns

Collective nouns represent a group of people but are usually considered **singular.** They usually take singular pronouns.

> 9. The *jury* reached *its* decision in three hours.
>
> 10. The debating *team* is well known for *its* fighting spirit.

- In sentence 9, *jury* is a collective noun. Although it has several members, the jury acts as a unit—as one. Therefore, the antecedent *jury* takes the singular pronouns *its*.

- In sentence 10, why does the collective noun *team* take the singular pronoun *its?*

Here is a partial list of collective nouns:

Common Collective Nouns		
class	family	panel
college	flock	school
committee	government	society
company	group	team
faculty	jury	tribe

PRACTICE 4   Read each sentence carefully for meaning. Circle the antecedent and then fill in the correct pronoun.

1. My family gave me all _____ support when I went back to school.

2. The government should reexamine _____ domestic policy.

3. The college honored _____ oldest graduate with a reception.

4. Eco-Wise has just begun to market a new pollution-free detergent that _____ is proud of.

5. The panel will soon announce _____ recommendations to the hospital.

6. The two teams gave _____ fans a real show.

7. The jury deliberated for six days before reaching _____ verdict.

8. After touring the Great Pyramid, the class headed back to Cairo in _____ air-conditioned bus.

PART C

Referring to Antecedents Clearly

A pronoun must refer *clearly* to its antecedent. Avoid vague, repetitious, or ambiguous pronoun reference.

1. Vague pronoun:		At the box office, *they* said that tickets were no longer available.
2. Revised:	{	The cashier at the box office said . . .
		or
3. Revised:		At the box office, I was told . . .

■ In sentence 1, who is *they? They* does not clearly refer to an antecedent.

■ In sentence 2, *they* is replaced by *the cashier.*

■ In sentence 3, the problem is avoided by a change of language.*

* For more work on using exact language, see Chapter 15, "Revising for Language Awareness," Part A.

4. Repetitious pronoun:	In the article, *it* says that Tyrone was a boxer.
5. Revised:	The article says that . . .
	or
6. Revised:	It says that . . .

- In sentence 4, *it* merely repeats *article,* the antecedent preceding it.
- Use either the pronoun or its antecedent, but not both.

7. Ambiguous pronoun:	Mr. Tedesco told his son that *his* car had a flat tire.
8. Revised:	Mr. Tedesco told his son that the younger man's car had a flat tire.
9. Revised:	Mr. Tedesco told his son Paul that Paul's car had a flat tire.

- In sentence 7, *his* could refer either to Mr. Tedesco or to his son.

PRACTICE 5 Revise the following sentences, removing vague, repetitious, or ambiguous pronoun references. Make the pronoun references clear and specific.

1. In this book it says that most ducks and geese travel between forty and sixty miles per hour.

   Revised: _____

   _____

2. On the radio they warned drivers that the Interstate Bridge was closed.

   Revised: _____

   _____

3. Sandra told her friend that she shouldn't have turned down the promotion.

   Revised: _____

   _____

4. In North Carolina they raise tobacco.

   Revised: _____

   _____

5. The moving van struck a lamppost; luckily, no one was injured, but it was badly damaged.

   Revised: _____

   _____

6. In this college, they require every entering student to take a hearing test.

   Revised: _____

   _____

7. Professor Grazel told his parrot that he had to stop chewing telephone cords.

   Revised: _____

   _____

8. Vandalism was so out of control at the local high school that they stole sinks and lighting fixtures.

   Revised: _____

   _____

9. On the news, it said that the president hopes to present his new tax bill to Congress in the next two weeks.

   Revised: _____

   _____

10. Mr. Highwater informed his cousin that his wholesale rug business was a success.

    Revised: _____

    _____

11. The saleswoman at Wigged Out, she said I look like a rock star in this wig.

    Revised: _____

    _____

12. I don't watch Sunday night wrestling because they show ten commercials an hour.

    Revised: _____

    _____

13. Keiko is an excellent singer, yet she has never taken a lesson in it.

    Revised: _____

    _____

14. Rosalie's mother said that she was glad that she had decided to become
    a nurse.

    Revised: _____

    _____

15. At my church, they run a soup kitchen for people who need a hot meal.

    Revised: _____

    _____

PART D

Special Problems of Case

Personal pronouns take different forms depending on how they are used in a
sentence. Pronouns can be **subjects, objects,** or **possessives.**
  Pronouns used as **subjects** are in the **subjective case:**

> 1. *He* and *I* go backpacking together.
> 2. The peaches were so ripe that *they* fell from the trees.

- *He, I,* and *they* are in the subjective case.

  Pronouns that are **objects of verbs** or **prepositions** are in the **objective
case.** Pronouns that are **subjects of infinitives** are also in the **objective case:**

> 3. A sudden downpour soaked *her.* (object of verb)
> 4. Please give this card to *him.* (object of preposition)
> 5. We want *them* to leave right now. (subject of infinitive)

- *Her, him,* and *them* are in the objective case.

  Pronouns that **show ownership** are in the **possessive case:**

6. The carpenters left *their* tools on the windowsill.

7. This flower has lost *its* brilliant color.

■ *Their* and *its* are in the possessive case.

Pronoun Case Chart

Singular	*Subjective*	*Objective*	*Possessive*
1st person	I	me	my (mine)
2nd person	you	you	your (yours)
3rd person	he	him	his (his)
	she	her	her (hers)
	it	it	its (its)
	who	whom	whose
	whoever	whomever	

Plural			
1st person	we	us	our (ours)
2nd person	you	you	your (yours)
3rd person	they	them	their (theirs)

Using the correct case is usually fairly simple, but three problems require special care.

1. Case in Compound Constructions

A **compound construction** consists of two nouns, two pronouns, or a noun and a pronoun joined by *and*. Make sure that the pronouns in a compound construction are in the correct case.

8. *Serge* and *I* went to the pool together.

9. Between *you* and *me*, this party is a bore.

■ In sentence 8, *Serge* and *I* are subjects.

■ In sentence 9, *you* and *me* are objects of the preposition *between*.

Never use *myself* as a substitute for either *I* or *me* in compound constructions.

PRACTICE 6   Determine the case required by each sentence and circle the correct pronoun.

1. (He, Him) and Harriet want to be correction officers.

2. A snowdrift stood between the entrance to the office building and (I, me).

3. He used the software and then returned it to Barbara and (I, me, myself).

4. The reporter's questions caught June and (we, us) off guard.

5. That price for a large-screen TV seemed fair to my brother and (I, me).

6. After work, Carl and (he, him) left for Bear Lake.

7. These charts helped (she, her) and (I, me) with our statistics homework.

8. Senator Grimley granted Diane and (she, her) an interview.

2. Case in Comparisons

Pronouns that complete **comparisons** may be in the **subjective, objective,** or **possessive** case:

> 10. His son is as stubborn as *he*. (subjective)
>
> 11. The cutbacks will affect you more than *her*. (objective)
>
> 12. This essay is better organized than *mine*. (possessive)

To decide on the correct pronoun, simply complete the comparison mentally and then choose the pronoun that naturally follows:

> 13. She trusts him more than I . . . (trust him).
>
> 14. She trusts him more than . . . (she trusts) . . . me.

■ Note that, in sentences 13 and 14, the case of the pronoun in the comparison can change the meaning of the entire sentence.

PRACTICE 7   Circle the correct pronoun.

1. Your hair is much shorter than (she, her, hers).

2. We tend to assume that others are more self-confident than (we, us).

3. She is just as funny as (he, him).

4. Is Hanna as trustworthy as (he, her)?

5. Although they were both research scientists, he received a higher salary than (she, her).

6. I am not as involved in this project as (they, them).

7. Sometimes we become impatient with people who are not as quick to learn as (we, us).

8. Michael's route involved more overnight stops than (us, our, ours).

3. Use of *Who* (or *Whoever*) and *Whom* (or *Whomever*)

Who and **whoever** are the **subjective** case. **Whom** and **whomever** are the **objective** case.

---

15. *Who* is at the door?

16. For *whom* is that gift?

17. *Whom* is that gift for?

- In sentence 15, *who* is the subject.

- The same question is written two ways in sentences 16 and 17. In both, *whom* is the object of the preposition *for.*

- Sometimes, deciding on *who* or *whom* can be tricky:

---

18. I will give the raise to *whoever* deserves it.

19. Give it to *whomever* you like.

- In sentence 18, *whoever* is the subject in the clause—*whoever deserves it.*

- In sentence 19, *whomever* is the object in the clause—*whomever you like.*

If you have trouble deciding on *who* or *whom,* change the sentence to eliminate the problem.

---

20. I prefer working with people *whom* I don't know as friends.
    or
    I prefer working with people I don't know as friends.

PRACTICE 8   Circle the correct pronoun or rewrite the sentence to eliminate the problem.

1. (Who, Whom) will deliver the layouts to the ad agency?

_____

2. To (who, whom) are you speaking?

_____

3. (Who, Whom) prefers hiking to skiing?

_____

4. For (who, whom) are those boxes piled in the corner?

_____

5. The committee will award the scholarship to (whoever, whomever) it chooses.

_____

6. (Who, Whom) do you wish to invite to the open house?

_____

7. At (who, whom) did the governor fling the cream pie?

_____

8. I will hire (whoever, whomever) can use a computer and speak Korean.

_____

PART E

Using Pronouns with *-Self* and *-Selves*

Pronouns with *-self* or *-selves* can be used in two ways—as reflexives or as intensives.

A reflexive pronoun indicates that someone did something to himself or herself:

> 1. My daughter Miriam felt very grown-up when she learned to dress *herself.*

■ In sentence 1, Miriam did something to *herself;* she *dressed herself.*

An intensive pronoun emphasizes the noun or pronoun it refers to:

> 2. Anthony *himself* was surprised at how relaxed he felt during the interview.

■ In sentence 2, *himself* emphasizes that Anthony—much to his surprise—was not nervous at the interview.

The following chart will help you choose the correct reflexive or intensive pronoun.

	Antecedent	Reflexive or Intensive Pronoun
Singular	I	myself
	you	yourself
	he	himself
	she	herself
	it	itself
Plural	we	ourselves
	you	yourselves
	they	themselves

Note that in the plural *-self* is changed to *-selves.*

■ *Be careful:* Do not use reflexives or intensives as substitutes for the subject of a sentence.

Incorrect: Harry and *myself* will be there on time.

Correct: Harry and *I* will be there on time.

PRACTICE 9 Fill in the correct reflexive or intensive pronoun. Be careful to make pronouns and antecedents agree.

1. Though he hates to cook, André _____ sautéed the mushrooms.

2. Rhoda found _____ in a strange city with only the phone number of a cousin whom she had not seen for years.

3. Her coffee machine automatically turns _____ on in the morning and off in the evening.

4. The librarian and I rearranged the children's section _____.

5. When it comes to horror films, I know that you consider _____ an expert.

6. They _____ didn't care if they arrived on time or not.

7. After completing a term paper, I always buy _____ a little gift to celebrate.

8. Larry _____ was surprised at how quickly he grew to like ancient history.

PRACTICE 10
Review

Proofread the following paragraph for pronoun errors. Then write the correct pronoun above the line.

Mikimoto, the Pearl King

(1) Few businesspersons can boast a career as meteoric as him: Kokichi Mikimoto began as a noodle maker and later became the king of the pearl industry.

(2) Born in 1858, Mikimoto began working even as a child. (3) He made noodles at night and sold it, along with other products, the next day. (4) In his early twenties, he revived the pearl business in Toba, his home town. (5) In Toba they had fishermen who made their money by selling oysters for food. (6) Mikimoto urged fishermen to harvest oysters only for pearls. (7) Since at that time oysters produced pearls only by chance, anyone who followed his advice risked losing their livelihood.

(8) Mikimoto, he changed all that. (9) He discovered, over a grueling twelve years of trial and error, how to cultivate these white gems. (10) With his own hands, he bedded thousands of oysters under water, inserting foreign matter into each shell. (11) A few years later, he dove to examine each of the oysters hisself to see if they had formed a pearl. (12) His wife complained that she lost her husband to an oyster; at one point, she even had to sell her best kimono to meet expenses. (13) Nevertheless, her and Mikimoto stayed

together. (14) In time, Mikimoto's oysters made not only pearls but also the most valuable kind—perfectly round ones.

(15) Mikimoto's real genius, however, it lay in aggressive merchandising. (16) By 1900, he was selling pearls throughout Japan; fifteen years later, they owned shops throughout the world. (17) He won legal battles in the United States and France in order to get his cultured pearls accepted as genuine, not artificial, gems. (18) He also knew how to generate publicity. (19) When fake pearls flooded the market during the 1930s, he bought quantities of it and dramatically burned them. (20) At the height of his career, Mikimoto's twelve million oysters were producing 75 percent of the world's pearls. (21) His company had become the largest one of their kind in the world. (22) Whomever wanted pearls probably bought from Mikimoto.

(23) As he prospered, Mikimoto set up model communities for his workers; each of the communities provided housing and education for their inhabitants. (24) At ninety, he was still juggling, a skill he learned as a youngster, for the amusement of his employees. (25) When he died in 1954 at the age of ninety-six, he was still actively in control of his pearl empire.

29

Prepositions

Prepositions are words like *about, at, behind, from, into, of, on,* and *with*.

Prepositions are often combined with other words to form fixed expressions. Determining the correct preposition in these expressions can sometimes be confusing. Below is a list of some troublesome expressions with prepositions. Consult a dictionary if you need help with others.*

Expressions with Prepositions

Expression	*Example*
according to	*According to* the directions, this flap fits here.
acquainted with	Tom became *acquainted with* his classmates.
addicted to	He is *addicted to* soap operas.
afraid of	Tanya is *afraid of* flying.
agree on (a plan)	Can we *agree on* our next step?
agree to (another's proposal or to do something)	Roberta *agreed to* her secretary's request for a raise.
angry about or at (a thing)	Jake seemed *angry about* his meager bonus.
angry with (a person)	Sonia couldn't stay *angry with* Felipe.
apply for (a position)	By accident, the twins *applied for* the same job.
approve of	Do you *approve of* bilingual education?
argue about (an issue)	I hate *arguing about* money.
argue with (a person)	Edna *argues with* everyone about everything.
capable of	Mario is *capable of* accomplishing anything he attempts.

* For more work on prepositions, see Chapter 21, "The Simple Sentence," Part B.

complain about (a situation)	Patients *complained about* the long wait to see the dentist.
complain to (a person)	Knee-deep in snow, Jed vowed to *complain to* a maintenance person.
comply with	Each contestant must *comply with* contest regulations.
consist of	This article *consists of* nothing but false accusations and half-truths.
contrast with	The light blue shirt *contrasts* sharply *with* the dark brown tie.
convenient for	A 10:00 A.M. appointment will be *convenient for* Ms. Belgrade.
correspond with (write)	We *corresponded with* her for two months before we met.
deal with	Ron *deals* well *with* temporary setbacks.
depend on	Miriam can be *depended on* to say the embarrassing thing.
differ from (something)	A typewriter *differs from* a word processor.
differ with (a person)	Kathleen *differs with* you on the gun control issue.
different from	Children are often *different from* their parents.
displeased with	Mr. Withers was *displeased with* his doctor's advice to eat less fatty foods.
fond of	Ed is *fond of* his pet tarantula.
grateful for	Be *grateful for* having so many good friends.
grateful to (someone)	The team was *grateful to* the coach for his inspiration and confidence.
identical with	Scott's ideas are often *identical with* mine.
inferior to	Saturday's performance was *inferior to* the one I saw last week.
in search of	I hate to go *in search of* change at the last moment before the toll.
interested in	Willa is *interested in* results, not excuses.
interfere with	That dripping faucet *interferes with* my concentration.
object to	Martin *objected to* the judge's comment.
protect against	This heavy wool scarf will *protect* your throat *against* the cold.

reason with	It's hard to *reason with* an angry person.
rely on	If Toni made that promise, you can *rely on* it.
reply to	He wrote twice, but the president did not *reply to* his letters.
responsible for	Kit is *responsible for* making two copies of each document.
sensitive to	Professor Godfried is *sensitive to* his students' concerns.
shocked at	We were *shocked at* the graphic violence in that PG-rated film.
similar to	Some poisonous mushrooms appear quite *similar to* the harmless kind.
specialize in	This disc jockey *specializes in* jazz of the 1920s and the 1930s.
succeed in	Oscar *succeeded in* painting the roof in under five hours.
superior to	It's clear that the remake is *superior to* the original.
take advantage of	Celia *took advantage of* the snow day to visit the science museum.
worry about	Never *worry about* more than one problem at a time.

PRACTICE Review   Proofread this essay for preposition errors. Cross out the errors and write corrections above the lines.

Dr. Daniel Hale Williams, Pioneer Surgeon

(1) In a lifetime of many successes, Dr. Daniel Hale Williams' greatest achievement was to pioneer open-heart surgery.

(2) Young Williams, an African American who grew up in the mid-1800s, knew poverty. (3) He relied to his wits to get by, becoming, in turn, a shoemaker, musician, and barber. (4) At the age of twenty-two, he met Dr. Henry Palmer, who soon saw he was capable on becoming a physician. (5) Williams' medical education, the usual one at the time, consisted in a two-year apprenticeship with Dr. Palmer, followed by three years at the Chicago Medical College, where he specialized on surgery.

(6) It was an exciting time in medicine, for surgeons had just started using antiseptics in order to protect patients for infection. (7) "Dr. Dan," as he was now called, became an expert on the new surgical techniques and a leader in Chicago's medical and African-American communities. (8) In 1891, he succeeded with opening Provident Hospital, the first inter-racial hospital in the United States. (9) There, African Americans were assured first-rate medical care; moreover, black interns and nurses received thorough professional training.

(10) It was to Provident Hospital that frightened friends brought James Cornish on the evening of July 9, 1893. (11) Near death, the young man had received a deep knife gash near his heart during a fight. (12) Sensitive to the dangerous situation, Dr. Williams decided to operate immediately. (13) According with eyewitnesses, he first made a six-inch incision and removed Cornish's fifth rib. (14) Then, he repaired a torn artery and stitched up the punctured sac surrounding the heart. (15) Fifty-one days later, Cornish left the hospital, recovered and deeply grateful for Dr. Williams to his life. (16) The age of open-heart surgery had begun.

(17) Much lay ahead for Dr. Williams. (18) He was responsible to reorganizing the Freedmen's Hospital at Howard University from 1894 to 1898; in 1913, he accepted an invitation from the American College of Surgeons and succeeded on becoming its only African-American charter member. (19) The high point of his life, however, remained that night in 1893.

30

Adjectives and Adverbs

PART A **Defining and Using Adjectives and Adverbs**
PART B **The Comparative and the Superlative**
PART C **A Troublesome Pair:** *Good/Well*

PART A

Defining and Using Adjectives and Adverbs

Adjectives and **adverbs** are two kinds of descriptive words. **Adjectives** describe or modify nouns or pronouns. They explain what kind, which one, or how many.

---

1. A *black* cat slept on the piano.

2. We felt *cheerful*.

3. *Three* windows in the basement need to be replaced.

- The adjective *black* describes the noun *cat*. It tells what kind of cat, a *black* one.

- The adjective *cheerful* describes the pronoun *we*. It tells what kind of mood we were in, *cheerful*.

- The adjective *three* describes the noun *windows*. It tells how many windows, *three*.

Adverbs describe or modify verbs, adjectives, and other adverbs. They tell how, in what manner, when, and to what extent.

4. Joe dances *gracefully*.

5. *Yesterday* Robert left for a weekend of camping.

6. Brigit is *extremely* tall.

7. He travels *very* rapidly on that skateboard.

■ The adverb *gracefully* describes the verb *dances*. It tells how Joe dances, *gracefully*.

■ The adverb *yesterday* describes the verb *left*. It tells when Robert left, *yesterday*.

■ The adverb *extremely* describes the adjective *tall*. It tells how tall (to what extent), *extremely* tall.

■ The adverb *very* describes the adverb *rapidly*, which describes the verb *travels*. It tells how rapidly he travels, *very* rapidly.

Many adjectives can be changed into adverbs by adding an *-ly* ending. For example, *glad* becomes *gladly*, *hopeful* becomes *hopefully*, *awkward* becomes *awkwardly*.

Note the pairs on this list; they are easily confused:

Adjectives	Adverbs
awful	awfully
bad	badly
poor	poorly
quick	quickly
quiet	quietly
real	really
sure	surely

8. The fish tastes *bad*.

9. It was *badly* prepared.

■ In sentence 8, the adjective *bad* describes the noun *fish*.

■ In sentence 9, the adverb *badly* describes the verb *was prepared*.

PRACTICE 1 Circle the correct adjective or adverb in parentheses. Remember that adjectives modify nouns or pronouns; adverbs modify verbs, adjectives, or adverbs.

1. Have you ever seen (real, really) emeralds?

2. Try to do your work in the library (quiet, quietly).

3. We will (glad, gladly) take you on a tour of the Crunchier Cracker factory.

4. Lee, a (high, highly) skilled electrician, rewired his entire house last year.

5. She made a (quick, quickly) stop at the photocopy machine.

6. It was (awful, awfully) cold today; the weather was terrible.

7. The fans from Cleveland (enthusiastic, enthusiastically) clapped for the Browns.

8. Are you (sure, surely) this bus stops in Dusty Gulch?

9. He (hasty, hastily) wrote the essay, leaving out several important ideas.

10. It was a funny joke, but the comedian told it (bad, badly).

11. Tina walked (careful, carefully) down the icy road.

12. Sam swims (poor, poorly) even though he spends as much time as he can posing on the beach.

13. Sasha the crow is an (unusual, unusually) pet and a (humorous, humorously) companion.

14. The painting is not (actual, actually) a Picasso; in fact, it is a (real, really) bad imitation.

15. It is an (extreme, extremely) hot day, and I (sure, surely) could go for some (real, really) orange juice.

PART B

The Comparative and the Superlative

The **comparative** of an adjective or adverb compares two persons or things:

> 1. Ben is *more creative* than Robert.
>
> 2. Marcia runs *faster* than the coach.

- In sentence 1, Ben is being compared with Robert.

- In sentence 2, Marcia is being compared with the coach.

The **superlative** of an adjective or adverb compares three or more persons or things:

---

3. Sancho is the *tallest* of the three brothers.

4. Marion is the *most intelligent* student in the class.

■ In sentence 3, Sancho is being compared to the other two brothers.

■ In sentence 4, Marion is being compared to all the other students in the class.

Adjectives and adverbs of one syllable usually form the **comparative** by adding *-er.* They form the **superlative** by adding *-est.*

Adjective	Comparative	Superlative
fast	fast*er*	fast*est*
smart	smart*er*	smart*est*
tall	tall*er*	tall*est*

Adjectives and adverbs of more than one syllable usually form the **comparative** by using *more.* They form the **superlative** by using *most.*

Adjective	Comparative	Superlative
beautiful	*more* beautiful	*most* beautiful
brittle	*more* brittle	*most* brittle
serious	*more* serious	*most* serious

Note, however, that adjectives that end in *-y* (like *happy, lazy,* and *sunny*) change the *-y* to *-i* and add *-er* and *-est.*

Adjective	Comparative	Superlative
happy	happ*ier*	happ*iest*
lazy	laz*ier*	laz*iest*
sunny	sunn*ier*	sunn*iest*

PRACTICE 2   Write the comparative or the superlative of the words in parentheses. Remember: Use the comparative to compare two items; use the superlative to compare more than two. Use -er or -est for one-syllable words; use *more* or *most* for words of more than one syllable.*

1. The ocean is _____ (cold) than we thought it would be.

2. Please read your lines again, _____ (slowly) this time.

3. She is the _____ (young) executive in the company.

4. Which of these two roads is the _____ (short) route?

5. Which of these three highways is the _____ (short) route?

6. Dimitri is the _____ (busy) person I know.

7. You painted the apartment _____ (quickly) last year.

8. That red felt hat with feathers is the _____ (outlandish) one I've seen.

9. Today is _____ (warm) than yesterday, but Thursday was the _____ (warm) day of the month.

10. The down coat you have selected is the _____ (expensive) one in the store.

11. Each one of Woody's stories is _____ (funny) than the last.

12. That trip to Mexico was the _____ (enjoyable) vacation our family has ever taken.

13. As a rule, mornings in Los Angeles are _____ (hazy) than afternoons.

14. Is Pete _____ (tall) than Louie? Is Pete the _____ (tall) player on the team?

15. If you don't do these experiments _____ (carefully), you will blow up the chemistry lab.

* If you have questions about spelling, see Chapter 34, "Spelling," Part F.

16. This farmland is much _____ (rocky) than the farmland in Iowa.

17. Learning those irregular verbs was _____ (easy) than I had thought it would be.

18. Therese says that Physics 201 is the _____ (challenging) course she has ever taken.

19. Tim's early experience proved _____ (valuable) than he once thought; growing up in an alcoholic home has made him a _____ (understanding) drug counselor than he might have been otherwise.

20. Mr. Wells is the _____ (wise) and _____ (experienced) leader in the community.

PART C

A Troublesome Pair: *Good/Well*

Adjective	Comparative	Superlative
good	better	best
bad	worse	worst
Adverb	**Comparative**	**Superlative**
well	better	best
badly	worse	worst

Be especially careful not to confuse the adjective **good** with the adverb **well:**

1. Jessie is a *good* writer.

2. She writes *well.*

- *Good* is an **adjective** modifying *writer.*

- *Well* is an **adverb** modifying *writes.*

Note that *well* can be used as an adjective meaning *in good health*. For example, *I feel well today.*

PRACTICE 3   Fill in either the adjective *good* or the adverb *well* in each blank.

1. How _____ do you understand Spanish?

2. He is a _____ tree surgeon who does his job _____.

3. Corned beef definitely goes _____ with cabbage.

4. He may not take phone messages very _____, but he is a _____ typist.

5. Alice is a _____ golfer; she performs _____ under pressure.

PRACTICE 4   Fill in the correct comparative or superlative of the word in parentheses.

1. Gina likes rock climbing _____ (good) than fishing.

2. Jason is the _____ (bad) mechanic on the lot.

3. Of the two sisters, Lee is the _____ (good) markswoman.

4. September is the _____ (good) month of the year for bird watching.

5. Your cold seems _____ (bad) today than it was yesterday.

**PRACTICE 5
Review**   Proofread the following essay for adjective and adverb errors. Correct errors by writing above the lines.

Julia Morgan, Architect

(1) Julia Morgan was one of San Francisco's most finest architects, as well as the first woman licensed as an architect in California. (2) In 1902, Morgan became the first woman to finish successful the program in architecture at the School of Fine Arts in Paris. (3) Returning to San Francisco, she opened her own office and hired and trained a very talented staff that eventual grew to thirty-five full-time architects. (4) Her first major commission was to reconstruct the Fairmont Hotel, one of the city's

bestest-known sites, which had been damaged bad in the 1906 earthquake. (5) Morgan earned her reputation by designing elegant homes and public buildings out of inexpensively and available materials and by treating her clients real good. (6) She went on to design more than eight hundred residences, stores, churches, offices, and educational buildings, most of them in California.

(7) Her bestest customer was William Randolph Hearst, one of the country's most rich newspaper publishers. (8) Morgan designed newspaper buildings and more than twenty pleasure palaces for Hearst in California and Mexico. (9) She maintained a private plane and pilot to keep her moving from project to project. (10) The most big and famousest of her undertakings was sure San Simeon. (11) Morgan worked on it steady for twenty years. (12) She converted a large ranch overlooking the Pacific into a hilltop Mediterranean village composed of three of the beautifullest guest houses in the world. (13) The larger of the three was designed to look like a cathedral and incorporated Hearst's fabulous art treasures from around the world. (14) The finished masterpiece had 144 rooms and was more larger than a football field. (15) San Simeon is now one of the most visited tourist attractions in California and seems to grow popularer each year.

31

The Apostrophe

PART A   The Apostrophe for Contractions
PART B   The Apostrophe for Ownership
PART C   Special Uses of the Apostrophe

The Apostrophe for Contractions

Use the **apostrophe** in a **contraction** to show that letters have been omitted.

> 1. *I'll* buy that coat if it goes on sale.
>
> 2. At nine *o'clock* sharp, the store opens.

- *I'll,* a contraction, is a combination of *I* and *will.* *Wi* is omitted.

- The contraction *o'clock* is the shortened form of *of the clock.*

Be especially careful in writing contractions that contain pronouns:

Common Contractions

I + am – I'm	you + have = you've
I + have = I've	you + will or shall = you'll
I + will or shall = I'll	we + are = we're
he + will or shall = he'll	let + us = let's
she + is or has = she's	they + are = they're
it + is or has = it's	they + have = they've
you + are = you're	who + is or has = who's

PRACTICE 1   Proofread these sentences and supply any missing apostrophes in the contractions above the lines.

1. Ansel Adams wasnt only a great photographer; he was also a conservationist who helped save wildlife areas and establish national parks.

2. Hes best known for his dramatic scenes of the wilderness, but he also made huge technical contributions to the field of photography.

3. Because of Adams, theres now a film-exposure system that controls light and dark contrasts in every part of a photograph.

4. Adams was a talented musician who had planned to become a concert pianist; he hadnt expected a career in photography at all.

5. Its a well-known fact that the fourteen-year-old Adams took his first photo while on a family vacation trip to Yosemite National Park in 1916.

6. His decision didnt happen overnight, but he eventually realized that music wouldnt be as satisfying a field for him to work in as photography.

7. People werent surprised when he transferred the great attention to detail that he had given his piano technique to developing sharp, clear prints.

8. Whats most unusual is how Adams worked with light, space, and mood when he photographed storms, mountains, and other natural scenes.

9. Before Adams, many people couldnt believe that photography would become an art form.

10. Theyve been proven wrong: Adams published books about photography as well as books of his own photographs, and he established photography departments in museums and universities throughout the United States.

One of Ansel Adams' photographs of Half-Dome and Merced River in Yosemite National Park appears on page 424.

PART B

The Apostrophe for Ownership

Use the apostrophe to show ownership: add an '*s* if a noun or an indefinite pronoun (like *someone, anybody,* and so on) does not already end in -*s*:

1. I cannot find my *friend's* book bag.
2. *Everyone's* right to privacy should be respected.
3. *John and Julio's* apartment has velvet wallpaper.

- The *friend* owns the book bag.
- *Everyone* owns the right to privacy.
- Both John and Julio own one apartment. The apostrophe follows the compound *John and Julio.*

    Add only an apostrophe to show ownership if the word already ends in *-s:*

4. My *aunts' houses* are filled with antiques.
5. The *knights'* table was round.
6. *Mr. Jonas' company* manufactures sporting goods and uniforms.

- My *aunts* (at least two of them) own the houses.
- The *knights* (at least two) own the table.
- *Aunts* and *knights* already end in -*s*, so only an apostrophe is added.
- *Mr. Jonas* owns the company. *Mr. Jonas* already ends in -*s*, so only an apostrophe is added.

Note that *possessive pronouns never take an apostrophe: his, hers, theirs, ours, yours, its:*

7. *His* car gets twenty miles to the gallon, but *hers* gets only ten.

8. That computer is *theirs; ours* is coming soon.

PRACTICE 2   Proofread the following sentences and add apostrophes where necessary to show ownership. In each case, ask yourself if the word already ends in -*s*. Put a *C* after any correct sentences.

1. Bills bed is a four-poster.

2. Martha and Davids house is a log cabin made entirely by hand.

3. Somebodys wedding ring was left on the sink.

4. During the eighteenth century, ladies dresses were heavy and uncomfortable.

5. Have you seen the childrens watercolor set?

6. Mr. James fried chicken and rice dish was crispy and delicious.

7. The class loved reading about Ulysses travels.

8. The Surgeon Generals latest report was just released.

9. Our citys water supply must be protected.

10. He found his ticket, but she cannot find hers.

11. Every spring, my neighbors porch is completely covered with old furniture for sale.

12. Jacks Health Club just opened at Locust and Broad.

13. Celias final, a brilliant study of pest control on tobacco farms, received a high grade.

14. The mens locker room is on the right; the womens is on the left.

15. It seems that your orders have been lost in transit.

Special Uses of the Apostrophe

Use an apostrophe in certain expressions of time:

> 1. I desperately need a *week's* vacation.

■ Although the week does not own a vacation, it is a vacation of a week—*a week's vacation.*

Use an apostrophe to pluralize letters, numbers, and words that normally do not have plurals:

> 2. Be careful to cross your *t*'s.
>
> 3. Your *8*'s look like *F*'s.
>
> 4. Don't use so many *but*'s in your writing.

Use an apostrophe to show omitted numbers:

> 5. The class of '*72* held its annual reunion last week.

PRACTICE 3   Proofread these sentences and add an apostrophe wherever necessary.

1. Cross your *t*s and dot your *i*s.

2. I would love a months vacation on a dude ranch.

3. Too many *and*s make this paragraph dull.

4. Those *9*s look crooked.

5. You certainly put in a hard days work!

**PRACTICE 4
Review** Proofread the following essay for apostrophe errors. Correct the errors by adding apostrophes above the lines where needed and crossing out those that do not belong.

The True Story of Superman

(1) Sometimes, things just dont work out right. (2) That's how the creators of Superman felt for a long time.

(3) Supermans first home wasnt the planet Krypton, but Cleveland. (4) There, in 1933, Superman was born. (5) Jerry Siegels story, "Reign of Superman," accompanied by Joe Shuster's illustrations, appeared in the boys own magazine, *Science Fiction.* (6) Later, the teenagers continued to develop their idea. (7) Superman would come to earth from a distant planet to defend freedom and justice for ordinary people. (8) He would conceal his identity by living as an ordinary person himself. (9) Siegel and Shuster hoped their characters strength and morality would boost peoples spirits' during the Great Depression.

(10) At first, the creators werent able to sell their concept; then, Action Comics' Henry Donnenfield bought it. (11) In June of 1938, the first Superman comic hit the stands. (12) Superman's success was immediate and overwhelming. (13) Finally, Americans had a hero who wouldnt let them down! (14) Radio and TV shows, movie serials, feature films, and generations of superheros' followed.

(15) While others made millions from their idea, Siegel and Shuster didnt profit from its' success. (16) They produced Superman for Action Comics for a mere fifteen dollars a page until they were fired a few years later, when Joe Shusters eyes began to fail. (17) They sued, but they lost the case. (18) For a long time, both lived in poverty, but they continued to fight. (19) In 1975, Siegel and Shuster finally took their story to the press; the publicity won them lifelong pensions. (20) The two mens long struggle had ended with success.

32

The Comma

PART A

Commas for Items in a Series

Use commas to separate the items in a series:*

> 1. You need *bolts, nuts,* and *screws.*
>
> 2. I will be happy to *read your poem, comment on it,* and *return it to you.*
>
> 3. *Mary paints pictures, Robert plays the trumpet,* but *Sam just sits and dreams.*

Do not use commas when all three items are joined by *and* or *or:*

> 4. I enjoy *biking* and *skating* and *swimming.*

* For work on parallelism, see Chapter 13, "Revising for Consistency and Parallelism," Part C.

PRACTICE 1   Punctuate the following sentences.

1. At the banquet, Ed served a salad of juicy red tomatoes crunchy green lettuce and stringless snap beans.

2. As a nursing assistant, Reva dispensed medication disinfected wounds and took blood samples.

3. Ali visited Santa Barbara Concord and Berkeley.

4. Our new gym is located in a modern air-conditioned glass skyscraper.

5. The police found TV sets blenders and blow dryers stacked to the ceiling in the abandoned house.

6. I forgot to pack some important items for the trip to the tropics: insect repellent sunscreen and antihistamine tablets.

7. Don't eat strange mushrooms walk near the water or feed the squirrels.

8. Everyone in class had to present an oral report write a term paper and take a final.

9. We brought a Ouija board a Scrabble set and a Boggle game to the party.

10. To earn a decent wage make a comfortable home and educate my children—that is my hope.

PART B

Commas with Introductory Phrases, Transitional Expressions, and Parentheticals

Use a comma after most introductory phrases of more than two words:*

---

1. *By four in the afternoon,* everybody wanted to go home.
2. *After the game on Saturday,* we all went dancing.

---

* For more work on introductory phrases, see Chapter 14, "Revising for Sentence Variety," Part C.

Use commas to set off transitional expressions:

> 3. Ferns, *for example,* need less sunlight than flowering plants.
>
> 4. Instructors, *on the other hand,* receive a lower salary than assistant professors.

Use commas to set off parenthetical elements:

> 5. *By the way,* where is the judge's umbrella?
>
> 6. Nobody, *it seems,* wants to eat the three-bean salad.

■ *By the way* and *it seems* are called parenthetical expressions because they appear to be asides, words not really crucial to the meaning of the sentence. They could almost appear in parentheses: (*By the way*) *where is the judge's umbrella?*

Other common parenthetical expressions are *after all, actually, as a matter of fact,* and *to tell the truth.*

PRACTICE 2   Punctuate the following sentences:

1. Frankly I always suspected that you were a born saleswoman.

2. General Marsh it seems to me trusted only one or two of his advisers.

3. At two o'clock in the morning we were awakened by garbage cans clanging.

4. All twelve jurors by the way felt that the defendant was innocent.

5. On every April Fool's Day he tries out a new, dumb practical joke.

6. In fact Lucinda should never have written that poison-pen letter.

7. Close to the top of Mt. Everest the climbers paused for a tea break.

8. To tell the truth that usher needs a lesson in courtesy.

9. My CD player I'm sorry to say gives me a shock every time I touch it.

10. These apples to tell the truth were organically grown in his back yard.

11. During the power blackout people tried to help one another.

12. Near the end of the driveway a large lilac bush bloomed and brightened the yard.

13. He prefers as a rule serious news programs to the lighter sitcoms.

14. To sum up Mr. Choi will handle all the details.

15. During my three years in Minnesota I learned how to deal with snow.

PART C

Commas for Appositives

Use commas to set off appositives:*

---

1. Yoko, *our new classmate,* is our best fielder.

2. *A humorous and charming man,* he was a great hit with my parents.

3. This is her favorite food, *ketchup sandwiches.*

■ Appositive phrases like *our new classmate, a humorous and charming man,* and *ketchup sandwiches* rename or describe nouns and pronouns— *Yoko, he, favorite food.*

---

4. Henry *the Fat* was a great king.

5. My friend *Bill* owns two stereos.

■ One-word appositives are generally not set off by commas.

PRACTICE 3   Punctuate the following sentences.

1. Hulk Hogan the popular wrestler and actor advises his fans to drink milk and say their prayers.

2. Long novels especially ones with complicated plots force me to read slowly.

* For more work on appositives, see Chapter 14, "Revising for Sentence Variety," Part D.

3. David a resident nurse hopes to become a pediatrician.

4. I don't trust that tire the one with the yellow patch on the side.

5. Tanzania a small African nation exports cashew nuts.

6. Watch out for Phil a man whose ambition rules him.

7. Sheila a well-known nutritionist lectures at public schools.

8. A real flying ace Helen will teach a course in sky diving.

9. We support the Center for Science in the Public Interest a consumer education and protection group.

10. The voters mostly blue-collar workers elected the new mayor by a wide margin.

PART D

Commas with Nonrestrictive and Restrictive Clauses

A **relative clause** is a clause that begins with *who*, *which*, or *that* and modifies a noun or pronoun. There are two kinds of relative clauses: **nonrestrictive** and **restrictive**.*

A **nonrestrictive relative clause** is not essential to the meaning of the sentence:

> 1. Raj, *who is a part-time aviator,* loves to tinker with machines of all kinds.

- *Who is a part-time aviator* is a relative clause describing *Raj*. It is a nonrestrictive relative clause because it is not essential to the meaning of the sentence. The point is that *Raj loves to tinker with machines of all kinds.*
- **Commas** set off the nonrestrictive relative clause.

A **restrictive relative clause** is essential to the meaning of the sentence:

> 2. People *who do their work efficiently* make good students.

---

* For more work on nonrestrictive and restrictive clauses, see Chapter 14, "Revising for Sentence Variety," Part D.

- *Who do their work efficiently* is a relative clause describing *people*. It is a restrictive relative clause because it is *essential* to the meaning of the sentence. Without it, sentence 2 would read, *People make good students.* But the point is that certain people make good students—*those who do their work efficiently.*

- Restrictive relative clauses *do not* require commas.

PRACTICE 4   Set off the nonrestrictive relative clauses in the following sentences with commas. Note that *which* usually begins a nonrestrictive relative clause and *that* usually begins a restrictive clause. Remember: Restrictive relative clauses are *not* set off by commas.

1. Olive who always wanted to go into law enforcement is a detective in the Eighth Precinct.

2. Employees who learn to use the new computers may soon qualify for a merit raise.

3. Polo which is not played much in the United States is very popular in England.

4. A person who always insists upon telling you the truth is sometimes a pain in the neck.

5. Statistics 101 which is required for the business curriculum demands concentration and perseverance.

6. Robin who is usually shy at large parties spent the evening dancing with Arsenio who is everybody's favorite dance partner.

7. This small shop sells furniture that is locally handcrafted.

8. His uncle who rarely eats meat consumes enormous quantities of vegetables, fruits, and grains.

9. Pens that slowly leak ink can be very messy.

10. Valley Forge which is the site of Washington's winter quarters draws many tourists every spring and summer.

PART E

Commas for Dates and Addresses

Use commas to separate the elements of an address:

> 1. I live at *300 West Road, Stamford, Connecticut.*
>
> 2. We moved from *10–15 Allen Circle, Morristown, New Jersey,* to *Farland Lane, Dubuque, Iowa.*

Use commas to separate the elements of a date:

> 3. The sociologists arrived in Tibet on *Monday, January 18, 1992,* and planned to stay for two years.
>
> 4. *By June 20, 1999,* I expect to have completed my B.A. in physical education.

Do not use a comma with a single-word address or date preceded by a preposition:

> 5. John DeLeon arrived from Baltimore *in January* and will be our new shortstop this season.

PRACTICE 5   Punctuate the following sentences.

1. The second Woodstock rock music festival began on Friday August 12 1994.

2. Many of the 350,000 people who traveled to Saugerties New York that summer wanted to relive the original festival.

3. The first Woodstock, held in Bethel New York from Friday August 15 1969 through that weekend, was a symbol of peace during wartime; people experienced kindness and camaraderie amidst mud, thunderstorms, and the most crowded conditions imaginable.

4. Over half a million people participated in the first Woodstock; they came from as far west as Portland Oregon and as far south as Miami Florida.

5. Ron Butler of 3001 Hughes Street Atlanta Georgia said that the high point of the original Woodstock was Jimi Hendrix's rendition of "The Star-Spangled Banner" on Monday August 18 at sunrise.

6. Hendrix was greatly missed at the second Woodstock; he died of a drug overdose on September 18 1970 in London England.

7. Another original Woodstock singer who didn't live to perform at the twenty-fifth reunion was Janis Joplin; she died on October 4 1970 in Los Angeles California also of a drug overdose.

8. Tracey Kelly from Chicago Illinois claimed that she could sense the presence of these two performers at the second festival.

9. Journalists, who came from as far as Rome Italy and Warsaw Poland reported that the mixture of the older and younger generations gave the festival a special feeling of reconciliation.

10. If a third Woodstock reunion is held in twenty-five years, it will probably take place from Friday August 9 2019 through Monday August 12 2019 but no one knows what that festival will be like.

PART F

Minor Uses of the Comma

Use a comma after answering a question with *yes* or *no*:

1. *No,* I'm not sure about that answer.

Use a comma when addressing someone directly and specifically naming the person spoken to:

> 2. *Alicia,* where did you put my law books?

Use a comma after interjections like *ah, oh,* and so on:

> 3. *Ah,* these coconuts are delicious.

Use a comma to contrast:

> 4. Harold, *not Roy,* is my scuba-diving partner.

PRACTICE 6　Punctuate the following sentences.

1. Yes I do think you will be famous one day.
2. Well did you call a taxi?
3. The defendant ladies and gentlemen of the jury does not even own a red plaid jacket.
4. Cynthia have you ever camped in the Pacific Northwest?
5. No I most certainly will not marry you.
6. Oh I love the way they play everything to a salsa beat.
7. The class feels Professor Molinor that your grades are unrealistically high.
8. He said "March" not "Swagger."
9. Perhaps but I still don't think that the carburetor fits there.
10. We all agree Ms. Crawford that you are the best jazz bassist around.

PRACTICE 7
Review
Proofread the following essay for comma errors—either missing commas or commas used incorrectly. Correct the errors above the lines.

The Pyramids of Giza

(1) A wonder of the ancient world the pyramids of Giza, Egypt still inspire awe. (2) Built nearly five thousand years ago the largest of these tombs, was ordered by Khu-fu, a powerful pharaoh of ancient Egypt. (3) The two smaller pyramids nearby belonged to his successors his son Khafre and his grandson Menkaure. (4) The three pyramids—together with the Sphinx many temples and causeways—comprised a ceremonial complex for the dead not far from the Nile River.

(5) We marvel today at the ability of this ancient people to build such colossal structures without the benefit of work animals or machinery not even the wheel. (6) The Great Pyramid for instance is 750 square feet and 480 feet high, roughly the size of Shea Stadium filled in with solid rock to a height of forty stories. (7) More than 100,000 workers, who were probably peasants forced into service cut two-and-a-half-ton limestone blocks from quarries on the other side of the Nile ferried them across the river, and then dragged them up ramps to be fitted exactly in place. (8) Experts estimate that 2.3 million blocks had to be moved over a period of more than twenty years, to complete the project.

(9) Perhaps the greatest wonder, however is that these structures have lasted. (10) Countless other buildings statues, and monuments have been constructed and admired, yet have fallen into ruin since these magnificent structures were built. (11) The pyramids are considered all but indestructible. (12) It has been said, in fact that they could withstand a direct hit by an atomic bomb.

33

Mechanics

PART A   Capitalization
PART B   Titles
PART C   Direct Quotations
PART D   Minor Marks of Punctuation

PART A

Capitalization

Always capitalize the following: *names, nationalities, religions, races, countries, cities, months, days of the week, documents, organizations,* and *holidays.*

> 1. The *Protestant* church on the corner will offer *Spanish* and *English* courses starting *Thursday, June* 3.

Capitalize the following *only* when they are used as part of a proper noun: *streets, buildings, historical events, titles,* and *family relationships.*

> 2. We saw *Professor Rodriguez* at *Silver Hall,* where he was delivering a talk on the *Spanish Civil War.*

Do not capitalize these same words when they are used as common nouns:

> 3. We saw the professor at the lecture hall, where he was delivering a talk on a civil war.

Capitalize geographic locations but not directions:

> 4. The tourists went to the *South* for their winter vacation.
>
> 5. Go south on this boulevard for three miles.

Capitalize academic subjects only if they refer to a specific named and numbered course:

> 6. Have you ever studied psychology?
>
> 7. Last semester, I took *Psychology* 101.

PRACTICE 1 Capitalize wherever necessary in the following sentences. Put a *C* after each correct sentence.

1. Anna Sewell was born on march 30, 1820, in a small town in england.

2. Raised in a loving quaker family, she bravely bore many misfortunes, including a childhood fall that disabled her for life.

3. When she was sixteen, her family moved to brighton, a seaside city south of london, where she wrestled with pain and accepted the fact that she would never walk without help again.

4. Sewell loved animals, particularly horses, and according to the biographer ms. margaret joyce baker, was always sensitive to their mistreatment.

5. When her family moved to lancing, she would drive her father in a horse-drawn carriage to the train station each day.

6. Along the busy coast road, she saw owners beating underfed, exhausted horses that were pulling loads much too heavy for them.

7. Inspired by an essay on animals written by an american religious writer, she decided that one day she would write a book that would make people more sympathetic to horses.

8. Her health gradually grew worse; bedridden in her home in Old catton, she took several years to write *Black Beauty*, which became the world's most beloved animal story.

9. Sewell wrote about a beautiful, loyal horse, from its gentle farm background to its life with a noble owner, squire gordon, and then with a cruel driver who overworked and mistreated it.

10. Published in 1877 by a company called jarrold and sons, the book was immediately popular in both britain and the united states.

11. When she died in the spring of the following year, several thousand copies of the book had been sold, and its influence had become enormous.

12. Even the royal society for the prevention of cruelty to animals distributed the book in order to change the way people treated pets and other animals.

13. Sewell's papers and many early editions of her book still can be found at the homer babbidge library on fairfield road in storrs, connecticut.

14. Perhaps you read this ever-popular novel as a child or even later, as a student in an english course, a sociology class, or a course such as children's literature 101.

15. You may want to give this unforgettable classic to a child as a birthday present, as a gift for christmas, hanukkah, or kwanzaa, or just as a treat for no special occasion.

PART B

Titles

Capitalize all the words of a title except for short prepositions, short conjunctions, and the articles *the*, *an*, and *a*. Always capitalize the first and last words of the title, no matter what they are:

> 1. I liked <u>The Color Purple</u> but found <u>The House on the River</u> slow reading.

Underline the titles of long works: *books,* newspapers and magazines,† television shows, plays, record albums, movies, operas,* and *films.*

Put quotation marks around shorter works or parts of longer ones: *articles, short stories, poems, songs, paintings, scenes from plays,* and *chapters from full-length books.*

> 2. Have you read Hemingway's "The Killers" yet?
>
> 3. We are assigned "The Money Market" in <u>Essentials of Economics</u> for homework in my marketing course.

- "The Killers" is a short story.

- "The Money Market" is a chapter in the full-length book *Essentials of Economics.*

Do not underline or use quotation marks around the titles of your own papers.

PRACTICE 2   Capitalize these titles correctly. Do not underline or use quotation marks in this practice.

1. the first immigrants

2. a trip through the Netherlands

3. making jams and jellies

4. a dangerous game

5. why every american should vote

6. nuclear power: safe or sorry?

7. how to build a sailboat

8. the quark theory

9. starting over

* The titles and parts of sacred books are not underlined and are not set off by quotation marks: Job 5:6, the Koran 1:14, and so on.
† However, do not capitalize or underline the word *the,* even when it begins the title of a newspaper or magazine.

10. a boy, a dog, and a murder

11. parents without partners

12. the value of friendship

13. what I would do with $50,000

14. three causes of world war II

15. the fate of the earth

PRACTICE 3 Wherever necessary, underline or place quotation marks around each title in the sentences below so that the reader will know at a glance what type of work the title refers to. Put a *C* after any correct sentence.

Example | Two of the best short stories in that volume are "Rope" and "The New Dress."

1. African-American writer Langston Hughes produced his first novel, Not Without Laughter, when he was a student at Lincoln University in Pennsylvania.

2. By that time, he had already been a farmer, a cook, a waiter, and a doorman at a Paris nightclub; he had also won a prize for his poem The Weary Blues, which was published in 1925 in the magazine Opportunity.

3. In 1926 Hughes wrote his famous essay The Negro Artist and the Racial Mountain, which appeared in the Nation magazine; he wanted young black writers to write without shame or fear about the subject of race.

4. Because he spoke Spanish, Hughes was asked in 1937 by the newspaper the Baltimore Afro-American to cover the activities of blacks in the International Brigades in Spain during the Spanish Civil War.

5. For the rest of his life, he wrote articles in newspapers such as the San Francisco Chronicle, the New York Times, and the Chicago Defender.

6. In fact, for more than twenty years he wrote a weekly column for the Chicago Defender, in which he introduced a character named Simple, who became popular because of his witty observations on life.

7. The stories about Simple were eventually collected and published in five books; two of those books are Simple Speaks His Mind and Simple Takes a Wife.

8. In 1938, Hughes established the Harlem Suitcase Theater in Manhattan, where his play Don't You Want to Be Free? was performed.

9. Because Hughes' poetry was based on the rhythms of African American speech and music, many of his poems have been set to music, including Love Can Hurt You, Dorothy's Name is Mud, and Five O'Clock Blues.

10. Few modern writers can rival Hughes' enormous output of fine poems, newspaper articles, columns, sketches, and novels.

PART C

Direct Quotations

Use quotation marks* to enclose the exact words of the speaker:

> 1. He said, "These are the best seats in the house."

- The direct quotation is preceded by a comma or a colon.
- The first letter of the direct quotation is capitalized.
- Periods always go *inside* the quotation marks.

> 2. He asked, "Where are my tickets?"
> 3. Stewart yelled, "I don't like beans!"

- Question marks and exclamation points go inside the quotation marks if they are part of the direct words of the speaker.

---

* For more work on direct and indirect quotations, see Chapter 13, "Revising for Consistency and Parallelism," Part D.

> 4. "That was meant for the company," he said, "but if you wish, you may have it."
>
> 5. "The trees look magnificent!" she exclaimed. "It would be fun to climb them all."

- In sentence 4, the quotation is one single sentence interrupted by *he said*. Therefore, a comma is used after *he said,* and *but* is not capitalized.

- In sentence 5, the quotation consists of two different sentences. Thus a period follows *exclaimed,* and the second sentence of the quotation begins with a capital letter.

PRACTICE 4   Insert quotation marks where necessary in each sentence. Capitalize and punctuate correctly.

1. The sign reads don't even think about parking here.

2. Can you direct me to the central bus stop he asked.

3. Alexander Pope wrote to err is human, to forgive divine.

4. Jim wondered why have I been having such good luck lately

5. Well, it takes all kinds she sighed

6. The report stated no one responded to the crisis in time.

7. He exclaimed you look terrific in those jeweled sandals

8. The article said Most American children do poorly in geography.

9. These books on ancient Egypt look interesting he replied but I don't have time to read them now.

10. Although the rain is heavy she said we will continue harvesting the corn.

11. Give up caffeine and get lots of rest the doctor advised.

12. This final is easy he whispered to himself it is a guaranteed *A*.

13. We haven't gone fishing for a month he complained and we really miss it

14. The label warns this product should not be taken by those allergic to aspirin.

15. Red, white, and blue Ronald said are my favorite colors

PART D

Minor Marks of Punctuation

1. The Colon

Use a colon to show that a direct quotation will follow or to introduce a list:*

> 1. This is the opening line of his essay: "The airplane is humanity's greatest invention."
>
> 2. There are four things I can't resist in warm weather: fresh mangoes, a sandy beach, cold drinks, and a hammock.

Use a colon to separate the chapter and verse in a reference to the Bible or to separate the hour and minute:

> 3. This quotation comes from Genesis 1:1.
>
> 4. It is now exactly 4:15 P.M.

2. Parentheses

Use parentheses to enclose a phrase or word that is not essential to the meaning of the sentence:

> 5. Herpetology (the study of snakes) is a fascinating area of zoology.
>
> 6. She left her home town (Plunkville) to go to the big city (Fairmount) in search of success.

3. The Dash

Use a dash to emphasize a portion of a sentence or to interrupt the sentence with an added element:

* Avoid using a colon after any form of the verb *to be* or after a preposition.

> 7. This is the right method—the only one—so we are stuck with it.

The colon, parentheses, and the dash should be used sparingly.

PRACTICE 5   Punctuate these sentences with colons, dashes, or parentheses.

1. Calvin asked for the following two light bulbs, a pack of matches, a lead pencil, and a pound of grapes.

2. They should leave by 1130 P.M.

3. The designer's newest fashions magnificent leather creations were generally too expensive for the small chain of clothing stores.

4. Harvey the only Missourian in the group remains unconvinced.

5. She replied, "This rock group The Woogies sounds like all of the others I've heard this year."

6. If you eat a heavy lunch as you always do remember not to go swimming immediately afterward.

7. By 9:30 P.M., the zoo veterinarian a Dr. Smittens had operated on the elephant.

8. Note these three tips for hammering in a nail hold the hammer at the end of the handle, position the nail carefully, and watch your thumb.

9. Whenever Harold Garvey does his birdcalls at parties as he is sure to do everyone begins to yawn.

10. Please purchase these things at the hardware store masking tape, thumbtacks, a small hammer, and some sandpaper.

PRACTICE 6
Review   Proofread the following essay for errors in capitalization, quotation marks, colons, parentheses, and dashes. Correct the errors by writing above the lines.

The Passion of Thomas Gilcrease

(1) Thomas Gilcrease, a descendent of creek indians, became an instant Millionaire when oil was discovered on his homestead in 1907. (2) He spent most of his fortune collecting objects that tell the story of the american frontier, particularly of the Native American experience. (3) The Thomas Gilcrease institute of american history and arts in Tulsa, oklahoma, is the result of his lifelong passion.

(4) This huge collection more than 10,000 works of art, 90,000 historical documents, and 250,000 native american artifacts, spans the centuries from 10,000 B.C. to the 1950s. (5) Awed visitors can view nearly 200 George Catlin paintings of Native American life. (6) They can walk among paintings and bronze sculptures by Frederic Remington with names like The Coming And Going Of The Pony Express that call up images of the West. (7) Museum-goers can admire Thomas Moran's watercolors that helped persuade congress to create yellowstone, the first national park. (8) In addition, visitors are treated to works by modern Native Americans, such as the display of wood sculptures by the cherokee Willard Stone.

(9) The museum also houses many priceless documents an original copy of the declaration of independence, the oldest known letter written from the new world, and the papers of Hernando Cortés. (10) A new glass storage area even allows visitors to view the 80 percent of the holdings that are not on display. (11) Thousands of beaded moccasins and buckskin dresses line the shelves, and a collection of magnificent war bonnets hangs from brackets.

(12) When the Gilcrease Museum opened its doors on May 2, 1949, *Life* declared "it is the best collection of art and literature ever assembled on the American frontier and the Indian. (13) Thousands of visitors agree.

Unit 7

Strengthening Your Spelling

34

Spelling

PART A   Suggestions for Improving Your Spelling

Accurate spelling is an important ingredient of good writing. No matter how interesting your ideas are, if your spelling is poor, your writing will not be effective.

Some Tips for Improving Your Spelling

- **Look closely at the words on the page.** Use any tricks you can to remember the right spelling. For example, "The *a*'s in *separate* are separated by an *r*," or "*Dessert* has two *s*'s because you want two desserts."

- **Use a dictionary.** Even professional writers frequently check spelling in a dictionary. As you write, underline the words you are not sure of and look them up when you write your final draft. If locating words in the dictionary is a real problem for you, consider a "poor speller's dictionary" or use the spelling-check feature of your word processor or computer.

- **Keep a list of the words you misspell.** Look over your list whenever you can and keep it handy as you write.

- **Look over corrected papers for misspelled words** (often marked *sp.*). Add these words to your list. Practice writing each word three or four times.

- **Test yourself.** Use flash cards or have a friend dictate words from your list or from this chapter.

- **Review the basic spelling rules explained in this chapter.** Take time to learn the material; don't rush through the entire chapter all at once.

- **Study the spelling list on pages 458–459,** and test yourself on these words.

- **Read through Chapter 35, "Look-Alikes/Sound-Alikes,"** for commonly confused words (*their, there,* and *they're,* for instance). The practices in that chapter will help you eliminate some common spelling errors from your writing.

PART B   Spotting Vowels and Consonants

To learn some basic spelling rules, you must know the difference between vowels and consonants.

> The **vowels** are *a, e, i, o,* and *u.*
> The **consonants** are *b, c, d, f, g, h, j, k, l, m, n, p, q, r, s, t, v, w, x,* and *z.*
> The letter *y* can be either a vowel or a consonant, depending on its sound:

> **daisy**   **sky**

- In each of these words, *y* is a vowel because it has a vowel sound: an *ee* sound in *daisy* and an *i* sound in *sky.*

> **yellow**   **your**

- In both *yellow* and *your, y* is a consonant because it has the consonant sound of *y.*

PRACTICE 1   Write *v* for vowel and *c* for consonant in the space on top of each word. Be careful of the *y.*

Example
$$\frac{\text{c v c v c}}{\text{h o p e d}}$$

1. ___ ___ ___ ___
   h a l l

2. ___ ___ ___ ___
   r e l y

3. ___ ___ ___ ___ ___ ___ ___
   p e r h a p s

4. ___ ___ ___ ___
   y a w n

5. ___ ___ ___ ___ ___ ___ ___
   i n s t e a d

6. ___ ___ ___ ___
   j u m p

7. ___ ___ ___ ___ ___ ___ ___
   q u a l i f y

8. ___ ___ ___ ___ ___ ___
   h i d d e n

9. ___ ___ ___ ___ ___
   f o r g e

10. ___ ___ ___ ___ ___ ___ ___ ___ ___
    b y s t a n d e r

PART C   Doubling the Final Consonant (in Words of One Syllable)

When you add a suffix or an ending that begins with a vowel (like *-ed, -ing, -er, -est*) to a word of one syllable, double the final consonant *if* the last three letters of the word are consonant-*vowel*-consonant or *c-v-c.*

> **plan + ed = planned**   **swim + ing = swimming**
>
> **thin + est = thinnest**   **light + er = lighter**

- *Plan, swim,* and *thin* all end in *cvc;* therefore, the final consonants are doubled.
- *Light* does not end in *cvc;* therefore, the final consonant is not doubled.

PRACTICE 2   Which of the following words should double the final consonant? Check to see whether the word ends in *cvc.* Then add the suffixes *-ed* and *-ing.*

	Word	Last Three Letters	*-ed*	*-ing*
Example	drop	cvc	dropped	dropping
	boil	vvc	boiled	boiling
	1. tan			
	2. brag			
	3. rip			
	4. mail			
	5. stop			
	6. peel			
	7. shift			
	8. wrap			
	9. ask			
	10. chat			

PRACTICE 3   Which of the following words should double the final consonant? Check for *cvc.* Then add the suffixes *-er* or *-est.*

	Word	Last Three Letters	*-er*	*-est*
Example	wet	cvc	wetter	wettest
	cool	vvc	cooler	coolest
	1. deep			
	2. short			
	3. fat			
	4. slim			
	5. red			
	6. green			
	7. moist			
	8. clean			
	9. dim			
	10. bright			

PART D   Doubling the Final Consonant (in Words of More Than One Syllable)

When you add a suffix that begins with a vowel to a word of more than one syllable, double the final consonant *if*

(1) the last three letters of the word are *cvc, and*

(2) the accent or stress is on the *last* syllable.

begin + ing = beginning   **control + ed = controlled**

- *Begin* and *control* both end in *cvc*.

- In both words, the stress is on the last syllable: *be-gin', con-trol'*. (Pronounce the words aloud and listen for the correct stress.)

- Therefore, *beginning* and *controlled* double the final consonant.

listen + ing = listening   **visit + ed = visited**

- *Listen* and *visit* both end in *cvc*.

- However, the stress is *not* on the last syllable: *lis'-ten, vis'-it*.

- Therefore, *listening* and *visited do not* double the final consonant.

PRACTICE 4   Which of the following words should double the final consonant? First, check for *cvc*; then check for the final stress. Then add the suffixes *-ed* and *-ing*.

	Word	Last Three Letters	*-ed*	*-ing*
Example	repel	cvc	repelled	repelling
	enlist	vcc	enlisted	enlisting
	1. expel			
	2. happen			
	3. polish			
	4. admit			
	5. offer			
	6. prefer			
	7. commit			
	8. pardon			
	9. compel			
	10. answer			

PART E   Dropping or Keeping the Final *E*

When you add a suffix that begins with a vowel (like *-able, -ence, -ing*), drop the final *e*.
When you add a suffix that begins with a consonant (like *-less, -ment, -ly*), keep the final *e*.

move + ing = moving   **pure + ity = purity**

■ *Moving* and *purity* both drop the final *e* because the suffixes *-ing* and *-ity* begin with vowels.

home + less = homeless   **advertise + ment = advertisement**

■ *Homeless* and *advertisement* keep the final *e* because the suffixes *-less* and *-ment* begin with consonants.

Here are some exceptions to memorize:

argument   manageable

awful   noticeable

courageous   truly

judgment   simply

PRACTICE 5   Add the suffix shown to each word.

Example | hope + ing = _hoping_
            | hope + ful = _hopeful_

1. love + able = _____   6. complete + ness = _____

2. love + ly = _____   7. enforce + ment = _____

3. pure + ly = _____   8. enforce + ed = _____

4. pure + er = _____   9. arrange + ing = _____

5. complete + ing = _____   10. arrange + ment = _____

PRACTICE 6   Add the suffix shown to each word.

Example | come + ing = _coming_
            | rude + ness = _rudeness_

1. guide + ance = _____   6. sincere + ly = _____

2. manage + ment = _____   7. notice + able = _____

3. dense + ity = _____   8. response + ible = _____

4. complete + ly = _____   9. judge + ment = _____

5. motive + ation = _____   10. fame + ous = _____

PART F Changing or Keeping the Final *Y*

When you add a suffix to a word that ends in -*y*, change the *y* to *i* if the letter before the *y* is a consonant.

Keep the final *y* if the letter before the *y* is a vowel.

happy + ness = happiness   **portray + ed = portrayed**

- The *y* in *happiness* is changed to *i* because the letter before the *y* is a consonant, *p*.

- The *y* in *portrayed* is not changed because the letter before it is a vowel, *a*.

However, when you add -*ing* to words ending in *y*, always keep the *y*:

copy + ing = copying   **delay + ing = delaying**

Here are some exceptions to memorize:

day + ly = daily   pay + ed = paid

lay + ed = laid   say + ed = said

PRACTICE 7   Add the suffix shown to each of the following words.

Example | marry + ed = _married_
            | buy + er = _buyer_

1. try + ed = _____   6. wealthy + est = _____

2. vary + able = _____   7. day + ly = _____

3. worry + ing = _____   8. duty + ful = _____

4. pay + ed = _____   9. display + s = _____

5. enjoy + able = _____   10. occupy + ed = _____

PRACTICE 8   Add the suffix in parentheses to each word.

1. beauty (fy)   _____   4. angry   (er)   _____
           (ful)   _____   (est)   _____
           (es)   _____   (ly)   _____

2. lonely (er)   _____   5. study   (es)   _____
           (est)   _____   (ous)   _____
           (ness) _____   (ing)   _____

3. betray (ed)   _____   6. busy   (ness) _____
           (ing)   _____   (er)   _____
           (al)   _____   (est)   _____

PART G   Adding -*S* or -*ES*

Nouns usually take an -*s* or an -*es* ending to form the plural. Verbs take an -*s* or -*es* in the third person singular (*he, she,* or *it*).

Add -*es* instead of -*s* if a word ends in *ch, sh, ss, x,* or *z* (the -*es* adds an extra syllable to the word):

box + es = boxes   **crutch + es = crutches**   **miss + es = misses**

Add -*es* instead of -*s* for most words that end in *o:*

do + es = does   **hero + es = heroes**

echo + es = echoes   **tomato + es = tomatoes**

go + es = goes   **potato + es = potatoes**

Here are some exceptions to memorize:

pianos   sopranos

radios   solos

When you change the final *y* to *i* in a word,* add -*es* instead of -*s:*

fry + es = fries   **marry + es = marries**   **candy + es = candies**

PRACTICE 9   Add -*s* or -*es* to the following nouns and verbs, changing the final *y* to *i* when necessary.

Example | sketch ___sketches_____

echo ___echoes_____

1. watch _____   6. piano _____

2. tomato _____   7. donkey _____

3. reply _____   8. dictionary _____

4. company _____   9. boss _____

5. bicycle _____   10. hero _____

PART H   Choosing *IE* or *EI*

Write *i* before *e,* except after *c,* or in an *ay* sound like *neighbor* or *weigh.*

achieve, niece   **deceive**   **vein**

- *Achieve* and *niece* are spelled *ie.*

- *Deceive* is spelled *ei* because of the preceding *c.*

- *Vein* is spelled *ei* because of its *ay* sound.

*See Part F of this chapter for more on changing or keeping the final *y.*

However, words with a *shen* sound are spelled with an *ie* after the *c: ancient, conscience, efficient, sufficient.*

Here are some exceptions to memorize:

either   seize

neither   society

foreign   their

height   weird

PRACTICE 10   Pronounce each word out loud. Then fill in either *ie* or *ei.*

1. bel __ __ ve   9. rec __ __ ve

2. __ __ ght   10. fr __ __ nd

3. effic __ __ nt   11. consc __ __ nce

4. n __ __ ther   12. h __ __ ght

5. cash __ __ r   13. ach __ __ ve

6. th __ __ r   14. v __ __ n

7. ch __ __ f   15. for __ __ gn

8. soc __ __ ty   16. perc __ __ ve

PRACTICE 11   Test your knowledge of the spelling rules in this chapter by adding suffixes
Review   to the following words. If you have trouble, the part in which the rule appears is
shown in parentheses.

	Part			Part
1. nerve + ous _____	(E)	11. carry + ing _____		(F)
2. feed + ing _____	(C)	12. tomato + s/es _____		(G)
3. beach + s/es _____	(G)	13. admit + ing _____		(D)
4. drop + ed _____	(C)	14. test + er _____		(C)
5. hope + ing _____	(E)	15. tasty + est _____		(F)
6. study + s/es _____	(G)	16. sip + ing _____		(C)
7. busy + ness _____	(F)	17. believe + able _____		(E)
8. manage + ment _____	(E)	18. commit + ment _____		(D)
9. radio + s/es _____	(G)	19. deny + al _____		(F)
10. occur + ed _____	(D)	20. day + ly _____		(F)

PRACTICE 12   Circle the correctly spelled word in each pair.
Review

1. writting, writing
2. receive, recieve
3. begining, beginning
4. greif, grief
5. grammer, grammar

6. piece, peice
7. resourceful, resourcful
8. argument, arguement
9. marries, marrys
10. thier, their

PART I   Spelling Lists

Commonly Misspelled Words

Here is a list of words that are often misspelled. As you can see, they are words that you might use daily in speaking and writing. The trouble spot, the part of each word that is usually spelled incorrectly, has been put in bold type.

To help yourself learn these words, you might copy each one twice, making sure to underline the trouble spot, or copy the words on flash cards and have someone test you.

1. across	18. doesn't	35. jewelry
2. address	19. eighth	36. judgment
3. answer	20. embarrass	37. knowledge
4. argument	21. environment	38. maintain
5. athlete	22. exaggerate	39. mathematics
6. beginning	23. familiar	40. meant
7. behavior	24. finally	41. necessary
8. calendar	25. government	42. nervous
9. career	26. grammar	43. occasion
10. conscience	27. height	44. opinion
11. crowded	28. illegal	45. optimist
12. definite	29. immediately	46. particular
13. describe	30. important	47. perform
14. desperate	31. integration	48. perhaps
15. different	32. intelligent	49. personnel
16. disappoint	33. interest	50. possess
17. disapprove	34. interfere	51. possible

52. **prefer**	60. ridic**ulous**	68. **taught**
53. pre**ju**dice	61. sep**arate**	69. **temperature**
54. privil**ege**	62. sim**ilar**	70. thor**ough**
55. pro**bably**	63. **since**	71. thought
56. **psychology**	64. speech	72. tired
57. pursue	65. stren**gth**	73. until
58. reference	66. success	74. wei**ght**
59. **rhythm**	67. surprise	75. written

Personal Spelling List

In your notebook, keep a list of words that *you* misspell. Add words to your list from corrected papers and from the exercises in this chapter. First copy each word as you misspelled it, underlining the trouble spot; then write the word correctly. Study your list often. Use this form:

As I Wrote It   **Correct Spelling**

1. probly _____   probably _____

2. _____   _____

3. _____   _____

4. _____   _____

5. _____   _____

PRACTICE 13
Review

Proofread the following essay for spelling errors. (Be careful: There are misspelled words from both the exercises in this chapter and the spelling list.) Correct any errors by writing above the lines.

The Fax Revolution

(1) The word *fax* is shortened from the word *facsimile*, which in Latin means "to make the same." (2) And "makking the same" is exactly what a fax (facsimile) system does. (3) It sends exact copys of writen or printed material by means of telephone lines.

(4) While not exactly an anceint invention, today's fax machine isn't really a new peice of equipment. (5) As a matter of fact, the fax is our oldest automated office technology, comming before the telephone or the telegraph. (6) It had its beginings in the 1800s and was patented in 1843 by the Scottish inventor Alexander Bain.

(7) A fax machine can be put on the same line as a telephone, but a seperate line is usually necesary. (8) The user puts a document in the machine and dials the telephone number of the machine that is to recieve the material. (9) The images on the document are immedietely converted into codes, which travel through the telephone lines. (10) The machine receiving the copy reconverts the images and prints them on paper. (11) It looks like magic! (12) While most people don't have much knowlege about how the fax works, they probly don't need to.

(13) The fax machine has become a very importent tool for both companys and individuals. (14) In fact, some people feel that the sucess of thier businesses depends on the fax machine. (15) It's certainly the fastest method for sending printed material, and nothing ever gets lost in the mail.

35

Look-Alikes/ Sound-Alikes

A/an/and

1. *A* is used before a word beginning with a consonant or a consonant sound.

    a man   *a* house

    a union (*u* in *union* is pronounced like the consonant *y*)

2. *An* is used before a word beginning with a vowel (*a, e, i, o, u*) or silent *h*.

    an igloo   *an* apple

    an hour (*h* in *hour* is silent)

3. *And* joins words or ideas together.

    Edward *and* Ralph are taking the same biology class.

    He is very honest, *and* most people respect him.

PRACTICE 1   Fill in *a, an,* or *and.*

1. The administration building is _____ old brick house on top of _____ hill.

2. _____ artist _____ two students share that studio.

3. The computer in my office has _____ amber screen _____ _____ hard-disk drive.

4. Joyce _____ Luis bought _____ lovely old rocker at the garage sale.

5. For lunch, Ben ate _____ ham sandwich, _____ apple, _____ two bananas.

Accept/except

1. *Accept* means to receive.

    That college *accepts* only women.   **I *accepted* his offer of help.**

2. *Except* means other than or excluding.

    Everyone *except* Ron thinks it's a good idea.

PRACTICE 2   Fill in *accept* or *except*.

1. Jan has read all of Shakespeare's comedies _____ one.
2. Please _____ my apologies.
3. Unable to _____ defeat, the boxer protested the decision.
4. Sam loves all his courses _____ chemistry.
5. _____ for Elizabeth, all of my friends went home after the intermission.

Affect/effect

1. *Affect* (verb) means to have an influence on or to change.

   Her father's career as a lawyer *affected* her decision to go to law school.

2. *Effect* (noun) means the result of a cause or an influence.

   Careful proofreading had a positive *effect* on the grades Carl received for his compositions.

3. *Effect* is also a verb that means to cause.

   The senate is attempting to *effect* changes in foreign policy.

PRACTICE 3   Fill in *affect* or *effect*.

1. You are mistaken if you think alcohol will not _____ your judgment.
2. Attractive, neat clothing will have a positive _____ on an employment interviewer.
3. Your cigarette smoke _____ my ability to think straight.
4. Hot, humid summers always have the _____ of making me lazy.
5. We will not be able to _____ these changes without the cooperation of the employees and the union.

Buy/by

1. *Buy* means to purchase.

   She *buys* new furniture every five years.

2. *By* means near, by means of, or before.

   He walked right *by* and didn't say hello.

   ***By* sunset, we had finished the harvest.**

PRACTICE 4   Fill in *buy* or *by*.

1. You can't _____ happiness, but many people try.
2. Lee _____ sand _____ the ton for his masonry business.

3. Please drop _____ the video store and _____ some blank tapes; I want to tape the football game.

4. _____ _____ out his partners, Joe became sole owner of the firm.

5. _____ the time he is thirty, Emil will have earned his M.A.

Been/being

1. *Been* is the past participle form of *to be*. *Been* is usually used after the helping verb *have, has,* or *had*.

   I *have been* to that restaurant before.

   She *has been* a poet for ten years.

2. *Being* is the *-ing* form of *to be*. *Being* is usually used after the helping verbs *is, are, am, was,* or *were*.

   They *are being* helped by the salesperson.

   Rhonda *is being* foolish and stubborn.

PRACTICE 5   Fill in *been* or *being*.

1. Have you _____ to Rib Heaven yet?

2. Pete thinks his phone calls are _____ taped.

3. Are you _____ secretive, or have I _____ imagining it?

4. Yoko has never _____ to Omaha!

5. _____ a dynamic teacher is Chris's goal.

It's/its

1. *It's* is a contraction of *it is* or *it has*. If you cannot substitute *it is* or *it has* in the sentence, you cannot use *it's*.

   It's a ten-minute walk to my house.   *It's* been a nice party.

2. *Its* is a possessive and shows ownership.

   The kitten rolled playfully on *its* side.

   Industry must do *its* share to curb inflation.

PRACTICE 6   Fill in *it's* or *its*.

1. Put the contact lens in _____ case, please.

2. _____ about time H.T. straightened up the rubble in his room.

3. Dan's truck has a dent in _____ fender.

4. The company offered some of _____ employees an early retirement option.

5. You know _____ cold when the pond has ice on _____ surface.

Know/knew/no/new

1. *Know* means to have knowledge or understanding.

2. *Knew* is the past tense of the verb *know*.

   Carl **knows** he has to finish by 6 P.M.

   The police officer **knew** the quickest route to the pier.

3. *No* is a negative.

   He is **no** longer dean of academic affairs.

4. *New* means recent, fresh, unused.

   I like your **new** hat.

PRACTICE 7   Fill in *know, knew, no,* or *new.*

1. I _____ he's _____ in town, but this is ridiculous.

2. If I _____ then what I _____ now, I wouldn't have made so many mistakes when I was young.

3. Abe _____ that he has _____ chance of winning the marathon.

4. Fran _____ when she bought this _____ chair that it was too big for the room.

5. _____, I don't _____ the way to Grandma's house, you hairy weirdo.

Lose/loose

1. *Lose* means to misplace or not to win.

   Be careful not to **lose** your way on those back roads.

   George hates to **lose** at cards.

2. *Loose* means too large, not tightly fitting.

   That shirt is not my size; it's **loose.**

PRACTICE 8   Fill in *lose* or *loose.*

1. When Ari studies in bed, he _____ the _____ change from his pockets.

2. Several layers of _____ clothing can warm you in winter.

3. Whenever my dog Rover gets _____ in the streets, all the neighborhood cats stay in hiding.

4. Don't _____ any sleep over tomorrow's exam.

5. If you _____ that _____ screw, the handle will fall off.

Past/passed

1. *Past* is that which has already occurred; it is over with.

    His *past* work has been satisfactory.

    Never let the *past* interfere with your hopes for the future.

2. *Passed* is the past tense of the verb *to pass.*

    She *passed* by and nodded hello.   **The wild geese *passed* overhead.**

PRACTICE 9   Fill in *past* or *passed.*

1. As Jake _____ the barn, he noticed a man talking to the reindeer.

2. To children, even the recent _____ seems like ancient history.

3. Mia _____ up the opportunity to see a friend from her _____.

4. The quarterback _____ the ball fifty yards for a touchdown.

5. This Bible was _____ down to me by my mother; it contains records of our family's _____.

Quiet/quit/quite

1. *Quiet* means silent, still.

    The woods are *quiet* tonight.

2. *Quit* means to give up or to stop doing something.

    Last year I *quit* drinking.

3. *Quite* means very or exactly.

    He was *quite* tired after playing handball for two hours.

    That's not *quite* right.

PRACTICE 10   Fill in *quiet, quit,* or *quite.*

1. The cottage is a _____ and beautiful place to study.

2. Nora is _____ dedicated to her veterinary career.

3. Don't _____ your job, even though you aren't _____ happy with the working conditions.

4. Each day when he _____ work, Dan visits a _____ spot in the park.

5. She made _____ an impression in red fake fur and a blond wig.

Rise/raise

1. *Rise* means to get up by one's own power.
   The past tense of *rise* is *rose*.
   The past participle of *rise* is *risen*.

   The sun *rises* at 6 A.M.

   Daniel *rose* early yesterday.

   He has *risen* from the table.

2. *Raise* means to lift an object or to grow or increase.
   The past tense of *raise* is *raised*.
   The past participle of *raise* is *raised*.

   ***Raise* your right hand.**

   She *raised* the banner over her head.

   We have *raised* one thousand dollars.

PRACTICE 11 Fill in the correct form of *rise* or *raise*.

1. The loaves of bread have _____ perfectly.

2. The new mayor _____ his arms in a victory salute.

3. Once the sun has _____, Pete _____ the shades and opens the window.

4. We all _____ as the bride walked down the aisle.

5. The money we have _____ will help build a shelter.

Sit/set

1. *Sit* means to seat oneself.
   The past tense of *sit* is *sat*.
   The past participle of *sit* is *sat*.

   ***Sit* up straight!**

   He *sat* down on the porch and fell asleep.

   She has *sat* reading that book all day.

2. *Set* means to place or put something down.
   The past tense of *set* is *set*.
   The past participle of *set* is *set*.

   Don't *set* your books on the dining room table.

   She *set* the package down and walked off without it.

   She had *set* the timer on the stove.

PRACTICE 12   Fill in *sit* or *set*.

1. Please _____ your briefcase here. Would you like to _____ down?

2. Have they _____ in on a rehearsal before?

3. Tom _____ the chair by the window and _____ down.

4. Maria _____ her alarm clock for 6:30 A.M.

5. Sorry, I wouldn't have _____ here if I had known you were returning.

Suppose/supposed

1. *Suppose* means to assume or guess.
    The past tense of *suppose* is *supposed.*
    The past participle of *suppose* is *supposed.*

    Brad *supposes* that the teacher will give him an *A.*

    We all *supposed* she would win first prize.

    I had *supposed* Dan would bring his trumpet.

2. *Supposed* means ought to or should; it is followed by *to.*

    He is *supposed* to meet us after class.

    You were *supposed* to wash and wax the car.

Remember: When you mean *ought to* or *should*, always use the *-ed* ending—*supposed.*

PRACTICE 13   Fill in *suppose* or *supposed.*

1. Why do you _____ wolves howl at the moon?

2. I _____ you enjoy reggae.

3. Detective Baker is _____ to address the Citizens' Patrol tonight.

4. Wasn't Erik _____ to meet us at five?

5. Ms. Ita says we're not _____ to guess in computer science class; we're _____ to know.

Their/there/they're

1. *Their* is a possessive and shows ownership.

    They couldn't find *their* wigs.   **Their children are charming.**

2. *There* indicates a direction.

    I wouldn't go *there* again.   **Put the lumber down *there*.**

There is also a way of introducing a thought.

> **There is a fly in my soup.**
>
> **There are two ways to approach this problem.**

3. *They're* is a contraction: *they + are = they're*. If you cannot substitute *they are* in the sentence, you cannot use *they're*.

> **They're the best tires money can buy.**   **If *they're* coming, count me in.**

PRACTICE 14   Fill in *their, there,* or *they're*.

1. If _____ not _____ on time, we will have to leave without them.

2. _____ two of the most amusing people I know.

3. _____ are two choices you can make, and _____ both risky.

4. Two mail carriers left _____ mail bags _____ on the post office steps.

5. Is _____ a doctor in the house?

6. The motorcycles roared _____ way into town.

7. _____ phone usually rings seven or eight times before they answer.

8. Don't worry about _____ performance in the race because _____ both tough.

Then/than

1. *Then* means afterward or at that time.

> **First we went to the theater, and *then* we went out for a pizza and champagne.**
>
> **I was a heavyweight boxer *then*.**

2. *Than* is used in a comparison.

> **She is a better student *than* I.**

PRACTICE 15   Fill in *then* or *than*.

1. First Cassandra kicked off her shoes; _____ she began to dance.

2. Jupiter's diameter is eleven times larger _____ Earth's.

3. If you're more familiar with this trail _____ I, _____ you should lead the way.

4. Fran lived in Chicago _____; now she lives in Miami.

5. If he is better prepared _____ you, what will you do _____?

Through/though

1. *Through* means in one side and out the other, finished, or by means of.

   The rain came *through* the open window.

   We should be *through* soon.

2. *Though* means although. Used with *as, though* means as if.

   ***Though* he rarely speaks, he writes terrific letters.**

   It was as *though* I had never ridden a bicycle before.

PRACTICE 16   Fill in *through* or *though.*

1. _____ study and perseverance, Charelle earned her degree in three years.

2. Dee usually walks to work, _____ she sometimes rides the bus.

3. Julio strode _____ the bank as _____ he owned it.

4. Clayton is a Texan _____ and _____.

5. I'm not really hungry; I will have an apple, _____.

To/too/two

1. *To* means toward.

   We are going *to* the stadium.

   To can also be combined with a verb to form an infinitive.

   Where do you want *to go* for lunch?

2. *Too* means also or very.

   Roberto is going to the theater *too*.

   They were *too* bored to stay awake.

3. *Two* is the number 2.

   There are *two* new accounting courses this term.

PRACTICE 17   Fill in *to, too,* or *two.*

1. Please take my daughter _____ the movies _____.

2. We'd like a table for _____ with a view of the sea.

3. Dan, _____, took _____ hours _____ complete the exam.

4. Luis went _____ Iowa State for _____ semesters.

5. This curry is _____ hot _____ eat and _____ good _____ resist.

Use/used

1. *Use* means to make use of.
   The past tense of *use* is *used.*
   The past participle of *use* is *used.*

   Why do you *use* green ink?

   He *used* the wrong paint in the bathroom.

   I have *used* that brand of toothpaste myself.

2. *Used* means in the habit of or accustomed to; it is followed by *to.*

   I am not *used* to getting up at 4 A.M.   **They got *used* to the good life.**

   Remember: When you mean *in the habit of* or *accustomed to,* always use the *-ed* ending—*used.*

PRACTICE 18   Fill in *use* or *used.*

1. Marie _____ to drive a jalopy that she bought at a _____ car lot.

2. We will _____ about three gallons of paint on this shed.

3. Can you _____ a _____ computer?

4. Pam _____ to _____ a pick to strum her guitar.

5. Shall I _____ contrast or illustration to develop this essay?

Weather/whether

1. *Weather* refers to atmospheric conditions.

   In June, the *weather* in Spain is lovely.

2. *Whether* implies a question.

   Whether or not you pass depends on you.

PRACTICE 19   Fill in *weather* or *whether.*

1. In fine _____, we take long walks in the woods.

2. _____ or not you like Chinese food, you'll love this dish.

3. The _____ person never said _____ or not it would snow.

4. I can't recall _____ you prefer tea or coffee.

5. In 1870 a national _____ service was established.

Where/were/we're

1. *Where* implies place or location.

   Where have you been all day?   **Home is *where* you hang your hat.**

2. *Were* is the past tense of *are*.

   We *were* on our way when the hurricane hit.

3. *We're* is a contraction: *we + are = we're*. If you cannot substitute *we are* in the sentence, you cannot use *we're*.

   We're going to leave now.   **Since we're in the city, let's go to the zoo.**

PRACTICE 20   Fill in *where, were,* or *we're.*

1. _____ going to Hawaii, _____ the sun always shines.

2. _____ you standing _____ we agreed to meet?

3. _____ working out three times a week.

4. There _____ two high-rise apartment houses _____ the ballpark used to be.

5. _____ determined to attend college, though we don't yet know _____.

Whose/who's

1. *Whose* implies ownership and possession.

   Whose term paper is that?

2. *Who's* is a contraction of *who is* or *who has*. If you cannot substitute *who is* or *who has*, you cannot use *who's*.

   Who's knocking at the window?

   Who's seen my new felt hat with the red feathers?

PRACTICE 21   Fill in *whose* or *who's.*

1. _____ Probe convertible is this?

2. Tanya, _____ in my history class, will join us for dinner.

3. We need someone in that position _____ dependable, someone _____ abilities have already been proven.

4. _____ biology textbook is this?

5. _____ going to clean the oven?

Your/you're

1. *Your* is a possessive and shows ownership.

   Your knowledge astonishes me!

2. *You're* is a contraction: *you + are = you're.* If you cannot substitute *you are* in the sentence, you cannot use *you're.*

   You're the nicest person I know.

PRACTICE 22   Fill in *your* or *you're.*

1. _____ sitting on _____ hat.

2. When _____ ready to begin _____ piano lesson, we'll leave.

3. Let _____ adviser help you plan _____ course schedule.

4. When _____ with _____ friends, _____ a different person.

5. If you think _____ lost, why not use _____ map?

Personal Look-Alikes/Sound-Alikes List

In your notebook, keep a list of look-alikes and sound-alikes that *you* have trouble with. Add words to your list from corrected papers and from the exercises in this chapter; consider such pairs as *adapt/adopt, addition/edition, device/devise, stationery/stationary,* and so forth.

   First, write the word you used incorrectly; then write its meaning or use it correctly in a sentence, whichever best helps you remember. Now do the same with the word you meant to use.

	Word	Meaning
1.	_____	_____
	_____	_____
2.	_____	_____
	_____	_____

PRACTICE 23
Review   The following essay contains a number of look-alike, sound-alike errors. Proofread for these errors, writing the correct word above the line.

Zora Neale Hurston

(1) Never will their be another person quiet like Zora Neale Hurston.

(2) Brilliant, restless, and unconventional, she was the most influential African-American female writer of the 1930s.

(3) Hurston came from Eatonville, Florida, a completely African-American community with it's own officials and culture. (4) In this all-black world, she learned the rich folklore and love of independence that effected her future writing. (5) An orphan at fourteen, young Zora worked her way north, attending Howard University in Washington, D.C. (6) In 1925, she moved to New York, becoming the first black woman to graduate from Barnard College (7) She than studied anthropology at Columbia University.

(8) During the 1930s, Hurston wrote five major works. (9) Too books explored the folklore of rural black cultures—those of Florida, Alabama, and Louisiana—as well as the voodoo of Haiti and Jamaica. (10) Hurston now saw the folklore of her youth though the trained eye of the social scientist. (11) She also turned her personal and scholarly knowledge into three fine novels. (12) Written in black dialect, her masterpiece, *Their Eyes Were Watching God*, tells the life of Janie, who's life of struggle leads to self-acceptance. (13) Hurston wrote a autobiography too, as well as many articles, essays, short stories, and plays. (14) In 1991, *Mule Bone*, one of her plays, finally reached Broadway.

(15) In her writings, Zora Neale Hurston showed the vitality of the African-American passed captured in oral folk tradition and the need of all people to attain emotional and spiritual freedom in there lives.

Unit 8

Reading Selections

Reading Strategies for Writers

We hope you will enjoy the reading selections that follow. These essays deal with many of the concerns you have as a student, as a worker, and as a member of a family. Your instructor may ask you to read and think about a selection for class discussion or for a composition either at home or in class.

The more carefully you read these selections, the better you will be able to discuss and write about them. Below are ten strategies that can help you become a more effective reader and writer:

1. Note the title. A title, of course, is your first clue as to what the selection is about. For example, the title "Strike Out Little League" lets you know that the selection will discuss negative aspects of organized sports for children.

A title may also tell you which method of development the author is using. For instance, a selection entitled "Husbands and Wives: Different as Night and Day" might be a comparison/contrast essay; one entitled "Using the Library—Electronically" might be a process piece explaining how to use a computerized library catalogue.

2. Underline main ideas. If you read a long or difficult selection, you may forget some of the important ideas soon after you have finished the essay. However, underlining or highlighting these key ideas as you read will later help you review more easily. You may wish to number main ideas to help you follow the development of the author's thesis.

3. Write your reactions in the margins. Feel free to express your agreement or disagreement with the ideas in a selection by commenting "yes," "no," "Important—compare to Alice Walker's essay," or "Is he kidding?" in the margins.

You will often be asked to write a "reaction paper," a composition explaining your thoughts about or reaction to the author's ideas. The comments that you have recorded in the margins will help you formulate a response.

4. Prepare questions. As you tackle more difficult reading selections, you may come across material that is hard to follow. Of course, reread the passage to see if a second reading helps. If it does not, put a question mark in the margin.

Ask a friend or the instructor to help answer your questions. Do not be embarrassed to ask for explanations in class. Instructors appreciate careful readers who want to be sure that they completely understand what they have read.

5. Note possible composition topics. As you read, you may think of topics for compositions related to the ideas in the selection. Jot these topics in the margins or write about them in your journal. They may become useful if your instructor asks you for an essay based on the selection.

6. Note effective writing. If you are particularly moved by a portion of the selection—a phrase, a sentence, or an entire paragraph—underline or highlight it. You may wish to quote it later in class or use it in your composition.

7. **Circle unfamiliar words.** As you read, you will occasionally come across unfamiliar words. If you can guess what the word means from its context—from how it is used in the sentence or in the passage—do not interrupt your reading to look it up. Interruptions can cause you to lose the flow of ideas in the selection. Instead, circle the word and check it in a dictionary later.

8. **Vary your pace.** Some essays can be read quickly and easily. Others may require more time if the material is difficult or if much of the subject matter is unfamiliar to you. Be careful not to become discouraged, skimming a particularly difficult section just to get through with it. Extra effort will pay off.

9. **Reread.** If possible, budget your time so you can read the selection a second or even a third time. One advantage of rereading is that you will be able to discuss or write about the essay with more understanding. Ideas that were unclear may become obvious; you may even see new ideas that you failed to note the first time around.

Another advantage is that by the second or third reading, your responses may have changed. You may agree with ideas you rejected the first time; you may disagree with ones you originally agreed with. Rereading gives you a whole new perspective!

10. **Do not overdo it.** Marking the selection as you read can help you become a better reader and writer. However, too many comments may defeat your purpose. You may not be able to decipher the mass—or mess—of underlinings, circles, and notes that you have made. Be selective.

The following essay has been marked, or annotated, by a student. Your responses might be different. Use this essay as a model to help you annotate other selections in this book—and reading material for your other courses as well.

*Could be a
process essay*

How Sunglasses Spanned the World

*staple—
standard item*

Like many of the world's inhabitants, you probably own at least one pair of sunglasses, chosen as much for the image they project as for their ability to protect your eyes from the sun. In fact, sunglasses have become a staple in almost every country; it is no longer surprising to spot sunglasses on robed Arabian sheiks, Bolivian grandmothers, or Inuit fisherman tramping Arctic snows. The process by which sunglasses have gained worldwide popularity is a fascinating one that began, surprisingly, in the justice system of medieval China. **1**

*Inuit—
Eskimo*

*Step 1—
really Stage 1*

Dark glasses with smoke-tinted quartz lenses existed for centuries in China prior to 1430, but they were not used for sun protection. Chinese judges wore the darkened lenses in court to conceal their eye expressions and keep secret their reactions to evidence until the end of a trial. In 1430, when vision-correcting glasses were introduced into China from Italy, these lenses, too, were smoke-tinted, but almost entirely for judicial use. Some people wore the darkened lenses for sun protection, but the idea never really caught on. **2**

*This is a
great idea.
judicial—
relating to
court*

*Stage 2— aviator
glasses invented*

Five hundred years passed before the popularity of sunglasses began to grow. In the 1930s, the U.S. Army Air Corps asked the optical firm of Bausch & Lomb to produce a highly effective spectacle that would protect pilots from the dangers of high-altitude glare. Company scientists perfected a special dark-green tint that absorbed yellow light from the spectrum. They also designed a slightly drooping metal frame to protect the aviator's eyes, which repeatedly glanced down at the plane's instument panel. **3**

*I wonder
why . . .*

*I own a pair
just like this!*

*spectrum—
range or
band (light
breaks
into a series
of colors)*

Stage 3

Soon this type of sunglasses was offered to the public as Ray Ban aviators, scientifically designed to ban the sun's rays. For the first time in history, large numbers of people began to purchase sunglasses. **4**

*Stage 4— sun-
glasses are chic*

The next step in the process—making sunglasses chic— was the result of a clever 1960s advertising campaign by the firm of Foster Grant. Determined to increase its share of the sunglass market, the company began to feature the faces of Hollywood celebrities wearing sunglasses above a slogan that read, "Isn't that . . . behind those Foster Grants?" Big stars of the day like Peter Sellers, Anita Ekberg, and Elke Sommer posed for the ads, and the public love affair with sunglasses took off. Behind those Foster Grants, everyone now could feel like a movie star. **5**

*Ah, yes.
What makes
anything
span the
world? Ad-
vertising.*

Stage 5—
designer shades

In the 1970s, the trend escalated further when well-known **6** fashion designers and Hollywood stars introduced their own brand-name lines, charging high prices for status sunglasses in the latest styles. A giant industry developed where only a few decades earlier none had existed, and shades became big business.

Stage 6

True. I know people who spend $200 for

Today sunglasses—like blue jeans and Coca Cola—circle **7** the globe. Protection against solar radiation is just part of their appeal. As women in ancient times had hidden seductively behind an expanded fan or a tipped parasol, modern women and men all over the world have discovered the mystery, sex appeal, and cosmopolitan cool of wearing sunglasses.

parasol— umbrella for the sun

wrap- arounds to wear danc- ing at night!

Writing ideas—
- *Research the development or origin of another popular item.*
- *Think more about the power of advertising to influence us.*
- *Observe sunglass wearers and write about them.*

Beauty:
When the Other Dancer Is the Self

Alice Walker

Being physically injured can be terrifying; coming to terms with a permanent disability can be a painful, difficult process. Alice Walker, a noted fiction writer, **poet, and author of *The Color Purple*, tells of her feelings and experiences before, during, and after an injury that changed her life.**

1   It is a bright summer day in 1947. My father, a fat, funny man with beautiful eyes and a subversive wit,[1] is trying to decide which of his eight children he will take with him to the county fair. My mother, of course, will not go. She is knocked out from getting most of us ready: I hold my neck stiff against the pressure of her knuckles as she hastily completes the braiding and then beribboning of my hair.

2   My father is the driver for the rich old white lady up the road. Her name is Miss Mey. She owns all the land for miles around, as well as the house in which we live. All I remember about her is that she once offered to pay my mother thirty-five cents for cleaning her house, raking up piles of her magnolia leaves, and washing her family's clothes, and that my mother—she of no money, eight children, and a chronic earache—refused it. But I do not think of this in 1947. I am two and a half years old. I want to go everywhere my daddy goes. I am excited at the prospect of riding in a car. Someone has told me fairs are fun. That there is room in the car for only three of us doesn't faze[2] me at all. Whirling happily in my starchy frock, showing off my biscuit-polished patent-leather shoes and lavender socks, tossing my head in a way that makes my ribbons bounce, I stand, hands on hips, before my father. "Take me, Daddy," I say with assurance; "I'm the prettiest!"

3   Later, it does not surprise me to find myself in Miss Mey's shiny black car, sharing the back seat with the other lucky ones. Does not surprise me that I thoroughly enjoy the fair. At home that night I tell the unlucky ones all I can remember about the merry-go-round, the man who eats live chickens, and the teddy bears, until they say: that's enough, baby Alice. Shut up now, and go to sleep.

4   It is Easter Sunday, 1950. I am dressed in a green, flocked, scalloped-hem dress (handmade by my adoring sister, Ruth) that has its own smooth satin petticoat and tiny hot-pink roses tucked into each scallop. My shoes, new T-strap patent leather, again highly biscuit-polished. I am six years old and have learned one of the longest Easter speeches to be heard that day, totally unlike the speech I said when I was two: "Easter lilies / pure and white / blossom in / the morning light." When I rise to give my speech I do so on a great wave of love and pride and expectation. People in the church stop rustling their new crinolines. They seem to hold their breath. I can tell

1. subversive wit: sarcastic, sharp sense of humor
2. faze: discourage

they admire my dress, but it is my spirit, bordering on sassiness (womanish-ness), they secretly applaud.

"That girl's a little *mess*," they whisper to each other, pleased.   **5**

Naturally I say my speech without stammer or pause, unlike those who   **6**
stutter, stammer, or, worst of all, forget. This is before the word "beautiful"
exists in people's vocabulary, but "Oh, isn't she the *cutest* thing!" frequently
floats my way. "And got so much sense!" they gratefully add . . . for which
thoughtful addition I thank them to this day.

It was great fun being cute. But then, one day, it ended.   **7**

I am eight years old and a tomboy. I have a cowboy hat, cowboy boots, check-   **8**
ered shirt and pants, all red. My playmates are my brothers, two and four
years older than I. Their colors are black and green, the only difference in
the way we are dressed. On Saturday nights we all go to the picture show,
even my mother; Westerns are her favorite kind of movie. Back home, "on
the ranch," we pretend we are Tom Mix, Hopalong Cassidy, Lash LaRue
(we've even named one of our dogs Lash LaRue); we chase each other for
hours rustling cattle, being outlaws, delivering damsels from distress. Then
my parents decide to buy my brothers guns. These are not "real" guns. They
shoot "BBs," copper pellets my brothers say will kill birds. Because I am a
girl, I do not get a gun. Instantly I am relegated to[3] the position of Indian.
Now there appears a great distance between us. They shoot and shoot at
everything with their new guns. I try to keep up with my bow and arrows.

One day while I am standing on top of our makeshift "garage"—pieces of   **9**
tin nailed across some poles—holding my bow and arrow and looking out
toward the fields, I feel an incredible blow in my right eye. I look down just
in time to see my brother lower his gun.

Both brothers rush to my side. My eye stings, and I cover it with my   **10**
hand. "If you tell," they say, "we will get a whipping. You don't want that to
happen, do you?" I do not. "Here is a piece of wire," says the older brother,
picking it up from the roof; "say you stepped on one end of it and the other
flew up and hit you." The pain is beginning to start. "Yes," I say. "Yes, I will
say that is what happened." If I do not say this is what happened, I know my
brothers will find ways to make me wish I had. But now I will say anything
that gets me to my mother.

Confronted by our parents we stick to the lie agreed upon. They place   **11**
me on a bench on the porch and I close my left eye while they examine the
right. There is a tree growing from underneath the porch that climbs past
the railing to the roof. It is the last thing my right eye sees. I watch as its
trunk, its branches, and then its leaves are blotted out by the rising blood.

I am in shock. First there is intense fever, which my father tries to break   **12**
using lily leaves bound around my head. Then there are chills: my mother
tries to get me to eat soup. Eventually, I do not know how, my parents learn
what has happened. A week after the "accident" they take me to see a doctor.
"Why did you wait so long to come?" he asks, looking into my eye and shak-
ing his head. "Eyes are sympathetic,[4]" he says. "If one is blind, the other will
likely become blind too."

3. relegated to: assigned
4. sympathetic: closely connected

This comment of the doctor's terrifies me. But it is really how I look that 13
bothers me most. Where the BB pellet struck there is a glob of whitish scar
tissue, a hideous cataract, on my eye. Now when I stare at people—a
favorite pastime, up to now—they will stare back. Not at the "cute" little
girl, but at her scar. For six years I do not stare at anyone, because I do not
raise my head.

Years later, in the throes[5] of a mid-life crisis, I ask my mother and sister 14
whether I changed after the "accident." "No," they say, puzzled. "What do
you mean?"

What do I mean?   15

I am eight, and, for the first time, doing poorly in school, where I have 16
been something of a whiz since I was four. We have just moved to the place
where the "accident" occurred. We do not know any of the people around us
because this is a different county. The only time I see the friends I knew is
when we go back to our old church. The new school is the former state peni-
tentiary. It is a large stone building, cold and drafty, crammed to overflowing
with boisterous,[6] ill-disciplined children. On the third floor there is a huge
circular imprint of some partition that has been torn out.

"What used to be there?" I ask a sullen girl next to me on our way past it 17
to lunch.

"The electric chair," says she.   18

At night I have nightmares about the electric chair, and about all the 19
people reputedly[7] "fried" in it. I am afraid of the school, where all the students seem to be budding criminals.

"What's the matter with your eye?" they ask, critically.   20

When I don't answer (I cannot decide whether it was an "accident" or 21
not), they shove me, insist on a fight.

My brother, the one who created the story about the wire, comes to my 22
rescue. But then brags so much about "protecting" me, I become sick.

After months of torture at the school, my parents decide to send me back 23
to our old community, to my old school. I live with my grandparents and the
teacher they board. But there is no room for Phoebe, my cat. By the time my
grandparents decide there *is* room, and I ask for my cat, she cannot be
found. Miss Yarborough, the boarding teacher, takes me under her wing, and
begins to teach me to play the piano. But soon she marries an African—a
"prince," she says—and is whisked away to his continent.

At my old school there is at least one teacher who loves me. She is the 24
teacher who "knew me before I was born" and bought my first baby clothes.
It is she who makes life bearable. It is her presence that finally helps me
turn on the one child at the school who continually calls me "one-eyed bitch."
One day I simply grab him by his coat and beat him until I am satisfied. It is
my teacher who tells me my mother is ill.

My mother is lying in bed in the middle of the day, something I have 25
never seen. She is in too much pain to speak. She has an abscess in her ear. I

5. throes: a condition of struggle
6. boisterous: rowdy and noisy
7. reputedly: supposedly

stand looking down on her, knowing that if she dies, I cannot live. She is being treated with warm oils and hot bricks held against her cheek. Finally a doctor comes. But I must go back to my grandparents' house. The weeks pass but I am hardly aware of it. All I know is that my mother might die, my father is not so jolly, my brothers still have their guns, and I am the one sent away from home.

"You did not change," they say.   26

Did I imagine the anguish of never looking up?   27

I am twelve. When relatives come to visit I hide in my room. My cousin 28
Brenda, just my age, whose father works in the post office and whose mother is a nurse, comes to find me. "Hello," she says. And then she asks, looking at my recent school picture, which I did not want taken, and on which the "glob," as I think of it, is clearly visible, "You still can't see out of that eye?"

"No," I say, and flop back on the bed over my book.   29

That night, as I do almost every night, I abuse my eye. I rant and rave at 30
it, in front of the mirror. I plead with it to clear up before morning. I tell it I hate and despise it. I do not pray for sight. I pray for beauty.

"You did not change," they say.   31

I am fourteen and baby-sitting for my brother Bill, who lives in Boston. 32
He is my favorite brother and there is a strong bond between us. Understanding my feelings of shame and ugliness he and his wife take me to a local hospital, where the "glob" is removed by a doctor named O. Henry. There is still a small bluish crater where the scar tissue was, but the ugly white stuff is gone. Almost immediately I become a different person from the girl who does not raise her head. Or so I think. Now that I've raised my head I win the boyfriend of my dreams. Now that I've raised my head I have plenty of friends. Now that I've raised my head classwork comes from my lips as faultlessly as Easter speeches did, and I leave high school as valedictorian, most popular student, and *queen*, hardly believing my luck. Ironically, the girl who was voted most beautiful in our class (and was) was later shot twice through the chest by a male companion, using a "real" gun, while she was pregnant. But that's another story in itself. Or is it?

"You did not change," they say.   33

It is now thirty years since the "accident." A beautiful journalist comes 34
to visit and to interview me. She is going to write a cover story for her magazine that focuses on my latest book. "Decide how you want to look on the cover," she says. "Glamorous, or whatever."

Never mind "glamorous," it is the "whatever" that I hear. Suddenly all I 35
can think of is whether I will get enough sleep the night before the photography session: if I don't, my eye will be tired and wander, as blind eyes will.

At night in bed with my lover I think up reasons why I should not appear 36
on the cover of a magazine. "My meanest critics will say I've sold out," I say. "My family will now realize I write scandalous books."

"But what's the real reason you don't want to do this?" he asks.   37

"Because in all probability," I say in a rush, "my eye won't be straight." 38

"It will be straight enough," he says. Then, "Besides, I thought you'd **39** made your peace with that."

And I suddenly remember that I have.   **40**

I remember: **41**

I am talking to my brother Jimmy, asking if he remembers anything **42** unusual about the day I was shot. He does not know I consider that day the last time my father, with his sweet home remedy of cool lily leaves, chose me, and that I suffered and raged inside because of this. "Well," he says, "all I remember is standing by the side of the highway with Daddy, trying to flag down a car. A white man stopped, but when Daddy said he needed somebody to take his little girl to the doctor, he drove off."

I remember: **43**

I am in the desert for the first time. I fall totally in love with it. I am so **44** overwhelmed by its beauty, I confront for the first time, consciously, the meaning of the doctor's words years ago: "Eyes are sympathetic. If one is blind, the other will likely become blind too." I realize I have dashed about the world madly, looking at this, looking at that, storing up images against the fading of the light. *But I might have missed seeing the desert!* The shock of that possibility—and gratitude for over twenty-five years of sight—sends me literally to my knees. Poem after poem comes—which is perhaps how poets pray.

On Sight

I am so thankful I have seen
The Desert
And the creatures in the desert
And the desert Itself.

The desert has its own moon
Which I have seen
With my own eye.
There is no flag on it.

Trees of the desert have arms
All of which are always up
That is because the moon is up
The sun is up
Also the sky
The stars
Clouds
None with flags.
If there *were* flags, I doubt
the trees would point.
Would you?

But mostly, I remember this: **45**

I am twenty-seven, and my baby daughter is almost three. Since her **46** birth I have worried about her discovery that her mother's eyes are different from other people's. Will she be embarrassed? I think. What will she say? Every day she watches a television program called "Big Blue Marble." It begins with a picture of the earth as it appears from the moon. It is bluish, a little battered-looking, but full of light, with whitish clouds swirling around it. Every time I see it I weep with love, as if it is a picture of Grandma's house. One day when I am putting Rebecca down for her nap, she suddenly focuses on my eye. Something inside me cringes, gets ready to try to protect myself. All children are cruel about physical differences, I know from experience, and that they don't always mean to be is another matter. I assume Rebecca will be the same.

But no-o-o-o. She studies my face intently as we stand, her inside and me **47** outside her crib. She even holds my face maternally between her dimpled little hands. Then, looking every bit as serious and lawyerlike as her father, she says, as if it may just possibly have slipped my attention: "Mommy, there's a *world* in your eye." (As in, "Don't be alarmed, or do anything crazy.") And then, gently, but with great interest: "Mommy, where did you *get* that world in your eye?"

For the most part, the pain left then. (So what, if my brothers grew up to **48** buy even more powerful pellet guns for their sons and to carry real guns themselves. So what, if a young "Morehouse man" once nearly fell off the steps of Trevor Arnett Library because he thought my eyes were blue.) Crying and laughing I ran to the bathroom, while Rebecca mumbled and sang herself to sleep. Yes indeed, I realized, looking into the mirror. There *was* a world in my eye. And I saw that it was possible to love it: that in fact, for all it had taught me of shame and anger and inner vision, I *did* love it. Even to see it drifting out of orbit in boredom, or rolling up out of fatigue, not to mention floating back at attention in excitement (bearing witness, a friend has called it), deeply suitable to my personality, and even characteristic of me.

That night I dream I am dancing to Stevie Wonder's song "Always" (The **49** name of the song is really "As," but I hear it as "Always"). As I dance, whirling and joyous, happier than I've ever been in my life, another bright-faced dancer joins me. We dance and kiss each other and hold each other through the night. The other dancer has obviously come through all right, as I have done. She is beautiful, whole and free. And she is also me. ▪

Discussion and Writing Questions

1. When did the author stop being "cute"? Is she happy about this change?

2. Why do you think her family insists that she did not change after the shooting?

3. Until her operation at age fourteen, Walker speaks of hating her injured eye. By the end of the essay, she dances with another "dancer," who is "beautiful, whole and free. And she is also me." What makes the author change her mind about her "deformity"?

4. The author uses particular words and phrases to indicate time or chronological order in her narrative. Find the words that indicate time order. At one point in her narrative, she breaks this time order to skip back into the past. In which paragraph does this flashback occur?

Writing Assignments

1. Write about an unpleasant event or experience that resulted in personal growth for you. Your writing need not focus on something as painful as Alice Walker's injury. What is important is how you came to terms with the experience and what you ultimately learned from it.

2. Tell a story about being thrust into a completely unfamiliar situation. You might describe your reaction to attending a new school, starting a new job, or moving to a new city. Present concrete details of your experience. Organize the story around your most vivid memories, like meeting new classmates for the first time, or your first few days on the new job.

3. Walker says that for a time she hated her blind eye. Do you think that this is a common reaction in people with a physical defect or illness?

In Search of Bruce Lee's Grave

Shanlon Wu

Most young people need heroes to respect or imitate. In this essay, Shanlon Wu discusses the lack of Asian heroes as he grew up in suburban New York in the 1950s. Then he saw his first Bruce Lee movie.

It's Saturday morning in Seattle, and I am driving to visit Bruce Lee's grave. I have been in the city for only a couple of weeks and so drive two blocks past the cemetery before realizing that I've passed it. I double back and turn through the large wrought-iron gate, past a sign that reads: "Open to 9 P.M. or dusk, whichever comes first."   1

It's a sprawling cemetery, with winding roads leading in all directions. I feel silly trying to find his grave with no guidance. I think that my search for his grave is similar to my search for Asian heroes in America.   2

I was born in 1959, an Asian-American in Westchester County, N.Y. During my childhood there were no Asian sports stars. On television, I can recall only that most pathetic of Asian characters, Hop Sing, the Cartwright family houseboy on "Bonanza." But in my adolescence there was Bruce.   3

I was 14 years old when I first saw "Enter the Dragon," the granddaddy of martial-arts movies. Bruce had died suddenly at the age of 32 of cerebral edema, an excess of fluid in the brain, just weeks before the release of the film. Between the ages of 14 and 17, I saw "Enter the Dragon" 22 times before I stopped counting. During those years I collected Bruce Lee posters, putting them up at all angles in my bedroom. I took up Chinese martial arts and spent hours comparing my physique with his.   4

I learned all I could about Bruce: that he had married a Caucasian, Linda; that he had sparred with Kareem Abdul-Jabbar; that he was a buddy of Steve McQueen and James Coburn, both of whom were his pallbearers.   5

My parents, who immigrated to America and had become professors at Hunter College, tolerated my behavior, but seemed puzzled at my admira-   6 tion of an "entertainer." My father jokingly tried to compare my obsession with Bruce to his boyhood worship of Chinese folk-tale heroes.

"I read them just like you read American comic books," he said. **7**

But my father's heroes could not be mine; they came from an ancient **8** literary tradition, not comic books. He and my mother had grown up in a land where they belonged to the majority. I could not adopt their childhood and they were wise enough not to impose it upon me.

Although I never again experienced the kind of blind hero worship I felt **9** for Bruce, my need to find heroes remained strong.

In college, I discovered the men of the 442d Regimental Combat Team, a **10** United States Army all-Japanese unit in World War II. Allowed to fight only against Europeans, they suffered heavy casualties while their families were put in internment camps. Their motto was "Go for Broke."

I saw them as Asians in a Homeric epic, the protagonists[1] of a Shake- **11** spearean tragedy; I knew no Eastern myths to infuse them with.[2] They embodied my own need to prove myself in the Caucasian world. I imagined how their American-born flesh and muscle must have resembled mine: epicanthic folds[3] set in strong faces nourished on milk and beef. I thought how much they had proved where there was so little to prove.

After college, I competed as an amateur boxer in an attempt to find my **12** self-image in the ring. It didn't work. My fighting was only an attempt to copy Bruce's movies. What I needed was instruction on how to live. I quit boxing after a year and went to law school.

I was an anomaly[4] there: a would-be Asian litigator.[5] I had always liked **13** to argue and found I liked doing it in front of people even more. When I won the first-year moot court competition in law school, I asked an Asian classmate if he thought I was the first Asian to win. He laughed and told me I was probably the only Asian to even compete.

The law-firm interviewers always seemed surprised that I wanted to **14** litigate.

"Aren't you interested in Pacific Rim trade?" they asked. **15**

"My Chinese isn't good enough," I quipped. **16**

My pat response seemed to please them. It certainly pleased me. I **17** thought I'd found a place of my own—a place where the law would insulate[6] me from the pressure of defining my Asian maleness. I sensed the possibility of merely being myself.

But the pressure reasserted itself. One morning, the year after graduat- **18** ing from law school, I read the obituary of Gen. Minoru Genda—the man who planned the Pearl Harbor attack. I'd never heard of him and had assumed that whoever did that planning was long since dead. But the general had been alive all those years—rising at 4 every morning to do his exercises and retiring every night by 8. An advocate of animal rights, the obituary said.

1. protagonists: main characters
2. infuse . . . with: put into
3. epicanthic folds: folds of the upper eyelid skin found in many Asian people
4. anomaly: oddity, unusual person
5. boisterous: rowdy and noisy
6. litigator: one who argues legal matters

I found myself drawn to the general's life despite his association with the **19** Axis powers. He seemed a forthright, graceful man who died unhumbled. The same paper carried a front-page story about Congress's failure to pay the Japanese-American internees their promised reparation[7] money. The general, at least, had not died waiting for reparations.

I was surprised and frightened by my admiration for General Genda, by **20** my still-strong hunger for images of powerful Asian men. That hunger was my vulnerability manifested,[8] a reminder of my lack of place.

The hunger is eased this gray morning in Seattle. After asking directions from a policeman—Japanese—I easily locate Bruce's grave. The head- **21** stone is red granite with a small picture etched into it. The picture is very Hollywood—Bruce wears dark sunglasses—and I think the calligraphy[9] looks a bit sloppy. Two tourists stop but leave quickly after glancing at me.

I realize I am crying. Bruce's grave seems very small in comparison to **22** his place in my boyhood. So small in comparison to my need for heroes. See- ing his grave, I understand how large the hole in my life has been, and how desperately I'd sought to fill it.

I had sought an Asian hero to emulate.[10] But none of my choices quite **23** fit me. Their lives were defined through heroic tasks—they had villains to defeat and wars to fight—while my life seemed merely a struggle to define myself.

But now I see how that very struggle has defined me. I must be my own **24** hero even as I learn to treasure those who have gone before.

I have had my powerful Asian male images: Bruce, the men of the 442d **25** and General Genda; I may yet discover others. Their lives beckon like fire- flies on a moonless night, and I know that they—like me—may have been flawed by foolhardiness and even cruelty. Still, their lives were real. They were not houseboys on "Bonanza." ■

Discussion and Writing Questions

1. Why did Wu see *Enter the Dragon* so many times?

2. Why did the author need so badly to find heroes? How did his situation differ from that of his parents?

3. Does Wu conclude his search for heroes?

4. This narrative begins in the present, then switches to the past, and then ends in the present. Why does the author switch tenses this way?

7. protagonists: main characters
8. infuse . . . with: put into
9. epicanthic folds: folds of the upper eyelid skin found in many Asian people
10. anomaly: oddity, unusual person

Writing Assignments

1. The search for a hero is the search for someone who sets an example or encourages you or teaches you. Write a narrative about your search for a hero, either in childhood or in the present day. In your narrative, include who this hero was, what he or she meant to you, and what your search taught you.

2. Discuss how it feels to be a stranger or an outsider. Perhaps you have felt like an outsider because your interests or ways of dressing are different from those of your classmates or neighbors; perhaps you have felt left out by your coworkers; or perhaps you have been treated as "different" because of your ethnic group or even your gender.

3. Write about a longing you felt as a child that was important in your development as a person—perhaps to have friends, to play music, or to make your parents happy. Was this longing ever filled? Do you think this longing has helped shape the person who you are today?

A Brother's Murder

Brent Staples

Brent Staples grew up in a rough, industrial city. He left to become a successful journalist, but his younger brother remained. Staples' story of his brother is a reminder of the grim circumstances in which so many young black men of the inner city find themselves today.

It has been more than two years since my telephone rang with the news that my younger brother Blake—just twenty-two years old—had been murdered. The young man who killed him was only twenty-four. Wearing a ski mask, he emerged from a car, fired six times at close range with a massive .44 Magnum, then fled. The two had once been inseparable friends. A senseless rivalry—beginning, I think, with an argument over a girlfriend—escalated[1] from posturing,[2] to threats, to violence, to murder. The way the two were living, death could have come to either of them from anywhere. In fact, the assailant had already survived multiple gunshot wounds from an accident much like the one in which my brother lost his life.   **1**

As I wept for Blake I felt wrenched backward into events and circumstances that had seemed light-years gone. Though a decade apart, we both were raised in Chester, Pennsylvania, an angry, heavily black, heavily poor, industrial city southwest of Philadelphia. There, in the 1960s, I was introduced to mortality, not by the old and failing, but by beautiful young men who lay wrecked after sudden explosions of violence. The first, I remembered from my fourteenth year—Johnny, brash lover of fast cars, stabbed to   **2**

---

1. escalated: increased
2. posturing: trying to appear tough

death two doors from my house in a fight over a pool game. The next year, my teenage cousin, Wesley, whom I loved very much, was shot dead. The summers blur. Milton, an angry young neighbor, shot a crosstown rival, wounding him badly. William, another teenage neighbor, took a shotgun blast to the shoulder in some urban drama and displayed his bandages proudly. His brother, Leonard, severely beaten, lost an eye and donned a black patch. It went on.

I recall not long before I left for college, two local Vietnam veterans— **3** one from the Marines, one from the Army—arguing fiercely, nearly at blows about which outfit had done the most in the war. The most killing, they meant. Not much later, I read a magazine article that set that dispute in a context. In the story, a noncommissioned officer—a sergeant, I believe— said he would pass up any number of affluent, suburban-born recruits to get hard-core soldiers from the inner city. They jumped into the rice paddies with "their manhood on their sleeves," I believe he said. These two items— the veterans arguing and the sergeant's words—still characterize for me the circumstances under which black men in their teens and twenties kill one another with such frequency. With a touchy paranoia born of living battered lives, they are desperate to be *real* men. Killing is only machismo taken to the extreme. Incursions[3] to be punished by death were many and minor, and they remain so: they include stepping on the wrong toe, literally; cheating in a drug deal; simply saying "I dare you" to someone holding a gun; crossing territorial lines in a gang dispute. My brother grew up to wear his manhood on his sleeve. And when he died, he was in that group—black, male and in its teens and early twenties—that is far and away the most likely to murder or be murdered.

I left the East Coast after college, spent the mid- and late 1970s in **4** Chicago as a graduate student, taught for a time, then became a journalist. Within ten years of leaving my hometown, I was overeducated and "upwardly mobile," ensconced[4] on a quiet, tree-lined street where voices raised in anger were scarcely ever heard. The telephone, like some grim umbilical, kept me connected to the old world with news of deaths, imprisonings and misfortune. I felt emotionally beaten up. Perhaps to protect myself, I added a psychological dimension to the physical distance I had already achieved. I rarely visited my hometown. I shut it out.

As I fled the past, so Blake embraced it. On Christmas of 1983, I traveled **5** from Chicago to a black section of Roanoke, Virginia, where he then lived. The desolate public housing projects, the hopeless, idle young men crashing against one another—these reminded me of the embittered town we'd grown up in. It was a place where once I would have been comfortable, or at least sure of myself. Now, hearing of my brother's forays[5] into crime, his scrapes with police and street thugs, I was scared, unsteady on foreign terrain.[6]

3. incursions: attacks, violations
4. ensconced: settled comfortably
5. forays: undertakings, trips
6. terrain: ground

I saw that Blake's romance with the street life and the hustler image had **6** flowered dangerously. One evening that late December, standing in some Roanoke dive among drug dealers and grim, hair-trigger losers, I told him I feared for his life. He had affected the image of the tough he wanted to be. But behind the dark glasses and the swagger, I glimpsed the baby-faced toddler I'd once watched over. I nearly wept. I wanted desperately for him to live. The young think themselves immortal, and a dangerous light shone in his eyes as he spoke laughingly of making fools of the policemen who had raided his apartment looking for drugs. He cried out as I took his right hand. A line of stitches lay between the thumb and index finger. Kickback from a shotgun, he explained, nothing serious. Gunplay had become part of his life.

I lacked the language simply to say: Thousands have lived this for you **7** and died. I fought the urge to lift him bodily and shake him. This place and the way you are living smells of death to me, I said. Take some time away, I said. Let's go downtown tomorrow and buy a plane ticket anywhere, take a bus trip, anything to get away and cool things off. He took my alarm casually. We arranged to meet the following night—an appointment he would not keep. We embraced as though through glass. I drove away.

As I stood in my apartment in Chicago holding the receiver that evening **8** in February 1984, I felt as though part of my soul had been cut away. I questioned myself then, and I still do. Did I not reach back soon enough or earnestly enough for him? For weeks I awoke crying from a recurrent dream in which I chased him, urgently trying to get him to read a document I had, as though reading it would protect him from what had happened in waking life. His eyes shining like black diamonds, he smiled and danced just beyond my grasp. When I reached for him, I caught only the space where he had been. ■

Discussion and Writing Questions

1. Staples says that he was "introduced to mortality" in Chester, Pennsylvania, in the 1960s (paragraph 2). What does he mean?

2. What does the author mean when he says his brother grew up to "wear his manhood on his sleeve" (paragraph 3)? Does he imply there are other ways of expressing masculinity?

3. Staples speaks of a dream in which he holds a document for his brother to read (paragraph 8). What do you suppose that document might say? What does this dream seem to say about communication between the two brothers?

4. Staples begins his narrative by describing the moment at which he hears of Blake's death. Why does he *start* with this event, instead of moving toward it?

Writing Assignments

1. Write a narrative about a shocking incident that took place in your neighborhood. Like Staples, you may want to start with the incident, and then narrate the smaller events in the story that led up to it. Or you can follow time order and end with the incident.

2. What is the most significant problem facing young people in the inner city today? Is it crime? Drugs? Lack of educational or employment opportunities? Discuss your opinion on this subject.

3. Do you think Brent Staples could have done more to change his brother? Can we really influence others to change their lives?

One More Lesson

Judith Ortiz Cofer

Judith Ortiz Cofer attended Augusta College, Florida Atlantic University, and Oxford University in England. Here she contrasts her memories of holidays in her native Puerto Rico and of later school experiences in Paterson, New Jersey, telling what she learned about love, prejudice, and the power of words. Her essay sheds light, too, on her decision to become a writer.

I remember Christmas on the Island by the way it felt on my skin. The temperature dropped into the ideal seventies and even lower after midnight when some of the more devout Catholics, mostly older women, got up to go to church—*misa del gallo,* they called it; mass at the hour when the rooster crowed for Christ. They would drape shawls over their heads and shoulders and move slowly toward town. The birth of Our Savior was a serious affair in our town.

At Mamá's house, food was the focal point of *Navidad.* There were banana leaves brought in bunches by the boys, spread on the table, where the women would pour coconut candy steaming hot, and the leaves would wilt around the sticky lumps, adding an extra tang of flavor to the already irresistible treat. Someone had to watch the candy while it cooled, or it would begin to disappear as the children risked life and limb for a stolen piece of heaven. The banana leaves were also used to wrap the traditional food of holidays in Puerto Rico: *pasteles,* the meat pies made from grated yucca[1] and plantain[2] and stuffed with spiced meats.

Every afternoon during the week before Christmas Day, we would come home from school to find the women sitting around in the parlor with bowls on their laps, grating pieces of coconut, yuccas, plantains, cheeses—all the ingredients that would make up our Christmas Eve feast. The smells that filled Mamá's house at that time have come to mean anticipation and a sensual joy during a time in my life, the last days of my early childhood, when I

1. yucca: a thick-stemmed tropical plant
2. plantain: a banana-like fruit

could absorb joy through my pores—when I had not yet learned that light is followed by darkness, that all of creation is based on that simple concept, and maturity is a discovery of that natural law.

It was in those days that the Americans sent baskets of fruit to our **4** barrio[3]—apples, oranges, grapes flown in from the States. And at night, if you dared to walk up to the hill where the mango tree stood in the dark, you could see a wonderful sight: a Christmas tree, a real pine, decorated with lights of many colors. It was the blurry outline of this tree you saw, for it was inside a screened-in porch, but we had heard a thorough description of it from the boy who delivered the fruit, a nephew of Mamá's, as it had turned out. Only, I was not impressed, since just the previous year we had put up a tree ourselves in our apartment in Paterson.

Packages arrived for us in the mail from our father. I got dolls dressed in **5** the national costumes of Spain, Italy, and Greece (at first we could not decide which of the Greek dolls was the male, since they both wore skirts); my brother got picture books; and my mother, jewelry that she would not wear, because it was too much like showing off and might attract the Evil Eye.

Evil Eye or not, the three of us were the envy of the pueblo.[4] Everything **6** about us set us apart, and I put away my dolls quickly when I discovered that my playmates would not be getting any gifts until *Los Reyes*—the Day of the Three Kings, when Christ received His gifts—and that even then it was more likely that the gifts they found under their beds would be practical things like clothes. Still, it was fun to find fresh grass for the camels the night the Kings were expected, tie it in bundles with string, and put it under our beds along with a bowl of fresh water.

The year went by fast after Christmas, and in the spring we received a **7** telegram from Father. His ship had arrived in Brooklyn Yard. He gave us a date for our trip back to the States. I remember Mother's frantic packing, and the trips to Mayagüez for new clothes; the inspections of my brother's and my bodies for cuts, scrapes, mosquito bites, and other "damage" she would have to explain to Father. And I remember begging Mamá to tell me stories in the afternoons, although it was not summer yet and the trips to the mango tree had not begun. In looking back I realize that Mamá's stories were what I packed—my winter store.

Father had succeeded in finding an apartment outside Paterson's "verti- **8** cal barrio," the tenement Puerto Ricans called *El Building*. He had talked a candy store owner into renting us the apartment above his establishment, which he and his wife had just vacated after buying a house in West Paterson, an affluent suburb. Mr. Schultz was a nice man whose melancholy[5] face I was familiar with from trips I had made often with my father to his store for cigarettes. Apparently, my father had convinced him and his brother, a look-alike of Mr. Schultz who helped in the store, that we were not the usual Puerto Rican family. My father's fair skin, his ultra-correct English, and his Navy uniform were a good argument. Later it occurred to me that my father had been displaying me as a model child when he took me to that store with him. I was always dressed as if for church and held firmly by the hand. I

3. barrio: district or neighborhood
4. pueblo: Spanish for *town*
5. melancholy: sad

imagine he did the same with my brother. As for my mother, her Latin beauty, her thick black hair that hung to her waist, her voluptuous[6] body which even the winter clothes could not disguise, would have been nothing but a hindrance to my father's plans. But everyone knew that a Puerto Rican woman is her husband's satellite; she reflects both his light and his dark sides. If my father was respectable, then his family would be respectable. We got the apartment on Park Avenue.

Unlike El Building, where we had lived on our first trip to Paterson, our **9** new home was truly in exile. There were Puerto Ricans by the hundreds only one block away, but we heard no Spanish, no loud music, no mothers yelling at children, nor the familiar *¡Ay Bendito!,* that catch-all phrase of our people. Mother lapsed into silence herself, suffering from *La Tristeza,* the sadness that only place induces and only place cures. But Father relished[7] silence, and we were taught that silence was something to be cultivated and practiced.

Since our apartment was situated directly above where the Schultzes **10** worked all day, our father instructed us to remove our shoes at the door and walk in our socks. We were going to prove how respectable we were by being the opposite of what our ethnic group was known to be—we would be quiet and inconspicuous.[8]

I was escorted each day to school by my nervous mother. It was a long **11** walk in the cooling air of fall in Paterson and we had to pass by El Building where the children poured out of the front door of the dilapidated[9] tenement still answering their mothers in a mixture of Spanish and English: "Sí, Mami, I'll come straight home from school." At the corner we were halted by the crossing guard, a strict woman who only gestured her instructions, never spoke directly to the children, and only ordered us to "halt" or "cross" while holding her white-gloved hand up at face level or swinging her arm sharply across her chest if the light was green.

The school building was not a welcoming sight for someone used to the **12** bright colors and airiness of tropical architecture. The building looked functional. It could have been a prison, an asylum, or just what it was: an urban school for the children of immigrants, built to withstand waves of change, generation by generation. Its red brick sides rose to four solid stories. The black steel fire escapes snaked up its back like an exposed vertebra. A chain-link fence surrounded its concrete playground. Members of the elite safety patrol, older kids, sixth graders mainly, stood at each of its entrances, wearing their fluorescent white belts that criss-crossed their chests and their metal badges. No one was allowed in the building until the bell rang, not even on rainy or bitter-cold days. Only the safety-patrol stayed warm.

My mother stood in front of the main entrance with me and a growing **13** crowd of noisy children. She looked like one of us, being no taller than the sixth-grade girls. She held my hand so tightly that my fingers cramped. When the bell rang, she walked me into the building and kissed my cheek. Apparently my father had done all the paperwork for my enrollment,

6. voluptuous: having a rounded, full shape
7. relished: enjoyed
8. inconspicuous: hard to notice
9. dilapidated: run-down

because the next thing I remember was being led to my third-grade classroom by a black girl who had emerged from the principal's office.

Though I had learned some English at home during my first years in **14** Paterson, I had let it recede deep into my memory while learning Spanish in Puerto Rico. Once again I was the child in the cloud of silence, the one who had to be spoken to in sign language as if she were a deaf-mute. Some of the children even raised their voices when they spoke to me, as if I had trouble hearing. Since it was a large troublesome class composed mainly of black and Puerto Rican children, with a few working-class Italian children interspersed,[10] the teacher paid little attention to me. I re-learned the language quickly by the immersion method.[11] I remember one day, soon after I joined the rowdy class when our regular teacher was absent and Mrs. D., the sixth-grade teacher from across the hall, attempted to monitor both classes. She scribbled something on the chalkboard and went to her own room. I felt a pressing need to use the bathroom and asked Julio, the Puerto Rican boy who sat behind me, what I had to do to be excused. He said that Mrs. D. had written on the board that we could be excused by simply writing our names under the sign. I got up from my desk and started for the front of the room when I was struck on the head hard with a book. Startled and hurt, I turned around expecting to find one of the bad boys in my class, but it was Mrs. D. I faced. I remember her angry face, her fingers on my arms pulling me back to my desk, and her voice saying incomprehensible things to me in a hissing tone. Someone finally explained to her that I was new, that I did not speak English. I also remember how suddenly her face changed from anger to anxiety. But I did not forgive her for hitting me with that hard-cover spelling book. Yes, I would recognize that book even now. It was not until years later that I stopped hating that teacher for not understanding that I had been betrayed by a classmate, and by my inability to read her warning on the board. I instinctively understood then that language is the only weapon a child has against the absolute power of adults.

I quickly built up my arsenal[12] of words by becoming an insatiable[13] **15** reader of books. ∎

Discussion and Writing Questions

1. Cofer writes that at some point after her early childhood she "learned that light is followed by darkness" (paragraph 3). What do you suppose she means by this?

2. How does the author seem to feel about her memories of Christmas in Puerto Rico? Is this feeling different from the one than she seems to have about her memories of Paterson?

3. Why does Cofer title her essay "One More Lesson"? What lesson does she learn? Why do you think she responded to her school experience by

10. interspersed: mixed in
11. immersion method: method of learning a foreign language in which the student is surrounded only by speakers of that language
12. arsenal: stockpile of weapons
13. insatiable: unable to be satisfied

becoming a reader (and later, a writer), when another child might have learned to hate school?

4. Cofer uses rich description in this essay. Choose one paragraph that you think contains excellent description. What words and details help you "see" Cofer's young world?

Writing Assignments

1. Compare two places that have been important to you. You may want to concentrate on the people in those two places, or you might discuss the smells and sounds or other physical details of each location. Focus on the most important details.

2. Write about a lesson you learned, especially an experience of prejudice, misunderstanding, or achievement that strongly affected your attitude toward English class, reading, or school.

3. Currently, educators are debating how English should be taught to speakers of foreign languages. Some believe that bilingual education, in which students are taught in their native languages as well as in English, helps students learn better than the "immersion method" Cofer writes about. Take a stand for bilingual education or for the immersion method. Which do you think is better for students in the long run?

Neat People Versus Sloppy People

Suzanne Britt

Suzanne Britt is a humorist and writer who likes to analyze people's behavior. In this essay from her book *Show and Tell,* she turns the commonly **accepted judgments about neatness and sloppiness upside down.**

I've finally figured out the difference between neat people and sloppy people. The distinction is, as always, moral. Neat people are lazier and meaner than sloppy people. 1

Sloppy people, you see, are not really sloppy. Their sloppiness is merely the unfortunate consequence of their extreme moral rectitude.[1] Sloppy people carry in their mind's eye a heavenly vision, a precise plan, that is so stupendous, so perfect, it can't be achieved in this world or the next. 2

Sloppy people live in Never-Never Land. Someday is their métier.[2] Someday they are planning to alphabetize all their books and set up home catalogs. Someday they will go through their wardrobes and mark certain items for tentative mending and certain items for passing on to relatives of 3

1. rectitude: righteousness, correctness
2. métier: specialty; work for which someone is especially suited

similar shape and size. Someday sloppy people will make family scrapbooks into which they will put newspaper clippings, postcards, locks of hair, and the dried corsage from their senior prom. Someday they will file everything on the surface of their desks, including the cash register receipts from coffee purchases at the snack shop. Someday they will sit down and read all the back issues of *The New Yorker*.

For all these noble reasons and more, sloppy people never get neat. They **4** aim too high and wide. They save everything, planning someday to file, order, and straighten out the world. But while these ambitious plans take clearer and clearer shape in their heads, the books spill from the shelves onto the floor, the clothes pile up in the hamper and closet, the family mementos accumulate in every drawer, the surface of the desk is buried under mounds of paper and the unread magazines threaten to reach the ceiling.

Sloppy people can't bear to part with anything. They give loving atten- **5** tion to every detail. When sloppy people say they're going to tackle the surface of the desk, they really mean it. Not a paper will go unturned; not a rubber band will go unboxed. Four hours or two weeks into the excavation, the desk looks exactly the same, primarily because the sloppy person is meticulously³ creating new piles of papers with new headings and scrupulously⁴ stopping to read all the old book catalogs before he throws them away. A neat person would just bulldoze the desk.

Neat people are bums and clods at heart. They have cavalier⁵ attitudes **6** toward possessions, including family heirlooms. Everything is just another dust-catcher to them. If anything collects dust, it's got to go and that's that. Neat people will toy with the idea of throwing the children out of the house just to cut down on the clutter.

Neat people don't care about process. They like results. What they want **7** to do is get the whole thing over with so they can sit down and watch the rasslin' on TV. Neat people operate on two unvarying principles: Never handle any item twice, and throw everything away.

The only thing messy in a neat person's house is the trash can. The **8** minute something comes to a neat person's hand, he will look at it, try to decide if it has immediate use and, finding none, throw it in the trash.

Neat people are especially vicious with mail. They never go through **9** their mail unless they are standing directly over a trash can. If the trash can is beside the mailbox, even better. All ads, catalogs, pleas for charitable contributions, church bulletins and money-saving coupons go straight into the trash can without being opened. All letters from home, postcards from Europe, bills and paychecks are opened, immediately responded to, then dropped in the trash can. Neat people keep their receipts only for tax purposes. That's it. No sentimental salvaging⁶ of birthday cards or the last letter a dying relative ever wrote. Into the trash it goes.

Neat people place neatness above everything, even economics. They are **10** incredibly wasteful. Neat people throw away several toys every time they walk through the den. I knew a neat person once who threw away a perfectly

3. meticulously: very carefully
4. scrupulously: conscientiously
5. cavalier: showing disregard; not having respect
6. salvaging: rescuing, saving

good dish drainer because it had mold on it. The drainer was too much trouble to wash. And neat people sell their furniture when they move. They will sell a La-Z-Boy recliner while you are reclining in it.

Neat people are no good to borrow from. Neat people buy everything in expensive little single portions. They get their flour and sugar in two-pound bags. They wouldn't consider clipping a coupon, saving a leftover, reusing plastic non-dairy whipped cream containers or rinsing off tin foil and draping it over the unmoldy dish drainer. You can never borrow a neat person's newspaper to see what's playing at the movies. Neat people have the paper all wadded up and in the trash by 7:05 a.m.   **11**

Neat people cut a clean swath[7] through the organic[8] as well as the inorganic[9] world. People, animals, and things are all one to them. They are so insensitive. After they've finished with the pantry, the medicine cabinet, and the attic, they will throw out the red geranium (too many leaves), sell the dog (too many fleas), and send the children off to boarding school (too many scuffmarks on the hardwood floors). ■   **12**

Discussion and Writing Questions

1. Britt says that the difference between neat and sloppy people is "moral" (paragraph 1). Which type of person does she claim to believe is superior? Is she serious about this? How do you know?

2. What does Britt mean when she says that "someday" is the "métier" for sloppy people (paragraph 3)?

3. The author characterizes neat people as "bums and clods" (paragraph 6). In what ways does she see neat people as heartless?

4. From her contrast essay, do you think Suzanne Britt is a neat or a sloppy person? Why do you think so?

Writing Assignments

1. Are you neat or sloppy? Does Britt accurately describe the reasons for your behavior? If not, discuss the reasons behind your neatness or sloppiness.

2. If you are a neat person, you may want to challenge Britt's arguments. Write a defense of neatness; explain from a neat person's point of view why neat people do what they do and how they are more "moral" than sloppy people.

3. Contrast the different personalities of two people you know. For instance, you might discuss two members of your study group, one a careless worker and one a perfectionist. Or you might contrast a pair of twins, one of whom is almost a hermit, while the other is very sociable. Or talk about the differences between your mountain-climbing aunt and her stay-at-home husband. Use humor if you wish.

7. swath: path, strip
8. organic: living
9. inorganic: nonliving

How to Get the Most out of Yourself

Alan Loy McGinnis

Why are some persons successful and productive while others struggle along unhappily? Alan Loy McGinnis, a psychotherapist, believes that the answer lies in self-image. In this essay, he presents numerous ways people can strengthen their self-image.

Our success at business, sports, friendship, love—nearly every enterprise **1** we attempt—is largely determined by our own self-image. People who have confidence in their personal worth seem to be magnets for success and happiness. Good things drop into their laps regularly, their relationships are long-lasting, their projects are usually carried to completion. To use the imagery of English poet William Blake, they "catch joy on the wing."

Conversely, some people seem to be magnets for failure and unhappi- **2** ness. Their plans go awry,[1] they have a way of torpedoing their own potential successes, and nothing seems to work out for them. As a counselor, I see many such persons. Their problems usually stem from a difficulty with self-acceptance. When I am able to help them gain more confidence, often their troubles take care of themselves.

I believe that anyone can change his self-perception. A person with low **3** self-image is not doomed to a life of unhappiness and failure. It *is* possible to get rid of negative attitudes and gain the healthy confidence needed to realize one's dreams. Here's how:

Focus on your potential—not your limitations. When Helen Hayes was **4** a young actress, producer George Tyler told her that, were she four inches taller, she could become one of the great actresses of her time. "I decided," she says, "to lick my size. A string of teachers pulled and stretched till I felt I was in a medieval torture chamber. I gained nary[2] an inch—but my posture was military-straight. I became the tallest five-foot woman in the world. And my refusal to be limited by my limitations enabled me to play Mary of Scotland, one of the tallest queens in history."

Helen Hayes succeeded because she chose to focus on her strong points, **5** not her weak ones.

Many clients tell me that because they are not as smart or good-looking **6** or witty as others, they feel inferior. Probably no habit chips away at our self-confidence quite so effectively as that of scanning the people around us to see how we compare. And when we find that someone is indeed smarter, better-looking or wittier, it diminishes our sense of self-worth.

The Hasidic rabbi Zusya was asked on his deathbed what he thought the **7** kingdom of God would be like. "I don't know," he replied. "But one thing I *do* know. When I get there I am not going to be asked, 'Why weren't you Moses? Why weren't you David?' I am only going to be asked, 'Why weren't you Zusya? Why weren't you fully you?'"

1. go awry: go off course
2. nary: not even one

Devote yourself to something you do well. There is nothing so common **8**
as unsuccessful people with talent. Usually the problem lies not in discover-
ing our natural aptitude but in developing that skill.

Young surgeons practice skills for months on end, such as tying knots in **9**
a confined space or suturing. The refining of these skills is the surgeon's
main method of improving total performance.

Many of us get interested in a field, but then the going gets tough, we see **10**
that other people are more successful, and we become discouraged and quit.
But it is often the boring, repetitive sharpening of our skills that will
ultimately enable us to reach our goals.

Horace Bushnell, the great New England preacher, used to say, "Some- **11**
where under the stars God has a job for you to do, and nobody else can do it."
Some of us must find our place by trial and error. It can take time, with dead
ends along the way. But we should not get discouraged because others seem
more skilled. Usually it is not raw talent but drive that makes the difference.

See yourself as successful. If I could plug into the minds of my patients **12**
and listen to the statements they make to themselves, I am convinced that
the majority of them would be negative: "I'm running late again—as usual."
"My hair looks terrible this morning." "That was a stupid remark I made—
she probably thinks I'm a dummy." Since thousands of these messages flash
across our brains every day, it is small wonder that the result is a diminished
self-image.

One daily exercise for building self-confidence is called "imaging" or **13**
"visualization." In order to succeed, you must *see* yourself succeeding.
Picture yourself approaching a difficult challenge with poise[3] and confidence. Athletes often visualize a move over and over in their minds; they
see themselves hitting the perfect golf or tennis shot. When we burn such
positive images into our minds deeply enough, they become a part of the
unconscious, and we begin to expect to succeed.

Author and editor Norman Cousins wrote: "People are never more inse- **14**
cure than when they become obsessed with their fears at the expense of
their dreams." There is no doubt that if we can envision beneficial things
happening, they have a way of actually occurring.

Break away from other people's expectations. It is a liberating step **15**
when we decide to stop being what other people want us to be. Although
opera singer Risë Stevens performed onstage with great poise, the self-
confidence she felt before audiences evaporated in social situations. "My
discomfort," she says, "came from trying to be something I was not—a
star in the drawing room as well as onstage. If a clever person made a joke,
I tried to top it—and failed. I pretended to be familiar with subjects I knew
nothing of."

Stevens finally had a heart-to-heart talk with herself: "I realized that I **16**
simply wasn't a wit or an intellectual and that I could succeed only as myself.
I began listening and asking questions at parties instead of trying to impress
the guests. When I spoke, I tried to contribute, not to shine. Almost at once
I started to feel a new warmth in my social contacts. They liked the real me
better."

---

3. poise: a look and feeling of self-assurance, calmness

If we are true to our instincts, most of us will find that we naturally **17** develop certain trademarks. The discovery and expression of that uniqueness is one reason we are on this planet. Resisting conformity and developing some small eccentricities[4] are among the steps to independence and self-confidence.

Build a network of supportive relationships. Many of my clients scramble to shore up[5] their self-images with various techniques, overlooking the source from which they will get help most readily—good friendships. **18**

One of the surest ways to improve confidence is to make certain you have **19** lots of love in your life, to go to whatever lengths are necessary to construct a network of sustaining and nurturing relationships. In building such supportive relationships, most of my patients think their problem is in meeting new people. But the answer, really, is in deepening the friendships you presently have.

The extended family can be a major source of support and nurture. A **20** friend who is 45 tells me that visiting her parents in Indiana is always "a mixed bag." She makes connections with some relatives she'd just as soon not see anymore, and she usually has at least one blow-up with her parents. "But it's important to be around my family," she says. "I always come back feeling that I have a clearer idea of who I am, where I came from, and where I want to go."

She is a wise woman. Such connections with our heritage make our identities more secure. As author John Dos Passos said, "A sense of continuity with the generations gone before can stretch like a lifeline across the scary present." **21**

The distribution of talents in this world should not be our concern. Our responsibility is to take the talents we have and ardently parlay[6] them to the highest possible achievement. **22**

When Yoshihiko Yamamoto of Nagoya City, Japan, was six months old, **23** physicians told his parents that he was mentally retarded. With a hearing loss that strangled his speech and an I.Q. that tested very low, Yamamoto faced a bleak future.

But a new special-education teacher, Takashi Kawasaki, took a special **24** interest in the boy. Gradually Yamamoto began to smile in class. He learned to copy the characters from the blackboard and cartoons from magazines. One day, Yamamoto drew an accurate sketch of Nagoya Castle. Kawasaki had the boy transfer his design to a wood block and encouraged him to concentrate on printmaking. Eventually Yamamoto won first prize in an art contest. Today, his work is much sought after.

It is not important that Yoshihiko Yamamoto has limitations. The important thing is that he has capitalized on his potential. **25**

Self-confidence, like happiness, is slippery when we set out to grab it for **26** its own sake. Usually it comes as a by-product. We lose ourselves in service or work, friendship or love, and suddenly one day we realize that we are confident and happy. ■

---

4. eccentricities: unusual or quirky personality traits or behavior
5. shore up: support, strengthen
6. parlay: turn into

Discussion and Writing Questions

1. McGinnis discusses several ways of overcoming poor self-esteem. What are these ways? Can you think of any he doesn't mention?

2. Which of these ways do you think is the most effective? The least effective? Why?

3. Identify the paragraphs in which McGinnis uses an anecdote, or brief story, to illustrate the topic sentence of the paragraph. Choose one or two of these paragraphs and illustrate the topic sentence with anecdotes from your own experience.

Writing Assignments

1. Give examples of ways a person might increase physical strength or some other capability or skill. For instance, tell what you or your friend did to train for a competitive event, such as a track meet or a football or basketball game. Use vivid details to make your illustration lively and interesting.

2. Write about someone whom you consider successful. What qualities or characteristics distinguish this person from others? The person need not be someone you know directly; he or she could be a politician, a rock star, a local personality, or an athlete. Be sure to choose someone about whom you know interesting details, so that your writing will engage your reader.

3. Choose one of the methods the author presents for improving self-esteem and restate the method as a topic sentence. Then write a paragraph that fully develops that topic sentence. For example, you could restate "Break away from other people's expectations" (paragraph 15) this way: "In order for me to break away from other people's expectations, I have to concentrate on what *I* want in life." The supporting details would then show how you concentrate on what you want. Remember to use details that clearly support the topic sentence.

Hunger of Memory

Richard Rodriguez

Growing up in California as a second-generation Mexican American, Richard Rodriguez wanted to understand the lives of *los pobres,* the poor Mexican laborers he saw around him. In this selection from *Hunger of Memory,* he tells of taking a summer job as a laborer and of learning about himself in the process.

It was at Stanford, one day near the end of my senior year, that a friend told **1**
me about a summer construction job he knew was available. I was quickly
alert. Desire uncoiled[1] within me. My friend said that he knew I had been
looking for summer employment. He knew I needed some money. Almost
apologetically he explained: It was something I probably wouldn't be interested in, but a friend of his, a contractor, needed someone for the summer to
do menial[2] jobs. There would be lots of shoveling and raking and sweeping.
Nothing too hard. But nothing more interesting either. Still, the pay would
be good. Did I want it? Or did I know someone who did?

I did. Yes, I said, surprised to hear myself say it.   **2**

In the weeks following, friends cautioned that I had no idea how hard   **3**
physical labor really is. ("You only *think* you know what it is like to shovel for
eight hours straight.") Their objections seemed to me challenges. They
resolved the issue. I became happy with my plan. I decided, however, not to
tell my parents. I wouldn't tell my mother because I could guess her worried
reaction. I would tell my father only after the summer was over, when I could
announce that, after all, I did know what "real work" is like.

The day I met the contractor (a Princeton graduate, it turned out), he   **4**
asked me whether I had done any physical labor before. "In high school,
during the summer," I lied. And although he seemed to regard me with
skepticism,[3] he decided to give me a try. Several days later, expectant, I
arrived at my first construction site. I would take off my shirt to the sun.
And at last grasp desired sensation. No longer afraid. At last become
like a *bracero*.[4] "We need those tree stumps out of here by tomorrow," the
contractor said. I started to work.

I labored with excitement that first morning—and all the days after. The   **5**
work was harder than I could have expected. But it was never as tedious as
my friends had warned me it would be. There was too much physical pleasure in the labor. Especially early in the day, I would be most alert to the sensations of movement and straining. Beginning around seven each morning
(when the air was still damp but the scent of weeds and dry earth anticipated
the heat of the sun), I would feel my body resist the first thrusts of the
shovel. My arms, tightened by sleep, would gradually loosen; after only several minutes, sweat would gather in beads on my forehead and then—a short
while later—I would feel my chest silky with sweat in the breeze. I would
return to my work. A nervous spark of pain would fly up my arm and settle to
burn like an ember in the thick of my shoulder. An hour, two passed. Three.
My whole body would assume regular movements; my shoveling would be
described by identical, even movements. Even later in the day, my enthusiasm for primitive sensation would survive the heat and the dust and the
insects pricking my back. I would strain wildly for sensation as the day came
to a close. At three-thirty, quitting time, I would stand upright and slowly let
my head fall back, luxuriating[5] in the feeling of tightness relieved.

1. uncoiled: loosened, unwound
2. menial: lowly, lacking status
3. skepticism: doubt
4. *bracero*: a Mexican living and working in the United States for a period of time
5. luxuriating: enjoying with deep pleasure

Some of the men working nearby would watch me and laugh. Two or **6**
three of the older men took the trouble to teach me the right way to use a
pick, the correct way to shovel. "You're doing it wrong, too fucking hard,"
one man scolded. Then proceeded to show me—what persons who work with
their bodies all their lives quickly learn—the most economical way to use
one's body in labor.

"Don't make your back do so much work," he instructed. I stood impa- **7**
tiently listening, half listening, vaguely watching, then noticed his work-
thickened fingers clutching the shovel. I was annoyed. I wanted to tell him
that I enjoyed shoveling the wrong way. And I didn't want to learn the right
way. I wasn't afraid of back pain. I liked the way my body felt sore at the end
of the day.

I was about to, but, as it turned out, I didn't say a thing. Rather it was at **8**
that moment I realized that I was fooling myself if I expected a few weeks of
labor to gain me admission to the world of the laborer. I would not learn in
three months what my father had meant by "real work." I was not bound to
this job; I could imagine its rapid conclusion. For me the sensations of exer-
tion and fatigue could be savored. For my father or uncle, working at compa-
rable jobs when they were my age, such sensations were to be feared. Fatigue took a different toll on their bodies—and minds.

It was, I know, a simple insight. But it was with this realization that **9**
I took my first step that summer toward realizing something even more
important about the "worker." In the company of carpenters, electricians,
plumbers, and painters at lunch, I would often sit quietly, observant. I was
not shy in such company. I felt easy, pleased by the knowledge that I was
casually accepted, my presence taken for granted by men (exotics[6]) who
worked with their hands. Some days the younger men would talk and talk
about sex, and they would howl at women who drove by in cars. Other days
the talk at lunchtime was subdued;[7] men gathered in separate groups. It
depended on who was around. There were rough, good-natured workers.
Others were quiet. The more I remember that summer, the more I realize
that there was no single *type* of worker. I am embarrassed to say I had not
expected such diversity. I certainly had not expected to meet, for example,
a plumber who was an abstract painter in his off hours and admired the work
of Mark Rothko. Nor did I expect to meet so many workers with college
diplomas. (They were the ones who were not surprised that I intended to
enter graduate school in the fall.) I suppose what I really want to say here is
painfully obvious, but I must say it nevertheless: The men of that summer
were middle-class Americans. They certainly didn't constitute[8] an oppressed
society. Carefully completing their work sheets; talking about the fortunes of
local football teams; planning Las Vegas vacations; comparing the gas
mileage of various makes of campers—they were not *los pobres*[9] my mother
had spoken about.

On two occasions, the contractor hired a group of Mexican aliens. They **10**
were employed to cut down some trees and haul off debris. In all, there were
six men of varying age. The youngest in his late twenties; the oldest (his

6. exotics: people who are quite unfamiliar
7. subdued: quiet, constrained
8. constitute: make up
9. *los pobres*: the poor people

father?) perhaps sixty years old. They came and they left in a single old truck. Anonymous men. They were never introduced to the other men at the site. Immediately upon their arrival, they would follow the contractor's directions, start working—rarely resting—seemingly driven by a fatalistic[10] sense that work which had to be done was best done as quickly as possible.

I watched them sometimes. Perhaps they watched me. The only time I **11** saw them pay me much notice was one day at lunchtime when I was laughing with the other men. The Mexicans sat apart when they ate, just as they worked by themselves. Quiet. I rarely heard them say much to each other. All I could hear were their voices calling out sharply to one another, giving directions. Otherwise, when they stood briefly resting, they talked among themselves in voices too hard to overhear.

The contractor knew enough Spanish, and the Mexicans—or at least the **12** oldest of them, their spokesman—seemed to know enough English to communicate. But because I was around, the contractor decided one day to make me his translator. (He assumed I could speak Spanish.) I did what I was told. Shyly I went over to tell the Mexicans that the *patrón*[11] wanted them to do something else before they left for the day. As I started to speak, I was afraid with my old fear that I would be unable to pronounce the Spanish words. But it was a simple instruction I had to convey. I could say it in phrases.

The dark sweating faces turned toward me as I spoke. They stopped **13** their work to hear me. Each nodded in response. I stood there. I wanted to say something more. But what could I say in Spanish, even if I could have pronounced the words right? Perhaps I just wanted to engage them in small talk, to be assured of their confidence, our familiarity. I thought for a moment to ask them where in Mexico they were from. Something like that. And maybe I wanted to tell them (a lie, if need be) that my parents were from the same part of Mexico.

I stood there. **14**

Their faces watched me. The eyes of the man directly in front of me **15** moved slowly over my shoulder, and I turned to follow his glance toward *el patrón* some distance away. For a moment I felt swept up by that glance into the Mexicans' company. But then I heard one of them returning to work. And then the others went back to work. I left them without saying anything more.

When they had finished, the contractor went over to pay them in cash. **16** (He later told me that he paid them collectively—"for the job," though he wouldn't tell me their wages. He said something quickly about the good rate of exchange "in their own country.") I can still hear the loudly confident voice he used with the Mexicans. It was the sound of the *gringo*[12] I had heard as a very young boy. And I can still hear the quiet, indistinct sounds of the Mexican, the oldest, who replied. At hearing that voice I was sad for the Mexicans. Depressed by their vulnerability. Angry at myself. The adventure of the summer seemed suddenly ludicrous. I would not shorten the distance I felt from *los pobres* with a few weeks of physical labor. I would not become like them. They were different from me. ∎

10. fatalistic: believing events to be predetermined; yielding to one's fate
11. *patrón*: boss
12. *gringo*: slang for a person from the United States

Discussion and Writing Questions

1. Why does the author decide to take the summer construction job?

2. Why does Rodriguez say he didn't mind shoveling the wrong way? As he says this, what does he realize about the men he works with?

3. Why does the experience with the Mexican laborers have such an impact on Rodriguez?

4. Rodriguez might have written his essay using comparison or contrast, discussing his feelings before and after his work on the summer construction crew. Why do you think he chose to write it as a narrative?

Writing Assignments

1. Retell Rodriguez's narrative from the point of view of one of the Mexican laborers. You could retell the story Rodriguez tells about speaking with the men, but this time from *your* point of view as a laborer. Or you could describe a typical day working for the *patrón*, doing various jobs at the construction site.

2. Tell what it is like to do a particular kind of work. You may choose, like Rodriguez, to describe hard, manual labor, or you may have a less strenuous form of work in mind. Whatever work you tell about, be sure to describe it in detail, so that your audience can picture exactly what the job involves.

3. Rodriguez writes of the labor his father or uncle would have known during a life of hard work. Write about a person of a generation older than yours. What kind of work did he or she do? Consider that person's job opportunities, or lack of them.

My Outing[1]

Arthur Ashe

Arthur Ashe was the first African-American to become a great tennis champion. After a heart attack ended his career, he contracted AIDS through a tainted blood transfusion. He kept his illness private for years while he pursued many business interests and human-rights projects. Then the possibility of a newspaper report forced him to reveal his condition to the public. The press conference he refers to in the essay was held in April 1992. Ashe died on February 6, 1993.

The day after my press conference, I made sure to keep the two appoint-   1
ments on my calendar because I was anxious to see how people would

---

1. "Outing" someone usually means revealing publicly, without permission, that he or she is homosexual. Although Ashe was not gay, he was "outed" as a person with AIDS.

respond to me after the announcement. I was thinking not only about the people I knew personally, even intimately, but also about waiters and bartenders, doormen and taxi drivers. I knew all the myths and fears about AIDS. I also understood that if I hadn't been educated in the harshest possible way—by contracting the disease and living with it—I would probably share some of those myths and fears. I knew that I couldn't spread the disease by coughing or breathing or using plates and cups in a restaurant, but I knew that in some places my plates and cups would receive special attention, perhaps some extra soap and hot water. Perhaps they would be smashed and thrown away.

That morning, I accompanied Donald M. Stewart, head of the College **2** Board testing service, on a visit to the offices of the New York Community Trust. We were seeking a grant of $5,000 to support the publication of a handbook aimed at student-athletes. The appointment went well; we got the money. And in the evening, I went in black tie to a gala dinner to celebrate the eightieth birthday of a man I had known for thirty years and regarded as one of my key mentors in New York City, Joseph Cullman III, a former chairman of Philip Morris. At the event, which took place at the Museum of National History in Manhattan, I felt anxiety rising as our taxi drew up to the curb. How would the other guests respond to me? The first person I saw was an old friend, John Reese. An investment banker now, in his youth John had been an up-and-coming star with me in junior tennis. He saw me, and hurried over. There was no mistaking the warmth of his greeting, his genuine concern but also his understanding of my predicament. We walked inside together and I had a fine time at the celebration. . . .

I was glad, in this context, that I had not concealed my condition from **3** certain people. I had reminded myself from the outset[2] that I had an obligation to tell anyone who might be materially hurt by the news when it came out. I have been both proud of my commercial connections and grateful to the people who had asked me to represent them or work for them in some other way. Several of them had taken a chance on me when they knew full well, from the most basic market research in the early 1970s, that having an African American as a spokesman or an officer might cost them business.

Among these organizations, the most important were the Aetna Life and **4** Casualty Company, where I was a member of the board of directors; Head USA, the sports-equipment manufacturer that had given me my first important commercial endorsement, a tennis racquet with my very own autograph on it; the Doral Resort and Country Club in Florida, where I had directed the tennis program; Le Coq Sportif, the sports-clothing manufacturer; Home Box Office (HBO), the cable-television network for which I worked as an analyst at Wimbledon;[3] and ABC Sports, for which I also served as a commentator.

Not one of these companies had dropped me after I quietly revealed to **5** their most important executives that I had AIDS. Now those executives had to deal with the response of the public. I would have to give them a chance to put some distance between their companies and me because I now carried the most abominable and intimidating medical virus of our age. In business, image is everything. And one would have to go back to leprosy, or the plague,

2. outset: beginning
3. Wimbledon: London, England, district where a major tennis tournament is held each year

to find a disease so full of terrifying implications as AIDS carries. AIDS was a scientific mystery that defied our vaunted[4] claims for science, and also a religious or spiritual riddle—at least to those who insisted on thinking of it as possibly a punishment from God for our evil on earth, as more than one person had publicly suggested. . . .

I waited for the phone calls and the signs that my services were no **6** longer needed. None came.

I read somewhere that in the two weeks following his announcement **7** that he was HIV-positive, Earvin "Magic" Johnson received thousands of pieces of mail, and that months later he was still receiving hundreds of letters a week. Well, I received nothing approaching that volume of correspondence following my press conference, but I certainly had a mountain of reading and writing to do in its aftermath. And every time I appeared on one of the few television interview shows I agreed to do, such as with Barbara Walters or Larry King, there was another surge of correspondence. I heard from the famous and the completely unknown, people I knew and people I had never met.

The most moving letters, without a doubt, came from people who had **8** lived through an AIDS illness, either their own or that of a loved one. Often the loved one was now dead. These writers, above all, understood why I had made such a fuss about the issue of privacy. Many probably understood better than I did, because they were more vulnerable than I am, and had suffered more. One Manhattan woman wrote to tell me about her father, who had received HIV-tainted blood, as I had, through a blood transfusion following heart surgery. Without knowing it, he had passed the infection on to her mother. For some years, they had kept their illness a secret from their daughter. After they could keep the secret from her no longer, she in turn had worked to keep their secret from other family members and friends, and from the world. Although both parents were now dead, she wrote, "I share your anger at that anonymous person who violated either your trust or their professional ethics." . . .

A grandmother in New England, HIV-positive after a transfusion, **9** shared with me her terror that the company she worked for would dismiss her if they found out; she was awaiting the passage of a law that might protect her. From Idaho, a mother told me about her middle-aged son, who had tried to keep his AIDS condition a secret even from her. "My son kept it to himself for six months before he told me and I'll never forget that day as we cried together." His ordeal included dementia,[5] forced incarceration in a state asylum, and ostracism[6] by relatives and friends. But mother and son had spent his last "four difficult months" together. "I'm so thankful to have had those days with him."

I heard from people whom I had not thought of in years, and some of **10** them had been touched by their own tragedy. A woman I remembered as a stunningly beautiful UCLA coed, as we called them in those days, told me about her younger brother, who had been diagnosed with full-blown AIDS about five years before. "He is gay," she reported, "and I saw how he lost so

4. vaunted: boastful
5. dementia: insanity
6. ostracism: exclusion, banishment

much self-esteem and hope" because of intolerance. "No one can speak as eloquently[7] as you and Magic to allow the stigma[8] to disperse[9] regarding this situation." Another letter illustrated the power of the stigma. Signed simply, "Sorry I can't identify myself, but you understand," it came from a man who had been diagnosed with HIV three years ago. "I'm the father of six children and many grandchildren. I'm not into needles or the gay life. Don't know where it came from (really)."

As for my daughter, Camera, more than one writer underscored my fears **11** about what she might have to undergo from insensitive people in the future. A woman whose son had died of AIDS about a year before, following the death of his wife, was now bringing up their young son: "I struggle with how this little child is going to deal with the insults and rejections that people will inflict on him when they find out that his father died from AIDS." . . .

Needless to say, I am grateful to all those who have taken the trouble to **12** write. Most of the letters left me humbled. ▪

Discussion and Writing Questions

1. In paragraph 3, Ashe says that he had told some business associates about his illness early on. Why had he done that? How had they reacted? Why, then, was Ashe concerned about the business community's reaction to his *public* announcement?

2. How did the general public react to Ashe's announcement? Which letters did Ashe find most moving? Why?

3. The privacy issue was extremely important to Ashe, who felt that he had been forced by the press to make an announcement he had not wanted to make. One letter he received said, "I share your anger at that anonymous person who violated either your trust or their professional ethics" (paragraph 8). What did the letter writer mean by this statement?

4. Arthur Ashe called his life story *Days of Grace*. On the basis of this essay, why do you think he chose that title? What example or examples of "grace" did he tell about?

Writing Assignments

1. Ashe believed that no newspaper had the right to tell the world that he had AIDS—that his right to privacy was greater than the public's need to know. The press argued that Ashe was a public figure and that whenever a public figure is ill, his or her condition is legitimate news. Do you think the press would have been justified in revealing Ashe's condition? Why or why not?

2. Have you ever prepared yourself for the worst—the ending of a relationship, a frightening medical test result, or other bad news—only to find

7. eloquently: skillfully, persuasively
8. stigma: mark of disgrace
9. disperse: disappear

that the worst did not happen? Discuss such a time: why you expected the worst, what you did to prepare, and what really happened.

3. Serious illness can force people to reevaluate their lives—their aspirations and their goals. Have you, or has someone you know, looked at life differently because of an illness or accident? Write a short account of your own or the other person's experience.

Some Thoughts About Abortion

Anna Quindlen

Since the *Roe vs. Wade* Supreme Court decision of 1973, the issue of abortion has gripped the United States as perhaps never before. In this essay, noted *New York Times* columnist Anna Quindlen describes her own mixed feelings about the subject, and at the same time gives persuasive reasons for keeping abortion legal.

It was always the look on their faces that told me first. I was the freshman dormitory counselor and they were the freshmen at a women's college where everyone was smart. One of them would come into my room, a golden girl, a valedictorian, an 800 verbal score on the S.A.T.'s, and her eyes would be empty, seeing only a busted future, the devastation of her life as she knew it. She had failed biology, messed up the math; she was pregnant. 1

That was when I became pro-choice. 2

It was the look in his eyes that I will always remember, too. They were as black as the bottom of a well, and in them for a few minutes I thought I saw myself the way I had always wished to be—clear, simple, elemental, at peace. My child looked at me and I looked back at him in the delivery room, and I realized that out of a sea of infinite possibilities it had come down to this: a specific person, born on the hottest day of the year, conceived on a Christmas Eve, made by his father and me miraculously from scratch. 3

Once I believed that there was a little blob of formless protoplasm[1] in there and a gynecologist went after it with a surgical instrument, and that was that. Then I got pregnant myself—eagerly, intentionally, by the right man, at the right time—and I began to doubt. My abdomen still flat, my stomach roiling with morning sickness, I felt not that I had protoplasm inside, but, instead, a complete human being in miniature to whom I could talk, sing, make promises. Neither of these views was accurate; instead, I think, the reality is something in the middle. And that is where I find myself now, in the middle—hating the idea of abortions, hating the idea of having them outlawed. 4

For I know it is the right thing in some times and places. I remember sitting in a shabby clinic far uptown with one of those freshmen, only three months after the Supreme Court had made what we were doing possible, 5

1. protoplasm: living matter

and watching with wonder as the lovely first love she had had with a nice boy unraveled[2] over the space of an hour as they waited for her to be called, degenerated[3] into sniping[4] and silences. I remember a year or two later seeing them pass on campus and not even acknowledge each other because their conjoining had caused them so much pain, and I shuddered to think of them married, with a small psyche in their unready and unwilling hands.

I've met fourteen-year-olds who were pregnant and said they could not **6** have abortions because of their religion, and I see in their eyes the shadows of twenty-two-year-olds I've talked to who lost their kids to foster care because they hit them or used drugs or simply had no money for food and shelter. I read not long ago about a teenager who said she meant to have an abortion but she spent the money on clothes instead: now she has a baby who turns out to be a lot more trouble than a toy. The people who hand out those execrable[5] little pictures of dismembered fetuses at abortion clinics seem to forget the extraordinary pain children may endure after they are born when they are unwanted, even hated, or simply tolerated.

I believe that in a contest between the living and the almost living, the **7** latter must, if necessary, give way to the will of the former. That is what the fetus is to me, the almost living. These questions began to plague me—and, I've discovered, a good many other women—after I became pregnant. But they became even more acute after I had my second child, mainly because he is so different from his brother. On two random nights eighteen months apart the same two people managed to conceive, and on one occasion the tumult[6] within turned itself into a curly-haired brunet with merry black eyes who walked and talked late and loved the whole world, and on another it became a blond with hazel Asian eyes and a pug nose who tried to conquer the world almost as soon as he entered it.

If we were to have an abortion next time for some reason or another, **8** which infinite possibility becomes, not a reality, but a nullity?[7] The girl with the blue eyes? The improbable redhead? The natural athlete? The thinker? My husband, ever at the heart of the matter, put it another way. Knowing he is finding two children somewhat more overwhelming than he expected, I asked if he would want me to have an abortion if I accidentally became pregnant again right away. "And waste a perfectly good human being?" he said.

Coming to this quandary[8] has been difficult for me. In fact, I believe the **9** issue of abortion is difficult for all thoughtful people. I don't know anyone who has had an abortion who has been casual about it. If there is one thing I find intolerable about most of the so-called right-to-lifers, it is that they try to portray abortion rights as something that feminists thought up on a slow Saturday over a light lunch. That is nonsense. I also know that some people who support abortion rights are most comfortable with a monolithic[9] position because it seems the strongest front against the smug and sometimes violent opposition.

2. unraveled: came apart
3. degenerated: became worse
4. sniping: bickering, arguing
5. execrable: disgusting

6. tumult: energetic movement
7. nullity: nonexistence
8. quandary: tough spot, predicament
9. monolithic: unified and solid

But I don't feel all one way about abortion anymore, and I don't think it   **10**
serves a just cause to pretend that many of us do. For years I believed that a
woman's right to choose was absolute, but now I wonder. Do I, with a stable
home and marriage and sufficient stamina and money, have the freedom to
choose abortion because a pregnancy is inconvenient just now? Legally I do
have the right; legally I want always to have that right. It is the morality of
exercising it under those circumstances that makes me wonder.

Technology has foiled[10] us. The second trimester has become a time of   **11**
resurrection; a fetus at six months can be one woman's late abortion,
another's premature, viable[11] child. Photographers now have film of embryos
the size of a grape, oddly human, flexing their fingers, sucking their thumbs.
Women have amniocentesis[12] to find out whether they are carrying a child
with birth defects that they may choose to abort. Before the procedure, they
must have a sonogram, one of those fuzzy black-and-white photos like a love
song heard through static on the radio, which shows someone is in there.

I have taped on my VCR a public television program in which somehow,   **12**
inexplicably,[13] a film is shown of a fetus *in utero*[14] scratching its face, seemingly putting up a tiny hand to shield itself from the camera's eye. It would
make a potent weapon in the arsenal of the antiabortionists. I grow sentimental about it as it floats in the salt water, part fish, part human being. It is
almost living, but not quite. It has almost turned my heart around, but not
quite turned my head. ■

Discussion and Writing Questions

1. Quindlen describes two positions she has taken about abortion. What are
   they?

2. In which paragraph does the author begin to express doubts about
   abortion? Why does she have these doubts?

3. By the end of her essay, how does Quindlen feel about abortion?

4. What types of proof does the author use in her argument?

Writing Assignments

1. Write on an issue about which you are, like Quindlen, undecided. Choose
   a topic you know fairly well so that you can present solid arguments for
   both sides. Be objective, but let your reader know which side you finally
   find more persuasive.

2. Do you believe that teenagers should be required to inform their parents
   before obtaining an abortion? Argue in favor of or against this position.

10. foiled: tricked, confused
11. viable: able to live
12. amniocentesis: a medical procedure for checking the amniotic fluid in the uterus
13. inexplicably: unexplainably
14. *in utero:* in the mother's uterus

3. Quindlen first gained experience with the abortion issue as a freshman dorm counselor. Write about a time that you once counseled, or gave advice, to a friend in need. Your friend might have been contemplating an abortion, like some of the young women Quindlen describes. She or he may have been fighting with a mate or having a problem with money, career decisions, or school.

On Kids and Couples

Francine Klagsbrun

In what ways does a new child change a couple's relationship? Francine Klagsbrun, in her interviews with a number of adults, uncovers many examples—some humorous, some quite serious.

Once a couple have a child, everything in life changes. Raising children may be the most rewarding job in the world, but it is also undoubtedly the most difficult—an "impossible profession," Salvador Minuchin[1] called it. Or in the words of one mother, "With kids, you're damned if you do and you're damned if you don't, meaning you never never know what's right." True, there are hundreds of experts out there telling us in books and articles what's right. The problem is that what's right with one is wrong with the next. Fashions in childrearing change and so does expert advice. In the end, as everyone knows, you and your spouse and your child have to figure out how to handle each other. **1**

Having a child is like getting married: you have to experience it to understand it. As prepared as anybody is, nobody is really prepared, at least not for the first child. The way you eat, the way you play, the way you work, the way you think—they all become different with the arrival of a baby. One of my favorite anecdotes[2] was told to me by a professor who described bringing his wife home from the hospital with their beautiful newborn son. They settled the baby in his sparkling bassinette, played with him for a while, then put on their coats and headed out to get some pizza. Partway through the door his wife cried, "Oh, my God, we left the baby alone," and ran back. They had simply forgotten that a new person had joined their lives and that many years would pass before they could casually leave the house together without thinking about him. **2**

For a couple, a child is an interruption—a constant interruption that needs to be fed, cared for, loved. The baby interrupts the flow between parents, the one-on-one intimacy that had existed before. A third being now becomes a focal point in the marriage; he or she also becomes a medium[3] through whom flow the issues and tensions with which partners themselves may be grappling. In her humorous but serious novel *Heartburn*, about the **3**

1. Salvador Minuchin: well-known family therapist
2. anecdotes: brief stories
3. medium: the means by which the parents communicate with each other

breakup of her marriage, Nora Ephron describes the effects of having a child this way:

"After Sam was born I remember thinking that no one had ever told me **4** how much I would love my child; now, of course, I realized something no one ever tells you: that a child is a grenade. When you have a baby you set off an explosion in your marriage, and when the dust settles, your marriage is different from what it was." And she goes on: "All those idiotically lyrical articles about sharing childrearing duties never mention that, nor do they allude to[4] something else that happens when a baby is born, which is that all the power struggles of the marriage have a new playing field. The baby wakes up in the middle of the night, and instead of jumping out of bed, you lie there thinking: whose turn is it? If it's your turn, you have to get up; if it's his turn, then why is he still lying there asleep while you're awake wondering whose turn it is?"

Among the people I interviewed, arguments were said to center around **5** children more than around any other issue in the marriage. Neither money nor sex nor in-laws nor work was mentioned as often as children as sources of disagreement in a marriage. For some couples, the tensions begin early on, almost as soon as the baby is born. A wife's deep involvement with a newborn baby can make her husband feel left out, almost like a sibling whose mother has abandoned him for the other child, the younger and cuter one. In turn, the husband's sullenness or jealousy can push the wife ever closer to the baby for comfort and emotional support. Even when a husband involves himself in caring for a baby, as so many do now, it may be hard for him to break through the physical and psychological closeness of a mother to her infant, especially if the mother is breast-feeding.

Added to this issue, a certain amount of sexual distancing often takes **6** place after the birth of a child. For a woman, the disinterest may be due to hormonal changes or to the enormous physical satisfaction she gets from holding and cuddling her baby. For both parents, there is the exhaustion and emotional drain of caring for an infant, an exhaustion that may continue even as a baby gets older and certainly as other children arrive. Children's demands and needs tire parents out, and the preoccupation with children in a family can shift interests and energies away from sexual desires. (They shift back again, of course, and many couples help things along by taking time out for themselves—getting a babysitter or a family member to stay with the baby during evenings or weekends while they concentrate on each other.)

Children may inhibit sex also simply because they are *there*, in the next **7** room or, at the most unexpected times, in parents' rooms. A topic of perennial[5] interest among parents is whether to lock their bedroom door so a child cannot enter when they may be making love, and what to say to a child who does see them in the act. In either case, a child's presence in a family may make sex between partners more self-conscious than ever before.

It may also raise career tensions. Many a couple, like Kimberly and **8** Randy, who are cool and confident before a child is born about their ability to handle a child and two careers, find the actuality more difficult than

4. allude to: hint at, refer to
5. perennial: happening again and again

expected. The smoothest-running dual-career families are those that can afford, and find, excellent help to care for home and children. In most others, partners constantly juggle and trade off time with each other. Who takes off from work to take the baby to the pediatrician, later to the dentist? Who stays home with a child when she's sick? And who loses a workday to go to a school play (an activity at which no one can substitute for a parent)? "When you're a working mother, you give up everything except your work and your family," said one woman. Working fathers make their sacrifices too, and the sorting out of who does what can generate anxieties in the marriage.

Then there are less expected work issues. For some men, liberation flies out the window when a baby is carried through the door. No matter how accepting they may be of a wife's work or career, once they have a child, they want their wives to be home, if not full time, then much of the time. They may be willing to "help out," and they may agree to hiring an outsider to handle some duties, but they expect, as their fathers expected, the major responsibility to rest with their wives. In such situations, the baby becomes the catalyst for a deeper struggle going on between the couple, the power struggle Nora Ephron describes, but even more, the struggle over roles and work and each spouse's interpretation of the marriage. **9**

"I just think," said one husband to me in front of his wife, "that a baby needs a parent at home. I think one of us needs to be here for him now, and one of us will need to be here later when he gets older and goes off to school and comes home from school." **10**

"Does she have to be the one who's here with the baby? Isn't it possible for you to be here some of the time?" I asked. **11**

"I can't organize my work that way," he answered quickly (he's a dentist), "but Debbie can find part-time work." **12**

Debbie shrugged. "We're negotiating," she said, as if wanting to stop the conversation before it got pushed into a track from which she knew she would have trouble extricating[6] it. "The problem for me is he makes more money than I do, so I'm on weaker grounds. But we'll work this thing out." **13**

I expect they will, but it will take quite a bit of negotiating. The baby has set in motion other conflicts between them that have to do with how they view themselves and each other. Had it not been for the baby, the dispute might have taken other forms or may not even have arisen for many years. It has arisen now, and the baby became the trigger for setting it off. **14**

Children can be explosives in other areas. The parents of four children portrayed their most heated battles as resulting from the kids' sloppiness and their way of strewing belongings in every room of the house. The husband would shout at the children, and when his wife tried to calm him down, they would get into a brawl of their own in which he would accuse her of being too easy on the children. The longer we spoke, however, the clearer it became to me (and to them too, I believe, although we didn't articulate it) that his anger at the children about their sloppiness was also an expression of his anger at his wife's careless housekeeping. "Gail can leave an open can of tomato sauce in the refrigerator for weeks, until it's covered with green mold, and not even notice," he said with a tight smile. Or "I've had friends come to visit and they go into the kitchen to see if the oven is as dirty as I **15**

6. extricating: getting out of a difficult situation

told them it is. And it is." Or "I'm used to seeing cobwebs wherever I look in this house." Instead of shouting directly at his wife about her habits, which may be too threatening to their relationship, he detours his anger through the kids. She responds by defending the children, which is also a way of defending herself, and both avoid an open battle around the things they dislike most about each other.

Children are sometimes used more openly as an excuse to cover up for **16** difficulties between parents. A spouse who wants to avoid sex, for example, may use the excuse that the children will hear, and then will complain that kids interfere with sex in marriage. In more serious situations, children become scapegoats[7] for the angers and disappointments of mates. The parents may blame the child for everything that is wrong between them—"If Tommy weren't doing so badly in school, we would have no problems in this family"—refusing to recognize that Tommy's difficulties may be not the cause but the result of family troubles. ▪

Discussion and Writing Questions

1. Klagsbrun describes several kinds of conflict that can arise between people when they have a child. What are they? Can you think of others that she doesn't mention?

2. The author points out that the child "becomes a medium" for a couple's issues and tensions (paragraph 3). What does she mean?

3. Which of the examples do you think is the most serious? Why?

4. Not every topic sentence of this essay supports the thesis statement directly, yet the essay is well organized. How does Klagsbrun develop her thesis? That is, how does she organize her essay?

Writing Assignments

1. As this reading selection illustrates, we all face stress in our lives: parenthood, job stress, family pressures. How we handle stress is important for our happiness and health. Write about effective ways of handling stress. You may want to give examples of techniques that have worked for you, such as getting some exercise, talking with a friend, or meditating on a peaceful scene.

2. Discuss how you balance two or more demands on your time. You might write about having a family and attending school or juggling family, school, and a job, for example. You might narrate a particular morning you remember as you prepared your child for school while getting yourself dressed. Or you may write about the process of a daily routine.

3. The author says that you have to experience the birth of a child in order to understand that event (paragraph 2). What event from your own life

7. scapegoats: people who take the blame unfairly for others

would you characterize this way? Perhaps you feel that you didn't really know what "going to college" was all about until you attended college. Or maybe you changed your notion of the ideal romance after you really fell in love. Try to retell the experience so vividly that the reader will be able to understand it.

Living with My VCR

Nora Ephron

Nora Ephron writes about many topics, often with humor. In this essay, she describes her complicated feelings about an item many of us take for granted: the video-cassette recorder, or VCR.

1 When all this started, two Christmases ago, I did not have a video-cassette recorder. What I had was a position on video-cassette recorders. I was against them. It seemed to me that the fundamental idea of the VCR—which is that if you go out and miss what's on television, you can always watch it later—flew in the face of almost the only thing I truly believed—which is that the whole point of going out is to miss what's on television. Let's face it: Part of being a grown-up is that every day you have to choose between going out at night or staying home, and it is one of life's unhappy truths that there is not enough time to do both.

2 Finally, though, I broke down, but not entirely. I did not buy a video-cassette recorder. I rented one. And I didn't rent one for myself—I myself intended to stand firm and hold to my only principle. I rented one for my children. For $29 a month, I would tape "The Wizard of Oz" and "Mary Poppins" and "Born Free," and my children would be able to watch them from time to time. In six months, when my rental contract expired, I would reevaluate.

3 For quite a while, I taped for my children. Of course I had to subscribe to Home Box Office and Cinemax in addition to my normal cable service, for $19 more a month—but for the children. I taped "Oliver" and "Annie" and "My Fair Lady" for the children. And then I stopped taping for the children—who don't watch much television, in any case—and started to tape for myself.

4 I now tape for myself all the time. I tape when I am out, I tape when I am at home and doing other things, and I tape when I am asleep. At this very moment, as I am typing, I am taping. The entire length of my bedroom bookshelf has been turned over to video cassettes, mostly of movies; they are numbered and indexed and stacked in order in a household where absolutely nothing else is. Occasionally I find myself browsing through publications like Video Review and worrying whether I shouldn't switch to chrome-based videotape or have my heads cleaned or upgrade to a machine that does six or seven things at once and can be set to tape six or seven months in advance. No doubt I will find myself shopping at some Video Village for racks and storage systems especially made for what is known as "the serious collector."

How this happened, how I became a compulsive[1] videotaper, is a mystery **5**
to me, because my position on video-cassette recorders is very much the
same as the one I started with. I am still against them. Now, though, I am
against them for different reasons: Now I hate them out of knowledge
rather than ignorance. The other technological break-throughs that have
made their way into my life after my initial pigheaded opposition to them—
like the electric typewriter and the Cuisinart—have all settled peacefully
into my home. I never think about them except when I'm using them, and
when I'm using them I take them for granted. They do exactly what I want
them to do. I put the slicing disk into the Cuisinart, and damned if the thing
doesn't slice things up just the way it's supposed to. But there's no taking a
VCR for granted. It squats there, next to the television, ready to rebuke[2]
any fool who expects something of it.

A child can operate a VCR, of course. Only a few maneuvers are required **6**
to tape something, and only a few more are required to tape something while
you are out. You must set the timer to the correct time you wish the record-
ing to begin and end. You must punch the channel selector. You must insert a
videotape. And, on my set, you must switch the "on" button to "time record."
Theoretically, you can then go out and have a high old time, knowing that
even if you waste the evening, your video-cassette recorder will not.

Sometimes things work out. Sometimes I return home, rewind the tape, **7**
and discover that the machine has recorded exactly what I'd hoped it would.
But more often than not, what is on the tape is not at all what I'd intended; in
fact, the moments leading up to the revelation of what is actually on my
video-cassettes are without doubt the most suspenseful of my humdrum[3]
existence. As I rewind the tape, I have no idea of what, if anything, will be on
it; as I press the "play" button, I have not a clue as to what in particular
has gone wrong. All I ever know for certain is that something has.

Usually it's my fault. I admit it. I have mis-set the timer or channel **8**
selector or misread the newspaper listing. I have knelt at the foot of my
machine and methodically, carefully, painstakingly set it—and set it wrong.
This is extremely upsetting to me—I am normally quite competent when it
comes to machines—but I can live with it. What is far more disturbing are
the times when what has gone wrong is not my fault at all but the fault of the
outside forces over which I have no control whatsoever. The program listing
in the newspaper lists the channel incorrectly. The cable guide inaccurately
lists the length of the movie, lopping[4] off the last 10 minutes. The evening's
schedule of television programming is thrown off by an athletic event. The
educational station is having a fund-raiser.

You would be amazed at how often outside forces affect a video-cassette **9**
recorder, and I think I am safe in saying that video-cassette recorders are
the only household appliances that outside forces are even relevant to. As a
result, my video-cassette library is a raggedy collection of near misses: "The
Thin Man" without the opening; "King Kong" without the ending; a football
game instead of "Murder, She Wrote"; dozens of PBS auctions and fund-

1. compulsive: obsessive, driven
2. rebuke: scold
3. humdrum: boring, ordinary
4. lopping: cutting

raisers instead of dozens of episodes of "Masterpiece Theater." All told, my success rate at videotaping is even lower than my success rate at buying clothes I turn out to like as much as I did in the store; the machine provides more opportunities per week to make mistakes than anything else in my life.

Every summer and at Christmastime, I re-evaluate my six-month rental **10** contract. I have three options: I can buy the video-cassette recorder, which I would never do because I hate it so much; I can cancel the contract and turn in the machine, which I would never do because I am so addicted to video-taping; or I can go on renting. I go on renting. In two years I have spent enough money renting to buy two video-cassette recorders at the discount electronics place in the neighborhood, but I don't care. Renting is my way of deluding[5] myself that I have some power over my VCR; it's my way of believing that I can still some day reject the machine in an ultimate way (by sending it back)—or else forgive it (by buying it)—for all the times it has rejected me.

In the meantime, I have my pathetic but ever-expanding collection of **11** cassettes. "Why don't you just rent the movies?" a friend said to me recently, after I finished complaining about the fact that my tape of "The Maltese Falcon" now has a segment of "Little House on the Prairie" in the middle of it. Rent them? What a bizarre suggestion. Then I would have to watch them. And I don't watch my videotapes. I don't have time. I would virtually have to watch my videotapes for the next two years just to catch up with what my VCR has recorded so far; and in any event, even if I did have time, the VCR would be taping and would therefore be unavailable for use in viewing.

So I merely accumulate video-cassettes. I haven't accumulated anything **12** this mindlessly since my days in college, when I was obsessed with filling my bookshelf, it didn't matter with what; what mattered was that I believed that if I had a lot of books, it would say something about my intelligence and taste. On some level, I suppose I believe that if I have a lot of video-cassettes, it will say something—not about my intelligence or taste, but about my intentions. I intend to live long enough to have time to watch my videotapes. Any way you look at it, that means forever. ■

Discussion and Writing Questions

1. Why does Ephron seem to have a love-hate relationship with her VCR?

2. Does the author indicate why she changed from (1) a person who refused to buy a VCR to (2) a person who taped movies "for the children" to (3) a person who taped compulsively?

3. Why do you suppose a person might become addicted to taping movies, watching TV, buying tools or gadgets, or engaging in some other, similar activity?

4. How do you know that this essay is not written with complete serious-ness? Give examples of sentences and paragraphs from the essay that suggest the author has a humorous attitude toward her subject.

5. deluding: fooling

Writing Assignments

1. Have you had an experience like Ephron's in which you moved from completely resisting something to completely embracing it? Or perhaps you've had the opposite experience, in which you enjoyed and accepted something at first but later rejected it. Discuss your experience. Try to show your reader just how you changed.

2. Write about the merits or drawbacks of a particular kind of technology. Like Ephron, you might choose to write about an item found in the home: the microwave, electric shaver, or pocket calculator. Or you may want to discuss a larger social issue: the reliance of modern medicine on drugs and surgery, the safety concerns associated with nuclear energy, or the effects on viewers of live television coverage of natural or human-caused disasters.

3. Using process, explain the steps to take in using a certain machine. You might write about operating a strange or difficult machine or one you know well. Write a humorous essay if you wish.

The Plot Against People

Russell Baker

Have you ever suspected that your appliances *plan* their breakdowns for the sole purpose of driving you crazy? Here, the Pulitzer Prize–winning author and humorist Russell Baker argues an absurd thesis: objects are out to defeat us.

Inanimate[1] objects are classified scientifically into three major categories— **1** those that break down, those that get lost, and those that don't work.

The goal of all inanimate objects is to resist man and ultimately to defeat **2** him, and the three major classifications are based on the method each object uses to achieve its purpose. As a general rule, any object capable of breaking down at the moment when it is most needed will do so. The automobile is typical of the category.

With the cunning peculiar to its breed, the automobile never breaks **3** down while entering a filling station which has a large staff of idle mechanics. It waits until it reaches a downtown intersection in the middle of the rush hour, or until it is fully loaded with family and luggage on the Ohio Turnpike. Thus it creates maximum inconvenience, frustration, and irritability, thereby reducing its owner's lifespan.

Washing machines, garbage disposals, lawn mowers, furnaces, TV sets, **4** tape recorders, slide projectors—all are in league with the automobile to take their turn at breaking down whenever life threatens to flow smoothly for their enemies.

1. inanimate: nonliving

Many inanimate objects, of course, find it extremely difficult to break 5 down. Pliers, for example, and gloves and keys are almost totally incapable of breaking down. Therefore, they have had to evolve[2] a different technique for resisting man.

They get lost. Science has still not solved the mystery of how they do it, 6 and no man has ever caught one of them in the act. The most plausible[3] theory is that they have developed a secret method of locomotion which they are able to conceal from human eyes.

It is not uncommon for a pair of pliers to climb all the way from the cel- 7 lar to the attic in its single-minded determination to raise its owner's blood pressure. Keys have been known to burrow three feet under mattresses. Women's purses, despite their great weight, frequently travel through six or seven rooms to find hiding space under a couch.

Scientists have been struck by the fact that things that break down 8 virtually never get lost, while things that get lost hardly ever break down. A furnace, for example, will invariably break down at the depth of the first winter cold wave, but it will never get lost. A woman's purse hardly ever breaks down; it almost invariably chooses to get lost.

Some persons believe this constitutes evidence that inanimate objects 9 are not entirely hostile to man. After all, they point out, a furnace could infuriate a man even more thoroughly by getting lost than by breaking down, just as a glove could upset him far more by breaking down than by getting lost.

Not everyone agrees, however, that this indicates a conciliatory[4] 10 attitude. Many say it merely proves that furnaces, gloves and pliers are incredibly stupid.

The third class of objects—those that don't work—is the most curious of 11 all. These include such objects as barometers, car clocks, cigarette lighters, flashlights and toy-train locomotives. It is inaccurate, of course, to say that they *never* work. They work once, usually for the first few hours after being brought home, and then quit. Thereafter, they never work again.

In fact, it is widely assumed that they are built for the purpose of not 12 working. Some people have reached advanced ages without ever seeing some of these objects—barometers, for example—in working order.

Science is utterly baffled by the entire category. There are many theo- 13 ries about it. The most interesting holds that the things that don't work have attained the highest state possible for an inanimate object, the state to which things that break down and things that get lost can still only aspire.[5] ▪

Discussion and Writing Questions

1. Part of the humor in this essay comes from Baker's imitation of scientific writing. Which sentence introduces the "scientific tone"? Which words establish that tone? Why is the end of that sentence funny?

2. evolve: develop
3. plausible: likely; apparently true
4. conciliatory: trying to be friendly
5. aspire: hope to achieve

2. How does Baker classify objects? That is, according to Baker, what are the three major categories into which objects can be divided?

3. Which category does Baker suggest is the "highest" of the three? Why?

4. "Objects" are nonliving things, but Baker constantly refers to them as "*inanimate* objects"—as if he needs to remind us that the objects are not alive. Why would he want to do that? Yet how does he also suggest that the objects really are alive? What is his purpose in doing so?

Writing Assignments

1. Have you had any frustrating experiences with objects such as Baker describes? Write about one object that always seems to get the better of you. What problems do you have with it? Do you ever feel that it has a mind of its own?

2. Have you developed a creative technique for finding lost or misplaced objects? For example, some people ask themselves where they might go if they were their own missing car keys. Describe a situation in which you lost something and then were able to find it by using an unusual or imaginative process.

3. In paragraph 11, Baker describes objects that never work or break down soon after they are purchased. Have you ever purchased an object that was defective and had to be returned to the store? Describe the incident. Were you upset? Was the clerk helpful or did he or she blame you for the problem? Did you have to prove that it wasn't your fault? What finally happened?

A Life Defined by Losses and Delights

Nancy Mairs

Nancy Mairs contracted multiple sclerosis (MS) when she was twenty-nine. In this essay, she defines who she is and is not in terms of this disease, as she describes the enormous impact MS has made on her life.

I am a cripple. I choose this word to name me. I choose from among several possibilities, the most common of which are "handicapped" or "disabled." I made the choice a number of years ago, unaware of my motives for doing so. People—crippled or not—wince at the word "cripple," as they do not at "handicapped" or "disabled." Perhaps I want them to wince. I want them to see me as a tough customer, one to whom the fates/gods/viruses have not been kind, but who can face the truth of her existence squarely. As a cripple, I swagger.   1

"Cripple" seems to me a clean word, straightforward and precise. As a **2** lover of words, I like the accuracy with which it describes my condition: I have lost the full use of my limbs. "Disabled," by contrast, suggests any incapacity, physical or mental. And I certainly don't like "handicapped," which implies that I have deliberately been put at a disadvantage, by whom I can't imagine, in order to equalize chances in the great race of life. These words seem to me to be moving away from my condition, to be widening the gap between word and reality. Most remote is the recently coined euphemism[1] "differently abled," which strikes me as pure verbal garbage designed, by its ability to describe anyone, to describe no one.

I haven't always been crippled, a fact for which I am grateful. To be **3** whole of limb is, I know from experience, infinitely more pleasant and useful than to be crippled; and if that knowledge leaves me open to bitterness at my loss, the physical soundness I once enjoyed (though I did not enjoy it half enough) is well worth the occasional stab of regret.

When I was 28 I started to trip and drop things. What at first seemed my **4** natural clumsiness soon became too pronounced to shrug off. I consulted a neurologist, who told me that I had a brain tumor. About a year and a half later I developed a blurred spot in one eye. I had, at last, the episodes requisite for a diagnosis: multiple sclerosis. I have never been sorry for the doctor's initial misdiagnosis, however. For almost a week, until the negative results of the tests were in, I thought that I was going to die right away. Every day for the past nearly 10 years, then, has been a kind of gift. I accept all gifts.

Multiple sclerosis is a chronic degenerative disease of the central ner- **5** vous system; during its course, which is unpredictable and uncontrollable, one may lose vision, hearing, speech, and ability to walk, control of bladder and/or bowels, strength in any or all extremities, sensitivity to touch, vibration, and/or pain, potency, coordination of movements—the list of possibilities is lengthy and, yes, horrifying. One may also lose one's sense of humor. That's the easiest to lose and the hardest to survive without.

In the past 10 years, I have sustained some of these losses; my disease **6** has been slowly progressive. My left leg is now so weak that I walk with the aid of a brace and a cane. I no longer have much use of my left hand. Now my right side is weakening as well. Overall, though, I've been lucky so far; the terrain left me has been ample enough to continue many activities that absorb me: writing, teaching, raising children and plants and snakes, reading, speaking publicly about MS and depression, even playing bridge with people honorable enough to let me scatter cards without sneaking a peek.

Lest[2] I begin to sound like Pollyanna, however, let me say that I don't **7** like having MS. I hate it. My life holds realities—harsh ones, some of them— that no right-minded human being ought to accept without grumbling: One of them is fatigue. I know of no one with MS who does not complain of bone-weariness; I wake up in the morning feeling the way most people do at the end of a bad day, and I take it from there.

---

1. euphemism: a word or phrase used instead of an offensive word or phrase
2. lest: out of fear that

I am lucky that my predilections[3] were already solitary, sedentary,[4] and **8** bookish. I am a superb, if messy, cook. I play a fiendish game of Scrabble. I like to sit on my front steps with my husband as we make sure that the sun gets down once more behind the sharp childish scrawl of the Tucson Mountains.

This lively plenty has its bleak complement, of course, in all the things I **9** can no longer do. I will never run, except in dreams, and I can no longer pick up babies, play piano, braid my hair. I am immobilized by acute attacks of depression, which may or may not be related to MS.

These two elements, the plenty and the privation,[5] are never pure, nor **10** are the delight and wretchedness that accompany them. The most important struts in the framework of my existence, of course, are my husband and children. Dismayingly few marriages survive the MS test, and why should they? Most 22- and 19-year-olds, like George and me, can vow in clear conscience, after a childhood of chicken pox and summer colds, to keep one another in sickness and in health so long as they both shall live. Not many are equipped for the dismay, the extra work, the boredom that a degenerative disease can insinuate[6] into a relationship. Children experience similar stresses when faced with a crippled parent, and they are more helpless, since parents and children can't usually get divorced. Deprived of legal divorce, the child can at least deny the mother's disability, even her existence, forgetting to tell her about recitals and PTA meetings, never inviting friends to the house. Many do.

But I've been limping along for 10 years now, and so far George and the **11** children are still at my left elbow, holding tight. Anne and Matthew vacuum floors and dust furniture and rake up dog droppings with just enough grumbling so I know that they don't have brain fever. And far from hiding me, they're forever welcoming gaggles[7] of friends while I'm wandering through the house in Anne's filmy pink baby doll pajamas. And they all yell at me, laugh at some of my jokes, in short, treat me as an ordinary human being. I think they like me. Unless they're faking. . . .

Faking. There's the rub. Tugging at the fringes of my consciousness **12** always is the terror that people are kind to me only because I'm a cripple. My mother almost shattered me once, with that instinct mothers have for striking blows along the fault-lines of their children's hearts, by telling me, in an attack on my selfishness, "We all have to make allowances for you, of course, because of the way you are." She was awfully angry but at the time I felt my worst fear, suddenly realized. I could bear being called selfish: I am. But I couldn't bear the corroboration[8] that those around me were doing what I'd always suspected them of doing, professing fondness while silently putting up with me because of the way I am. A cripple. I've been a little cracked ever since.

3. predilections: interests, inclinations
4. sedentary: pertaining to sitting or not being active
5. privation: lack
6. insinuate: work slowly
7. gaggles: groups
8. corroboration: confirmation, assurance

Along with this fear comes a relentless pressure to please. Part of the **13** pressure arises from social expectations. In our society, anyone who deviates[9] from the norm had better find some way to compensate. Like fat people, who are expected to be jolly, cripples must bear their lot meekly and cheerfully. A grumpy cripple isn't playing by the rules. And much of the pressure is self-generated. Early on I vowed that, if I had to have MS, by God I was going to do it well. This is a class act, ladies and gentlemen.

Because I hate being crippled, I sometimes hate myself for being a crip- **14** ple. Over the years I have come to expect—even accept—attacks of violent self-loathing. Physical imperfection, even freed of moral disapprobation,[10] still defies and violates the ideal, especially for women, whose confinement in their bodies as objects of desire is far from over. Today's ideal woman, who lives on the glossy pages of dozens of magazines, seems to be between the ages of 18 and 25; her hair has body, her underarms are dry; she has a career but is still a fabulous cook, especially of meals that take less than 20 minutes to prepare; she jogs, swims, plays tennis, sails, but does not bowl. Though usually white and often blonde, she may be black, Hispanic, Asian, or Native American, so long as she is unusually sleek. She may be old, provided she is selling a laxative or is Lauren Bacall. But she is never a cripple.

At my age, however, I don't spend much time thinking about my appear- **15** ance. The burning egocentricity of adolescence, which assures one that all the world is looking all the time, has passed; I'm also too old to believe in the accuracy of self-image. The self-loathing I feel is neither physically nor intellectually substantial. What I hate is not me but a disease.

I am not a disease. **16**

And a disease is not—at least not single-handedly—going to determine **17** who I am.

I learned that one never finishes adjusting to MS. One does not, after all, **18** finish adjusting to life, and MS is simply a fact of my life—not my favorite fact, of course—but as ordinary as my nose and my yellow Mazda station wagon. It may at any time get worse, but no amount of worry can prepare me for a new loss. My life is a lesson in losses. I learn one at a time.

The absence of a cure often makes MS patients bitter toward their doc- **19** tors. Doctors are, after all, the priests of modern society whose business is to heal. Doctors too think of themselves as healers, and for this reason many have trouble dealing with MS patients, whose disease in its intransigence[11] defeats their aims and mocks their skills. Too few doctors, it is true, treat their patients as whole human beings, but the reverse is also true. I have always tried to be gentle with my doctors, who often have more at stake in terms of ego than I do. I may be frustrated by the incurability of my disease, but I am not diminished by it, and they are.

This gentleness is part of the reason I'm not sorry to be a cripple. I didn't **20** have it before. It has opened my life enormously.

If a cure were found, would I take it? In a minute. I may be a cripple, but **21** I'm only occasionally a loony and never a saint. Anyway, in my brand of theology God doesn't give bonus points for a limp. ∎

9. deviates: turns away from, does not conform
10. disapprobation: blame, condemnation
11. intransigence: stubbornness

Discussion and Writing Questions

1. Why does the author call herself "a cripple" (paragraph 1)? Why does she prefer that word to any other currently in use?

2. How limiting does Mairs find MS to be? Does she find any positive aspects to having the disease?

3. Why does the author worry so much that underneath their helpfulness people might just feel sorry for her? Do you think this is a common concern among people in her situation?

4. In which paragraphs does the author present definitions? What words does she define?

Writing Assignments

1. Write about a personality trait or a physical fact that you believe defines who you are. For instance, you may see yourself as "fun-loving," "people-pleasing," "overweight," or "athletic." Define this trait for the reader and describe its importance in your life.

2. Use comparison and contrast to write about the good that can arise from a bad situation. First, state the problem itself (like an illness, an accident, being fired from a job, or running out of money while taking a trip). Then discuss the good that came out of it.

3. Mairs discusses how having an illness has clarified for her what she enjoys most in her life. Is there an activity you feel you couldn't do without? Describe this activity and explain why you would always want to be able to pursue it.

Three Types of Resistance to Oppression

Martin Luther King, Jr.

Martin Luther King, Jr., the great civil rights leader of the 1960s, studied the teachings of Mahatma Gandhi, the spiritual leader who struggled for Indian independence from British rule. Gandhi, and King after him, preached nonviolent resistance as a means of achieving social goals.

Oppressed people deal with their oppression in three characteristic ways. 1
One way is acquiescence:[1] the oppressed resign themselves to their doom. They tacitly[2] adjust themselves to oppression, and thereby become conditioned to it. In every movement toward freedom some of the oppressed prefer to remain oppressed. Almost 2800 years ago Moses set out to lead the

1. acquiescence: acceptance
2. tacitly: quietly, implicitly

children of Israel from the slavery of Egypt to the freedom of the promised land. He soon discovered that slaves do not always welcome their deliverers. They become accustomed to being slaves. They would rather bear those ills they have, as Shakespeare pointed out, than flee to others that they know not of. They prefer the "fleshpots of Egypt" to the ordeals of emancipation.

There is such a thing as the freedom of exhaustion. Some people are so **2** worn down by the yoke of oppression that they give up. A few years ago in the slum areas of Atlanta, a Negro guitarist used to sing almost daily: "Ben down so long that down don't bother me." This is the type of negative freedom and resignation that often engulfs the life of the oppressed.

But this is not the way out. To accept passively an unjust system is to **3** coöperate with that system; thereby the oppressed become as evil as the oppressor. Noncoöperation with evil is as much a moral obligation as is coöperation with good. The oppressed must never allow the conscience of the oppressor to slumber. Religion reminds every man that he is his brother's keeper. To accept injustice or segregation passively is to say to the oppressor that his actions are morally right. It is a way of allowing his conscience to fall asleep. At this moment the oppressed fails to be his brother's keeper. So acquiescence—while often the easier way—is not the moral way. It is the way of the coward. The Negro cannot win the respect of his oppressor by acquiescing; he merely increases the oppressor's arrogance and contempt. Acquiescence is interpreted as proof of the Negro's inferiority. The Negro cannot win the respect of the white people of the South or the peoples of the world if he is willing to sell the future of his children for his personal and immediate comfort and safety.

A second way that oppressed people sometimes deal with oppression is **4** to resort to physical violence and corroding hatred. Violence often brings about momentary results. Nations have frequently won their independence in battle. But in spite of temporary victories, violence never brings permanent peace. It solves no social problem; it merely creates new and more complicated ones.

Violence as a way of achieving racial justice is both impractical and **5** immoral. It is impractical because it is a descending spiral ending in destruction for all. The old law of an eye for an eye leaves everybody blind. It is immoral because it seeks to humiliate the opponent rather than win his understanding; it seeks to annihilate rather than to convert. Violence is immoral because it thrives on hatred rather than love. It destroys community and makes brotherhood impossible. It leaves society in monologue rather than dialogue. Violence ends by defeating itself. It creates bitterness in the survivors and brutality in the destroyers. A voice echoes through time saying to every potential Peter, "Put up your sword." History is cluttered with the wreckage of nations that failed to follow this command.

If the American Negro and other victims of oppression succumb[3] to the **6** temptation of using violence in the struggle for freedom, future generations will be the recipients of a desolate[4] night of bitterness, and our chief legacy to them will be an endless reign of meaningless chaos. Violence is not the way.

---

3. succumb: give in
4. desolate: empty, barren

The third way open to oppressed people in their quest for freedom is the   **7**
way of nonviolent resistance. Like the synthesis[5] in Hegelian[6] philosophy,
the principle of nonviolent resistance seeks to reconcile the truths of two
opposites—acquiescence and violence—while avoiding the extremes and
immoralities of both. The nonviolent resister agrees with the person who
acquiesces that one should not be physically aggressive toward his opponent;
but he balances the equation by agreeing with the person of violence that
evil must be resisted. He avoids the nonresistance of the former and the violent resistance of the latter. With nonviolent resistance, no individual or
group need submit to any wrong, nor need anyone resort to violence in order
to right a wrong.

It seems to me that this is the method that must guide the actions of the   **8**
Negro in the present crisis in race relations. Through nonviolent resistance
the Negro will be able to rise to the noble height of opposing the unjust
system while loving the perpetrators of the system. The Negro must work
passionately and unrelentingly for full stature as a citizen, but he must
not use inferior methods to gain it. He must never come to terms with
falsehood, malice,[7] hate, or destruction.

Nonviolent resistance makes it possible for the Negro to remain in the   **9**
South and struggle for his rights. The Negro's problem will not be solved by
running away. He cannot listen to the glib[8] suggestion of those who would
urge him to migrate en masse[9] to other sections of the country. By grasping
his great opportunity in the South he can make a lasting contribution to the
moral strength of the nation and set a sublime example of courage for generations yet unborn.

By nonviolent resistance, the Negro can also enlist all men of good will   **10**
in his struggle for equality. The problem is not a purely racial one, with
Negroes set against whites. In the end, it is not a struggle between people
at all, but a tension between justice and injustice. Nonviolent resistance
is not aimed against oppressors but against oppression. Under its banner
consciences, not racial groups, are enlisted.

If the Negro is to achieve the goal of integration, he must organize him-   **11**
self into a militant and nonviolent mass movement. All three elements are
indispensable. The movement for equality and justice can only be a success
if it has both a mass and militant character; the barriers to be overcome
require both. Nonviolence is an imperative in order to bring about ultimate
community.

A mass movement of militant quality that is not at the same time com-   **12**
mitted to nonviolence tends to generate conflict, which in turn breeds anarchy.[10] The support of the participants and the sympathy of the uncommitted
are both inhibited by the threat that bloodshed will engulf the community.
This reaction in turn encourages the opposition to threaten and resort

5. synthesis: the combining of separate elements to form a whole
6. Hegelian: pertaining to the nineteenth-century German philosopher Georg Hegel
7. malice: ill will
8. glib: unthinking, too easy
9. en masse: as a group, all together
10. anarchy: lawlessness

to force. When, however, the mass movement repudiates[11] violence while moving resolutely[12] toward its goal, its opponents are revealed as the instigators[13] and practitioners of violence if it occurs. Then public support is magnetically attracted to the advocates of nonviolence, while those who employ violence are literally disarmed by overwhelming sentiment against their stand. ■

Discussion and Writing Questions

1. According to King, what are the three ways in which oppressed people respond to their oppression?

2. What does the author mean by "the freedom of exhaustion" (paragraph 2)?

3. King writes that violence as a response to oppression is "impractical and immoral" (paragraph 5). Do you agree? Are there cases in which violence is justified?

4. Does King present the three types of resistance to oppression in any particular order? Least to most important? Most to least? Explain your reasoning.

Writing Assignments

1. Classify three different types of love, hate, or friendship that someone can experience. The categories for love might be spiritual love, romantic love, and friendly love, for example. Make sure that each of your categories relates directly to your thesis statement.

2. Discuss the differences between a person who gives in to hardship (illness, poverty, or some other difficulty) and one who refuses to give in. How are the two people different?

3. Since the time of the civil rights movement, many obstacles to achieving racial equality in this country have been removed. On the other hand, inequalities in employment, housing, educational opportunities, and health care still exist. Discuss your views on the state of racial equality.

11. repudiates: rejects
12. resolutely: with determination
13. instigators: people who start something

Quotation Bank

This collection of wise and humorous statements has been assembled for you to read, enjoy, and use in a variety of ways as you write. You might choose quotations that you particularly agree or disagree with and use them as the basis of journal entries and writing assignments. Sometimes when writing a paragraph or an essay, you may find it useful to include a quotation to support a point you are making. Or you may simply want to read through these quotations for ideas and for fun. As you come across other intriguing statements by writers, add them to the list—or write some of your own.

Education

Knowledge is power.   **1**
—*Francis Bacon*

Everyone is ignorant, only on different subjects.   **2**
—*Will Rogers*

Never be afraid to sit awhile and think.   **3**
—*Lorraine Hansberry*

Experience is a good teacher, but she sends in terrific bills.   **4**
—*Minna Antrim*

A mind stretched by a new idea can never go back to its original   **5**
dimensions.—*Oliver Wendell Holmes, Jr.*

Education makes a people . . . easy to govern but impossible to enslave.   **6**
—*Henry Peter, Lord Brougham*

Our minds are lazier than our bodies.   **7**
—*François, Duc de la Rochefoucauld*

This thing called "failure" is not the falling down, but the staying down.   **8**
—*Mary Pickford*

The main hope of a nation lies in the proper education of its youth.   **9**
—Erasmus

Wisdom consists of anticipating the consequences.   **10**
—Norman Cousins

We learn something by doing it. There is no other way.   **11**
—John Holt

The greatest obstacle to discovery is not ignorance—it is the illusion of   **12**
knowledge.
—Daniel J. Boorstin

Work and Success

The harder you work, the luckier you get.   **13**
—Gary Player

All glory comes from daring to begin.   **14**
—Anonymous

It is not because things are difficult that we do not dare; it is because we   **15**
do not dare that they are difficult.
—Seneca

Show me a person who has never made a mistake, and I'll show you a   **16**
person who has never achieved much.
—Joan Collins

Nice guys finish last.   **17**
—Leo Durocher

Never look behind you. Something may be gaining on you.   **18**
—Satchel Paige

Winning isn't everything; it is the only thing.   **19**
—Vince Lombardi

Life is a succession of moments. To live each one is to succeed.   **20**
—Corita Kent

Should you not find the pearl after one or two divings, don't blame the   **21**
ocean! Blame your diving! You are not going deep enough.
—P. Yogananda

I've always tried to go a step past wherever people expected me to end up.   **22**
—Beverly Sills

It is good to have an end to journey towards, but it is the journey that matters in the end.
—*Ursula K. LeGuin*

23

Sometimes, it is more important to discover what one can't do than what one can do.
—*Lin Yutang*

24

Nothing is really work unless you would rather be doing something else.
—*J. M. Barrie*

25

I merely took the energy it takes to pout and wrote some blues.
—*Duke Ellington*

26

Tomorrow is often the busiest day of the year.
—*Spanish proverb*

27

I'm a slow walker, but I never walk back.
—*Abraham Lincoln*

28

I write when I'm inspired, and I see to it that I'm inspired at nine o'clock every morning.
—*Peter de Vries*

29

Love

If you want to be loved, be lovable.
—*Ovid*

30

After ecstasy, the laundry.
—*Zen saying*

31

The only true love is love at first sight; second sight dispels it.
—*Israel Zangwill*

32

A successful marriage requires falling in love many times, always with the same person.
—*Mignon McLaughlin*

33

The first duty of love is to listen.
—*Paul Tillich*

34

There is no surprise more magical than the surprise of being loved.
—*Charles Morgan*

35

Love is a fire, but whether it's going to warm your hearth or burn down your house, you can never tell.
—*Dorothy Parker*

36

The way to love anything is to realize that it might be lost. 37
—*G. K. Chesterton*

It's like magic. When you live by yourself, all your annoying habits are 38
gone!
—*Merrill Marko*

Love does not consist in gazing at each other but in looking together in the 39
same direction.
—*Antoine de Saint-Exupéry*

Someday, after we have mastered the winds, the waves, the tides and 40
gravity, we shall harness for God the energies of love. Then for the second
time in the history of the world, [we] will have discovered fire.
—*Pierre Teilhard de Chardin*

The story of a love is not important—what is important is that one is 41
capable of love. It is perhaps the only glimpse we are permitted of eternity.
—*Helen Hayes*

Friends and Family

Love is blind; friendship closes its eyes. 42
—*Anonymous*

Friendship with oneself is all important, because without it one cannot be 43
friends with anyone else in the world.
—*Eleanor Roosevelt*

What is a friend? A single soul dwelling in two bodies. 44
—*Aristotle*

You do not know who is your friend and who is your enemy until the ice 45
breaks.
—*Eskimo proverb*

The closest friends I have made all through life have been people who also 46
grew up close to a . . . loving grandmother or grandfather.
—*Margaret Mead*

Your children need your presence more than your presents. 47
—*Jesse Jackson*

I have founded charitable organizations, run them, and raised hundreds of 48
thousands of dollars to support them. I have lectured around the world to
many thousands of people, and I have written a number-one best-selling
book. Raising a child is harder.
—*Marianne Williamson*

How times change: it used to be kids would ask where they came from.   **49**
Now they tell you where to go.
—Ann Landers

Children begin by loving their parents; as they grow older they judge them;   **50**
sometimes they forgive them.
—Oscar Wilde

Children need love, especially when they do not deserve it.   **51**
—Harold S. Hulbert

My mother was dead for five years before I knew that I loved her so much.   **52**
—Lillian Hellman

Ourselves in Society

When spider webs unite, they can tie up a lion.   **53**
—Ethiopian proverb

Be kind, for everyone you meet is fighting a hard battle.   **54**
—Plato

Freedom does not always win. This is one of the bitterest lessons of history.   **55**
—A. J. P. Taylor

We can do no great things, only small things with great love.   **56**
—Mother Teresa

If you think you're too small to have an impact, try going to bed with a   **57**
mosquito.
—Anita Koddick

Courage isn't the absence of fear; it is action in the face of fear.   **58**
—S. Kennedy

Perfect courage is to do without witnesses what one would be capable of   **59**
doing with the world looking on.
—François, Duc de la Rochefoucauld

For the sake of one's children, in order to minimize the bill *they* must pay, **60**
one must be careful not to take refuge in any delusion—and the value placed
on the color of the skin is always and everywhere and forever a delusion.
—James Baldwin

What women want is what men want: they want respect.   **61**
—Marilyn Vos Savant

The same heart beats in every human breast.   **62**
—Matthew Arnold

Basically people are people . . . but it is our differences which charm,   **63**
delight, and frighten us.
—*Agnes Newton Keith*

There is a call to us, a call of service—that we join with others to try to   **64**
make things better in this world.
—*Dorothy Day*

Wisdom for Living

One who wants a rose must respect the thorn.   **65**
—*Persian proverb*

To live a creative life, we must lose our fear of being wrong.   **66**
—*Joseph Chilton Pearce*

Laughter can be more satisfying than honor, more precious than money,   **67**
more heart cleansing than prayer.
—*Harriet Rochlin*

People who keep stiff upper lips find that it's damn hard to smile.   **68**
—*Judith Guest*

Self-pity in its early stages is as snug as a feather mattress. Only when it   **69**
hardens does it become uncomfortable.
—*Maya Angelou*

When three people call you a donkey, put on a saddle.   **70**
—*Spanish proverb*

Never criticize a man until you have walked a mile in his moccasins.   **71**
—*Native American proverb*

Everyone is a moon and has a dark side which he never shows to anybody.   **72**
—*Mark Twain*

Self examination—if it is thorough enough—is always the first step towards   **73**
change.
—*Thomas Mann*

If you can't change your fate, change your attitude.   **74**
—*Amy Tan*

The older I grow, the more I distrust the familiar doctrine that age brings   **75**
wisdom.
—*H. L. Mencken*

Time is a dressmaker specializing in alterations.   **76**
—*Faith Baldwin*

Money can't buy friends, but you can get a better class of enemy. **77**
—*Spike Milligan*

Living in the lap of luxury isn't bad, except you never know when luxury is **78**
going to stand up.
—*Orson Welles*

Egoist. A person of low taste, more interested in himself than me. **79**
—*Ambrose Bierce*

Envy is a kind of praise. **80**
—*John Gay*

What doesn't destroy me strengthens me. **81**
—*Friedrich Nietzsche*

Life shrinks and expands in proportion to one's courage. **82**
—*Anaïs Nin*

I'm not afraid to die. I just don't want to be there when it happens. **83**
—*Woody Allen*

ACKNOWLEDGMENTS *(continued from copyright page)*

Pages 480–485: "Beauty: When the Other Dancer Is the Self" from *In Search of Our Mothers' Gardens.* Copyright © 1983 by Alice Walker. Reprinted by permission of Harcourt Brace Jovanovich, Inc., and David Higham Associates Limited.

Pages 486–488: "In Search of Bruce Lee's Grave" by Shanlon Wu. Copyright ©1990 by The New York Times Company. Reprinted by permission.

Pages 489–491: "A Brother's Murder" by Brent Staples. Copyright © 1986 by The New York Times Company. Reprinted by permission.

Pages 492–495: "One More Lesson" from *Silent Dancing: A Partial Remembrance of a Puerto Rican Childhood* by Judith Ortiz Cofer (Houston: Arte Publico Press, University of Houston, 1991). Reprinted with permission from the publisher.

Pages 496–498: "Neat People Versus Sloppy People" by Suzanne Britt. Copyright © 1993 by Suzanne Britt. Reprinted by permission of the author.

Pages 499–501: "How to Get the Most Out of Yourself" from *Confidence: How to Succeed at Being Yourself* by Alan Loy McGinnis. Copyright © 1987 Augsburg Publishing House. Used by permission of Augsburg Fortress and from the March 1988 Reader's Digest.

Pages 502–505: "Hunger of Memory" from *Hunger of Memory* by Richard Rodriguez. Copyright © 1982 by Richard Rodriguez. Reprinted by permission of David R. Godine, Publisher.

Pages 506–509: "My Outing" from *Days of Grace* by Arthur Ashe and Arnold Rampersad. Copyright © 1993 by the Estate of Arthur Ashe and Arnold Rampersad. Reprinted by permission of Alfred A. Knopf Inc.

Pages 510–512: "Some Thoughts About Abortion" from *Living Out Loud* by Anna Quindlen. Copyright © 1987 by Anna Quindlen. Reprinted by permission of Random House, Inc., and International Creative Management.

Pages 513–516: "On Kids and Couples" from *Married People: Staying Together in the Age of Divorce* by Francine Klagsbrun. Copyright © 1985 by Francine Klagsbrun. Used by permission of Bantam Books, a division of Bantam Doubleday, Dell Publishing Group, Inc., and The Charlotte Sheedy Agency, Inc.

Pages 517–519: "Living with My VCR" by Nora Ephron. Copyright © 1985 by Nora Ephron. Reprinted by permission of International Creative Management, Inc.

Pages 520–521: "The Plot Against People" by Russell Baker. Copyright © 1968 by The New York Times Company. Reprinted by permission.

Pages 522–525: "A Life Defined by Losses and Delights" from "On Being a Cripple" by Nancy Mairs, from *Plaintext* (Tucson: University of Arizona Press). Copyright © 1986 by the Arizona Board of Regents. Reprinted by permission.

Pages 526–529: "Three Types of Resistance to Oppression" from *Stride Toward Freedom* by Martin Luther King, Jr. Copyright © 1958 by Martin Luther King, Jr. Copyright renewed 1986 by Coretta Scott King. Reprinted by arrangement with The Heirs to the Estate of Martin Luther King, Jr., c/o Joan Daves Agency as agent for the proprietor.

ESL Reference Guide

Index

Rhetorical Index

The following index first classifies the paragraphs and essays in this text according to rhetorical mode and then according to rhetorical mode by chapter. (Those paragraphs with built-in errors for students to correct are not included.)

Rhetorical Modes

Illustration

Narration

Description

Rhetorical Modes by Chapter

Persuasion

Few Americans stay put, 292
Millions of law-abiding Americans, 293
Music is the speech of angels, 294
Thus, if race relations, 295
Students who follow their hearts, 295
Illness related to, 296

Rhetorical Modes in the Reading Selections

Illustration

How to Get the Most Out of Yourself (Alan Loy
    McGinnis), 499–501
My Outing (Arthur Ashe), 506–509
Some Thoughts About Abortion (Anna Quindlen),
    510–512
On Kids and Couples (Francine Klagsbrun), 513–516

Narration

Beauty: When the Other Dancer Is the Self (Alice
    Walker), 480–485
In Search of Bruce Lee's Grave (Shanlon Wu), 486–488
A Brother's Murder (Brent Staples), 489–491
One More Lesson (Judith Ortiz Cofer), 492–496
Hunger of Memory (Richard Rodriguez), 502–505
My Outing (Arthur Ashe), 506–509
A Life Defined by Losses and Delights (Nancy Mairs),
    522–525

Process

How Sunglasses Spanned the World, 477–479
Living with My VCR (Nora Ephron), 517–519

Definition

How to Get the Most of Yourself (Alan Loy McGinnis),
    499–501
A Life Defined by Losses and Delights (Nancy Mairs),
    522–525

Comparison and Contrast

One More Lesson (Judith Ortiz Cofer), 492–496
Neat People Versus Sloppy People (Suzanne Britt),
    496–498

Classification

Three Types of Resistance to Oppression (Martin Luther
    King, Jr.), 526–529
The Plot Against People (Russell Baker), 520–521

Persuasion

How to Get the Most Out of Yourself (Alan Loy
    McGinnis), 499–501
Some Thoughts About Abortion (Anna Quindlen),
    510–512
A Life Defined by Losses and Delights (Nancy Mairs),
    522–525
Three Types of Resistance to Oppression (Martin Luther
    King, Jr.), 526–529

Evergreen

11

Adam Corbett
Lenora Mitton
Rebecca Penner   Jan 16/04
Lori Wamboldt
Lori Wamboldt